CHEVELLE
Restoration
AND AUTHENTICITY GUIDE
1970–1972

Dale McIntosh and Rick Nelson

CarTech®

CarTech®

CarTech®, Inc.
6118 Main Street
North Branch, MN 55056
Phone: 651-277-1200 or 800-551-4754
Fax: 651-277-1203
www.cartechbooks.com

© 2019 by Rick Nelson and Dale McIntosh

All rights reserved. No part of this publication may be reproduced or utilized in any form or by any means, electronic or mechanical, including photocopying, recording, or by any information storage and retrieval system, without prior permission from the Publisher. All text, photographs, and artwork are the property of the Author unless otherwise noted or credited.

The information in this work is true and complete to the best of our knowledge. However, all information is presented without any guarantee on the part of the Author or Publisher, who also disclaim any liability incurred in connection with the use of the information and any implied warranties of merchantability or fitness for a particular purpose. Readers are responsible for taking suitable and appropriate safety measures when performing any of the operations or activities described in this work.

All trademarks, trade names, model names and numbers, and other product designations referred to herein are the property of their respective owners and are used solely for identification purposes. This work is a publication of CarTech, Inc., and has not been licensed, approved, sponsored, or endorsed by any other person or entity. The Publisher is not associated with any product, service, or vendor mentioned in this book, and does not endorse the products or services of any vendor mentioned in this book.

Edit by Wes Eisenschenk
Layout by Connie DeFlorin

ISBN 978-1-61325-809-5
Item No. SA428P

Library of Congress Cataloging-in-Publication Data

Names: Nelson, Rick, 1961- author. | McIntosh, Dale, 1946- author.
Title: Chevelle restoration and authenticity guide 1970-1972 / Rick Nelson and Dale McIntosh.
Description: Forest Lake, MN : CarTech, [2019]
Identifiers: LCCN 2018045942 | ISBN 9781613254295
Subjects: LCSH: Chevelle automobile–Conservation and restoration. | Automobiles–Conservation and restoration.
Classification: LCC TL215.C48 N45 2019 | DDC 629.28/722–dc23
LC record available at https://lccn.loc.gov/2018045942

Written, edited, designed, and printed in the U.S.A.

CarTech books may be purchased at a discounted rate in bulk for resale, events, corporate gifts, or educational purposes. Special editions may also be created to specification. For details, contact Special Sales at 6118 Main Street, North Branch, MN 55056 or by email at sales@cartechbooks.com.

DISTRIBUTION BY:

Europe
PGUK
63 Hatton Garden
London EC1N 8LE, England
Phone: 020 7061 1980 • Fax: 020 7242 3725
www.pguk.co.uk

Australia
Renniks Publications Ltd.
3/37-39 Green Street
Banksmeadow, NSW 2109, Australia
Phone: 2 9695 7055 • Fax: 2 9695 7355
www.renniks.com

Canada
Login Canada
300 Saulteaux Crescent
Winnipeg, MB, R3J 3T2 Canada
Phone: 800 665 1148 • Fax: 800 665 0103
www.lb.c

CONTENTS

Acknowledgments 4
About the Authors 4
Introduction 6

Chapter 1: Acquisition 12
Chapter 2: Preparation 18
Chapter 3: Body Disassembly 26
Chapter 4: Chassis, Suspension, and Brake Work 29
Chapter 5: Engine and Driveline 73
Chapter 6: Body and Paint Work 106
Chapter 7: Electrical 133
Chapter 8: Interior 161
Chapter 9: Details, Facts, and Myths 202

Appendix A: Pre-Restoration Checklist 231
Appendix B: Chassis and Engine Compartment Paint Colors 233
Appendix C: Engine Assembly Process 235
Appendix D: Driveshaft Stripe Colors 238
Source Guide 240

ACKNOWLEDGMENTS

Unless otherwise noted, the photos in this book were taken either by Rick Nelson of Musclecar Restoration and Design or Dale McIntosh.

Both of us would like to take this opportunity to thank all the people and companies that supplied us with photos and text where applicable: Chris White, Dane Belden of Belden Speed & Engineering, Dave Castine, Bill Garcia, David Hagan, Warren Leunig, Derek Love of Painless Performance Products, Ray McAvoy of Ray's Chevy Restoration Site, Mark Redmon, Tom Rightler, Les Saville, Dominick Scorziello, Arne Skog, and Mark Wilson.

A special thank you to Jamie Cooper. Jamie had his first experience in a body shop in 1988 as a freshman in high school. Gary Goss, owner of Goss Automotive and a member of a United Methodist Church where Jamie's father was a pastor, hired Jamie to keep the shop clean and lend a hand where needed. A year later, Jamie purchased his first car, and with the help and supervision of Gary and fellow-employee Barry Smith, the learning of the trade began. After high school, Jamie attended Vale Technical Institution, graduating first in his class and receiving the directors award for maintaining a 3.5 GPA or higher. After working in three different body shops for the next 20 years, his dream of being a shop owner came true in 2014, when he and his partner Joe Griffith opened Super Car Restoration.

ABOUT THE AUTHORS

Rick Nelson

Many people ask Rick when he became interested in cars, and the generic answer is the ever-commonly used "I was born with a wrench in my hand." In this case, it is all but true. His father was a master sergeant in the US Air Force and was an Airframe and/or Powerplant (A&P) mechanic. Rick's older brother also grew up loving cars and was a radar technician in the air force as well. His brother raced cars, so Rick was exposed to wrenching at a very early age when his brother would bring his car buddies home. Rick was often exposed to these cars in his driveway and taken for many rides.

By the time Rick was 18, he had already owned several muscle cars, some of which included SS427 Impalas and a 1969 Chevelle SS with a transplanted 450-hp 427. His Chevelle was one of the fastest cars in town, and it became a car to watch out for at Friday and Saturday night

street races. Shortly after that, Rick started bracket racing in earnest, and by 1981 he was wrenching on a Pro Stock team running a 1981 Camaro. After graduating from high school, Rick went to Dunwoody Industrial Institute with hopes of becoming a mechanic, but he realized shortly after joining the working ranks that wrenching was more of a hobby and not a career, at least from a repair standpoint. He did finally land a job with Corvette Specialties in Minnesota, and within a short period of time, Rick was restoring Bloomington Gold Corvettes for many customers. This was more in line with what he was looking for, and the future had been set.

Not being happy working for someone else and not making enough as a restorer, Rick set his sights on a corporate job. He continued doing restorations on the side for customers. By the time he was in his mid-20s, he had restored several cars for friends and customers and was making a name for himself. In 1984, one of his cars was featured in three different car magazines, and that exposure started the blood flowing in earnest as well as the pay. Rick continued to restore many cars on the side.

In 2001, one of his customer restorations, a 1970 LS6 Chevelle, scored as the second-highest scoring Chevelle in the country under the Diamond Certification process. From then on, the cars came to him with high demands and with enough requests that it was time to make a change. Rick started Musclecar Restoration and Design and worked out of his home shop. Then in 2008, Rick moved to a small town in central Illinois and opened a large shop where he was able to restore several cars at a time. Business boomed, and within a few short years Rick was overwhelmed with work. He hired on a full-time restorer to help.

Though not a journalist by any stretch, Rick helped write several magazine feature articles and also provided several authors with information and photographs that were needed to write their books. This gave Rick an opportunity to see how things were done in automotive publications. Rick's business is booming, and his restorations are some of the best in the country. It is not a job; it is an obsession.

In addition to restorations and writing, Rick also travels the country inspecting LS6 Chevelles. He was instrumental in helping Lane Collectables build and design its first diecast LS6 Chevelle with Rick providing more than 600 photographs and technical information to make it one of the highest detailed diecasts available.

Dale McIntosh

Dale has always had an interest in cars, especially Chevelles. He purchased his first 1967 SS396 in the fall of 1967 while home in Overland Park, Kansas, on leave from US Army basic training. Dale's Advanced Individual Training was done at Fort Sill in Lawton, Oklahoma. Dale did not want to leave his new car at home, so he took it with him to Fort Sill. During his eight weeks of training, he would leave Saturday at noon and drive his Chevelle the seven-hour one-way trip to Overland Park to meet up with his friends and go out Saturday night. On Sunday around noon, he would make the seven-hour trek back to Fort Sill. When he learned that he would be leaving for a tour in Korea, it became obvious he could not take the car with him, so he enlisted his best friend to make the final trek from Overland Park to Fort Sill, and his friend drove the car back to Dale's home. His parents cared for the car during his 16-month stint in Korea, keeping it registered and driving it occasionally to keep everything running in good order.

As is often the case, life came along with responsibilities. After returning from Korea, Dale had several automotive mechanic jobs, worked the counter at numerous auto parts stores, and did a second stint in the army with a tour in Germany. After all of that, Dale decided it was time to really settle down and plant roots. As luck would have it, Dale was stationed again at Fort Sill after his tour of duty in Europe.

Dale's tour in Europe had introduced him to computers, and he put those skills to use. After leaving the military, Dale continued as a civil servant with those computer skills. Upon retiring from civil service, he combined those computer skills with his long love of and interest in Chevelles. Today, he has several Chevelle-related websites, including ChevelleStuff.net. Dale hosts several Chevelle car club websites and had a number of Chevelle-related registries; many are specialty registries such as 1970 Chevelles with the LS6 engine option, 1970–1972 Chevelles with the LS5 engine, SS396 series, and SS396-optioned Chevelles. One of Dale's websites is ChevelleCD.net, where he offers signed copies of his books along with numerous Chevelle-related information CDs.

In May 2015, Dale was approached by CarTech to write an information guide on 1964–1972 Chevelles. This effort, *Chevelle Data and ID Guide*, was introduced in August 2016. A second book, the first in a series by CarTech on muscle cars of the 1960s and 1970s called *1970 Chevrolet Chevelle SS* quickly followed. A third book was released in 2018: *The Definitive Chevelle SS Guide*. Rick Nelson was a valuable asset with proofreading, photos, etc. for all three books along with many other Chevelle owners supplying photos of their cars and several proofreaders.

This book is a collaborative effort between Rick and Dale with Rick supplying the majority of the photos and technical expertise and Dale handling the writing and editing chores. Other contributors of photo images and technical expertise, as in the past, will be noted where applicable.

We both hope you find the information educational and a worthwhile addition to your reference material collection.

INTRODUCTION

In the 1960s, the Chevrolet division of General Motors saw the need to add a midsize model to its lineup—something between the Chevy II/Nova line and the full-size Chevrolet. The design and engineering departments set out to create such a car, and on September 26, 1963, the Chevelle family was introduced to the public. The Chevelle's main competitor outside of General Motors was Ford's midsize Fairlane. From inside the GM family, Buick redesigned the Buick Special from its previous unibody construction to the A-body form of body on frame. Oldsmobile followed suit with its F-85, and Pontiac joined in with its Tempest. Cadillac was GM's luxury line and never felt the need to enter into the midsize market.

The Chevelle would have multiple bodystyles, series names, creature comforts, and options over the years, much like its internal GM rivals of Buick, Oldsmobile, and Pontiac. With Baby Boomers coming of age and looking for inexpensive transportation that had style and performance, GM's lineup offered a myriad of choices for the buyer. Since Chevrolet was the bread-and-butter of General Motors and offered a lower entry cost for the young consumer, the Chevelle has something for everyone from entry level 300/300 Deluxe series with minimal trim and creature comforts to the Malibu and SS396 series with upgraded trim and interiors. There were also station wagons for the young family, convertibles for the drop-top enthusiast, and the sedan pickup (El Camino) half-truck, half-car that was resurrected into the Chevelle family; there was truly something for everyone.

GM's Pontiac division broke the performance barrier with the GTO option on its 1964 Tempest. John DeLorean, Bill Collins, and Russ Gee were responsible for the GTO in 1964. Although GM's management banned divisions from involvement in racing, Pontiac disregarded GM policy of limiting the midsize A-body platform to a maximum of 330 ci. Pete Estes was president of the Pontiac division from 1961 to 1965, and he approved the Pontiac 389-ci engine with the GTO option. With its 3x2 carburetor setup, the GTO pumped out an amazing 348 hp. Buick and Oldsmobile had nothing to compete with Pontiac, and Chevrolet's best initial offering was their tried-and-true 283-ci engine with 220 hp. Chevrolet did respond in March with a 250-hp version of the 327-ci engine and again in June with a 300-hp version. It was still far short of the 348-hp 389-ci monster that the GTO option offered.

Pete Estes became the president of the Chevrolet division in 1965, and he started the ball rolling for the largest division of General Motors. He remained in this position until he was promoted to executive vice president of General Motors in 1972. During these years, the Chevrolet division saw the beginning (and end) of Chevrolet's participation in the horsepower wars of the 1960s and 1970s.

Through the 1960s and into the 1970s, this cubic inch/horsepower war would rage within General Motors, as well as Ford Motor Company, Chrysler Corporation, and, to some extent, American Motors. The peak was reached with the 1970 Malibu with the SS454 option, which was its 454-ci 450-hp LS6 monster. The December 1969 introduction of the Chevelle became the highest advertised horsepower-rated engine in any production car on the market for the 1970 model year and would not be surpassed by any other muscle car of the era. A total of 4,475 Regular Production Option (RPO) LS6 engine options were sold in three Chevelle Malibu bodystyles: the sport coupe, the convertible, and the custom El Camino. Transmission choices were limited to the heavy-duty Muncie RPO M22 4-speed or the heavy-duty RPO M40 Turbo-Hydramatic 400 (TH400) 3-speed automatic.

The Tonawanda, New York, engine plant production figures do show that 3,525 LS6 engines were built for a manual transmission (obviously the M22) and 1,923 were built for the automatic (heavy-duty TH400) for a total of 5,448 LS6 engines. Of those, 4,475 went into production Malibus and 973 were service engines. One can take those figures and guess or calculate a statistical number of how many production LS6 Malibus were equipped with either transmission, but it is still a guess because the M40 transmission, as an RPO number, was available with the newly introduced LS3 402-ci 330-hp engine along with the L34, L78, LS5, and LS6.

The same can be said for specific engines versus bodystyles. The number of LS6 engines sold is not broken down by the particular bodystyle

INTRODUCTION

they were sold in. One can extrapolate a statistical distribution of sport coupes, convertibles, and El Caminos that received the LS6 engine, but like the engine/transmission combination, it is only a calculated, distributive number. Throw in things such as the RPO ZL2 cowl-induction hood (which could also be ordered with the two 396-ci engine options), and you can see how claims of "1-of-X" LS6 4-speed convertibles with the ZL2 hood option can get a bit silly.

The 1960s and 1970s were days of "race on Sunday and sell on Monday." Chevrolet's Chevelle was never really that competitive in oval track racing (such as NASCAR) like Ford and Chrysler, but straight-line performance in drag racing was another story. There were two 1970 Malibus on the drag racing circuit that were famous. One was the Ray Allen–piloted Briggs Chevrolet LS6 Fathom Blue convertible, which was tuned by performance specialists Ralph Truppi and Tommy Kling. It pretty much dominated the National Hot Rod Association (NHRA) SS/EA class by never losing a class race except on those occasions when he might red-light himself out of competition. Although the NHRA required at least 50 cars be built for a particular class, it has been claimed the NHRA relaxed the rules a bit to allow the Ray Allen car to compete; so, whether there were actually at least 50 LS6 convertibles built will continue to be a question as GM's production records were destroyed years ago. The other famous car was Bob Hamilton's LS6 Cranberry Red *Red Alert* sport coupe in SS/DA class. It was so well known that AMT model car kit company introduced a 1:25 scale model of *Red Alert* (albeit a 1972 Malibu model) and became a primary sponsor on the car for a number of years.

Valuable Chevelle Malibus and SS396 Chevelles

These two race cars aside, the LS6 Chevelle is still arguably the most sought-after 1970 Chevelle, and the cars typically have six-figure selling prices. Correctly restored LS5 Malibus and even the L34 and L78 Malibus can bring a hefty price in the upper five-figure range at private sales as well as auctions, and 1971/1972 Malibus are growing in popularity.

Well-done restorations of 1970 Malibus with the other three engines: RPO L34 396/350 hp, RPO L78 396/375 hp, and RPO LS5 454/360 hp, can still command mid-to-high five-figure prices along with the 1971 and 1972 LS5-powered Malibus. Remember, aside from the unique pieces of the 1970 LS6 driveline, it costs just as much in bodywork, chassis work, paint, interior, etc. to properly restore a 1970 Chevelle with the other three engines; something to keep in mind whether you are looking at a roller to restore or buy one that has been recently restored. The same holds true for the 1971 and 1972 model years; aside from engine/transmission options, the bodywork, chassis work, etc. costs can run the same. Generally, other years of Chevelles are not as costly to restore due to the relatively lower cost of those hard-to-find items.

Some engine/model combinations, such as the 1970 L78 convertible, are relatively rare due to the short production time of the L78 engine being an option for 1970. The 1965 RPO Z16-optioned Malibu

This rare 1970 convertible in Fathom Blue and white convertible top with RPO L78 engine was optioned with RPO ZL2 Special Ducted Hood Air System and complemented with white stripes. Given the short life span of the L78, engine availability in 1970, and being a convertible, these are highly sought after by Chevelle enthusiasts. (Photo Courtesy L78 Registry)

INTRODUCTION

A two-door station wagon made a brief comeback in the Chevelle lineup, but it only lasted for two years: 1964 and 1965. The two-door station wagon was only available in the base Chevelle 300 series. One can only imagine the interest these would have sparked if they had been a Malibu SS series with the nostalgia chrome trim on the tailgate.

SS396 is certainly considered one of the rarest and arguably the most desirable Chevelle today. Of the 201 built, only about 70 are known to exist, so finding a real unknown RPO Z16 Malibu SS396 today is not very likely.

As with any collectible item, rarity doesn't always mean desirability or potential value. There were quite a number of low-production-volume Chevelles built between the 1964 and 1972 model years. One example is the 1968 Malibu four-door station wagon with a 6-cylinder engine; only five were built and only a few people would consider them collectible and spend the money necessary to bring one back to showroom condition. On the other hand, the 1964 and 1965 Chevelle 300 two-door station wagon brings back the nostalgia days of the 1955–1957 Nomad station wagon. Owners will spend the money to restore them, particularly those with the optional high-horsepower V-8 engine of the day and 4-speed manual transmission.

COPO Chevelles

Many think the COPO acronym is magic and that anything outside the norm is a COPO Chevelle. The only true COPO Chevelles were 323 Malibu sport coupes built in 1969 with Chevrolet's RPO L72 427 425-hp engine. Because General Motors had a 400-ci limit on engine size prior to the 1970 model year, these 323 1969 Malibus were built under the COPO process with several COPO codes for various performance items.

There are a number of 1970 Malibus that were special ordered and equipped a bit differently from normal-production-run Malibus, but these are limited to minor items such as requesting a different paint color from the normal selection, changing D88 Hood and Deck stripe color from Chevrolet's suggested color, or not having D88 Hood and Deck stripes painted when the RPO ZL2 Special Ducted Hood Air System is ordered, since stripes were part of the ZL2 option. These changes were ordered through the Fleet & Special Order (F&SO) process, not the COPO process.

1964–1965 Malibu SS Features

The 1964 and 1965 Malibu SS was Chevelle's sporty option. Both years of the Malibu SS could be ordered with any 6- or 8-cylinder engine available at the time; they were the only SS Chevelles to hold this distinction. Bucket seats were standard equipment in both years and, when ordered with either the 2-speed Powerglide automatic transmission or the 4-speed manual transmission, would also include a center console.

Bucket seats were only available as an option in Malibu-series El Caminos of the day, not as regular production option (RPO) A51 but simply an optional seat and color choice for the interior. Bucket seat color choices were limited in the 1964 model year El Camino to light fawn, medium aqua, and medium red. In 1965, the El Camino was limited to light fawn, medium turquoise, and medium red. Bucket seats would not become an RPO until the 1966 model year.

The 1965 model year saw the introduction of the blacked-out grille and tail panel area for the Malibu SS with the exception of black Malibu SSs that received silver highlighted

INTRODUCTION

tail panels. The 1964 and 1965 Malibu SS Chevelles were the only years an amp gauge, oil pressure gauge, and water temperature gauge were standard equipment.

1966–1968 SS396 Features

The Malibu SS series of 1964 and 1965 gave way to the SS396 series in 1966 and would continue as a separate series through the 1968 model year. These years continued the blacked-out grille and, to a limited number of 1966 SS396s, a blacked-out tail panel. It is believed some very early 1966 model year and possibly some very late model year 1966 Atlanta-built SS396 Chevelles had their tail panels blacked out, but for the most part, 1966 SS396s have lower body panel colored tail panels.

The SS396 was now more performance-oriented with only three 396-ci engines available. The 396/325-hp engine was the base V-8 in the SS396 with two optional 396-ci engines: RPO L34 (rated at 360 hp in 1966 but 350 hp in 1967 and 1968) and RPO L78 396-ci engine rated at 375 hp.

Bench seats were standard equipment along with a heavy-duty 3-speed manual transmission. Optional were several 4-speed manual transmissions, the 2-speed Powerglide automatic transmission, and for 1967 and 1968 the 3-speed Turbo-Hydramatic 400 automatic transmission.

Bucket seats and gauges (including a tachometer) were options, even on the SS396. The term "SS Gauges" is a misconception. The RPO U14 gauge option was available on any V-8 Malibu or SS396 sport coupe, convertible, or sedan pickup.

1969 Chevelle SS Features

In 1969, the SS396 as a series was gone. The SS396 was an option under RPO Z25 SS396 Equipment. Still available in the Malibu-series sport coupe, convertible, and El Camino, 1969 also offered the Z25 option with the 300 Deluxe coupe and sport coupe.

Bench seats were standard equipment along with a heavy-duty 3-speed manual transmission. Optional were several 4-speed manual transmissions and the 3-speed Turbo-Hydramatic 400 automatic transmission. The 2-speed Powerglide automatic transmission was no longer available with the SS396 Equipment option. For the first time, power front disc brakes were included in the SS396 Equipment option package.

Bucket seats and gauges/tachometer were options, even on the SS396, but bucket seats were not an option in the 300 Deluxe series.

1970 SS Features

The 1970 model year saw two SS Equipment–option packages. RPO Z25 is the SS396 package, and RPO Z15 is the SS454 package. Both were available as options on the Malibu-series sport coupe, convertible, and El Camino.

A bench seat was still standard fare for 1970 Chevelles, even when optioned with one of the two SS option packages. The Malibu sport coupe bench seat is a cloth and vinyl combination with an all-vinyl seat option costing an additional $12.65. Both the Malibu-series

All SS396 and SS-optioned Malibus (as well as 300 Deluxe coupes and sport coupes in 1969) came standard with a bench seat. Bucket seats and/or console were optional on all Malibu sport coupe, convertible, and El Camino Chevelles after 1965. The 1970 Chevelle shown here has the optional all-vinyl bench seat option. (Photo Courtesy L78 Registry)

convertible and El Camino came standard with an all-vinyl bench seat. Bucket seats and/or console were optional-cost items.

RPO Z25 was the SS396 option package that included the 350-hp 396-ci engine as the base engine with the RPO L78 375-hp engine as an option. The L78 engine would only last through early to mid-December, while the L34 would remain the entire model year. The LS5 454 is the base engine for the Z15 option with the LS6 being optional.

Since the 396-ci L34 and 454-ci LS5 were the base engines in the two SS option packages, they were not considered "options" as such, and there are no published figures for the number of L34 or LS5 engines that went into Z25 or Z15 Malibus. However, since the 396-ci L78 and 454-ci LS6 were optional engines, one can easily calculate how many Z25s were built with the L34 or L78 and how many Z15s were built with the LS5 or LS6. Sales reports show there were 53,599 Z25 options sold in 1970. By subtracting the number of optional L78 engines (2,144), you can see there would be 51,455 SS396 Malibus with the base L34 engine. Likewise by subtracting the number of optional LS6 engines (4,475) from the total number of Z15 options sold (8,773), you can see there were 4,298 LS5-powered Malibus and actually fewer LS5 Malibus than LS6 Malibus in 1970. The number of LS5 engines sold in Malibus *does not* include the 3,823 LS5 engines sold with the Monte Carlo SS option; those are separate.

The cowl-induction hood, RPO ZL2, is one of the very few options one could only order with one of the two SS options. While the RPO LS3 402-ci Mark IV big-block was available in all non-SS Malibus in 1970, the ZL2 hood package was exclusive to an SS-optioned Malibu; no LS3-powered 1970 Malibu could order the ZL2 hood package. It is believed the 4.10:1 gear ratio was only available with the LS6 engine option as well because no other engine package has been found with a documented 4.10:1 gear set to date.

Any exterior paint color and any interior color were available with any Chevelle within restrictions imposed by Chevrolet, such as a green interior could not be in a red or blue Chevelle. Since both SS options could only be ordered with a Malibu sport coupe, convertible, or El Camino, any interior seat/material available for a non-SS-optioned Malibu was also possible with the two SS options. No special colors or interiors were reserved for the two SS options.

RPO D88 stripes were optional on non-SS-optioned Malibu sport coupes, convertibles, and El Caminos as well as optional on both SS options when the ZL2 option was not ordered. D88 stripes were part of the RPO ZL2 package, along with hood pins, but could be deleted on request. In this case, the term "stripe delete" would be appropriate, and the stripe deletion required approval from the F&SO office. On an SS-optioned Malibu without the ZL2 option, stripe delete is no more appropriate than radio delete, positraction delete, etc. If someone did not order an option, it cannot be considered a "delete" item.

Aside from the engine size, the two SS options (RPO Z25 and RPO Z15) were pretty much the same as far as standard equipment went. Both came standard with front power disc brakes and F41 suspension, except El Caminos. While the Z25 SS396 option could be ordered with the wide-ratio Muncie M20, close-ratio Muncie M21 4-speed transmission, or the M40 Turbo-Hydramatic 3-speed automatic transmission, the Z15 SS454 option required either the heavy-duty close-ratio M22 4-speed transmission or a heavy-duty M40 Turbo-Hydramatic 3-speed automatic transmission. The Z15 did come with a stronger rear end than its Z25 counterpart.

Both SS options came standard with a black dash carrier assembly, black steering column, and black steering wheel with a centered SS emblem. A Cushion Rim steering wheel was optional under RPO NK1, and this optional steering wheel could be ordered with or without one of the two SS options. The basic SS dash carrier gave the owner three large, round gauge pods with fuel gauge, speedometer, and a blank along with three small gauge pods for warning lamps for generator, water temperature, and oil pressure.

RPO U14 Instrument Panel Gauges was optional, even on SS-optioned Malibus. The U14 option included an ammeter, water temperature gauge, tachometer, and electric clock. The tachometer replaced the fuel-level gauge in the large left-most pod, the speedometer/odometer remained in the large center-most pod, and the clock replaced the blank in the large right-most pod. An ammeter gauge was installed in the small left-most pod above the headlamp switch, replacing the generator warning lamp; a water temperature gauge was installed in the small, upper right-most pod, replacing the water temperature warning lamp; and the fuel-level gauge was moved to the small, lower-most pod, replacing the oil pressure warning lamp. For some unknown reason, 1970 would see the end of an oil pressure gauge. The oil pressure warning lamp was retained but moved to the bottom of the tachometer face.

1971 and 1972 SS Features

The 1971 and 1972 model years saw a change in Chevrolet's approach to the youth market. Whether due to rising insurance costs or federal EPA regulations, or maybe both, the 1971 and 1972 model years saw the SS become more of a styling and handling package than a performance one. The two 1970 SS options were cut to one option, RPO Z15, and any optional V-8 with any optional transmission (except the 2-speed Powerglide) could be ordered with the SS Equipment package. The two optional 350-ci engines (RPO L65 and RPO L48) with a manual 3- or 4-speed transmission or 3-speed automatic TH350 transmission were available with the SS package. The RPO L34 396-ci engine was dropped in 1971, and the 402-ci LS3 (first introduced in 1970) could be ordered with a manual 3- or 4-speed or 3-speed automatic TH400 transmission. All three of these engines could be ordered with the SS option, but they could also be ordered without the SS option. Only the RPO LS5 454-ci engine required the SS option in both years. The LS5 could only be ordered with the heavy-duty Muncie M22 4-speed manual transmission or heavy-duty TH400 automatic transmission.

A bench seat was still standard for 1971 and 1972 Chevelles, even when optioned with the SS-option package. The Malibu sport coupe bench seat is a combination cloth and vinyl with an all-vinyl seat optional for an additional $19. Both the Malibu-series convertible and El Camino came standard with an all-vinyl bench seat. Bucket seats and/or console were optional-cost items.

Since the availability of the two 350-ci V-8s and the LS3 was such that neither required the SS package, without documentation showing one of those engines along with RPO Z15, it is difficult to verify a Malibu sport coupe, convertible, or El Camino with one of these three engines as SS optioned.

Many of the same features applied to the 1971 and 1972 model year SS with a few differences. All SS-optioned Malibus came with the same domed hood as 1970, but hood pins were now standard on all SS hoods. The ZL2 option was reserved for the LS3 and LS5 only and added RPO D88 sport stripes just as 1970 did. D88 sport stripes could still be ordered on any Malibu sport coupe, convertible, or El Camino whether SS optioned or not. The D88 option is listed at $79 for 1971 and $81.10 for 1972. As was the case in 1970, some exterior paint colors were restricted to the color of stripe that could be ordered.

As in 1970, all SS-optioned Malibus came with a round-pod instrument panel with U14 Instrument Panel Gauges still an option. The 1971 and 1972 grilles received the typical SS black-out treatment appropriate for the year along with a centered SS emblem. Gone was the black rear bumper pad of 1970 in favor of an SS emblem on the rear bumper, which meant rear bumper guards could be ordered on any 1971 or 1972 SS-optioned Malibu sport coupe or convertible where they could not be ordered on an SS-optioned 1970 Malibu sport coupe or convertible. All 1971 and 1972 SS-optioned Malibu sport coupes and convertibles received an "SS" emblem on the front fenders, but only the LS5 454 received engine size numbering. El Caminos retained their El Camino script on the front fenders and SS emblems on the tailgate with only the 454-ci engine option getting the engine size badge as well.

Added to the SS option in 1971 and 1972 was a remote control driver-side mirror (an option in 1970). Changed were the wheel and tire sizes: 1971 and 1972 SS-optioned Malibus were shod with 15x7 wheels and F60x15 tires.

As with 1970, any exterior paint color or interior material/seat type available in any Malibu was fair game for the SS-optioned ones as well.

Choosing a Good Candidate

As noted earlier, all things being equal, it will take as much time and effort into restoring a 1970 SS396-optioned Malibu as it will an SS454-optioned Malibu or any 1971 or 1972 SS-optioned Malibu. Given you have the correct engine and driveline components, the bodywork, chassis work, interior work, etc. will be the same, so be sure you have either the skills and knowledge to restore your Chevelle yourself or expect to pay about the same for a premium restoration regardless of which Chevelle you start with. Depending on the condition of the Chevelle you start with, ensure your expectations are within your budget.

If you are looking for a six-figure Chevelle when you are finished, expect to invest at least a five-figure price to get it done. Of course, the more work you can do yourself the less the overall costs are going to be.

CHAPTER 1

ACQUISITION

When looking for a 1970–1972 Chevelle candidate to restore, you should have in mind what the finished product is going to be used for. Are you looking for a daily driver, a weekend family cruiser, something for the local car show crowd, or are you expecting to do a full concours restoration for perfection? Your expectations will dictate the amount of labor and money it will take to achieve your goal.

Determine Your Goals

With a straight body, good paint, and sound mechanicals to start with, your investment for a daily driver (okay, maybe an only-good-weather daily driver) can be kept to a minimum, and you can add dress-up and power options as time and your wallet permits. Something a bit nicer for family and friends cruises and competing at local car shows in a restored class can cost a bit more because you may need to do some bodywork, invest in a quality paint job, refresh the interior, and ensure original or original-type components are used. That can take a bit more time and money to accomplish.

If you are planning on a full, no-expenses-spared concours restoration, you will want to start with something as complete and original as possible. Maybe not so much the body, interior, and mechanicals condition, as those will be rebuilt and/or replaced anyway. But, if you are looking at a concours-quality L34, L78, LS5, or LS6 candidate, having original driveline components is paramount because some items can be expensive to obtain and it is difficult to locate correctly dated pieces.

Know What You Are Looking For

Nobody likes to get duped into buying a car that is not what it is represented to be, especially if you are looking for a true SS-optioned Chevelle. The 1964 model year is easy to determine as a Malibu SS: the vehicle identification number (VIN) will begin with 457 or 458;

Whether you start with a running, driving car or a rolling shell, carefully inspect the Chevelle for what is present and what is missing. If you have doubts about it being a true SS Chevelle, get a professional inspection.

ACQUISITION

the 1965 Malibu SS VIN will begin with 13737/67 or 13837/67; 1966 through 1968 SS396 VIN will begin with 13817/37/67/80, depending on the year. There is nothing in the VIN for 1969 through 1971 Chevelles that will tell you if one is a true SS-optioned Malibu (or 300 Deluxe in the 1969 model year only). It was fairly easy to clone/fake/recreate 1969–1972 Malibus. So, know what you are looking for.

The 1972 VIN will only be an aid in one case: in 1972, Chevrolet began putting the particular engine size in the VIN with a letter code in the fifth character position. If this fifth letter is the letter W, it indicates the LS5 454-ci engine was originally installed in the car, and the LS5 454-ci engine could only be ordered with the SS option. Basically, the same is true for 1970 and 1971 in regard to the 454-ci engine being SS-specific, but nothing in the 1970 or 1971 VIN indicates which original engine was installed in the car.

Protect-O-Plate

In 1971 and 1972, any optional V-8 engine could be ordered with the SS option. The problem here is these three optional V-8 engines could also be ordered without the SS option. So, documentation such as a warranty card (Protect-O-Plate) showing the original engine identification is of no help in determining if the SS option was also ordered, and a matching-numbers 350- or 402-ci engine cannot be used as a determining factor in 1971 or 1972 of the SS option.

Cowl Tag

The Fisher Body number plate—also known as a trim tag, cowl tag, or firewall tag—typically does not list options on a US-built Malibu. The Oshawa, Ontario, assembly plant did show RPO codes Z15 or Z25 on an SS454- and SS396-optioned Malibus in 1970. The practice did not continue in 1971 or 1972, making it much more difficult to visually identify an SS-optioned, Canadian-built Malibu. The Kansas City assembly plant is suspected to denote the SS option on its trim tags with the letter *L* stamped below the lower body color number. This is believed to mean a change in body trim from standard Malibu trim to SS trim, but while it is a popular belief, there is currently no published documentation to support this theory. Suffice it to say a Kansas City-built Malibu without this *L* is most likely *not* an SS-optioned Malibu but possibly is if the letter exists on the trim tag.

Beginning about February 1970, Kansas City-built Malibus began appearing with either the letters B or W stamped below the upper-body-color number/letter to indicate black or white sport stripes. The RPO D88 sport stripes could be ordered on any Malibu sport coupe, convertible, or El Camino without the SS option as well, so either B or W could be stamped without the L letter. While not definitive proof, it is something to look for.

None of the other 1970–1972 assembly plants put any identifying codes on their trim tags that might help.

Hire a Professional

If you are not well versed with how to determine if your candidate is a legitimate car, it is worth a few thousand dollars to have the car inspected by someone who does concours restorations for a living and get their well-respected and expert advice before the purchase. This could save you thousands of dollars in the end by not paying a premium for a, shall we say, highly suspect or fake car to begin with. This inspection can also determine what original and correct parts are on the car now and what is needed to be purchased or rebuilt. The inspector can also look for overall signs of previous restorations to determine how much labor might be involved to bring the car up to quality standards.

The inspection can also determine if the correct and original driveline is intact or if the car has been rebodied or the engine ID stamp and partial VIN stamps are legitimate. All of these factors will then give you a good feeling about proceeding with the car or turning it down and continuing your search for a better candidate.

Always use an inspector who is an expert on the type of car you are interested in purchasing. Do not use a generic classic car inspector, as they will not know any of the nuances that an expert in a specific car will know. Ask for a detailed inspection report. More often than not, the inspection report can be used as a bargaining tool to negotiate the price of the car. In almost all cases, the lowered price will cover the entire cost of the inspection, so in essence, it cost you nothing and gives you peace of mind as well as a valuable report to keep with the car.

I'm not suggesting that car appraisers cannot be helpful as well, but often they do not know what to look for in determining a true SS-optioned Chevelle and may be biased toward the person paying for the appraisal.

CHAPTER 1

How Do I Know the Car Is What It Is Claimed to Be?

Documentation for a car is always good and can give you peace of mind on an initial purchase. This is particularly true in the case of 1970–1972 Chevelles and their assembly plant broadcast sheets, commonly called build sheets. These build sheets will show when the car was built and what options it was built with. Assuming the build sheet is authentic, it can go a long way in determining just how real the car you are buying and/or restoring truly is. A build sheet will also give you the car's original exterior color, interior color, and seat type.

Be careful with build sheets. There are a lot of unscrupulous people out there who will create a fake build sheet for a car and even age it to look authentic, plus charge several hundred dollars for their work. Luckily, these build sheet creators have not perfected their art yet and often use broadcast codes or verbiage from a different plant, making them fairly easy to spot as being fakes. Some assembly plants put some numbers on the Fisher Body Number Plate from the build sheet, so this is one method of checking a build sheet against a particular car.

Body Broadcast and Chassis Broadcast Build Sheets

Prior to late 1969, only the Fremont, California, and the Framingham, Massachusetts, assembly plants used the build sheet form. Other plants have two forms of paperwork used to build Chevelles: a body broadcast copy sheet and a chassis broadcast copy sheet. The former was used on the Fisher Body side of the plant and the latter by the final

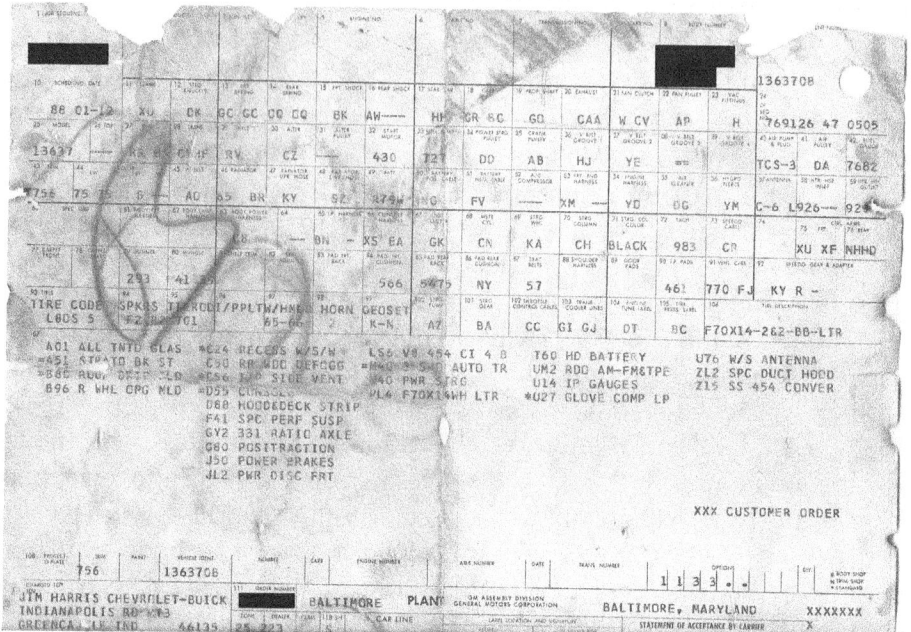

In 1970, the Baltimore build sheet showed the Z15 SS 454 CONVER option verbiage for the SS454 option along with the optional LS6 V-8 454 CI 4 B verbiage for the LS6 engine. A build sheet such as this is invaluable in documenting your Chevelle. (Photo Courtesy LS6 Registry)

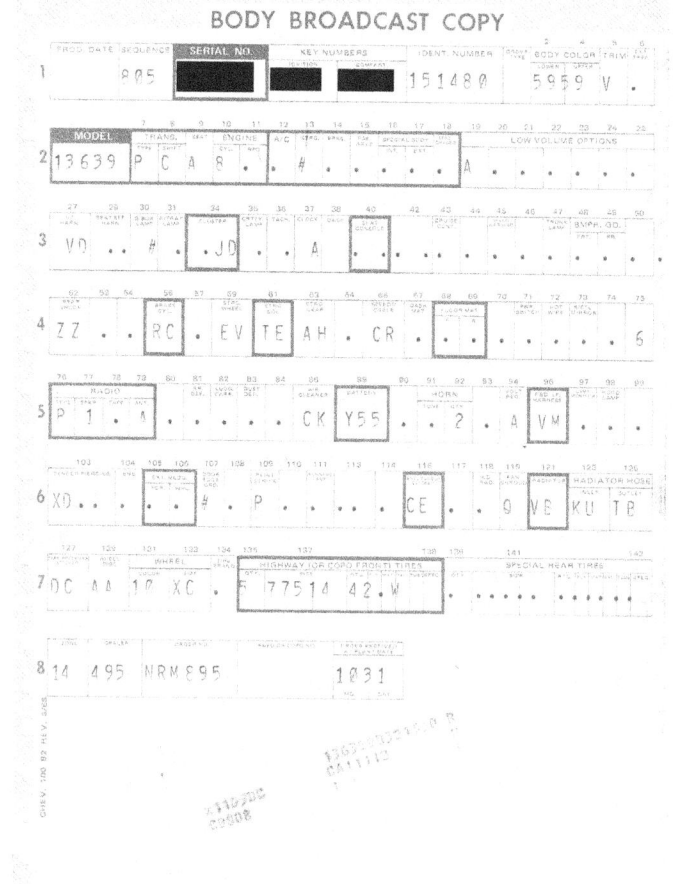

While the SS396 option is not specifically noted, there are several clues in this 1969 Chevelle body broadcast copy sheet. First is the model at the beginning of line 2: 13639 is a Malibu sport sedan, so it is automatically disqualified as an SS396-optioned Chevelle. The engine option code entry in line 2, box 11 has a single dot where an internal RPO code would be used for an optional engine. The dot indicates the standard V-8, or 307-ci engine in this case, was to be installed. (Photo Courtesy ChevelleStuff.net)

ACQUISITION

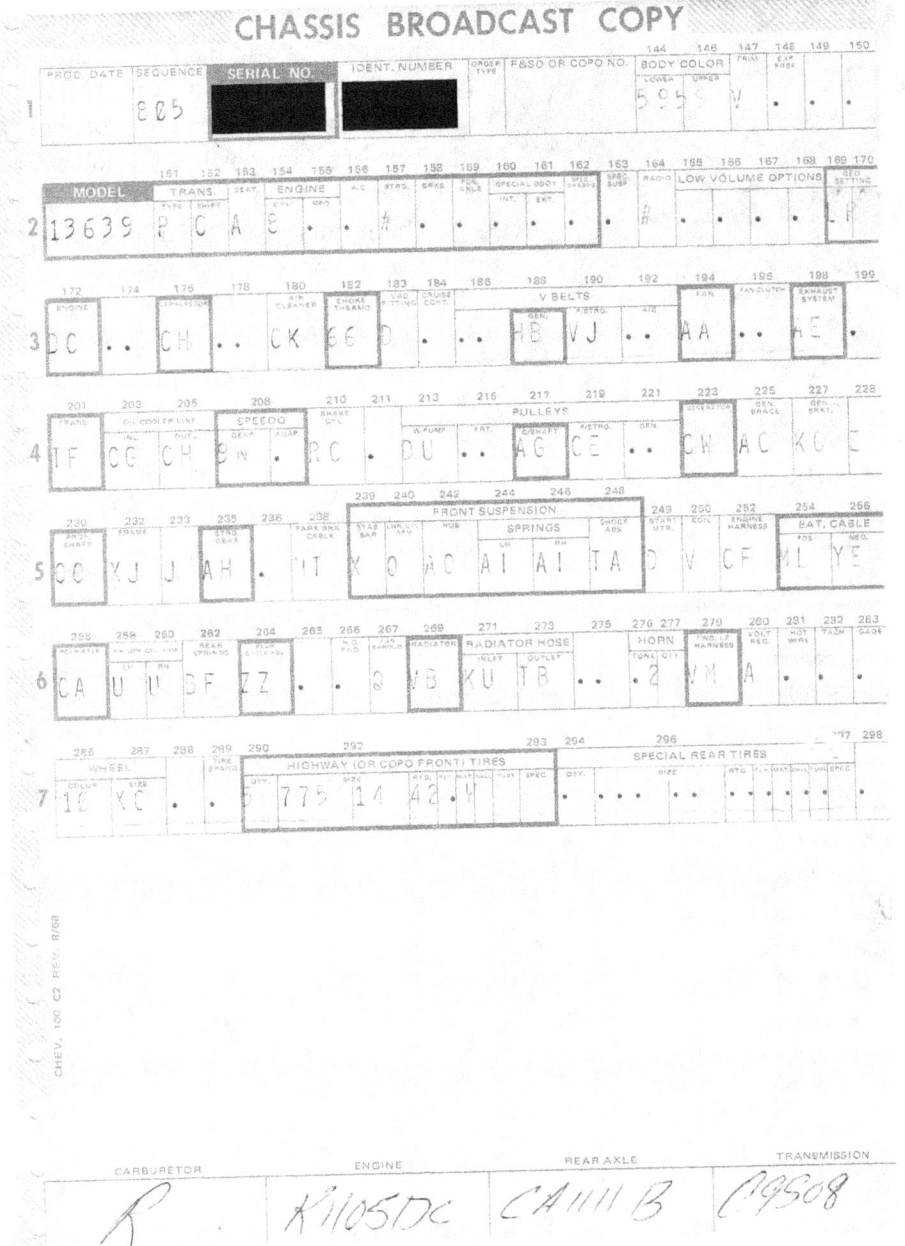

Where the body broadcast copy sheet was used on the Fisher Body side of the assembly plant, the chassis broadcast copy sheet was used on the final assembly side. The car's model, engine type, and several other pieces of information match the body broadcast copy information. In addition, the chassis broadcast copy sheet has the engine identification code on line 3, box 172: DC is for the base 307-2 engine.

assembly side of the plant.

Typically, a body broadcast copy sheet will show the series/bodystyle along with the build sequence number. The series/bodystyle, model year, plant designator, and sequence number make up the VIN. The chassis broadcast copy sheet will show the same VIN information along with the engine code.

A typical chassis broadcast copy sheet shows parts to be used for final assembly. It will include an internal sequence number, body color, engine identification code, transmission type, various pulleys to be used on the engine, front suspension pieces, and various other parts used to complete the car.

Warranty Card

Another form of verification is the warranty card, or Protect-O-Plate, first used in 1965. This metal card was created at the assembly plant and lists the car's VIN, original engine identification information (engine build date and identifying suffix code), transmission type and date, and rear end date and ratio code. Be aware these are now being reproduced as well, so again, buyer beware. The original warranty card will verify a 1970 SS-optioned Chevelle by the engine code for the L34 or L78 396-ci engine or the LS5 or LS6 454-ci engine. For 1971 and 1972, since both 350-ci engines and the 402-ci engine could be ordered with or without the Z15 SS option, the card will only verify the original engine, not whether it was ordered with the Z15 SS option or not. Only a warranty card for the LS5 454-ci engine will truly verify a 1971 Z15 SS-optioned Malibu.

The Protect-O-Plate was stamped by humans and often errors or variations did occur. For example, the engine identification code for the RPO L34 396-ci engine such as CTX may be stamped with just TX. This anomaly hasn't been found (yet) on any 454-ci engines, but there may be some out there. The engine assembly plant and date portion never includes the year, only the month and day. The rear end identification code shows the ratio designation, the month, day, and assembly plant letter. The transmission is shown in several formats, depending on the

CHEVELLE RESTORATION AND AUTHENTICITY GUIDE: 1970–1972

CHAPTER 1

The original buyer of the car received a metal card with warranty information, commonly called a POP (for Protect-O-Plate). This contained the car's full VIN, carburetor type (R for Rochester), engine assembly date and identification code (T0616CRT), rear end type and date (CRV1215B), and transmission (P0E01) identification along with a code for the month the car was built (6). The label information has the original owner's name and address along with the date the car was sold.

proving a mid-December rear end is most likely original to the car.

Selected options are depicted on a warranty card with numbers in any one of seven positions, and the location of the numbers is critical. For the model years 1970 through 1972, there is only one number possible for each position: either the number 1 or the number 3. On earlier years there could be up to one of four numbers

transmission itself. This example is for a Muncie manual 4-speed as noted by the letter "P," which is followed by the model year it was intended for ("0" for 1970 here) and the month and date it was built. E01 is May on this example. Plants varied in how the Muncie manual transmission is depicted beyond the P0E01 example. Some will add A, B, or C for the M20, M21, or M22, respectively. Some may add the broadcast code WB, WL, or WO as well. It should be noted again that these were stamped by humans and variations and mistakes occur.

Although the warranty card was not intended to document a car, it has become a valuable tool in doing so. Typically, the major components such as engine, transmission, and rear end are dated fairly close to the car's build date. But, as shown here, these major components can be dated well before the car's final assembly. The warranty card becomes invaluable in

A Kansas City car shipper invoice shows the Z15 SS 454 Equipment option verbiage with the optional LS6 450-HP Turbo-Jet 454 V-8 engine verbiage along with all other options and exterior color choice. (Photo Courtesy Warren Leunig)

16   CHEVELLE RESTORATION AND AUTHENTICITY GUIDE: 1970–1972

ACQUISITION

Type Dlr. Ord. No.	Serial Number Options and Extra Equip.	Description	Suggested Retail Price	Dlr. Inv. Amt. Car & Options	D & H	Amount
13637	136370A▇▇▇	8 MALIBU SPT COUPE	2809.00	2128.68	156.00	2284.68
	06AK1BA	SEAT BELTS& FRT SHOULD	12.15	8.97	.65	9.62
	06A51AB	STRATO-BUCKET FRONT SE	121.15	89.70	6.15	95.85
	06B93AA	DOOR EDGE GUARDS	4.25	3.12	.25	3.37
	06C08AA	VINYL ROOF COVER/BLACK	94.80	70.20	4.80	75.00
	06C60VA	4-SEASON AIR CONDITION	376.00	278.46	19.00	297.46
	06D55BP	CENTER CONSOLE	53.75	39.78	2.75	42.53
	06G80AA	POSITRACTION AXLE	42.15	31.20	2.15	33.35
	06M40BC	TURBO HYDRA-MATIC	221.80	172.20	11.80	184.00
	06N40AZ	POWER STEERING	105.35	78.00	5.35	83.35
	06PL4AD	F70X14 BELTED WHITE LE	.00	.00	.00	.00
	06T60AL	HEAVY-DUTY BATTERY	15.80	11.70	.80	12.50
	06UM1AT	STEREO TAPE WITH AM RA	194.85	144.30	9.85	154.15
	06ZL2AK	COWL INDUCTION HOOD	147.45	109.20	7.45	116.65
	06Z15AA	SS 454 EQUIPMENT	503.45	372.84	25.45	398.29
	06756AC	BLACK VINYL INTERIOR	.00	.00	.00	.00
	06931AA	14-14 CORTEZ SILVER	.00	.00	.00	.00
TNK561	KEY NOS. ▇▇▇▇	DESTINATION CHARGE				78.75

This is an example of a 1970 Atlanta dealer invoice showing the SS 454 Equipment option verbiage. Since the LS5 454 engine was the base engine for the SS 454 Equipment option, it is not shown on the dealer invoice. (Photo Courtesy Warren Leunig)

used in certain positions. Why only 1 or 3 for 1970 through 1972? You'd have to ask General Motors, that's just the way it is.

The options in position order from left to right are:
1 = Power Steering
1 = Power Brakes
3 = Radio
3 = Disc Brakes
1 = Four Season Air-Conditioning
3 = Power Windows
3 = Four-way Power Seats

Only two of these options were standard equipment on any SS-optioned Malibu: power brakes and disc brakes. So those two should be present on any warranty card of an SS-optioned Malibu and must be in positions number-2 and number-4, other options may or may not be present on the warranty card. The same option numbers and their physical location are also shown on the build sheet in box number-108 and should match.

Often you can even score the original order form for the car, the car shipper, or even the dealer's original invoice.

CHAPTER 1

CHAPTER 2

PREPARATION

The first thing you probably need to ask yourself is, "Do I have the skills and tools to do what I need to do?" Well, that depends on a lot of factors. What is your overall objective for the car? If the objective is to build a nice driver-quality car and you have some skills in bodywork and things mechanical along with the garage space to do the work, you probably have most of the skills needed. Major steps such as rebuilding the engine or transmission may require you to send the engine block, heads, etc. to a machine shop for cleaning and/or necessary machining of parts. You will also need confidence in your ability to reassemble it and get it running.

Many cannot afford to have a professional restoration done and decide to carry out the task between themselves and their buddies. Many say it is not possible, while many others enthusiastically accept the challenge. In reality, it can be done in most home garages using home mechanic tools. Yes, some items will have to be farmed out, but then again, even most professional shops farm out at least some of their work. Every month I get dozens of calls and e-mails at the shop asking me for help in how to restore their car.

Set a Budget

The most important item I can stress when undertaking a project like this is to have a budget set and stick to that budget. Have the funds already set aside before the project is started. Nothing can be more harmful to a project then getting underway and then running out of money. The car will sit for months while more funds are being raised. In the meantime, other important items come up such as repairing the bathroom or taking a family vacation, and before you know it, the project is on permanent hold, making all the work and money spent to date mostly a waste of time. Seldom are projects picked up and started moving again, and more often than not the interest is lost and the car will

All you need is a little space, some fairly basic tools, a little know-how, and lots of money, and you too can be successful at restoring your car. The fruits of your labor will be enjoyed for many years to come.

once again sit and be forgotten as the excitement has worn off.

Gather Documentation

Once you have determined you are serious about the project, you must go back to the very beginning to when the car was first acquired. By this, I mean gather as much information, documentation, history, and photos of the restoration candidate before a single bolt is loosened.

The type of restoration you will be doing will dictate what information you must gather. If all you intend to do is restore the car bearing no resemblance to what it once was and then drive the heck out of it, then its history and documents are likely unimportant. However, if you intend to restore it to a show or concours level and duplicate exactly what it was coming off the assembly line, then items such as color, interior type, options, etc. will be very important, especially in preserving your investment.

Knowing its history will also help in explaining any hidden battle scars encountered during the tear down, as well as make it a little more interesting. It will also help in locating issues that may be there but until now have remained unseen. The more valuable the car, the more important the car's history, documentation, old photos, owner history, and many other items will come into play.

Reference Sources

I strongly recommend purchasing as many books and reference materials as you can afford. Items such as assembly manuals, chassis service manuals, and model-specific books are priceless when doing a complete restoration. Wiring schematics for your year can be invaluable. While these are fairly generic and will not cover many options, they are still worth obtaining in color if possible.

Buy any manuals and reference material you can get your hands on. Chevrolet printed any number of manuals for a given model year, and there are good reference books that break down information such as paint codes, interior trim codes, engine codes, rear end codes, etc. to help you with your search for, and restoration of, that dream Chevelle of yours.

Road Test the Car

If the car is drivable, I have always found it very beneficial to take the car out on a road test. Check out every system, such as brakes, heater, radio, shifting, engine, etc., and make note of any issues no matter how small. This will help during the restoration process so that things like a non-functioning fuel gauge will be checked out and repaired before the dash is restored and set back in the car only to find out you forgot to fix it.

Engine, transmission, and rear end issues will also be helpful for the rebuilder to be aware of so that they can look for internal issues during the rebuild. Telling the rebuilder that the rear end made a clunking noise while going around a corner will alert them to make sure to find the cause.

Thoroughly Examine the Condition

Give the car a good going over, noting what can be saved and what needs to be repaired or replaced. If you find electrical items that do not work, such as the wipers, gas gauge, horn, turn signals, etc., it is best to fix them now if possible rather than to face the same issue when you are putting the car back together. If it is a wiring issue, fix it and make note of the fix so when you install that new wiring harness you can be assured the component worked before installing

An item such as this battery tray can be purchased later in the restoration if you deem it beyond saving, so we will be sure to add it to the list of things to thoroughly inspect. (Photo Courtesy Steve Lubkey)

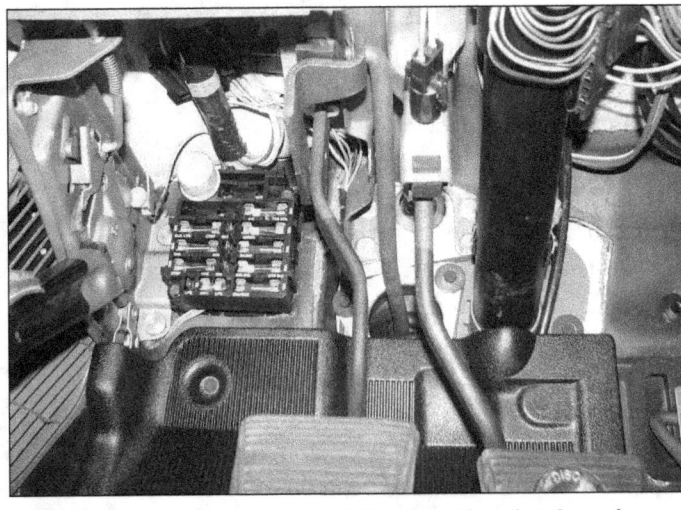
Note details such as the paint lines on the clutch and brake pedals. While these are serviceable and can be cleaned, make note of how much of the pedal is painted and how much is left natural. Photos of details like this will be valuable when it comes time to refurbish the part and reassemble the car.

the wiring harness. If it is something like wipers not working, turn signals not working, etc., hunting gremlins after installing new wiring may not be the best way to go only to find out your wiper motor is bad or you have a bad ground in the light wiring. If the issue is the part itself, such as the fuel gauge or the tank sending unit, now is the time to note that and get replacement parts ordered or at least on the list of parts to find or order. Any engine, transmission, brake, or suspension issues can be addressed when it comes time to rebuild/replace those components.

Keep a list with the item needing repair/replacement. This will help you prioritize and keep track of what you still need to buy and do. Some things you will need pretty quickly; some can easily wait. Components that are relatively easy to find but will not be installed until late in the restoration can probably wait. If you need new brake components, those can probably wait until you begin work on the chassis and suspension.

Appendix A has a checklist sample of some things to look for. Many items on the checklist you will want to replace as a matter of safety, such as brake pads/shoes, front suspension pieces, tires, engine belts, hoses, etc. But, do not throw those old parts away just yet. You may need them to compare the replacement items you will be buying in the future to ensure those replacement parts are correct.

Note details of the car and write them down or photograph them. Details such as the paint lines on the clutch and brake pedals, how much of the pedal is painted, and how much is left natural will be helpful as you reassemble your restoration.

You may need to send the body or frame to a specialty shop for cleaning, stripping, and in many cases straightening. If you are confident enough to do the bodywork and chassis assembly, then by all means use that to save for potential cost to other areas of your restoration. You may even be fortunate enough to have paint skills and a safe place to paint your car. Even if you do not have painting skills, you can do the bodywork and prep the car to have it painted by an outside source and then reassemble the car yourself, often with the help and advice of good friends. Just remember, everything you have to farm out to an outside source adds time and money to your project.

If you are planning to buy new wiring harnesses, be sure to have a list of all the options your car has such as air-conditioning, factory gauges, power windows, etc. to ensure your supplier can get you the correct harnesses. Use as many of the hundreds of online forums as you can. There are many knowledgeable people on these boards who can help answer your many questions, and you will be able to compare photos of similar cars to yours to help you in the disassembly or assembly process. Gather as many reproduction catalogs for your type of car as you can or use

PREPARATION

their online catalogs to shop for the best products, prices, and terms.

Repair or Replace List

As you take the car apart, check the pieces and determine if they can be used as is with a little cleanup or if they need to be repaired, rebuilt, or replaced. Separate the must-be-replaced items and make a plan for the timing of when they need to be ordered for installation. When possible, it is always better to repair an item if it can be repaired than to replace it with parts from a donor car or reproduction parts. It is good to remember that these almost 50-year-old cars were not built with the laser and robot precision that cars are built with today. Reproduction parts often are not up to the quality of original parts in fit and finish, so it can take quite a bit of tweaking to get them to fit properly. Aftermarket suppliers do not always have the same quality parts as originals. Even new old stock (NOS) replacement pieces, especially body panels, do not match the fit, finish, and quality of original body panels.

Factory Correct Parts

GM service replacement parts often are not the same as original parts. If General Motors discovers that a part can be serviceable for several years and/or models of GM cars, it will be sold by dealers. Often, tweaking is necessary to get them to fit correctly, and they may or may not have the correct casting number or even the casting date or markings for your specific application. There may have been a production change during the year, such as the 1966 and 1970 hood panels where only the later version is available.

Aftermarket suppliers are becoming more aware of the demand for correctly marked pieces and offer quality reproductions with correct markings, such as engine hoses, fuel lines, etc. One good example for 1970 of aftermarket versus original equipment body panels is this driver-side front fender.

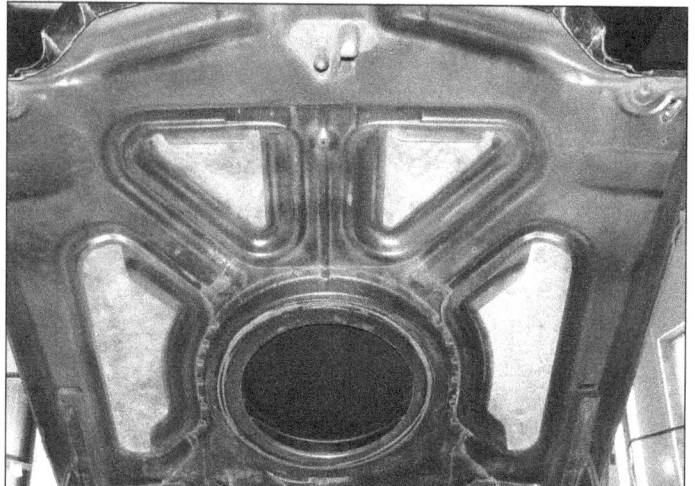

The underside of the early version of the RPO ZL2 hood had different-shaped cutouts and no creases for a crush zone, which would have allowed the front of the hood to buckle on impact and distribute the energy.

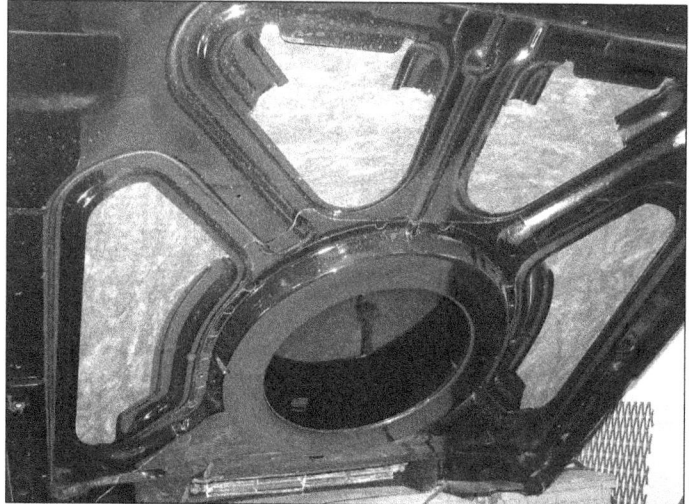

The late version of the RPO ZL2 Special Ducted Hood Air system had different cutout shapes on the underside with horizontal creases to create a crush zone. Also note the four cutouts are a new design.

This late version of the underside of a standard SS domed hood had creases for a crush zone and redesigned cutout areas. The change from early to late occurred around the April/May time frame in most plants.

CHAPTER 2

Note different cutout shapes and the horizontal creases to create a crush zone on the underside of this late version of a normal SS domed hood. Assembly plants would continue to use the early version until supplies of the early hood had expired.

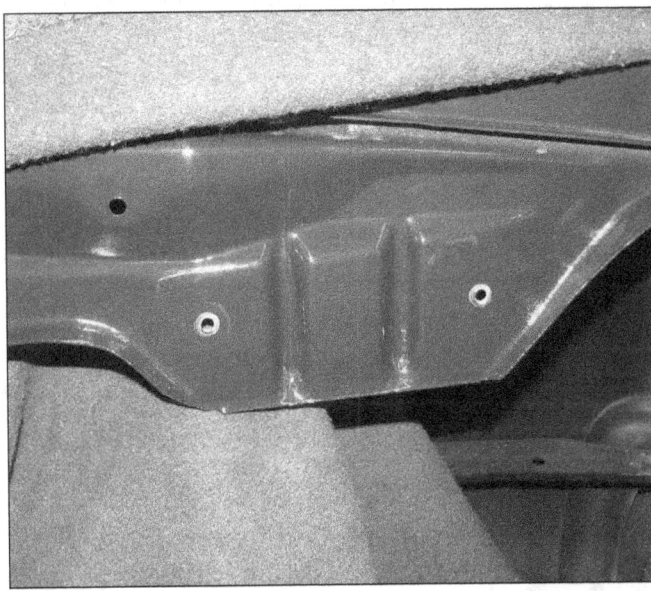

This is the location of the two holes used on an original equipment driver-side fender to mount the windshield wiper fluid bottle.

Compare the original equipment driver-side fender with a typical aftermarket replacement. Not only are the two windshield wiper fluid bottle holes located incorrectly, but the overall bracing structure of the sheet metal itself is vastly different.

Find Discounts on Parts

I contact several different dealers to obtain the best price and terms for parts. Let them know that this is an ongoing project and work out the details beforehand. For example, many dealers offer a 10-percent discount on purchases more than $1,000. Let them know that in all likelihood you will not spend $1,000 on each order but will spend several times that over the coming year. In doing so, many will assign you an account number to ensure you get the discount every time you order regardless of how small.

One very important point I can make is not to always order based on price alone. Shipping costs, lead times, customer service, return policy, and product quality all come into play. Usually, there is a reason someone can offer you the lowest price, and it is not always to your benefit.

Find Work Space and Parts Storage

Set aside a work portion in your garage, barn, pole building, or your basement and ensure it is large enough to accommodate the entire restoration. Workable space and storage to perform the task—and not have it interrupted by garage sales or the family's bikes, portable basketball hoop, and lawn equipment, etc.—is advisable. All that does is help deter your interest in completing the restoration.

Set up shelves to place items on once they are removed from the car and catalog them. I recommend buying quality zipper-type plastic storage bags in various sizes to accommodate various size parts as well as a permanent marker to label not only the bags but also the parts when applica-

PREPARATION

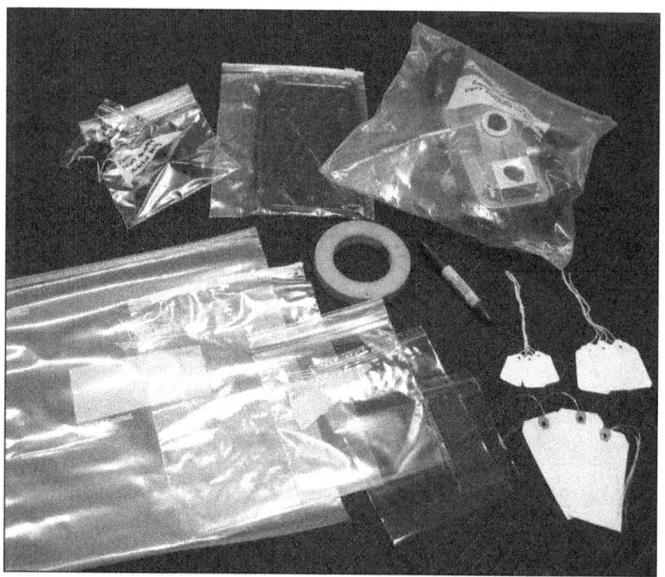

Use plastic bags of various sizes for nuts, bolts, and any number of small parts. Use non-stick tape to keep smaller items together in a group, and use wire and string tags to label larger pieces. The labels will come in very handy in six months when you are ready to reassemble your Chevelle.

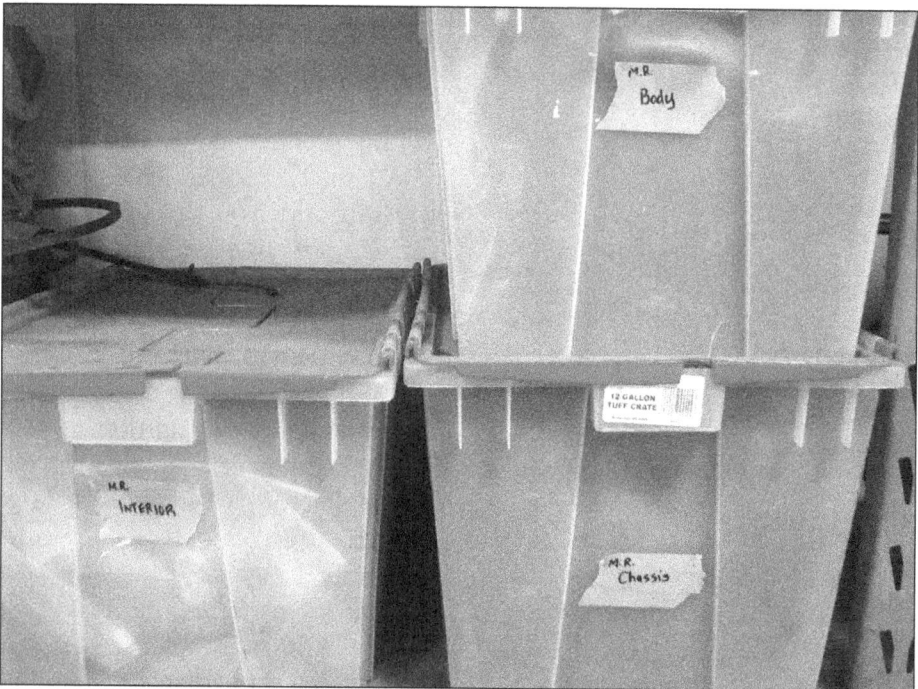

Large, portable storage boxes can be used to store larger pieces both before they are refurbished and after while waiting for reassembly. Engine pieces being sent out or stored, such as starter, carburetor, distributor, etc., can be stored in one container, while chassis and suspension pieces can be stored in another. All those plastic bags you've filled with small pieces can be stored in the larger boxes so they don't get lost.

ble. Buying cheap bags does not work here, as they will tear easily, so go with quality heavy-duty ones. Label every bag with the contents, such as "right front fender bolts," and put them onto a shelf near other bags from similar areas of the car. Never simply put all the bolts in a box or coffee can. It will only come back to haunt you later. String tags also come in very handy. Since I am often doing multiple cars at a time, I am in the habit of putting string tags on many parts, but it can also work well for the home restorer. You may not recognize that left front bumper support or those fuel line clips in six months.

Photograph Everything!

I cannot stress this enough: take photographs, and take a lot of them. Let's face it, with the advent of digital cameras and almost unlimited space on our computers for storage, there is no excuse not to take lots of them. I have more than 70,000 photos in my library and have only just started using my available disk space.

Check each photo after taking it to ensure it is in focus and shows what you want it to show. If you cannot read it now (yes, you know what it is . . . now) you will not be able to read it or recognize it when it comes time to identify the part. When taking photographs, pay special attention to detail more so than taking a picture to show your buddies or post on Facebook. These detailed photos will come in very handy during the reassembly process.

Take photos of everything, including how the wires were routed under the dash, quantity of alignment shims installed on a given suspension part, or as a reminder that a certain bolt was installed differently than one would assume. These are just a few of the many reasons why photos are so important.

Before I ship parts to a subcontractor, such as when having plating done, I lay the parts out, photograph them, and make a written list of all of the parts. This helps you, and it also helps the subcontractor know what parts they should have. This can also help ensure you get back the same parts that you shipped out originally. I also engrave many parts in an inconspicuous place with a job number or customer initials.

Factory Markings and Overspray

If you are restoring a car back to concours standards, then you should also document overspray, how primers were laid on, and how and where the factory sound deadener was sprayed on. These are just some of the things that will help the painter finish the car exactly how it was originally built. On original cars, I also use photos to document bolt-head logos to show how sometimes one bolt type was used on one side of the car, while a different bolt head was used on the opposite side as it was going down the assembly line.

Documenting inspection marks and paint daubs are yet another reason for taking photos. I photograph these areas before, during, and after the cleanup process. In the case of firewall markings, I duplicate what I find in a similar-colored crayon or grease pencil and then photograph it again to document it. From there, I make templates that can be precisely duplicated during the reinstallation process.

Keep a notebook handy and take notes. During the disassembly process, I make notes on parts that are missing, parts that cannot be reused and will have to be ordered, parts that need to be plated, etc. I also note any issues I encounter along the way that will need to be addressed at a later date. Another good step is to list the order in which something was taken apart, such as removing a complete dash to aid in the remounting of that particular item so that you do not forget a ground wire or bolt.

Gather Your Tools

Your skills will probably determine what tools you have on hand, can borrow from friends, or can rent. If you only own a small set of sockets, a nine-piece wrench set in a bag, a couple of screwdrivers, an adjustable 6-inch wrench, and a pair of pliers, you do not have the tools needed to rebuild your Chevelle. If your Chevelle shares the same garage with your family SUV, your kid's bicycles, the washer and dryer, etc., you probably do not have the space to truly rebuild your Chevelle.

Not to put a damper on your enthusiasm for the project but, realistically, it takes more than enthusiasm. Sure, you can do small tasks such as adding custom wheels or adding some engine dress-up items in your cramped garage, but even a minimal restoration takes some skill, tools, and space to match your enthusiasm for the project.

For a restoration project, you will need a lot of specialty tools that you may only use once, unless you do a number of restorations. Air-powered tools such as impact drivers, paint guns, grinders, etc. require a quality air compressor and ancillary items such as air hoses and compressor filters. If you need to repair or replace body pieces including quarter panels or floorpans, you will need a spot-weld cutter, welder with supplies, cut-off wheels, grinder, etc. To blend the bodywork, you may need dollies, specialty hammers, fillers, sanders, etc. Plus, it can be invaluable in getting debris and trash out of those hard-to-clean areas and generally cleaning up the shop after work. The home-size 10-gallon compressor used to air up your tires or inflatable swimming pool is just not going to cut it. You will need at least a 50- to 100-gallon tank with at least 10 cfm at 90 psi to get any serious work done. A good hydraulic press will allow you to remove and install bearings, bushings, ball joints, and similar items. A quality bead-blast cabinet or portable sandblaster can quickly clean paint, surface rust, and years of crud off smaller parts.

Engine-Specific Tools

Rebuilding an engine, transmission, or rear end can also require specialty tools such as valve spring compressors, micrometers (both inside and outside), and dial indicators to measure piston top dead center (TDC) or gear backlash, and specialty pliers for those E-clips, C-clips, and various retainer clips. If you do not do a lot of engine, transmission, or rear end work, it will be easier to farm these tasks out to qualified shops.

Jacks

At least one good floor jack and at least two but preferably four or more jack stands are needed to raise the car off the ground and support the chassis. A set of car dollies can be of great assistance if you plan on moving your rolling chassis around your garage or shop as well.

Bench Grinder

A bench grinder with both grinding and polishing heads is handy for touch-up finishing and final polishing of trim pieces. Adhesives for gaskets, weatherstripping, and special lubricants for brakes, windows tracks, etc. will also be needed.

Naturally, if you do not have or cannot borrow or rent these items, you will need to find a reputable body shop that is willing to take on the project and do the work. It is often difficult to find a local body shop to do a good restoration or even a passable one. The bulk of their business is insurance collision repair, and your project can sit for months with nothing being done and parts getting lost. Get a solid estimate up front of not only the work to be done and a price but the time frame for its completion. Most body shops will not make near as much money on your restoration as they do on collision work, so your car will always be the second priority in their shop, sometimes making the project last years.

Taking on Someone Else's Project

Probably 60 to 70 percent of all projects get stalled at some point, and owners decide to move on. Extreme caution should be taken if considering another owner's project. There are many questions to consider including: How much work has been done, and is it quality work? How much of the original driveline is left, and is it all there? Were removed parts tagged or bagged? Few things are as daunting as buying a roller with the engine and transmission out of the car; no trim or windows on the body; 15 milk crates of parts; and a few coffee cans of nuts, bolts, small trim pieces, etc. and none of it marked.

A project that has been assembled is much easier to work with. You will know exactly what has and has not been done and if all small pieces are there. A car that you purchased in primer and were told is "ready for paint" is usually not, and you have no way of knowing if the prep work was done correctly. If they did not acid wash the metal and remove all traces of oil or other contaminants from the body prior to priming, the paint will never stay on the car.

If you started the project yourself and decide it is more than what you bargained for or decide you want a concours restoration rather than a simple rebuild to drive, ensure you have all of your pieces and parts sorted in such a matter that the shop doing the rest of the work has everything you removed and tagged. Decide up front if you want the shop to call you and see if you can locate any parts needed or if you will opt to let the shop track down the missing parts. Missing parts can often hold up one area of the restoration, but work can still possibly continue in other areas. One important fact to keep in mind is a restoration shop will always charge you more for a project you started and didn't complete than one that was brought to them from the beginning. That is even assuming you can find a shop willing to take on your already-started project.

Where to Start

We are going to begin with the assumption you are doing a concours-quality body-off-frame restoration. If your plan is something less, you can adjust your plan of attack accordingly.

Once you begin your project, get organized. Tag and/or bag every piece you remove along with a note of when in the process it was removed, so you can reinstall the pieces in correct order. After you reinstalled the dash assembly is not the time to remember you need to replace/repair the heater controls or the radio. Get a quality digital camera and document disassembly details with photos. Download them to your computer after each work session and note what you did and any difficulties encountered in the day's work. In six months or a year, when you are putting it back together, you will forget something or misremember how it came apart. I also make separate files for the photos to make them easier to find when needed, such as body, chassis, drivetrain, interior, etc.

Lastly, I cannot emphasize enough to save all of your old parts until the restoration is complete. Many times, I refer back to the original part when I receive a replacement or donor-car part. This will ensure that what goes back on the car will be similar to what originally came off. You may also be able to use parts of the old part if needed.

Even if you plan on farming out the entire process of restoring your Chevelle, you should be aware of the time, effort, materials, etc. that your selected shop must invest in the restoration. While the factory could build a complete car in four or five days, it took hundreds of employees at numerous subassembly stations to put the car together. Quite a number of those major parts, such as driveline components, came pretty much assembled by scores of other employees at other plants.

The assembly plants did not have to worry about patching rusted body panels, stripping old paint, tearing out old interior and wiring, or waiting for a third party to complete the assembly of a major component. A concours restoration can take months, even years, to complete from chasing down those hard-to-find correctly dated parts that were changed and/or lost long ago to the quality of a small team of experts to assemble the car and, last but not least, to your finances.

CHAPTER 2

CHAPTER 3

Body Disassembly

Overcome the urge to dig right in and start unbolting pieces; get organized up front. Have a general plan of attack for the day. If today's task is to disassemble the front sheet metal, have a place in mind to store the hood, fenders, bumper, radiator support, etc. beforehand. These large items can be difficult to store due to their size, and keeping them out of the way once they have been removed can be a challenge. Protect them from warpage; do not lay fenders on their sides, as they tend to flatten out over time. I buy the cheap $25 body-panel stands and set them on there. Take care that your hood and other body panels are not sitting on a wet or damp garage floor; this will only add to your rust issues. Take care of the hood corners.

Large plastic dairy crates are great for larger heavy items but tend to gather dust when stored for a time. Heavy-duty boxes will help with dust issues, but you cannot see what is inside the box. Be sure to label boxes clearly. I find that those large plastic totes are the best and are not very expensive. I then tag them with pieces of tape and separate them by category: body, interior, chassis, engine, etc. This makes it much easier when it comes time to reassemble the car, as you grab only the tote and its parts for the area you are currently working on.

Clear plastic bags can be used for the smaller items such as nuts, bolts, alignment shims, etc. Be sure to note which side (driver's side versus passenger's side) with items such as fender alignment shims. Assuming the body panels were hanging nicely on the car when you disassembled it, I like making a shim map showing the location of the shims and what overall thickness was present in that area. This will give you a starting point come assembly time.

With camera, bags, and a marker in hand, it is time to get started. Unless you have a dozen friends and a camera crew filming everything, do not expect to have your car stripped in an afternoon like you will often see on television. Take your time during

The interior needs to be completely gutted along with all wiring removed and any mechanical attachments, such as steering linkage, transmission linkage, etc., removed, as you see here. Two heavy-duty bumper jacks are used here to lift the body from the frame, but any safe method you have available to you will work.

BODY DISASSEMBLY

disassembly as you photograph the steps and mark and bag trim pieces, screws, bolts and nuts, etc.

Removal Methods

There are two ways to attack a restoration depending on your skills, space, access to specialty equipment, or just your preference. Is the body going to be removed from the chassis? Some prefer to do bodywork with the body on the chassis, and some prefer to remove the body as quickly as possible and either put it on a rotisserie or a donor frame, or just lift the body and support it with 55-gallon drums and 4x4s for support.

Two-Post Lift

One way to lift the body off the chassis is with a two-post lift, a pair of large end jacks, or even an engine hoist or two.

It is always a good idea to temporarily weld in some square tube bracing if you are taking the body off the chassis. This is especially important on a convertible, as the body will flex and make your assembly that much more difficult.

Hoist

Another way is to use an engine hoist and lift the front and rear of the car. From there you can transfer onto a jigging cart, a donor rolling frame, the 55-gallon drum/4x4 method, or simply homemade sawhorses.

Since this is a convertible body, extra bracing should be temporarily welded at critical stress points of the body to keep it from bending during removal. This needs to be done before the body is removed from the frame. Once removed, the body can be attached to a rotisserie jig for easy access.

This convertible body, properly braced and off the frame, illustrates the amount of materials that should be removed from the body and interior components before the body is removed from the frame. Everything you can remove from the interior prior to lifting the body off is less that you have to deal with once it is off.

This is one of the preferred methods of lifting a body off a frame because it is quick and easy. It is always a good idea to have a rotisserie jig or some stand ready to support the body once you roll the chassis out from underneath. Sometimes you just have to do what you can and use the tools available to you at the time.

If you are on a tight budget, one storage solution for the body is homemade sawhorses. This alternative works pretty well, is inexpensive to build, and still gives you access to do some cleanup work. If you need to replace sheet metal or quarter panels, this may not be a viable solution for obvious reasons. (Photo Courtesy Bill Garcia)

This rolling chassis is in final prep stages to remove the body. On this particular car, the engine and transmission have been removed prior to removing the body. As long as all physical connections between the body and the driveline have been disconnected, it is simply a matter of choice whether to remove the engine and/or transmission beforehand.

At this early stage of disassembly, all front sheet metal has been removed, cooling and engine oil drained, radiator support removed, and all wiring disconnected and removed that would hinder removing the body. Note in this instance the windshield and rear window have been removed before taking the body off the frame. Do whatever works for you.

Disassembly

If you are planning to remove the body from the frame, leave the doors on the car for now. They will add rigidity to the body when it is lifted from the frame.

Whether you plan on removing the engine now or later is up to you. The engine and driveline could be left in place and removed once the body is lifted from the chassis. I remove every body I restore from their respective frames, mount them on a cart or a straight donor frame, and send them over to my body shop. In the case of the do-it-yourself restorer, you may want to leave the body on its frame while you do all the bodywork and panel replacement or welding, as this will ensure the body does not move or flex while off the frame. If not, when you try mounting the body back onto the frame you may find things not lining up. When completed, or at the very least when in primer, you can then remove the body and restore the rolling chassis.

Set the engine and transmission aside for now. Put the engine on a stand, tape and seal up all of the openings, and leave it for now. There is no sense in rebuilding the engine and having it gather dust in your shop/garage while you are doing body or chassis work. It will be a while before you are ready to fire it up and get it running properly. If there are some hard-to-find items missing such as the A.I.R. system, correct intake or exhaust manifolds, carburetor, distributor, or brackets/braces/pulleys, now would be the time to start the search for those pieces. Until then, hold off until you are close to putting the engine and transmission back in the chassis.

The same goes for the transmission. If you have made notes on what needs to be repaired or replaced, leave it alone until it comes close to reassembly time.

CHAPTER 4

CHASSIS, SUSPENSION, AND BRAKE WORK

The chassis is usually one of the dirtiest and most worn-out parts of the restoration you will encounter due to the fact that it is mostly out of sight and therefore neglected. The undercarriage is usually in very bad shape with pitting, many bent areas due to previous wrecks or hastily put floor jacks, welds showing ill-gotten repairs, oily residue, and cracked or worn-out bushings, just to name a few of the problems. All of these issues will have to be addressed on a restoration.

Chassis Disassembly

To what length you decide to take it will be up to you, taking into account whether the car will be a daily driver or a trailer queen. It will also depend on how much time and money you are willing to spend on that part of the restoration. Many people will not put much emphasis on the chassis due to it being unseen, while others will expect the same attention to detail on the chassis as will go into the body. Regardless of your intentions, keep a notebook and pen handy and make notes of your findings and, more importantly, document which parts will need to be found or purchased as you remove the defective part from the car.

Cleaning and Inspecting the Frame

The body has likely been removed prior to this task, so this will leave the chassis fully exposed for you to now start your inspection and restoration. It is highly recommended you begin with a good pressure wash to get as much of the oily film, road grime, and remaining residue removed from the car before you begin the teardown.

Before you begin to pressure wash the frame, look for any factory

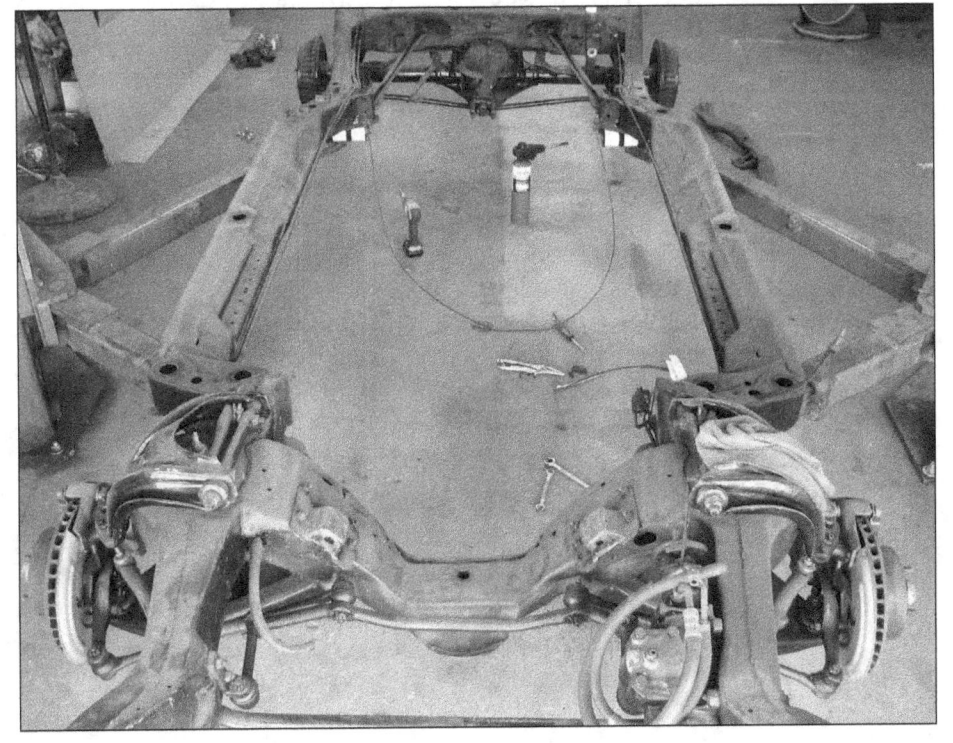

One of the most neglected parts of your Chevelle is the frame, and it will require a lot of work to bring it back to its original condition. Make sure to fully document its state with photographs before you disassemble the frame.

CHAPTER 4

Make special note of items such as the frame motor mount with regard to how the bolts are oriented. Some plants installed them with the bolt head on the top side, while others installed them with the nuts and lock washers on the top (shown).

This is an example of the frame decal that the author has personally only ever found on the driver-side rear axle hump. The decal has always been inverted likely due to the frame being assembled upside down. These are often obliterated by road grime or are missing altogether. If still in place, it should read XU for coupe, XV for convertible, and XX for El Camino, at least for 1970.

tags or decals and document them. Keep in mind that all of the removed grime will have to go somewhere, and it is illegal in most residential areas for these types of contaminants to go down the storm drain in the streets. You may want to drag it to the local self-wash car wash, as they generally have catch tanks designed for this runoff, and they are legal.

After a good cleaning and scraping, photograph every part of the frame and its bolt-on parts for component placement, damage, brake and fuel-line placement, the location of specific clamps, cracks, inspection marks, and stampings, just to name a few. Do an initial inspection and photograph it. Do it again when it is fully disassembled for areas that may have been missed. Not all frames were assembled the same throughout the seven different plants, so if you are reasonably sure that your frame has been unmolested, document its assembly, especially motor mount-to-frame bolt orientation, crossmember-to-frame bolt orientation, the different types of clamps used on the brake and fuel lines, etc.

With regard to VIN stampings on the frame, keep in mind, these VIN stamps were put there by assembly workers. It was a general practice and a federal mandate that they all be stamped, but for reasons unknown, not all plants or line workers did what they were supposed to. Most plants stamped the frames with VIN numbers (some at least three times), while other plants, such as the Kansas City Leeds plant, rarely did, at least not in 1970.

It is a good idea to start a separate file within your car's main restoration file and call it something like "Frame and Chassis Components" so that you can easily track all the facts and progression of the restoration. If you are doing a concours restoration and the condition allows for it, make sure to document any component parts that have decals still attached and the type of finish that particular component may have had.

Authentication

You will also want to carefully clean and document the frame part number, assembly date stamp, manufacturing code, and VIN (if found). The VIN can usually be found on a variety of places on the rear half of the frame and usually on the top side. You may not find any, or you may find as many as three stamps. When originally stamped, they were very faint even when new; after almost 50 years of weathering, they can be difficult to find. Some plants did not follow the mandate of stamping the frame with a VIN.

Decals (such as the frame prefix code, coil spring, shock, power steering gear, rear axle, and many others) should be documented for future replacement. The color and part number on the decal and location

CHASSIS, SUSPENSION, AND BRAKE WORK

You will always find the manufacturer's information on the driver-side rear framerail aft of the rear tire. This information provides the manufacturer (in this case Parish for Parish Pressed Steel), the part number 3960733 (a coupe), the date code (4 14 70 or April 14, 1970), and the shift (in this example, second shift).

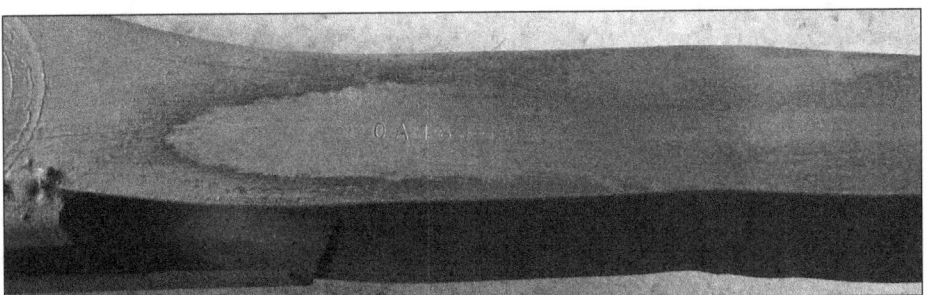

This particular Atlanta Chevelle had the frame stamped with its VIN in three different locations. One was in the conventional location on the top side of the driver-side rear rail; two additional stamps were on the top side of the passenger-side rear rail. Make sure to look everywhere for the possible VIN stamp, but do not be alarmed if one is not found.

An example of one of the many decals that might still be on your chassis is shown. It may be found with careful disassembly. This particular rear coil spring decal is actually from a 1969 Chevelle for example purposes and denotes code GV and part number 3952817. It can be found under a variety of Chevelles.

should also be noted. This is also a good time to do a preliminary documentation of the colored-paint inspection marks commonly found throughout the front suspension and rear differential components. These are vitally important to replicate on a highly valuable collector car to bring the degree of the restoration to a higher level. A more in-depth documentation can be done during the individual-parts-cleaning process as well, which will be covered later in the reassembly part of this chapter.

Once you have documented everything that you can, very carefully try and remove all of the decals. You will likely not be able to save them, but you can use them later as a reference and replace them with decals that closely resemble the ones you removed and documented. If you are only doing a driver-quality restoration, you may not be concerned with these items, so use your own judgment.

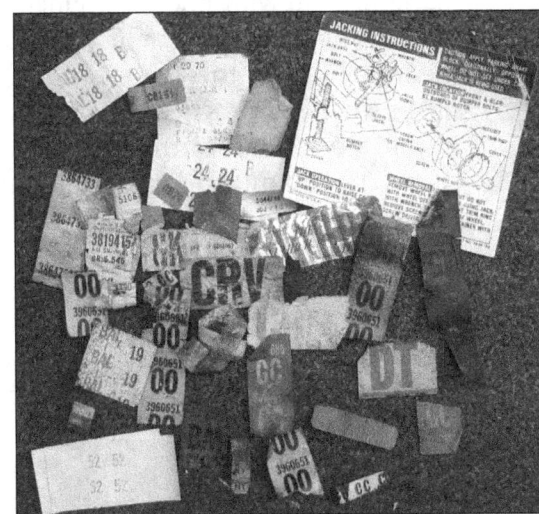

Save all the decals you can from the car and chassis as you find them. This is just a small selection of decals you might find on your Chevelle during your restoration. They can be helpful in replicating them and also confirming and documenting what your car was originally.

CHEVELLE RESTORATION AND AUTHENTICITY GUIDE: 1970–1972

Inspection Markings

You may also find many paint or grease pencil markings throughout your chassis and even in places on the body. These were placed there for a variety of reasons. Most of the time, it helped the assembly line pick the part that went on that particular car based on color markings. Other times, the independent supplier marked the items as they were being manufactured or assembled to denote things such as bolts that had been tightened to spec, if heat treating was performed, that machining was completed, the placement of welds, inspections that were done, etc. In a lot of cases, such as front-suspension paint markings, there seems to be no rhyme or reason as to their application, and seldom are any two alike in either color or placement.

Your best bet is to replace what you found exactly as you found it, backing it up with photo documentation of where and how it looked. Restoring one of these cars is much like what an archeologist goes through when unearthing a treasure. The utmost care and patience needs to be used to preserve and document everything that was found to help solidify your car's roots and provenance.

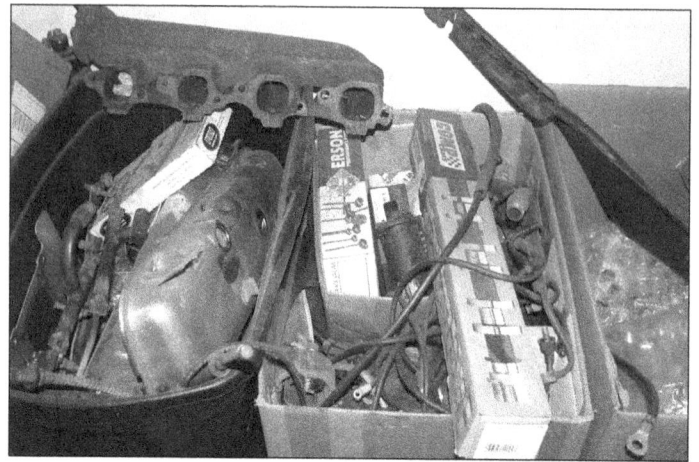

Keep all old parts in a separate tote during the restoration, even if they are not salvageable. There are many small pieces off these components that can be reused if the replacement component parts are not to your liking or don't fit. You can also use the original parts for comparison to the replacement ones. If you are restoring a car for a customer, let them decide what gets thrown away and what they may want to keep.

Save Those Old Parts

As with most areas of the restoration and with rare exception, save all old parts that you know you will not be using in separate marked bins. This way, you can refer back to them if you are having fitment, function, finish, or design issues with replacement parts. Sometimes comparing the new to the old will solve a problem. Just as importantly, you can sometimes take pieces off your old parts and use them along with the new parts. Even completely unsalvageable parts such as weatherstripping can provide you with little things like the small white push pins if you come up short or they went missing from the new weatherstripping package.

If you are restoring a Chevelle for a customer, it is a good idea to keep all of their parts until the car is ready for delivery, thereby allowing them to make the final decision to throw parts away or to keep them. In the case of a highly valuable collector car, these original parts can also add to the sale and story of the car if or when it comes time to sell it. Broken parts—such as a transmission case or exploded differential housing—can round out the picture in a story of how the transmission came apart just as you slammed second gear while being a car length in front of your opponent. It will also prove the beginnings of the car since you will still possess the original part with the car's VIN number on it even if it cannot be used. In most of the do-it-yourself restorers' cases, you just need to keep them for reference and parts salvage.

Suspension Disassembly

Now it is time to start the disassembly in earnest. First, make note

Just one example of the many paint or grease pencil markings you might find on your Chevelle is shown. These particular yellow paint markings are commonly found on Chevelle 12-bolt differentials as well as others to denote the placement of the pocket welds that held the axle tubes into the center carrier. These were done before the welding took place, evidenced by the burned paint around the weld.

of any shims located in the front upper control arm area. This is one very good way to determine if your frame has been involved in any significant damage. If the car was ever in an accident where the frame was knocked out of alignment, the frame and body shop would have to compensate for that alignment issue with the use of shims and/or a replacement offset cross shaft, assuming they were not able to pull the frame back to its original state. If you notice significantly more shims on one side versus the other or a lot of shims on both sides, this is a likely sign of a pending frame alignment issue.

Another sign of severe damage is if the upper control arm shaft has been replaced with an offset shaft to make up for more needed camber or caster. When the frame is totally disassembled and with a GM frame dimension sheet in hand, this would be the time to have the frame brought back to its original form.

Suspension Failures

Also look for any obvious wrinkles, tears, or broken welds on the frame. This is also an indicator of extremely hard usage or damage. These issues will need to be addressed during the restoration to ensure the car will sit and ride according to the manufacturer's specifications. It is rare that a 50-year-old Chevelle would not have been involved in an accident or drag raced in its lifetime, so this will more often than not be the norm.

Pay close attention for signs of damage to all parts of the frame, including the rear differential, rear crossmember, control arms, trailing arms, and frame to name a few. Any

This particular frame had seen severe use and damage in its lifetime primarily due to drag racing. Notice the pulled and stretched oval tie-down hole, the badly damaged and rusted core support–mounting hole on the top, and several holes drilled and then damaged in the inside rail. Dents found in the frame like the one near the core support mount often lead to more severe damage elsewhere that needs to be addressed before you can consider any bodywork and paint on the frame.

Note the excessive amount of shims used on this upper control arm, which is usually a good indicator of other damage somewhere in the frame or suspension. The cross shaft shown here was also not used on the Chevelle but was used on other GM A-bodies, so this is another indicator that someone replaced some suspension pieces, likely because they were bent.

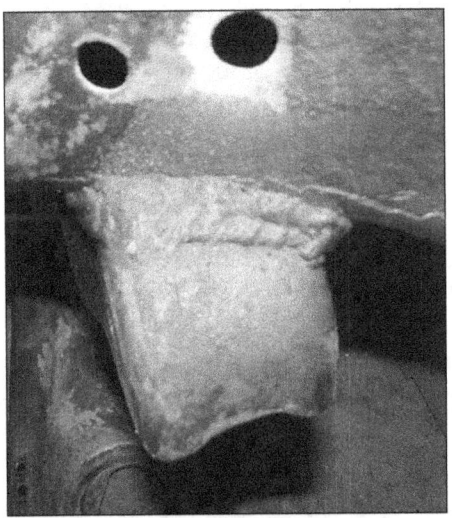

Some less-than-quality shops will try and repair cracks in suspension mounts using less-than-stellar welding techniques. As can be seen in this photo, it did not stop by simply welding; the crack just continued down the frame. When not addressed in the correct manner, it can lead to catastrophic results.

This particular Chevelle was used extensively for drag racing in its early life. Many hard launches caused the axle tube to break the plug welds loose. This not only caused the tube to walk itself out a 1/4 inch but also rotated the tube slightly. Had this not been addressed during the restoration, you would continue to have issues, some of which could have had an ill-fated outcome.

damage will all have to be addressed during the restoration. Especially look for things you would normally not even consider looking for in most cases, such as axle tube damage. A badly or heavily abused car may have axle tube twist or separation, and you or your mechanic must address these during the rebuild.

Engine, Transmission, and Driveshaft Removal

If you have not already done so, it is time to remove the engine, transmission, and driveshaft. Again, fully document everything you disassemble. Start by disconnecting any components related to the drivetrain, such as electrical, fuel lines, exhaust, and any remaining transmission or carburetor linkages. If you are saving your exhaust—and this cannot usually be done very well—carefully remove the exhaust tips, tailpipes, mufflers, and the head pipes. Once those are removed, proceed by removing all the hangers. If you do not intend to save the exhaust, then just cut them apart using a tool, such as an exhaust cutter.

Engine Removal Preparation

Unbolt the engine mount through bolts found on either side of the engine. If this is an original or unmolested car, make note of the direction of the bolts and motor mounts. Original assembly-line engine mounts had a swaged nut on one side of the engine mount, allowing the assembly worker to simply install the bolt through the mount and not have to worry about putting a wrench on the nut on the other side. Replacement mounts did not come with this and required installing a nut and lock washer onto the bolt. However, when reassembling the engine onto the frame, you can still simulate factory mounts by at the very least installing the bolts in the same direction as the factory did. On the driver's side, the bolt was installed from the rear toward the front. The passenger's side is just the opposite since it uses the same part-numbered engine mount, and the bolt was installed into the front side of the mount.

On assembly-line engine mounts, the nuts are swaged onto the mount and do not require two tools when tightening. If you no longer have the original mounts, you can simulate this by using thin nuts and orientating the bolts from back to front on the driver's side and front to back on the passenger's side.

Unbolt the two bolts that hold the transmission mount to the crossmember. Take special note of how the washers are placed on automatic cars: two large washers should be mounted between the transmission tailshaft housing and the transmission mount on either side. This aids in pinion alignment and is very important.

Remove or cut the rubber fuel line(s) running from the frame-mounted fuel hard line to the

Either of these two tools will work well to remove your old exhaust system. If you already own a Sawzall, that is the quickest and easiest way to remove it. The exhaust pipe cut-off tool can be purchased for less than $30, which is also a good alternative. In a pinch, simply use a hacksaw.

CHASSIS, SUSPENSION, AND BRAKE WORK

This is just one example of the stripes that you may encounter on your driveshaft. The color codes will be found in box 19 of your build sheet and in this case marked PK-BL. It is widely believed that the thin orange stripe denotes that the shaft has been through the balancing process.

Note how there is a large washer installed between the top of the transmission mount and the transmission tailhousing. This is only on automatic cars and must be put back in this way, as it affects the pinion angle. People often install the large washer under the lock washer and bolt on the top mount to tailhousing bolts, and that would be incorrect.

The meaning of this yellow grease pencil marking on the aft part of the driveshaft has not yet been determined, but it has been found on many 454 shafts and always at the rear. It is likely that it is just another way of marking that a part of the machining or assembly has been completed and checked or tells the installer to put that at the rear during installation.

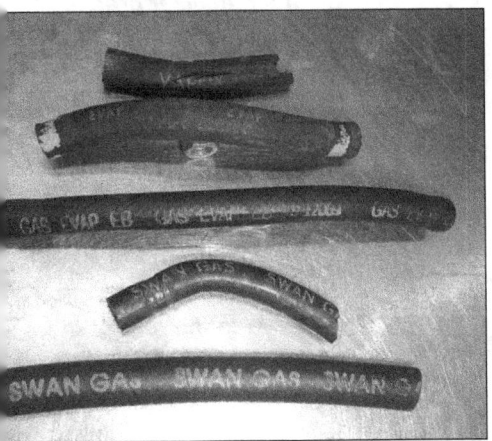

These are just some of the many types of fuel and evaporator lines you may encounter during your restoration. Keep your original lines and replicate the markings if you so choose. Some of these lines are available in the aftermarket, but with most you will need to replicate the stamps and stamp your own. Many of these will also have date codes on them.

fuel pump. Inspect the fuel line(s) to see if they may be an original with ink stamping such as "SWAN GAS" or "EVAP" so that these can be replicated during the restoration process.

Driveshaft

Remove the driveshaft at this time. Before doing so, have a pan ready and lay it underneath the transmission output shaft to collect transmission fluid that may leak. If not already done, drain the engine oil at this time as well. Be aware that even more antifreeze, engine oil, and transmission fluid may leak from these areas when the engine and transmission are tilted up for removal, so prepare containers to catch these fluids.

Remove the four universal-joint U-bolts or through bolts, nuts, and straps, whichever your car has at the rear U-joint. Wrap duct or electrical tape around the U-joint so that the bearing caps do not fall off the U-joint and cause the loss of some of your needle bearings. Carefully set the rear end of the driveshaft on the ground (if you are not using a hoist), then pull the front slip yoke from the transmission tailhousing.

Place the driveshaft in a safe and secure area so it does not fall; it can be easily dented. The U-joints will be replaced later on in your restoration, and we will cover that part of the restoration at that time. As always, make note of any markings you may find. The assembly-line shafts have paint stripes on them that correlated with box 19 of the build sheet. The assembly worker would look on the build sheet for the stripe colors and would pick the correct shaft from the bank to install on the car. Other paint markings can be found on the shaft as well as the pinion flange and slip yoke, so look around.

Pulling the Engine

Remove the carburetor and distributor so they are not damaged during the engine-removal process. Have an engine stand, dolly, old tire, wood blocks, or whatever else you intend to use to set the engine on at the ready. It is recommended to use an engine hoist (or cherry picker as some are called) to remove the engine and try to have a buddy available to help negotiate the engine and transmission from the frame if needed.

Always use grade 3 or higher bolts and a chain suited for the task. This is one area you never want to skimp on when it comes to safety. Lift the engine and transmission from the frame as a unit for ease of removal. Once on the ground, the engine and transmission can be separated. At this point, the transmission can be stored in a safe place—preferably on a dolly—and the engine mounted on a stand to ease in its disassembly.

Parking Brake Removal

The parking or emergency brake (as it is commonly called) cables can now be removed; they are in three separate assemblies. The front main cable that was separated from the body during the body removal section in chapter 3 can now be removed from the frame. Note that the cable comes downward and into the front corner of the driver-side framerail. From there, it runs through a hole at the rear portion of that part of the frame and is held there by what is commonly called a butterfly clip.

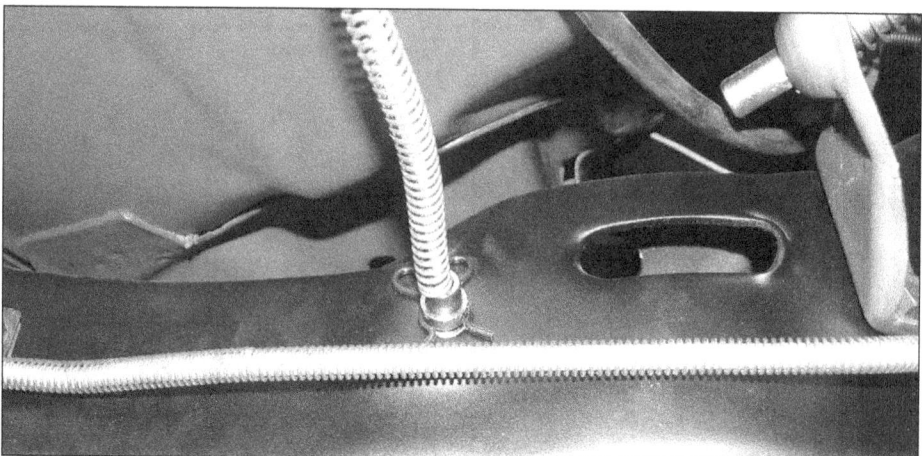

The primary parking brake cable will come through the front framerail just behind the driver-side front tire on the rear side of that rail. After the intermediate cable equalizer and large C-hook have been removed, go back and remove the small butterfly clip.

The primary cable attaches to the intermediate cable by way of a stabilizer bracket, and tension is applied via two nuts. Remove these and the large C-hook from the intermediate cable as well as the two smaller S-hooks from the body and let the cable drop. Move to the rear of the intermediate cable and remove the U-brackets.

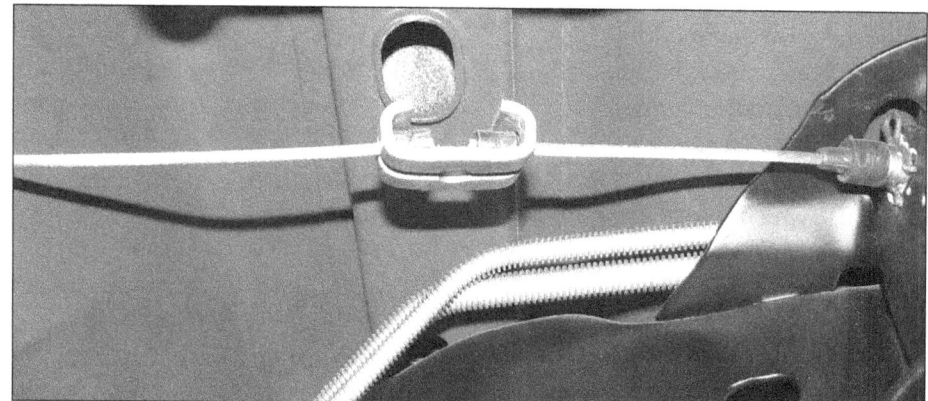

Moving to the rear of the intermediate cable, remove the C-brackets that hold the intermediate cable to the rear cable. Note that the rear parking brake cable is also held to the frame with butterfly clips.

CHASSIS, SUSPENSION, AND BRAKE WORK

Determine if your crossmember is correct for your manual-transmission (shown here) or the automatic-transmission application. The manual-transmission crossmember will have the extra bracket welded to the rear of the crossmember for mounting of the shifter bracket to it.

Pay special attention to the bolts mounting the crossmember to the frame, assuming they are original and have never been molested. The assembly manual shows that these should be mounted from the top down, but we rarely see them this way. They are usually mounted from the bottom up. This is likely due to the frame being assembled at the plant upside down.

Near the end of this cable, you will find an intermediate brake-cable equalizer. It will have the intermediate cable running through it. Just behind the equalizer are two nuts that lock together and adjust the cable tension. Remove these two nuts and slide the equalizer and intermediate cable off of the front cable as well as the large C-hook that stabilizes the intermediate cable. The C-hook is attached to the transmission crossmember just to the right of the transmission tailhousing.

Now remove the intermediate cable from the equalizer. Place the hardware and any other parking brake parts in the bag you already labeled back when the body was removed from the frame. The two C-shaped hooks that held the intermediate cable to the floorpan will already be in that bag. Now that you have all of that hardware removed, go back and remove the butterfly clip from the primary cable and pull the cable upward and out of the frame.

At the rear of the intermediate cable, you will find two U-brackets that hold the intermediate cable to the rear differential cables. Place the U-brackets in your bag and put the front main and intermediate cable in a safe place for restoration or replacement. Normally these cables are worn, stretched, and rusted and will require replacement.

With the drivetrain and emergency brake cables out of the way, now is a good time to remove the transmission crossmember. Chevrolet used one type for manual transmissions and another for automatic transmissions. The manual version had an additional bracket welded to the rear of it for the manual-shifter mounting bracket, so make sure you have the correct one. Also, note how the four bolts that hold the crossmember to the frame are positioned. The assembly manual states to install them facing downward, but some plants installed them facing up.

Suspension Removal

From this point, place the frame on jack stands in four locations, or—better yet—use a two-post lift if you have one available. Start by placing the jack stands on the front and rear corners of the main framerail under the door area or two at the rear of the frame. Raise the frame so that the tires are just off the ground. I found that this will best support the frame: the stands are (for the most part) out of your way, and you can remove the tires when the time comes without jacking up the frame. If you are using a car lift, this will work even better because you can raise and lower the frame to better suit the area that you are working on. When using the lift, strap the frame to the hoist arms for added security.

Now that you documented everything and stabilized the frame, you can remove the wheels and tires. Once you have them removed and neatly stacked out of your way, start removing all the frame component parts.

CHAPTER 4

Usually the best location to place the jack stands is under the frame to keep them mostly out of your way during disassembly when removing both the front and rear suspension. Be very careful not to accidently lean on or move the frame while disassembling because this could cause the stands to move and the frame to fall off, causing severe damage and injury. Shown here is a completely disassembled frame to give an unobstructed view of the locations to place the stands.

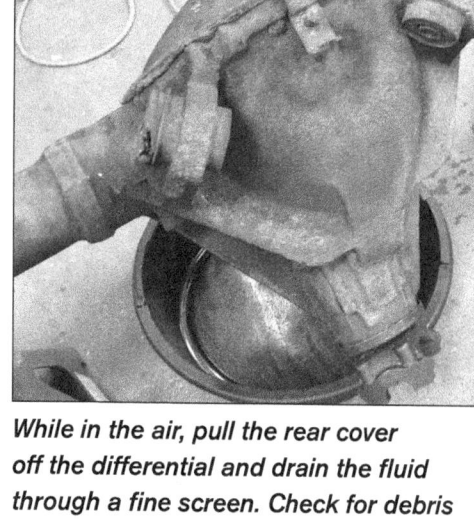

While in the air, pull the rear cover off the differential and drain the fluid through a fine screen. Check for debris and other foreign matter to get an idea of what you may be dealing with.

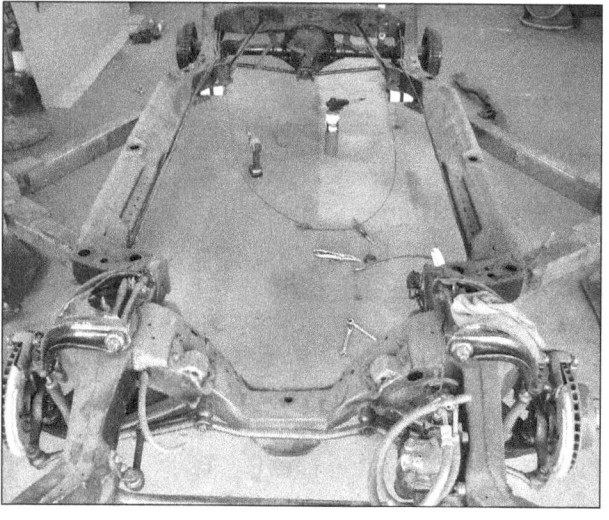

Place your rolling frame on a two-post lift. This will allow you to raise and lower the frame to a comfortable height while you work on each facet of the disassembly. It is a good idea to use straps and wrap them around the frame at each lift arm for added security so that the frame does not walk off the lift arms.

The order in which you do this is entirely up to you. However, it is best to get the bulky and heavy items out of the way first, such as the front and rear suspension. This allows for a little cleaner access area to the rest of the components to remove them later on.

Rear Differential Removal

The rear differential is the next major component to remove. If not previously done, now is the time to remove the rear cover and drain the differential fluid. It is best to drain it through a strainer so that you can retain any filings or metal chips that will help you to determine if there may be an issue with the internals of the differential beyond normal wear. This will need to be addressed with a potential complete overhaul. Also, note if there is any water or other foreign material in the differential lube.

Start by placing a drain pan under the differential and slightly loosening all the bolts on the cover. Leave the top couple of bolts a little tighter, which will allow the fluid to drain but not gush out and cover you and everything else with fluid. Once the fluid has been drained, put all the bolts back into their respective holes and slightly tighten them for the time being until you address the differential overhaul.

Trailing Arms Removal

There are two upper and two lower trailing arms as well as the flexible brake line, emergency brake cables, and sway bar that are attached to the rear differential. The frame is already being supported by jack stands, so you can use a floor jack under the differential to support it and later for removal. Before placing it there, remove the four bolts holding the sway bar (if so equipped) to the lower trailing arms and remove the sway bar. Note the quantity and placement of any shims between the trailing arms and sway bar–attaching points, if any were present.

CHASSIS, SUSPENSION, AND BRAKE WORK

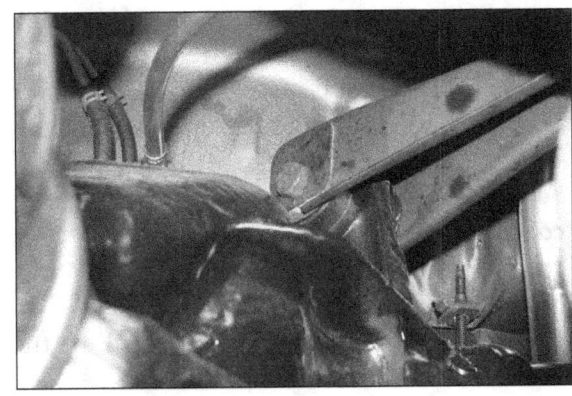

Cars that came equipped with the F41 suspension option will have a reinforcement plate spot welded onto the driver-side upper trailing arm. It will always be on the upper driver's side.

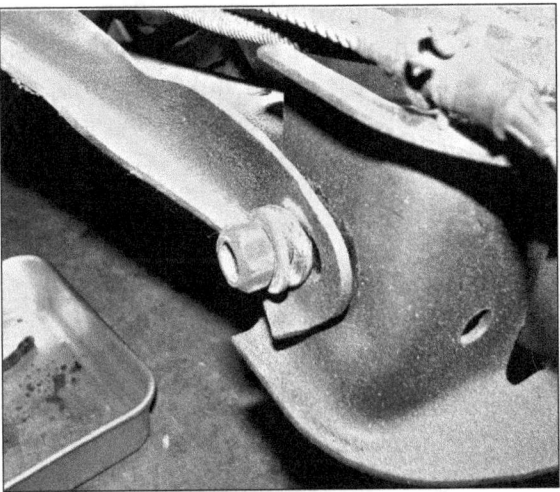

When removing any components of the suspension, always make note of the bolts, nuts, and washers. The front lower rear trailing arm has unique hardware from the integral washer-headed bolt to the washer(s) found under the frame-reinforcement bars, if so equipped. You will usually only find one washer per side, but in this case there were two. Also note the direction of the bolt.

After removal of the differential from the frame, you can either leave it on your floor jack for the time being or move it to a small caster cart to make it more mobile and keep it out of your way. If you are not going to be doing anything to it for a time, simply store it out of the way.

and out of the way. Lift the differential up until it starts to raise the frame. This will take the load off of it and make it easier to remove the bolts.

Moving on to the upper trailing arms, remove the four bolts from the attaching points at the differential. On F41-equipped cars, make sure the heavy-duty reinforcing tab is there and take note of which side it is located. This particular arm should be attached on the driver's side.

Move to the lower trailing arms and remove the two front and two rear bolts holding the trailing arms onto the differential. On heavy-duty suspension cars, you will have an additional frame-reinforcement bar that mounts to the front side of the bottom rear trailing arm and runs up to the front top mount of the rear upper trailing arms. Remove these at the same time as you remove the bolts.

Take special note of the types of bolts and their orientation when removing them, as all the rear suspension bolts need to be installed in the correct direction. Also make note that the frame through bolt holding the lower trailing arm to the frame gusset in the front of the trailing arm is different than any other suspension bolt; it has an integral washer head on it, whereas none of the other ones do. You should also find large washers under the stop nuts on cars equipped with the frame-reinforcement bars attached to this same point.

Check all four trailing arms for bushing wear to the point that the through bolt has worn through the bushing and into the trailing arm. If you find this, the arm will either need to be replaced or, if the damage

Place the floor jack under the differential carrier and use a strap to hold it so it cannot roll off when it is separated from the trailing arms.

Remove the two butterfly clips from the front of the parking brake cable attaching points outlined earlier, and pull the cables through the hole

CHAPTER 4

If you have access to a two-post hoist, simply lower the hoist near the ground and remove the bolts holding the control arms to the rear differential. Place the differential on a small four-caster dolly and move it out of the way. Then simply raise the frame back in the air, where it is easier to work on, and remove the balance of the rear suspension pieces.

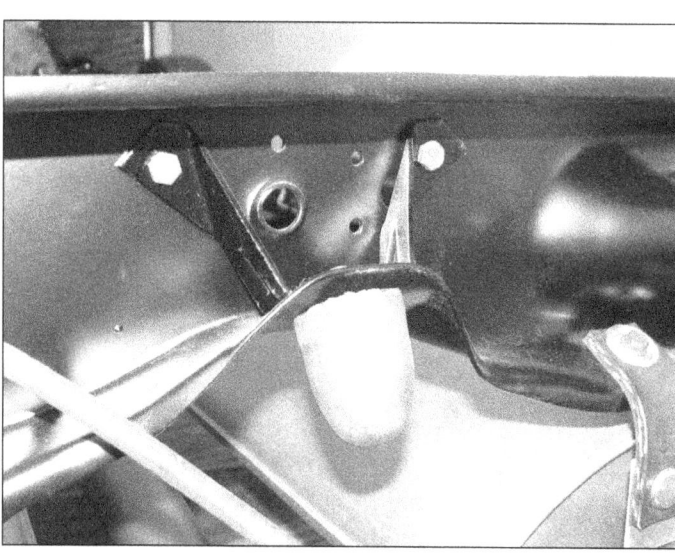

Remove the snubber and bracket from the frame. Pay attention to the orientation of the bolts. I have never seen them mounted any other way than with the bolts installed from the rear of the crossmember and facing the front of the car.

is minor, some welding and grinding will be required.

Remove the clip and remove the brake flex line from the upper rear crossmember area. It is best to put some sort of cap or plug in the line so you do not drip brake fluid everywhere. Now that you have the differential completely loose, remove the bolts and either leave the differential on the floor jack or transfer the differential onto an inexpensive four-wheel caster dolly and push it out of the way for the time being.

If you are using a two-post hoist, you can simply lower the frame until the differential is sitting on jack stands or that same inexpensive caster dolly. Remove all the attaching hardware, and then lift the frame up and away from the differential using the hoist.

The last thing you need to remove will be the pinion snubber. This is held on the crossmember by not only two bolts, nuts, and washers but also with a nut holding the pinion snubber through the crossmember and into the snubber bracket. Remove the hardware, snubber, and bracket and place them in a separate bag. Also, note the original finish of the pinion bracket; I have seen both natural steel and black dipped.

Front Suspension Removal

The front suspension will be the last major component to remove from the frame assembly. It is best to remove all of the small components—such as tie rods, steering arms, the center link, idler arm, and sway bar—first to get them out of the way before you move on to the bigger parts. This would also be a good time to check most of the components for wear or other defects.

Check all the tie-rod joints for looseness by having a buddy turn the steering wheel back and forth about an inch while you hold your hand around the joint, testing one joint at a time. If you feel any clunking or obvious looseness, make note of that so it can be replaced during your restoration. Ball joints can also be tested at this time, but it is recommended that you automatically replace all bushings and joints if you are doing a full restoration.

Sway Bar Removal

Separate the sway bar from the sway bar end links. Bag and tag those pieces as you have been doing. Now, carefully remove the sway bar brackets from the frame. If you have a friend helping you, have them hold the sway bar as you remove the brackets. If you do not have help, a floor jack placed in the center of the sway bar will hold it in place while you remove the hardware.

Remove all the cotter pins from all the attachment points on the

CHASSIS, SUSPENSION, AND BRAKE WORK

These are just some of the tools that can be used on the front suspension to remove tie rods, pinion arms, and other pieces. The use of these tools will allow you to safely remove the part without damage to it or its associated parts, other than the pickle fork, which should not be used unless you intend to replace everything.

Using either an electric, rechargeable, or pneumatic impact wrench will greatly simplify the removal of the pitman arm nut. Without it, you may have your work cut out for you and could likely damage the internal gears of the steering gear. These are usually very rusty, so it is best to presoak it in penetrant before attempting to remove the nut.

It is imperative that you use the correct tool for the job, especially on something such as the pitman arm removal. Use of incorrect tools will lead to potential damage and costly repairs if care is not taken. With the pitman arm tool, getting the arm off is a snap.

articulating suspension pieces. Then loosen all the castle nuts. Leave them attached with a few threads so that they do not simply fall to the ground when the parts are separated. Removing these joints can be tricky. It is best to use a tool designed specifically for tie rod removal to limit any damage to the tie rod or boot. The pullers are the best tool to use because they will not damage any part of the joint, whereas the pickle fork will most certainly damage the boot. It is also not recommended to use any type of hammer to remove the joints unless you intend to replace them; this will not only damage the outside of the tie rod but in some cases will actually distort the tapered joint that the tie rod knuckle fits into. Heat can also be your friend here, but caution needs to be used with regard to the boot as well as any combustible material nearby. If you are replacing the boots, this is a good option along with one of the tools discussed.

Drag Link and Pitman Arm Removal

Once you remove the tie rods, loosen the drag link (or center link, as many call them) joints at the steering gear pitman arm on the driver's side and the frame-mounted idle arm on the passenger's side. Use the same methods and procedures that you previously used on the tie rods.

It can be difficult to remove the drag link with the steering gear attached because the drag link will hit the protruding frame center section. It is best that you now loosen the steering gear so you can move it around and remove the drag link joint. Regardless of which steering you have, be it power assisted or manual, remove the pitman arm nut and lock washer and set them aside.

If you do not intend to rebuild the steering gear, it may not be necessary to remove the arm, and you can ignore this step. It is best and far easier to use an impact wrench and a 1-5/16 socket. If this is not available and you must use a large wrench, it is imperative that you do not turn the arm all the way to the steering gear stop; this will likely damage the internal parts of the steering gear. Using heat here will also sometimes help, but damage to the shaft rubber seal is likely; unless you intend to rebuild the gear, do not use heat in this area.

Steering Gear Removal

Remove the three bolts going through the frame and into the side of the steering gear. This may require a helper to hold the steering gear from falling while the other removes the bolts. These attaching bolts can sometimes be rusty, so both heat and a rust penetrant can help you here.

This is a very heavy unit, so be prepared to catch it as the last bolt is removed.

Once the gear has been separated from the frame, remove the drag link to pitman arm joint and place the steering gear out of the way for now. You have already removed the large pitman arm bolt and lock washer, so now you can remove the pitman arm. Removal of this arm will almost always require a removal tool to separate the arm from the shaft so neither part is damaged. Using any other method may cause damage.

Idle Arm Removal

Now you can remove the drag link and place it out of the way. This will leave only the idle arm, which is attached to the frame with two bolts and lock nuts. Insert a long extension and 9/16 socket through the frame while holding a 9/16 wrench on the lock-nut side. It is easier to remove the nut first and then carefully pull the bolt out of the frame using your socket or better yet a magnet. These bolts can sometimes fall down into the frame, and retrieving them can often be difficult. Use caution and patience here.

Drum Brake Removal

The spindle and brake assembly can be removed as a complete assembly or as individual parts. It is actually better to remove the assembly piece by piece so that you are using the frame as a jig to hold the parts rather than wrestle with them on a bench. This will also allow you to take better photos if you find inspection marks, decals, or issues with the individual parts.

Drum brakes are slightly different in the disassembly process than disc brakes. On a front drum-brake assembly, first remove the flexible brake line from the frame-mounting point using the appropriate-sized line wrench. Not using the correct tool here will cause you bigger headaches. Do the same at the other end where it attaches to the wheel cylinder.

Move on to the brake drum. In some cases, the shoes may have ground a groove into the inside of the drum due to excessive wear, or the shoes may have welded themselves to the drum from sitting for so long. Both will inhibit easy removal of the drum, and both of these situations can be a major headache.

If the drum cannot be turned, it is likely the shoes are stuck to it. You can try and dislodge them using a large rubber or plastic mallet and hitting the drum quite hard to try and loosen the shoes. It is very hard to get it inside the drum, but spraying some penetrant so that it gets onto the shoes may also help loosen them. Sometimes there are adjustment holes that have been opened on the backside of the drum, and it can be sprayed through there as well.

In rare cases, you may have to use a lot of heat and a sledge hammer to jar the drum free. However, using this method will most surely require replacement of the drum, so use it as a last resort.

Spindle Dust Cap Removal

Once you have removed the drum, you will see the spindle, bearing flange, and the brake hardware. Remove the spindle dust cap using a dust cap–removal tool or simply a

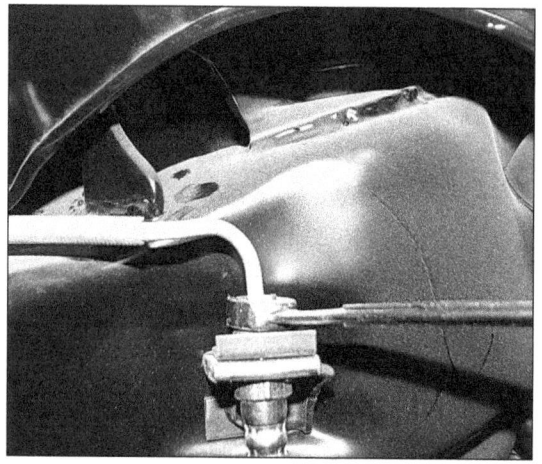

Use of a flare nut or line wrench here is imperative because using a conventional wrench will only round the edges of the nut, ruining the fitting and making it much more difficult to remove. This is yet another good area to use a penetrant or heat, but as always be very careful not to burn the hose. The fluid will also be extremely hot, so care must be taken not to burn yourself.

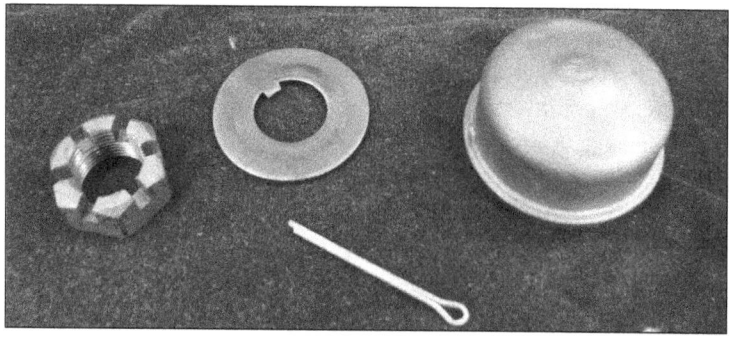

A dust cover will keep the bearing free of dirt and moisture. It will also contain grease so that it does not drip everywhere and contaminate the wheel. Behind the cover you will find the nut, tabbed washer, and cotter pin. Care must be taken to not damage the spindle threads.

CHASSIS, SUSPENSION, AND BRAKE WORK

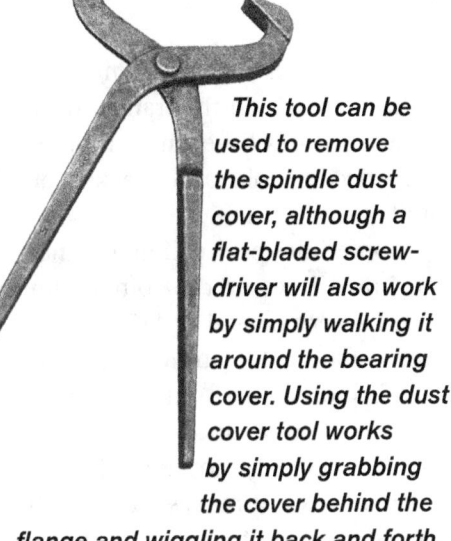

This tool can be used to remove the spindle dust cover, although a flat-bladed screwdriver will also work by simply walking it around the bearing cover. Using the dust cover tool works by simply grabbing the cover behind the flange and wiggling it back and forth. Place the nut, washer, and cotter pin in the dust cap and then into a bag for safe keeping.

large flat-bladed screwdriver. Place the blade behind the raised ridge at the rear of the cap, walk the screwdriver around the cap, and gently pry it loose without damaging the cap or flange. You will now see a large nut, washer, and cotter pin.

Removing the Drum

Remove the cotter pin by bending the tabs with pliers and pulling the pin with a pin puller tool or simply using a side cutter (dikes) and leverage the pin out from its hole. In rare cases, the pin may have rusted into the hole or break off and you will have to drill the damaged pieces out.

After the pin is removed, gently remove the nut using either a socket or a crescent wrench. Using a gripping type of tool like channel-lock pliers may damage the surface of the nut and is not recommended. Now, simply wiggle the spindle flange, and the outer bearing will walk out onto the spindle. Take a paper towel, remove the bearing, and set it aside.

While in this position, a trick for removing the inner bearing and seal (if you are replacing the bearing) is to put the nut back on the spindle, pull the drum out until the nut contacts the roller bearing, and give it a forceful tug toward you. The nut will force the bearing and seal from the back of the drum and spindle flange. It may require a few tugs before it separates itself. You can now remove the spindle flange/drum assembly.

Bearing and Spindle Analysis

Regardless of the type of restoration you are doing, it is recommended to clean and re-grease the inner and outer bearings. Based on the cost and the fact that you are this far into it, replacement of the bearings and seal makes more sense. If you choose to clean and reuse your bearings, you will still need to replace the inner seal on the backside of the drum and bearing hub.

Before you decide to keep the bearings, clean them thoroughly and check for any roughness, expanded cages, missing bearings, etc. You will also want to clean the spindle and check for any blued, galled, or damaged areas where the bearing race rides as well as for bad threads on the shaft itself. Very minor damage can be massaged and cleaned up with emery cloth, but damage beyond that will require replacement of the spindle itself. If you can feel a groove in the spindle with your fingernail, chances are the damage is too severe and replacement of the spindle will be necessary. If the spindle is badly blued, it is also time to replace it. The bluing was caused by severe heat, and this can cause the spindle to become brittle and break.

If you chose to replace the bearings and/or drum and bearing hub, you will also need to remove the bearing races in most cases; they should be matched to the bearings.

Carefully inspect the spindle for any damage to the threads or the bearing race surface as well as bluing. Minor damage can be repaired, but in a case such as this one where the bearing actually galled the bearing surface, it will need to be replaced.

Using a brass drift inserted inside the bearing hub, place on the back side of the bearing race in the relief cut-out area within the hub. Gently tap this on both sides and remove the bearing race, being very careful not to damage the mating surface of the bearing race.

Looking inside the drum mounting flange, you will see the backs of the bearing races with only a very small cutout area for a driver tool to reach the backside of the bearing race. Using a small brass drift and small hammer, very carefully drive the race out, tapping from side to side until the race falls out. Be very careful not to damage the surface the bearing race lays against. Flip the rotor over and repeat for the other bearing race.

Miscellaneous Suspension Removal

Now that the flange is out of the way, take several photographs, paying particular attention to the location of the springs, their color, and their orientation. Also note that the brake adjusters are left- and right-handed and that the brake shoes have two different lengths of pads on them, which are better known as primary and secondary shoes. The shorter pad will always face the front of the car.

Once you document these, you can proceed to remove the springs, shoes, brake hardware, and wheel cylinder. Start by removing the flexible brake hose at the rear of the backing plate. Remove the retainer clip and loosen the nut on either end

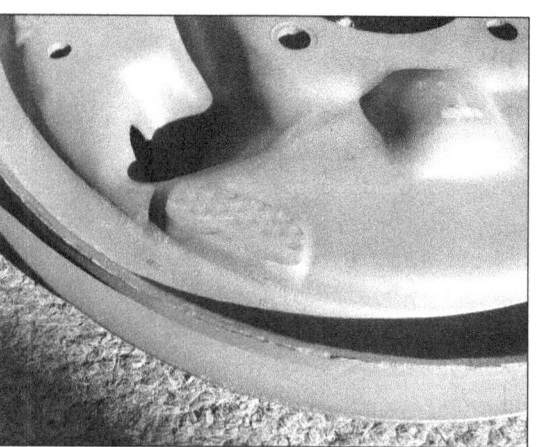

Inspect all drum brake backing plates in the area of the pads where the brake shoes ride. If grooves are found, either weld and grind this area or replace the backing plate as these grooves will cause the shoes to hang up.

Brake Tools

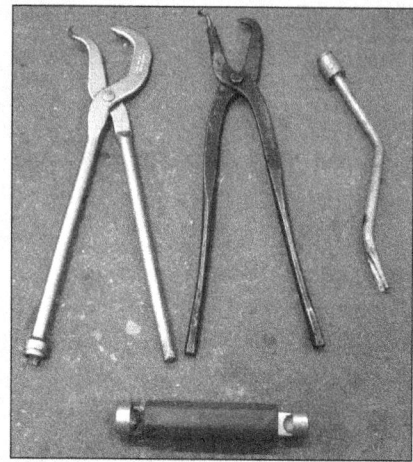

It is best to purchase an assortment of brake tools or buy them in a kit form. They make doing brake work much easier, and there is less chance of damaging the tool, the part, or yourself. It will also speed up disassembly and reassembly.

A variety of brake tools are available specifically for doing brake work. However, most standard tools in your toolbox will work just as well to remove the springs, hardware, wheel cylinder, and shoes. Once removed, place them all in a bag or a box and label them as to which wheel they came off of. You should now be left with a bare brake backing plate. Carefully inspect it for cracks or other defects. Pay close attention to the pads on the backing plate where the brake shoes ride. If there is a groove cut into these pads, either replace the backing plate or weld the groove and grind flat, as this will cause the shoes to hang up if left as is. At this point, you can either remove the backing plate or leave it attached to the spindle or axle flange. ■

of the flex hose where it meets the brake hard line on the frame. Always replace this flex hose with a new one. They become old and cracked and can be very brittle.

Sometimes heat will help remove the brake lines at the joints. However, be very careful as DOT 3 brake fluid is flammable and can catch fire as you loosen the joint. At the very least, it could be under pressure and will be extremely hot and will cause severe burns if it makes contact with your skin. Use of a propane torch is advised, as this will provide more than enough heat for your needs.

Disc Brake Removal

Much of the removal process for disc brakes is the same as the drum brakes with minor exceptions. Starting with the caliper, remove the flex line from the frame mount as before, then move on to the caliper side where the banjo bolt holds it to the caliper using a copper washer on either side of the line. Take caution because these lines are full of brake fluid and will damage paint if spilled.

Look for and remove the two long internal 3/8-inch headed bolts that hold the caliper onto the caliper bracket. Loosen these until they no longer thread out, then pull them the rest of the way and set them aside. Check for damage or excessive wear at the head and along the shaft of the bolt and set them aside. The caliper is now free, but due to the piston being forced out against the brake pads, it may still not want to come off the caliper. Using a medium-size pry bar or large screwdriver, pry the caliper back and forth against the rotor face in an attempt to force the piston back, giving it more wiggle room to be removed from the rotor.

Now, place the same tool between the outer race of the rotor and the caliper on both sides of the caliper bracket. Gently pry upward on both ends to pull the caliper up and away from the rotor. Once removed, the caliper assembly can be set in a drain pan until it has fully drained.

Spindle Hub Removal

Move on to the spindle hub. Remove the bearing dust cap from the face of the rotor hub. You can now see the cotter pin, nut, and washer that are attached to the spindle. Remove these, allowing the rotor to be freed from the spindle. Regardless of the type of rotors, place the palms of your hands on either side of the rotor and gently wiggle or push inward. This will cause the outer bearing to come out of the spindle, where you can now grab and remove it. Set it aside.

As stated earlier in the drum brake removal section, a trick for removing the inner bearing and seal is to put the nut back on the spindle, pull the rotor out until the nut contacts the inner roller bearing, and give it a forceful tug toward you. This will move the nut, forcing the bearing and seal from the back of the rotor and/or bearing hub. It may require a few tugs before it separates itself. The rotor will now come off the spindle and can be set aside.

One-Piece and Two-Piece Rotors

Early Chevelles had what is referred to as a two-piece rotor. In this case, the machined rotor can be separated from the bearing hub and can then be replaced or re-machined without doing anything to the bearings or hub other than unbolting it from the rotor, which is not the case on a one-piece rotor. In both cases and after the caliper has been removed and out of the way, the rotor (one piece) or rotor/hub assembly (two piece) is simply removed and separated from the bearing hub and can be set aside.

You will need to determine if the rotor is within spec or if it needs to be turned. If not enough material remains on the rotor face, a replacement will need to be located and can be sourced from restoration parts suppliers. In the case of the one-piece rotor, it will need to be machined as a unit; with the two-piece rotor, if there is not enough material left to machine, it will need to be discarded and replaced as a unit.

Bearing Hub Disassembly

Removing the bearing hub on two-piece rotors is done the same way. The inner and outer bearing races, the inner bearing, and the seal will all stay within the hub unless you use the seal-removal trick stated earlier. The bearing hub can then be

Using a seal puller in the manner shown, gently pry up on the bearing seal with the removal tool while walking around the circumference of the seal. If a seal removal tool is not available, a large flat-bladed screwdriver can also be used. Regardless of what tool you use, the seal must be replaced.

separated from the rotor by removing the five bolts attaching the rotor to the hub. If you did not remove the inner bearing and hub using the trick before, do so now by placing the rotor and/or hub face down on the floor and using a seal-removal tool or another device that works to gently pry up on the seal and remove it.

Bearing Race

If you are doing a more thorough restoration and replacing the bearings and/or rotor, you will also need to remove the bearing races in most cases. It should be mentioned again that during a restoration it is best to replace the bearing as opposed to cleaning and repacking, but that is up to you. If you insist on using the original bearings, thoroughly clean them of all grease and dry them off. *Do not* use an air hose and spin the bearings; this can not only damage them but they can also explode the cage and severely injure you. If you turn the bearing and do not feel any roughness or excessive looseness, then grease and reinstall it after the rotors have been restored or replaced.

As was already covered in the drum brake removal section, look inside the rotor mounting flange (on two-piece rotors) or the rotor itself (on one-piece units) to find the backs of the bearing races with only a very small cutout area for a driver tool to reach the bearing race. Using a brass drift and small hammer, very carefully drive the race out, tapping from side to side until the race falls out. Flip the rotor over and repeat for the other bearing race.

Spindle Removal

Before removing the spindle, loosen and remove the two bolts at the bottom that go through the backing plate, through the spindle, and out the steering arm. Also remove the top center bolt holding the backing plate onto the spindle. The disc brake caliper bracket is also attached with these same bolts and can be removed at the same time. Once all are removed, the steering arm, backing plates, and caliper bracket can be removed and placed out of the way. Each of these items have to be put back on their correct side during reassembly.

Coil Spring Removal

Now comes the interesting part: removing the coil spring. It is best to use a spring compressor designed for this very job, and there are several varieties on the market that can be used. It is best to wrap a chain or strap around the coil and attach it to the frame to stop the spring from flying out and striking you if something goes awry. A ratchet strap with a hooked end also will do the job.

Once you have the coil spring compressor installed, remove the cotter pins from the upper and lower ball joints. Loosen the nuts several threads but be very cautious and leave enough threads attached to

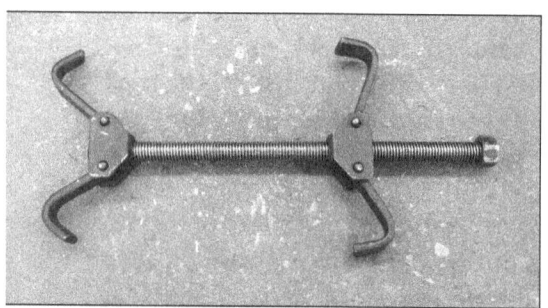

Get yourself a conventional coil spring removal tool. These are readily available at most automotive parts stores and can be rented from most of them, as well as rental shops. This will make coil spring removal and installation much easier.

Creating Your Own Spring Compressor Tool

You can also have a tool fabricated similar to what I use. It consists of a stainless steel threaded rod that is inserted through the upper shock mount hole. It should have a long stainless threaded rod, long tubular spacer, phenolic spacer to protect the control arm, washer, and roller bearing that works very well to compress the spring. At the bottom of the threaded rod, you can use the lower spring retainer hook from a conventional spring-compressor tool.

This has the same result as a normal spring compressor but is much easier to use and does not get in the way as much. It is suggested that you also hook one end of a ratchet strap to the coil spring and the other end to a part of the frame on the opposite side of the car, so in case of a mishap, the spring will not fly out and hit you. It is also best to protect the area surrounding the coil spring on the lower control arm, but this is more important during reinstallation. ■

If you are more of a fabricator, you can make your own tool, consisting of a stainless steel all-thread rod, steel spacer, phenolic spacer, washer, bearing, and bottom coil spring retainer from a conventional spring compressor. This makes the job far easier and is much safer to use.

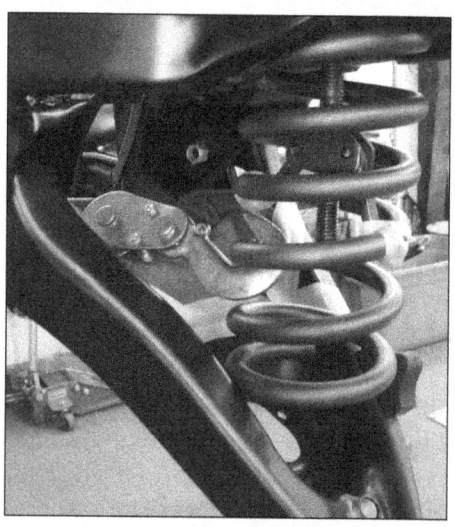

This homemade tool not only makes the job easier but the through rod also helps hold the coil spring in place in case of an accident. The use of a hooked ratchet strap will greatly aid in the removal and installation as well as add to the safety factor.

hold the nut on the spindle as the coil spring is under a great deal of tension.

Using the same tools and/or methods that you used to separate the tie rods, separate the spindle from the upper and lower control arms while leaving the spindle nuts slightly attached at this time. Applying some localized heat to the area of the ball-joint stud will greatly help in separating the two from each other.

During this procedure, you may hear a loud bang and should notice that the spindle is now tight up against the nuts. This means the ball-joint studs have separated themselves from the spindle bore.

Using the spring compressor of your choice, compress the spring enough to take tension back off the spindle where it attaches to the ball

CHASSIS, SUSPENSION, AND BRAKE WORK

Notice how the spring tension has aided the separation of the spindle from the ball joint stud, eliminating the need to impact the spindle with a hammer. Always make sure you leave plenty of threads on the castle nut to retain the spindle for the time being and so that it cannot completely separate, allowing the coil spring to fly off and cause bodily injury.

joints. Once that tension has been removed, remove the nuts holding the spindle to the control arms, and you are ready for the next step.

Depending on which method of overall restoration you are taking, you can also use several other tools and equipment to help here. If the body is still on the frame, simply place a floor jack under the ball joint on the lower control arm. Using whichever method works best for you to separate the ball joint from the spindle, do so at this time using extreme caution. Once separated, slowly lower the floor jack and allow the lower control arm to slowly pivot downward, allowing the tension of the coil spring to be gently released.

If you have a two-post hoist available and the body has been removed from the frame, you can ratchet strap the frame to the hoist and secure it from moving and also use it as a tool. Lower the hoist all the way to the floor so that the lower control arms are resting on the floor. Once you have the spindle nuts loose, you can separate the spindle from the ball joints. Once that takes place, very slowly raise the hoist, letting the lower control arm stay resting on the floor. This allows the tension on the coil springs to gently be released. Once again, it is suggested that you use a chain or ratchet strap around the coil spring to hold it from flying out. Once the spindle has been separated from the upper and lower ball joints, remove it and place it aside.

Upper and Lower Control Arms Removal

Now you can remove the upper and lower control arms. Each lower arm is attached by two through bolts and lock nuts. Remove these followed by the arm. Be cautious because these are heavy and may drop out on their own when the bolts are removed.

The upper control arm is attached to the frame using two bolts on each side that run through the control arm cross shaft. Remove the lock nuts and sometimes lock washers and wiggle the control arm toward the center of the frame and off the bolts. Slight tapping with a rubber mallet will help in the removal process. Remove the control arms and place aside.

If you are doing a full concours restoration, you may want to consider removing the upper control arm attaching bolts from the frame and replacing them with new ones that are available from a variety of sources, or if they are in good shape, simply restore the originals. A few light taps with a hammer and pin punch will drive them out of the frame. Caution must be used to not damage the threads.

Note that the head end of the bolt shank has knurling on it. This helps keep the bolt from spinning in the frame when you attach the lock nuts. New through bolts are usually good enough to keep them from spinning as long as the bolt holes in the frame are still good. In rare cases, these holes are wallowed out, and a simple trick is to use a body hammer and dolly to compress the hole slightly. While holding the dolly on one side, hit the other with the body hammer thereby compressing the metal and making the hole smaller. This will compress the metal slightly enough to give the bolt some bite when reinstalling it. In severe cases, it may be required to ever so slightly weld the hole around the perimeter and redrill the hole or simply tack weld the bolt head to the frame. Make sure to cover the threads during the painting or powder coating process. As with any part of a restoration, always wear gloves as well as face and eye protection.

After all the pieces have been removed from the upper control arm, check for any damage, such as a bent arm, damaged bushing holes, damaged rivet holes for the ball joints, etc. There is no point using the control arm if it has severe damage and will require a replacement. If there is only minor damage and you possess a welder, small repairs may be made. It is very common on the upper control arms to have bushings that are so worn that the cross shaft will have actually worn a groove in the bushing bore of the control arm. If not severe, this can be welded and repaired. If these are extremely worn, it will again require replacement of the arm. Also, check the cross shaft for severe damage as they too would need to be replaced.

Check the cross shafts as well to ensure they are not replacement

CHAPTER 4

Take note on the frame-mounted motor mounts how the bolts were installed at the factory. Plants varied as to how they installed this with regard to which way the bolts faced, so it is best to replicate what you found, assuming they have not been previously removed.

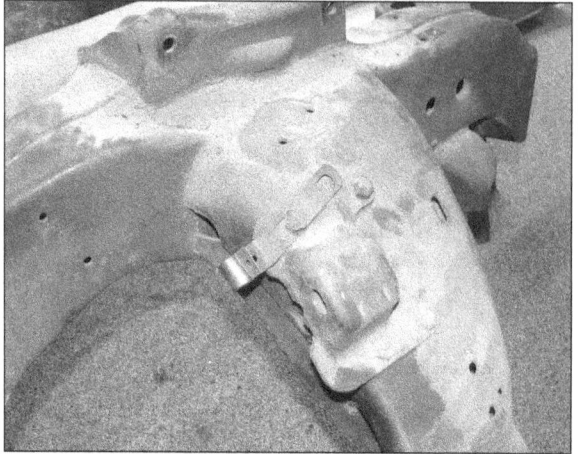

Make note on both frame mounts as to which mount has the elongated through-bolt hole and which one has the round hole. Also, photograph the way the battery cable holder bracket is mounted to the frame mount. It is different than you would think it would mount. Notice on this original mount that the mount bolts go downward through the frame with no lock washers under the head, unlike what the manual shows.

As with any part of your restoration, examine all of the component parts for damage. Minor damage can be repaired with a welder and grinder, but if the damage is too severe, it may require replacement of the entire control arm. Also check the cross shaft for damage.

offset shafts. Offset replacement shafts would have been used if there was severe frame or suspension damage and the repair shop chose to replace the shafts in order to get the car in alignment rather than replace the control arm or repair the frame. These are readily apparent by the obvious offset in the shaft from the center line as well as the use of a large lock nut holding the bushing on compared to a fine-threaded bolt normally found on the Chevelle. However, the control arms may also be from another GM A-Body car, such as a Cutlass or Tempest. These cars commonly used a large lock nut as well, whereas the Chevelle never used that method. Assuming you will be repairing those areas during your restoration, it will now make these offset cross shafts no longer necessary, and a set of originals will need to be obtained.

Going back to the lower control arms, check them over thoroughly for any signs of damage. The most common signs are bent arms due to contact with a curb or other low obstructions. Minor bending of the arm flange can be heated and repaired, but severe bending will require replacement of the arm because it will be difficult to ever get the car aligned again. Severe bushing damage here is not as common but should be checked regardless. Ball joint bore damage is also somewhat common, so look closely at that area as well. Most damage can be repaired using heat and a welder. As with many other parts of the restoration, replace all the bushing found on the suspension, as these are inexpensive replacement items and now is the time to do them.

Upper Control Arm Bumper Removal

Now that you have all the front suspension out of the way, remove the upper control arm bumpers found underneath where the upper control arm had been mounted. These will need to be replaced. Simply pry them from the frame.

Motor Mounts Removal

Since the lower control arms are no longer in the way, this will give you much better access to the frame-mounted motor mounts. Take note and photograph the orientation of the bolts holding them on, which side has the elongated engine through bolt, and if there is a battery cable bracket mounted on

CHASSIS, SUSPENSION, AND BRAKE WORK

the passenger-side mount and how it is mounted. Remove all eight nut, bolt, and washer combinations from both mounts and remove them from the frame.

Fuel Hard Lines

You now have all of the large and heavy items out of the way. It is now time to remove all of the small brackets, clips, and lines from the frame. Starting with the fuel lines, there may be one or two hard lines, depending on engine size and date of assembly. Here again, you will want to photo document the placement of the lines, line brackets, and straps as well as the bolts. They will vary along with the attachment points and the color of the clips. You will be able to use these photos for later refinishing and reinstallation of them.

Remove the fuel lines by lifting them up and over the axle crossmember and pulling them back out through the frame, where they run along and inside the front passenger frame horn. Take note of where they run in the frame and out of the front crossmember as this will help you understand where they need to run come reinstallation time. You will find it easier to remove them one at a time, but both can be done at one time. Try to not damage or bend these as you are removing them; you may want to use them to compare to the new lines to ensure you not only have the correct replacement lines but also that the new ones are bent accurately. Once these are removed safely, drain them and set them out of the way.

Brake Hard Lines

Moving on to the driver's side of the frame, start by photographing the placement and shape of the brake lines on the frame. Your original photos can be used later as a reference if you are having trouble with the replacement lines and how they are bent.

Now that you have that done, begin by removing the brake lines at the front. You already removed the flex lines running from the drums or rotors to the front frame brackets during the front disassembly process, so go directly to the hard lines. Separate the crossover line on the front crossmember and the short line running from the distribution

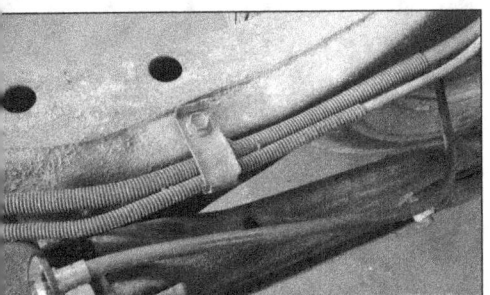

Just like on the brake lines, this bracket may be the flat type or the full-round-encased type (shown). There seems to be no rhyme or reason as to which was used, so document which your car has as well as the attaching bolt.

Make note of how your fuel lines run and take special note of the area around the passenger-side rear coil-spring tower. This area can get interesting when installing the new lines. Photo documentation of how the originals were routed will aid in your installation of the new ones.

The fuel-line clips are different depending on if used on a single line or dual line, so document what type you have, the color of each clip, and the placement and bolt-head design of each. Also note if the coiled sleeve is on the line in the area of the clip or not as this too will make a difference on which size clip was used.

Loosen and remove all the brake lines at the distribution block while it is still bolted to the frame. Depending on its condition, heat may be required for this step. Use precautionary methods when handling a torch and hot brake fluid, as severe injuries may occur if hot brake fluid spills on you.

Pay attention to each clamp and bolt when removing. You may find several different sizes, colors, and styles of clamps. It is important to document these and replace them in the original location during the restoration. Also make note of the head markings and type of bolt.

Pay attention to this bracket; there can be two different styles used on these cars. Usually there is one open flat bracket and one looped closed bracket. There does not seem to be any rhyme or reason as to which type was used or when. The fuel line uses a similar bracket, so don't get them confused.

valve mounted on the frame on the driver's front to the left front brake. Remove the clips from the crossover line again, noting their original color. If the two lines running from the distribution valve up the master cylinder have not yet been removed, go ahead and do so at this time. As before, heat may be required to get these to break loose, so use the same precautions as you did before.

Moving rearward, disconnect the main line from the rear of the distribution valve. Chevelles used at least two different designs for the distribution valves: one being cast iron and the other is brass. Remove the valve from the frame and put it and its bolt in a separate bag. Note which valve you have because they will be restored differently.

Remove the main brake line from the frame while again noting the different-size brake line clamps, location, color, and different bolt markings and type. Clamps are different depending on the diameter of the line at that particular location, including the dimension of the protective spring sleeve, and will also be color coded. These coil sleeves are installed to protect vulnerable areas of the brake line from road debris, such as rocks, as well as protecting some of the main bends from kinking or crushing. Tag the clamps while again noting their location and bolt usage and put them into a bag.

On disc-brake cars, another valve was used at the driver-side rear crossmember just in front of the driver-side rear wheel. This valve is called the brake hold-off valve, and it is only found on cars with disc brakes. If it is not there, it is because you have four-wheel drum brakes or someone incorrectly replaced brake lines and left it out. Lack of use of this valve on disc-brake cars will cause the car to nose dive during braking.

As in other areas, heat may be required to loosen the lines. Since you already removed the rear flex hose at the time you dropped the differential from the frame, your brake line removal is now complete. It is a good idea to put the flex line and bracket in your bag tagged for brake line hardware.

The hold-off valve is found on the driver-side rear crossmember. Loosen the lines to and from the valve and use heat if needed to separate them. In rare cases, these valves will need to be replaced or rebuilt. Both rebuild kits and replacement valves are available aftermarket. Place it in your bag with your other brake line pieces.

Restoration and Assembly of the Frame

Congratulations! This marks the completion of your frame disassembly and the beginning of the restoration of the frame and all associated bolt-on hardware items. Here is where the excitement begins and you will start to see the fruits of your labor.

For ease of understanding, let's

Doing your homework, taking your time, and using quality products will give you the end result that will make you feel great about the time and money you put into your project.

restore the frame and chassis in the same order you disassembled it. It was touched on earlier, but the very first thing you will want to do is examine the frame and determine if it is the right candidate for restoration. If it has any major issues, such as rust holes, bends, or cracks, it may be a good time to locate a good donor frame to use for your project. Frames for Chevelles vary slightly between years, and there are also differences between the body-styles (coupe, wagon, convertible, El Camino, two-door versus four-door), so make sure you are replacing it with the right donor. In most cases, you can also use a frame from another GM A-Body car.

Frame Cleaning

It is best to take your frame and sandblast it or use other means of media removal, such as aluminum oxide, walnut shells, or plastic media. Sand and aluminum oxide are usually fairly inexpensive, not very time consuming, and allow you to start with fresh bare metal as well as remove rust, unlike some forms of media blasting that will not remove rust. There are other means of paint removal, but most of them are very time consuming or expensive.

You might also want to consider hiring a company that will do on-site blasting with their equipment, though your local surroundings will dictate if this will work or not. There are several varieties of these services as well, including high-pressure water, walnut, glass, plastic media, etc. If you are not close to a blasting facility, you can purchase a do-it-yourself compact blaster for little money; although, a fairly high-volume, high standard cubic feet per minute (SCFM) air compressor would be necessary. If you are using silica sand, you must also use a fresh-air hood and blast upwind of your project.

For the best bang for your buck—and regardless if you are doing the work or farming it out—you are better off if you put most of the parts

Before hiring a blaster or doing it yourself, get all of the heavy pieces together in one place and blast all at once to save on expenses. However, be ready to treat each piece of bare steel immediately after blasting, or flash rust may occur.

that need blasting aside and wait to do them all at one time. It is not suggested to sandblast any large sheet metal items, however, as warpage can be a major problem. If forced to, turn the pressure down as low as you can and still remove material. This will help by not heating the metal as much.

Powdercoating

Powdercoating will be covered more extensively later in this chapter as well as in the paint and body chapter. With that in mind, if you are going to powdercoat the frame and there are no repairs that are needed, now would be a good time—but only after acid washing the frame—to remove all oils, contaminants, and blasting residue. If your frame needs any amount of bodywork to repair pitting or other issues, powdercoating may not be the answer for you due to the high heat used in the baking process. However, you can do welding repairs prior to the coating. If you are not concerned about seeing those types of defects, then powdercoating is a much cheaper and quicker way to apply paint to your frame and is suggested for a daily driver car.

Regardless of your paint removal and application method, you must treat the metal within hours of blasting, otherwise flash rusting will begin. You also need to be careful to not allow contaminants onto the bare metal, as this can cause issues during the painting process. Even handling the bare metal with ungloved hands will allow contaminants in the metal. If you are able to keep the frame out of the elements or high humidity, you can begin any needed repairs to the frame, such as cracks, broken welds,

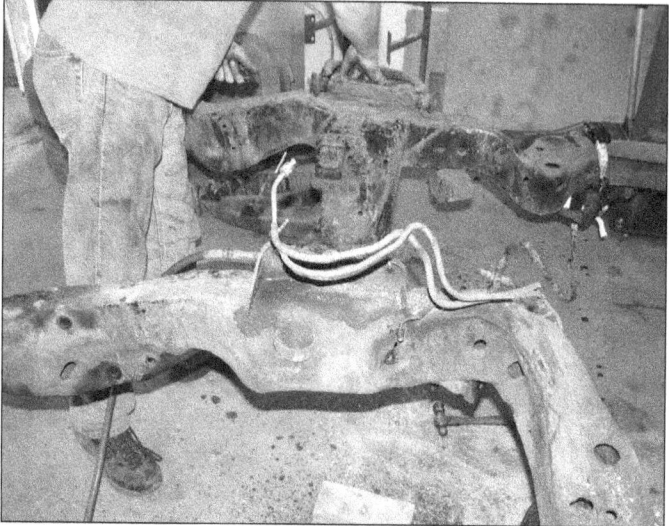

This frame was badly damaged in a frontal collision, and these impacts can telegraph rearward and cause the frame to get out of square. The cost to straighten it is likely more than what a donor frame would cost. Let your frame shop be the judge on what is salvageable.

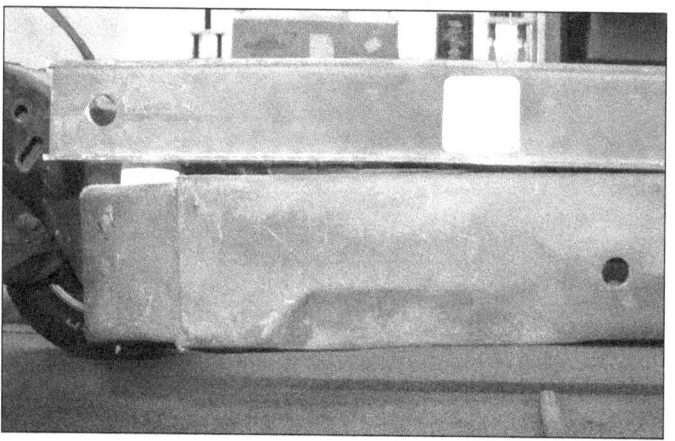

Using a straightedge shows a very apparent issue with this frame, and this would have to be repaired before moving forward. Not addressing this would cause great difficulty in body and sheet metal fitment later on.

bent rails or other areas, repairing mounting pads, etc. Once completed, the frame can be washed in an acid solution to remove all oils and other contaminants prior to priming it.

Carefully examine every square inch of the frame and look for bends, scrapes, pitting, rusted areas, thin portions of the frame due to rust, rusted body mounting pads, or other issues, such as cracks. All should be addressed prior to moving forward for safety reasons.

It is rare that an almost 50-year-old frame will not have been involved in at least a minor altercation at some time in its life. Many issues can be straightened at a reputable frame shop, but both you and they must know your limits. It can also be very costly, depending on how severe the frame damage is. Decide which would be best before you waste the money: fix or replace. There are sites on the internet where you can obtain a copy of the frame measurements on your particular Chevelle, such as chevellestuff.net/qd/frames.htm. Many of the measurements are also available in the assembly manual. Check these and determine what steps need to be taken before getting started.

Check every weld joint for any signs of issues such as cracking or incomplete welds. Reweld those areas at this time. Any cracks you find in

CHASSIS, SUSPENSION, AND BRAKE WORK

Not only is this part of the frame one of the first places to contact obstructions, it is also one of the most common areas of a frame needing attention. If you are powdercoating the frame, you need to realize that this damage will not be hidden, so other means of repair or paint may be necessary.

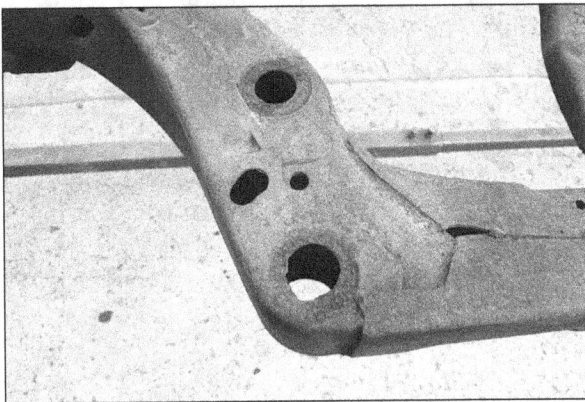

A very common sight on 50-year-old frames is rusted body-mount holes. These must be repaired for proper body alignment and safety. The area around this rust is too thin and cannot support the body safely.

Start by tracing around a replacement piece, such as a washer, while making sure your placement is exactly centered over the original. Cut out the area you have traced and weld in the replacement steel followed by grinding.

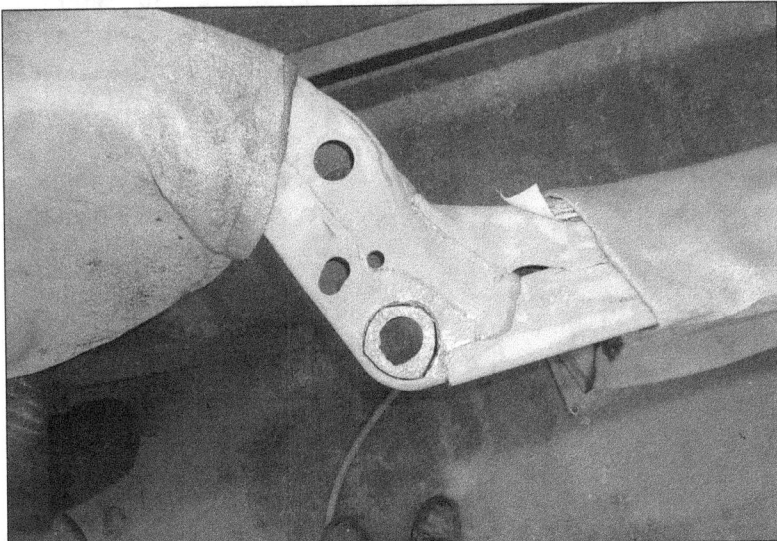

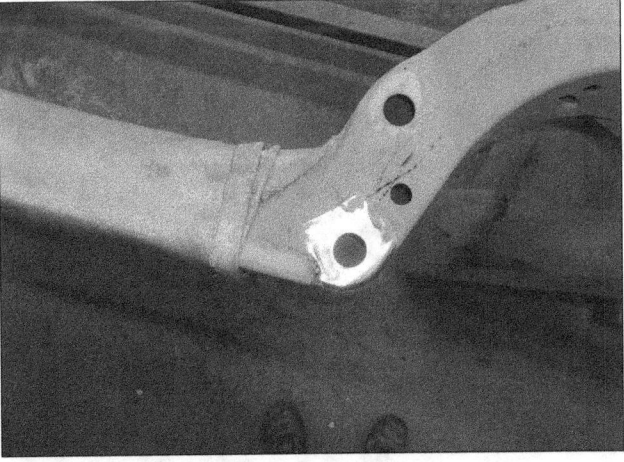

Post repairs show a perfectly strong and usable hole to mount your body-mount bushing. If done correctly, no one will ever know that there had been rust damage here before, and the body will stay where it is placed on the frame without the mounts pulling through.

the metal of the frame should also be V-grooved, welded, and ground smooth. V-grooving is the process of opening up a crack by grinding a V-shaped groove in the area of the crack and allowing the weld to penetrate into the substrate of the crack; it makes for a much stronger weld. This can be accomplished using a V-shaped grinding tool. Look over the rest of the frame to ensure that you fixed any damaged areas that you found, straightened the framerails caused by poor placement of floor jacks, or any other gouges, rips, or tears.

It is also a good idea to roll the frame over onto its back so you have a better view of the bottom side. Another area to pay attention to is the front crossmember. This is usually the first area that makes contact with ground obstructions, and it is very likely you will find severe damage here. This should be addressed if you want a good-looking frame.

CHEVELLE RESTORATION AND AUTHENTICITY GUIDE: 1970–1972

Other common areas of concern are the body-mount holes in the frame. These are often corroded through or at the very least have become thin. This area must be cut out, repaired, and finished just like any other damaged part of the car, or it may impede proper alignment of body panels later on. A simple way to fix this area is to use a large washer or a similar-thickness piece of donor steel and trace a hole around it, making sure you have your dead centers perfectly matched the best you can with the original hole or by using the frame measurements discussed earlier.

You will also want to find or modify a washer with the same inside diameter as the outside diameter of the body mount where it fits down into the frame. Otherwise, you will need to open that hole up to match the body-mount extension. After tracing, cut out the damaged area in a circle and weld in the washer. Once completed, grind and fill the welds. You now have a new strong body-mount hole that will last for years. When all bodywork is completed, you are ready for paint application. The painting instructions will be covered more in depth later in this chapter.

Suspension Rebuilding

For the most part, all suspension components of the Chevelle are fairly simple to remove, rebuild, or replace using common tools found in your toolbox. On some occasions, you may have to rent or purchase some tools to complete the task or hire a professional shop to complete the task. Rebuilding the suspension on these cars in not that difficult, and most home mechanics are perfectly capable of doing these repairs, thereby saving themselves a lot of money.

Upper Control Arm Shaft and Bushing Removal

The next step at this point is to remove the upper control arm shaft and bushings. Start by removing the bolt, lock washer, and large bushing washer from the ends of the cross shafts. Normally it will require the use of a pneumatic chisel to pry the bushing out of the control arm, and

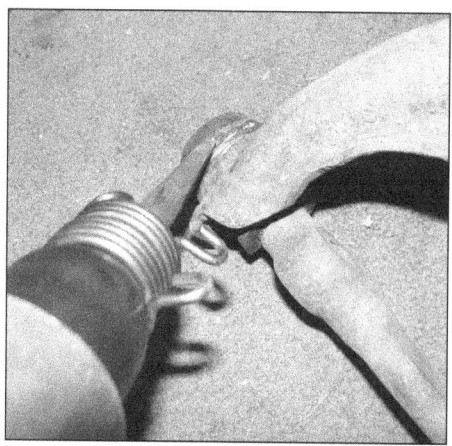

Remove the cross-shaft bushings using the same pneumatic chisel. Simply walk the tool around the flanged head of the bushing and walk it out. It may first require compressing the bushing from the inside by putting a V-groove on the backside of the bushing perpendicular to the flanged head.

more often than not you can simply lay your chisel head under the flange of the bushing and use it to walk the bushing out. Be very careful not to damage the bushing mating surface or the cross shaft.

In severely rusted conditions, it may require a little more effort and strategy. Sometimes the inner metal sleeve may have rusted itself to the cross shaft, making it very difficult to remove the bushing.

As touched on earlier—and as with any part of the suspension with bushings—inspect the bushing race in the control arm for any damage. If a bushing is badly worn, the through bolt or cross shaft will eventually wear into the bushing race and start to wear on it. If you encounter this, you can sometimes repair minor damage by welding and grinding. In severe cases, it will require you to replace the entire control arm.

Original versus Aftermarket Offset Cross Shaft

After both bushings have been removed, the shaft will simply come out of the control arm. As mentioned before, check the cross shafts for damaged threads and damage to the bushing shank or mounting holes. Also look to make sure it is not an offset shaft. The centerline of the entire shaft should be in line with the bushing sleeve mounting surface.

Always check your bushing races and through-bolt holes for any signs of damage, hole elongation, and/or cracks. If you find any, this must be repaired, or you can replace the control/trailing arm since not repairing it will not allow the bushing to be seated correctly or tight enough to hold it in place and the arm may move around on the through bolt.

CHASSIS, SUSPENSION, AND BRAKE WORK

Compare the aftermarket offset cross shaft on the left with an original on the right. Notice the offset from the center line of the aftermarket. Do not reuse these if you have completely replaced or repaired your original suspension. Also note the method of bushed retention from the original to the replacement.

Using a pneumatic air chisel, cut the heads off the rivets. It may also require pushing the rest of the rivet remains through its hole using a pneumatic pin punch. The ball joint will separate when all four heads have been cut off and removed. If the joints had been previously replaced with aftermarket units, simply remove the bolts and replace the joint.

Most home restorers will not have the capability to install the upper ball joints back with the same-style factory rivets that were used on the assembly line. If you must go this route, locate a shop with the rivets and tooling that can do this step for you.

If the shaft centerline is offset one way or the other with that surface, it was replaced and an offset was put in its place.

Assuming all alignment issues and frame and suspension damage were addressed during the restoration, these offset cross shafts cannot be used. They will impede correct alignment settings. Lastly, make sure your bushing retainer washers were held onto the cross shaft by a fine-threaded bolt and not a large lock nut (also used on aftermarket offset shafts). This method of mounting was used on some A-Body cars but not Chevelles to the best of my knowledge, so make sure you use the fine-threaded bolt version. They will interchange but are not considered correct.

Ball Joint Replacement

With the bushing and cross shaft out of the way, move on to the ball joints. During any restoration, it is a good idea to replace both upper and lower ball joints since you now have the suspension completely torn down. Originals will likely be worn, and since you are so deep into the project, this is the best time to attack them.

The replacements may or may not be in good working order, but why take a chance, considering the low cost to replace them. Originals were held on with rivets, while replacements are attached with hardened bolts and nuts. Originals were also 1/4 inch in diameter, while replacements are generally 5/16 inch in diameter, requiring the holes in the control arms to be enlarged. If an aftermarket ball joint is in place, simply remove the bolts and the joint.

Even if you think your joint may be in good shape, it would be suggested to replace it now because these are inexpensive and far easier to replace now than after the car is assembled. If the joint is an original, it will require either grinding off the rivet head, which can be difficult due to space, or chiseling off the head. When replacing the old joint with a new one, enlarge the four holes to accommodate the larger bolts and reattach the new joint.

We will not go into replacing the ball joints with NOS versions using the rivet method of attachment. There are very few people in the country who offer this service, and average home restorers are not capable of re-riveting their own rivets. Original ball joints are also nearly impossible to find today and are very expensive. If you desire having original ball joints installed, search the internet for these as well as shops that offer this service.

CHAPTER 4

Lower Control Arm Disassembly

Now that you have the upper control arms disassembled, move on to the lowers that were previously removed. The lower control arm does not use a cross shaft, so all that is needed is to knock the bushings and ball joints out. Because of a much larger surface area, you will have to either press these out, use a bushing-removal tool, or (since most people have access to one) use a pneumatic chisel. Look for any spot welds on the bushings before you attempt to remove them. If you find spot welds, you will need to carefully grind them off before attempting to remove the bushings.

The easiest way to remove the bushing if you do not have the tools designed for it is to take your pneumatic chisel and make an indentation in the bushing in line with the through bolt and on the inside portion of the arm where the bushing protrudes. This will not only help collapse the bushing in on itself but will also help knock any rust loose. Once this has been accomplished, you can push or walk the bushing out with your chisel. Though both bushings are different sizes, they are removed the same.

As with the upper control arm, check the lowers for any damage that needs to be addressed before proceeding with restoring yours. Pay special attention to the bushing bores for any damage. It will need to be repaired before attempting to press in new bushings.

Again, it is advised to remove and replace the lower ball joint at this point in your restoration rather than later. This can be easily accomplished with a press or with a little more effort using a pneumatic driver. If you cannot obtain either of these tools, it would be advisable to bring the control arm to an auto-repair facility and let them remove and replace the ball joint.

Rear Trailing Arms

Moving on to the rear upper and lower trailing arms, these are very similar in regard to bushing replacement procedures as the front. Again, check for damage to the arm and bushing area. If the damage is too severe, they should to be replaced. There are different varieties of these arms based on which RPO code suspension the car came with as well as design dates, so look to make sure you are replacing it with a similar arm.

Check all the bushings, but with any full restoration, it is advisable to replace them all at this time. The rear bushings may also have been spot welded, so again check for this and grind the welds before attempting to remove the bushing. Care must also be taken when reinstalling the bushings in the front control arms and rear trailing arms as you can easily collapse the two halves if they are not supported with the proper spacer or tool while pressing in the new bushings.

If you do not have the proper tools or press, bring all the arms to an auto repair shop and have them pressed in for you. I find it better to press the bushings into all the control arms before the painting procedure so you do not damage the paint during the press-in process. You can simply mask off the bushings prior to painting.

Pressing the bushings into the rear differential is much the same as with the others you have encountered so far. It should only be done after the rear differential has been rebuilt unless you are only doing a cosmetic restoration in which case you can press them in any time. It is

Before attempting to remove your bushing, check to make sure if any are spot welded in. This was fairly common on the front lower control arms, and these will have to be ground off in order to remove the bushing from the control arm.

The differential bushings can only be installed from one direction, which is the same as all the other bushings. It is best to use a bushing-installation tool, but other means can also be employed that will get the job done. Wait until the differential is completely rebuilt before installing these.

easiest to use a bushing-installation tool designed to press the bushings in, but other methods may be used as well. However, using a large hammer and block of wood is not one of them. Care must be taken with the cast-iron ears of the differential to not break them off if using one of the more primitive means to install the bushings. Take note that due to the flange diameter of the bushing, it can only be pressed in one direction due to the interference with the center carrier housing. This now completes the bushing installation of the suspension on your Chevelle.

Front Suspension Restoration

Moving back to the front suspension, we will examine and restore each piece one at a time. You have previously checked your spindles, steering arms, and the rest of your suspension to make sure they were all usable. At this time, very carefully clean all the front suspension pieces with one of the many available water-based solvents or a mild automotive solvent, such as kerosene, using extreme caution. Using a soft bristle brush, this will hopefully expose the inspection paint marks. Do not soak any rubber parts such as the seals or tie-rod boots in the solvent, as it will destroy them.

After removing the rubber pieces, soaking the rest of the parts will allow you to remove the grease and grime without disturbing the painted on inspection marks if they can still be seen. If found, carefully take photos of these markings so you can replicate them as well as make note of their color and size by using a measuring device. Once you have the parts completely cleaned, look them over thoroughly again for any defects.

Check both upper and lower ball-joint spindle bores to make sure they are still round and have not been made oblong from improper removal techniques. If you find that the bores are not round, these individual pieces must be replaced. Once you are satisfied, proceed to remove all rust, corrosion, grit, and paint from the suspension pieces by bead blasting, paint remover, or by other means. Protect the machined spindle area with duct tape if you are going to blast the part so it does not tarnish the machined bearing surfaces.

Once you have the suspension pieces completely cleaned and documented, move on to restoring these parts. The spindle, steering arm, tie-rod ends, idler arm, pitman arm, center link (or drag link, as some are called), and coil springs were all natural cast iron when produced and seldom had any paint applied. If you find any black paint, the odds are it was sprayed on by the receiving dealer to cover any flash rust. Some people restore these as painted black while the more-correct method would be a darker cast-iron-colored appearance.

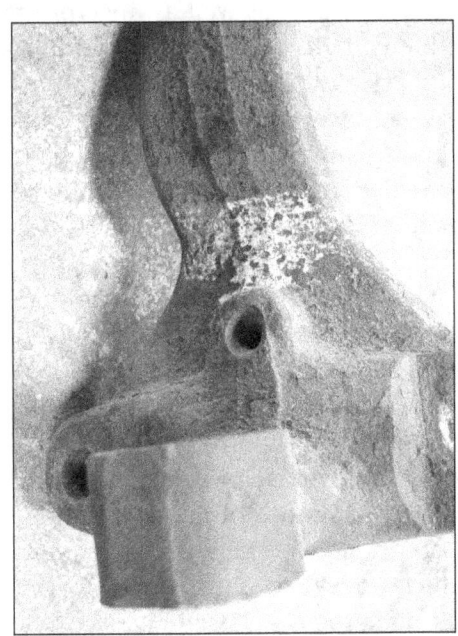

After thoroughly cleaning the spindles, steering arms, and the rest of the suspension, look for and photo document paint markings so they can be replicated. It is best to use an oil-based art paint and sponge brush to reapply these.

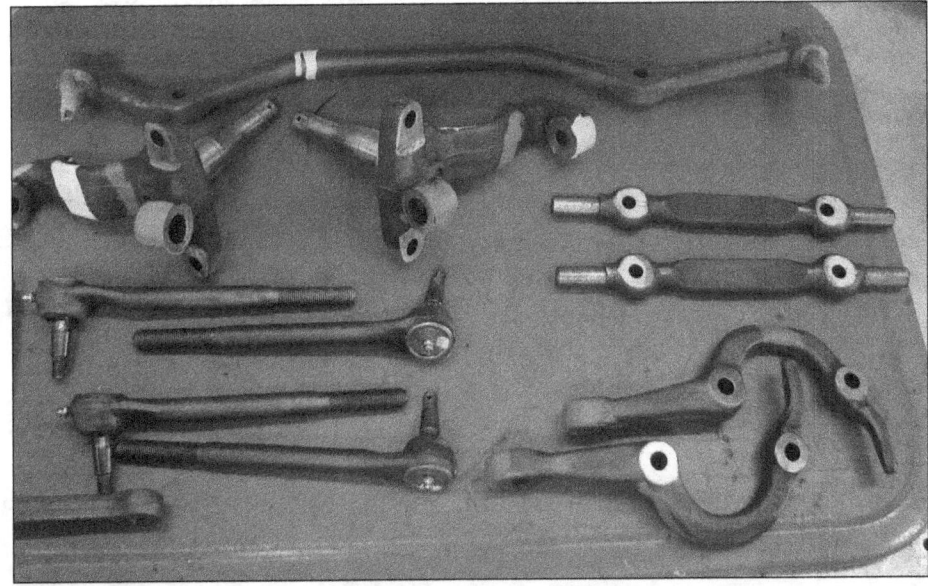

With a little time and effort and not very much expense, you can make your front suspension look as it did when it was newly assembled once again. A little extra care in this area will really make a restoration stand out from the rest.

As with any steel part that is going to be painted, acid wash and prep it so that it is totally free of any contaminants as well as fingerprints that will inhibit the paint from sticking. Hang these parts in an appropriate and well-ventilated area or spray booth and proceed to paint them the desired color. The tie-rod sleeves and clamps were natural steel. These can either be painted with a stainless steel–colored paint or seal the bare steel with Boeshield or its equivalent to give you that natural look.

When it is dry, add all the various colored inspection marks back onto each individual piece based on the photos you took of them. When that is completed, you will have a very nicely restored and stock-appearing front suspension assembly.

Restoring the Dust Shields

The dust shields found on disc brake cars can also be restored to like-new condition with a little effort. Contrary to popular belief, these pieces were not zinc plated; instead, they were stamped from a sheet of galvanized steel. Many people replate them in zinc, which is not technically correct, but it does somewhat resemble the original appearance and for a nominal cost.

Regalvanizing these parts would be expensive. It is also a different process today than it was in the 1970s, so today's process has a different look. It is possible to make them appear to be galvanized. One way to restore these with a similar appearance to galvanizing is to mottle them with various colors of silver paint, giving them that galvanized look. This is also inexpensive to replicate but does take a little practice to get them to look correct and fairly smooth. Spray silver paint onto a newspaper, then dip a crumpled-up piece of cellophane in the paint and dab it onto the backing plate. Use a tamping manner in an attempt to create dots of various colors of galvanizing. Do this several times over the entire piece with multiple shades of grey and silver to achieve a very close look to the real thing.

Once the paint is applied, add the correct two-digit part code decal that can be found on your build sheet, if you have one. If you do not have your car's build sheet, these codes are readily found on the internet. Once completed, spray a very fine thin coat of satin clear paint over the entire piece will help seal your work.

Caliper Bracket Replating

Since it takes some time in the shipping and plating process, it is suggested that you send off your caliper brackets to be plated to allow time to get them back so you can reassemble them. These can be plated in gold cadmium, which resembles the originals. It is suggested to chemically strip any paint that may be on them as opposed to bead blasting. Blasting will etch them and give the gold a flatter look instead of the desired rainbow appearance.

An exception is plastic or walnut blasting, as that will not etch the metal. However, soft media blasting will not remove the rust. If badly

Original backing plates were stamped from a sheet of galvanized steel. With a little effort you can replicate this process by tamping various shades of silver paint onto the plates using a piece of crumpled up cellophane. When dry, add your decals for a very nicely restored piece.

Calipers were plated in gold cadmium, which has a slight rainbow color effect. To achieve this same color, the metal must be cleaned and smooth in finish. Any roughness from blasting them will translate into the plating and give a flatter appearance that what is desired.

rusted, you may just want to find a donor set of brackets that are much cleaner to start with. If you are not bothered by the flat gold appearance of the brackets that have been blasted, thoroughly clean and plate them.

Caliper Rebuilding

When it comes to your front calipers, you will want to either rebuild your originals or simply replace them with auto store rebuilt units. It is actually cheaper to replace your originals than it is to rebuild them. However, if you are into original numbers, you will likely want to rebuild your own.

You must first determine if your original calipers are salvageable. Are the outsides badly pitted and unsightly or are they just showing average wear? Are they damaged or bent? Are they the correct part-numbered unit for your car? If you decide to rebuild your own, proceed with the next part.

Using a large C-clamp or piston-compression tool that you used when you removed the calipers, slowly compress the brake pads and/or piston back into its bore. Once again, keep in mind the fluid you may displace will have to go somewhere, so plan accordingly and have rags and a pan ready to catch this fluid as it comes out of the rear of the caliper.

Once the pistons are compressed, remove the pads if you have not done so already. Place a 1-inch-thick board or a hammer handle between the piston and the outer housing of the caliper. While keeping your fingers clear of the piston area, apply a small amount of pressurized air into the brake line hose-attachment hole and make sure the bleeder screw is closed. Tap your air gun with a few short bursts of air into the hole. It is best if your air gun has a rubber-coned tip that will allow you to tightly seal it to the hose inlet hole. The piston will come up out of its bore, and you will now be able to remove it by hand.

Once the piston is out of the way, remove the piston dust boot and rubber piston ring and discard it. These will come in a new rebuild kit and can be replaced at that time. Carefully check the piston for pitting. If it has any amount of pitting, you must replace the piston, which is readily available from your favorite auto parts store.

Remove the four O-rings from the mounting tabs on the caliper and discard them. These sometimes are included in the rebuild kit. Once the caliper is completely disassembled, thoroughly clean and blow-dry it off. It is best if you media blast the unit after cleaning to remove the scale that has accumulated over the years. If that is not available, simply use a wire brush or wheel to remove the scale. If you do media blast yours, make sure to remove any remaining media.

After cleaning, paint your calipers in either cast-iron colored paint or in a semigloss black and start the reassembly using the kit's directions. Carefully use either DOT 3 or DOT 5 fluid as a lubricant when reassembling any of the rubber parts, being careful to not get brake fluid on the painted surface. Either DOT 3 or DOT 5 can be used in your car's braking system. DOT 5 is a silicone fluid and will not harm the paint. Reassemble the piston seal, piston, and piston dust boot onto the caliper. Reinstall the new O-rings in the mounting pads of the caliper and apply anti-seize to the mounting bolts. Set aside the completed units until it comes time to mount them back on the front calipers.

Sway Bar Restoring

Proceed to restore the front and rear sway bars. These should be treated much the same as the other suspension pieces. Completely strip them of all rust, grime, paint, etc. and acid wash to get them clean, or at the very least, use a solvent that leaves no film. From there, they can be primed and painted. These were natural or painted black from the factory, and you must decide which color to paint yours, either a semigloss black or cast-iron color. Painting them a natural color will give your suspension a bit of contrast.

With your completed suspension restoration, you have a very nicely detailed and correct-appearing chassis with minimal expense and lots of elbow grease. This detail is the difference between a nicely restored car and a wannabe.

The same goes for the front sway-bar brackets, as both natural-steel and black-painted clamps have been found. As with every part of your restoration, carefully examine your original parts to determine exactly how they were manufactured and finished on your particular car. Do not just rely on what you have heard or been told. For the natural steel look, use stainless steel–colored paint, or strip your originals and seal them with a quality bare-steel sealer, such as Boeshield. Keep in mind that if yours are pitted, body filling and painting may be the suggested manner as the pits will be very evident if you are leaving it natural. The sway-bar standoffs (or towers, as they are often called) can be left natural and sealed with Boeshield to keep them from flash corroding.

Rear Differential Restoration

If you had chosen to have your differential completely rebuilt or if you just simply want to freshen it up, you will want to restore the outside to match the condition of the rest of the frame restoration. It has been found that rear differential assemblies were delivered to General Motors in both a natural finish as well as painted a semigloss paint, depending on plant and other factors. When painted, there was usually just enough paint to keep the differential from flash rusting while being rail transported. It has also been found both ways from the same plant, so either could be considered correct.

Another known fact is that dealers often painted some of the undercarriage of the car with a flash coat of black paint to hide any signs of flash rusting while the car sat on the dealer's parking lot, especially in arid climates. In these cases, usually only the rear portions of the differential were painted for visual reasons. Detective work and research needs to be performed on your particular Chevelle to determine how your car was originally assembled if you chose to restore it that way. If you intend to use your Chevelle as a daily driver, it would be better to paint the entire differential black to protect it.

We will discuss both methods here and let you decide. On original cars that were painted all black, this would include the completely assembled rear differential and brakes with backing plates and drums installed. Brake lines have also been found to have been painted as well.

Starting with a completely restored or freshened-up differential, attach the subassemblies onto the rear assembly, such as the brake backing plates, rear brake hardware, and finally the axles and brake drums. The rear backing plates are very similar, but you must install each backing plate so that the emergency brake cable hole is mounted toward the front of the vehicle. Brake drums and the brake hardware were originally installed during the paint process,

When restoring your differential in a natural finish, you can achieve the appearance of the various types of steel and cast-iron items using various colors of paint. You may also want to add inspection marks that were used during the assembly and pre-machining stages of the assembly.

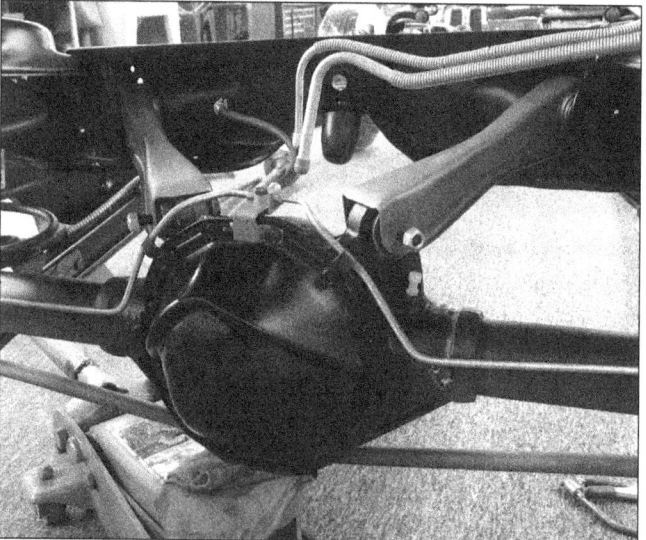

If choosing to restore your differential in the more-common black finish, you can add inspection marks prior to the paint process and put a light coat of black over the entire differential as was done originally, which will also allow the inspection marks to bleed through and be slightly seen.

CHASSIS, SUSPENSION, AND BRAKE WORK

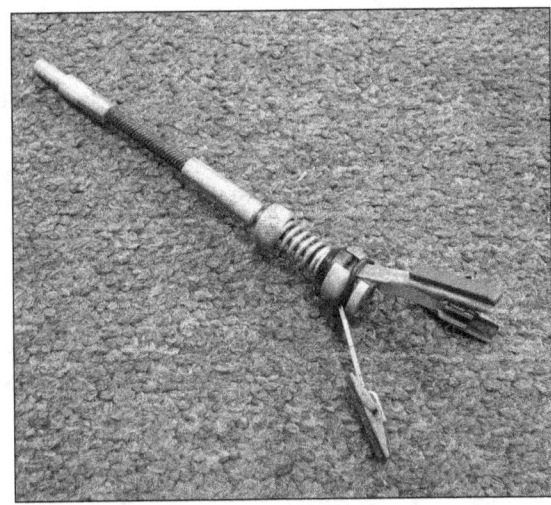

Available from most tool suppliers or automotive parts suppliers is a brake hone made for honing out wheel cylinders. Make sure to purchase the correct size for your cylinder and hone to a nice smooth finish.

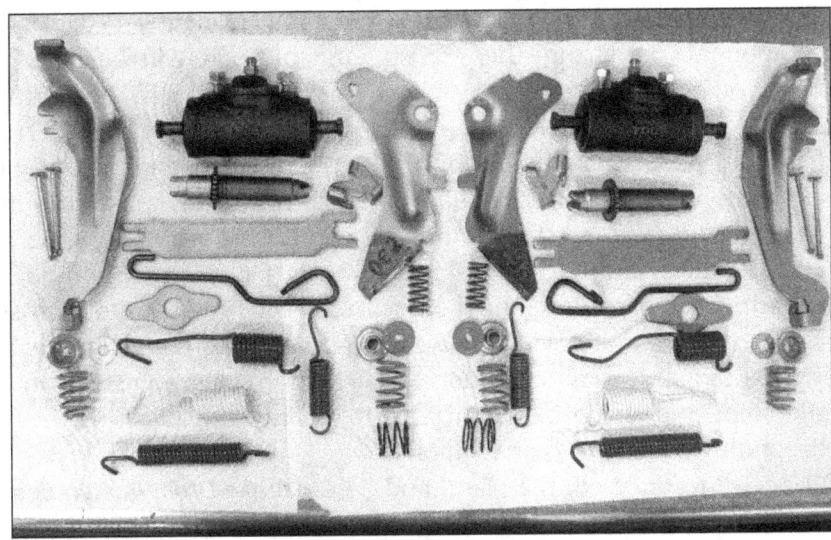

Before installing the hardware, lay all of it out on a towel with the left and right side separated. This will give you a visual on what needs to be installed. Do one side and then the other.

The axle has been removed to show how the hardware is installed. Use this as a guide for the color and installation of the springs, shoes, levers, and adjusters. Notice these shoes are the original bonded type and not the current riveted type.

so you will want to restore this area prior to painting the complete differential assembly.

The inside portion of the backing plate would have been bare steel when original. To ward off future rusting and to make this area look correct, it is suggested to paint the inside of the backing plate with a stainless steel– or bare steel–colored paint. Once cured, you can add the brake hardware onto the backing plate. If you are rebuilding the rear differential, it would be suggested to paint the inside of the backing plate prior to installing the axel shafts to obtain a more complete coverage with nothing in your way as you paint them.

Your backing plates are now ready for assembly. Install your brake hardware starting with the rebuilt or replacement wheel cylinders. On a car that will be used as a weekend car, it is much cheaper and easier to replace the wheel cylinders with a pair from your auto parts store. If this will be a concours restoration, you can often rebuild your own original Delco Moraine cylinders by simply disassembling, bead blasting, and honing them smooth using a brake cylinder hone available from most auto parts or tool suppliers. You can also buy wheel cylinder–rebuild kits to replace the spring, pistons, and seals found within the cylinder.

If you find the bores on your originals to be too badly pitted where the hone will not remove the pitting, it will require that you replace them, or you can send them off to a reputable service company and have them resleeved. This will give you a brand-new bore surface that you can then reassemble using a rebuild kit. This can be very expensive and time consuming, so plan ahead for these.

Restore all your brake hardware for a concours restoration or replace it with a complete hardware kit from your auto parts supplier. If you chose to restore, it is easiest to put them in paint stripper or bead blast all the component parts and then finish them off in the appropriate color. Make sure to keep the right- and left-hand parts separated during the restoration process because many of these must be reinstalled on the correct side. Before you bead blast or strip your parts, document what color and shade of color they were. There can be some variation to the color and shade of these parts, depending on which parts supplier General Motors used, the plant, and the year, so refer to the notes you took during the disassembly process. Once you have cleaned and washed all the parts, hang them for painting. After they have dried, you can lay them out on a towel or a piece of cardboard for ease of installation; again, keep the two sides separated.

From this point, assemble the driver- and passenger-side brake hardware on their appropriate sides of the rear axle. Have your new brake shoes handy as well before you start. The first item to take care of is to lubricate the six brake shoe–contacting pads on the backing plate with lithium grease. As stated earlier in the chapter, if these have a deep groove in them, the backing-plate pads either need to be welded and ground smooth or replaced; otherwise, the shoes will not move in and out as designed.

Make sure to always install the primary shoe (the shoe with the shorter brake pad of the two) toward the front of the car; otherwise, the brakes will not apply correctly. Assemble all the hardware and shoes per the assembly manual and check for free movement. You will also need to install your rear emergency brake cables at this time. The cable should be inserted through the hole near the front lower edge of the backing plate. It will be installed completely when you hear the locking tabs click as they are inserted. Now, attach the tail end of the cable to the emergency brake application lever behind the secondary shoe.

Pay close attention to the bottom shoe-to-shoe holding spring. If not installed correctly, it will inhibit the star-wheel adjuster from working correctly and adjusting the brakes.

Rear Brake Drum Restoration

As for the rear brake drum, you will want to sandblast or aluminum-oxide media blast these to remove any rust. First ensure that they have adequate thickness left on the drum to be able to be turned. Once they are blasted, you can paint them overall cast-iron color. If not done already, this would be a good time to turn them. If they are turned before painting, you will need to give them a very good bath to remove any oil film that might get on them during the handling and turning process.

Perform any needed bodywork, such as filling pits in the axle tube area or backing plates. The differential center housing was cast iron and will have many pock marks from the casting process. As a general rule, those do not need to be filled unless you chose to do it for a smoother look or if it is badly pitted.

Painting the Rear Differential

Once sanding and all bodywork is completed, it is time to paint the assembly. One of the simplest ways to paint your differential is to hang it from something like an engine cherry picker using a chain or other sufficient means from the upper trailing arm mounts so that it is unobstructed when painting. Once hung, wash down the entire assembly using Prep-Sol and do not handle any of it with bare hands; then, prepare

For ease of bodywork and paint, it is best to hang the assembly from a hoist or engine cherry picker to gain full access to all areas of the differential. Always wash down your components with a metal prep prior to painting for good primer and paint adhesion.

it for painting. Mask off any areas that you do not want to get paint on, such as the trailing-arm bushings, the previously installed emergency brake cable, pinion flange, and the oil slinger on the front of the differential.

The complete painting techniques are covered in the paint and body section, so we will only skim over what is necessary here. After you are done doing your body filling, sanding, and cleaning, it is time to apply primer to protect the metal and give the paint a good base. Cleanliness is paramount, so make sure you have everything once again wiped down with a metal prep and a tack cloth before priming.

Whether you are using a spray can or a spray gun to apply your paint, make sure that the paint is mixed thoroughly, you have adequate ventilation, and that the temperature of the area you are painting in is suitable for paint application. Cover your entire differential with a light coat of primer, let it tack up a bit, and then follow it with a couple of good coats to completely seal it. After the primer has cured per the manufacturer's directions, wet sand the entire area to give the surface a texture to receive the paint coat. Completely blow off the dust as well as any water that may have been trapped during the wet-sand process, and follow that by thoroughly wiping it down with the tack cloth just prior to color painting.

Cast-Iron Look

If you intend to finish your differential in a natural, as-built finish, understand that the steel axle tubes and backing plates will be a different color than the cast-iron center section. Regardless of which paint application method you are using to paint the differential, it is suggested to use a stainless steel– or natural steel–colored paint for the axle tubes and backing plates and a cast-iron color for the center section. Mask off the axle tubes and the rear cover (if installed).

The rear cover on a natural-colored differential is usually found to be bare steel with black phosphate bolts. It is best to use paint stripper on the cover instead of media blasting to retain the natural steel look. If it is badly pitted, you will need to perform the necessary bodywork followed by a steel-colored paint. If leaving natural steel, you can treat it with a clear paint or a brush/spray-on protector like T9 Boeshield. Use this method only when leaving it natural because you will not be able to top coat the cover with any type of paint due to the waxy finish that Boeshield leaves.

Assuming that you are painting your differential in a natural finish because you are looking for an authentic as-built appearance, it is also assumed that you may want to apply your inspection paint marks after the paint has dried to replicate an as-delivered differential to Chevrolet. If you intend to paint your differential black, then apply these colored inspection marks before you spray the black and cover it lightly, allowing some of the inspection marks to bleed through.

Differential Inspection Marks

There are several inspection marks that have been found on rear differentials. I have mainly seen yellow and blue marks that are usually painted on the differential in similar manners. However, these were documented on 454-ci engine cars for

If you choose to restore your differential in its natural finish, be sure to add the manufacturing plant inspection marks to the rear after you have simulated its natural appearance. If you choose to paint the differential black, many of these inspection marks should be slightly covered in paint.

Prior to completed machining, the differential assembly plant applied paint marks to various parts of the assembly to denote where things were to be welded and for other reasons yet understood. In the case of these yellow markings, they were applied to the center housing prior to the axle tubes being welded into the housing. Once welding was applied, it burned off much of the yellow paint and left bluing where the welded area heated up.

For reasons unknown, other inspection marks can be found on other parts of the rear differential and axle tubes. These may be to signify that the welds on the brake line retainer clips were intact, while others may be done to signify that the assembly was inspected and cleared for the next step in the assembly process.

Sometimes dealers chose to apply some black-out paint to parts of the suspension so potential customers did not have to look at flash rust that developed while cars sat in the elements on the dealer's lots. These black-out coats were haphazardly applied, so poor coverage and drips were common. Brake lines were also often painted over in the process.

The most common way that rear differentials are restored is in an overall semi-gloss black finish. How much coverage is applied is up to the restorer, whether they are just looking to replicate how the assembly plant painted it or if they intend to drive the car frequently and just want it to look good.

the most part, so other rear differentials may vary, depending on 10- or 12-bolt and 396-ci or 454-ci equipped cars, so use this only as a guide.

The yellow marks have been found on the bottoms and tops of the center housing as well as the plug-weld areas where the axle tubes were welded into the center housing. After welding, portions of the yellow paint burned off and left a bluing appearance around the weld from the intense heat. With a little experimenting and experience, this can easily be replicated.

Other markings have been found on or near the axle-tube areas as well. Careful cleaning during the disassembly process may possibly expose these marking so that they can be replicated during the restoration. Many inspection markings that have been found on these cars have no rhyme or reason to their colors, layout, or consistency, so it is often best to replicate only what you find and exactly how you found it.

Another option is to restore your differential in the natural finish and then give it a slight black-out. Many times, dealers would dress up their cars after they received them and perform a clean-up process after the cars arrived at their dealerships. Many dealers did not want customers to see flash rusting on parts of the suspension and undercarriage, so they would spot-paint black-out paint in those areas to make the car more appealing. Great care was not taken during this process, so you will see black overspray on surrounding areas of the car other than where it was intended as well as drips since the applicator was not too worried about how perfect it was as long as it hid the rust. Many restorers want to replicate this look.

CHASSIS, SUSPENSION, AND BRAKE WORK

The last option is to paint your differential in complete semigloss black paint coverage. This is strongly recommended on a Chevelle that will be driven frequently. All the same preparation steps need to be taken as outlined previously. For a more appealing appearance, you can leave the brake lines off until the differential has been painted. It is best to install the brake drums and put an overspray coat of black around the finned area, as most of the time the entire drum did not get fully covered in black paint. However, there is no right or wrong way as far as how much paint and how large or small an area of coverage. These were painted by humans and may vary. Perfection was not a prerequisite.

The upper and lower trailing arms were usually finished in the same manner as the rear differential, though they can still vary; so again, research is your best friend here. It is fairly common to find Baltimore, Atlanta, and Arlington Chevelles with all-natural differentials and trailing arms, although some have been found with either or both of the differential and/or trailing arms painted black as well. Finish these using the same techniques as you used painting the rear differential. Chevelles have also been found to have natural upper arms, while the lowers were painted. There just does not seem to be any rhyme or reason to how they were done—not the assembly plant or assembly date.

Bodywork and Primer

You are now ready for bodywork and primer for your frame and components. As stated many times previously, before you do any bodywork and priming, you must prep the metal on the frame and all of the component parts just prior to doing bodywork. Prep-Sol or another acid wash will be required to clean the frame thoroughly enough to accept the paint process. From this point on, avoid all contact with those parts with bare hands, dirty rags, or airborne contaminants because this will again contaminate the bare steel and cause issues with the paint process. You should use no less caution and preparation on a frame and its components as you would on the body, so do not skimp here either.

With regards to bodywork, priming, and painting, we will not get too technical here (painting techniques are covered at length in the chapter 6). If you are doing a concours restoration, you will have a professional spray out these parts for you, or if you are educated enough, you already know what you are doing here. With the home restorer in mind, I will cover the basics.

Protecting the Frame

If you are choosing the more conventional painting method, the first step after cleaning these parts is to either cover the bare steel with a rust inhibitor such as POR 15, which is widely available over the internet and in many parts stores, or sandblast followed by the appropriate bodywork, priming, and painting. For POR 15 usage, follow the instructions on the can and either brush or spray the frame and components to seal them from future rust that was not completely removed. You will still need to topcoat over the entire area because it is not a final sealer, and this method should only be used on a driver-quality frame.

For a concours-restored frame, all of the imperfections must be filled and sanded smooth. If you are very detail oriented, you do not want to cover or destroy the factory stretch marks, welds, or stamping wrinkles that were made when the framerails and pieces were initially stamped. Filling of all the rust pits is imperative if you want a show-quality job, but it is very time consuming, so be forewarned. There are several types and brands of body filler on the market. Bondo is just one and is not only a brand name but also the generic name when talking body filler. It can be obtained from a variety of automotive parts stores, retail stores, and online.

Fixing Imperfections

Using an applicator from your auto body and paint supplier, fill all imperfections with body filler, let it dry thoroughly, and sand it smooth, using progressively finer grits of sandpaper. There are also several other types of sanding products available, such as Scotch-Brite pads, sanding disks, and screens. The use of pneumatic sanders will also greatly improve your sanding time if these are available to you. Talk with your paint and body supplier and purchase what is best for your needs.

You may have to apply more than one coat of filler, depending on the depth of the damage, pits, or imperfections. Again, refer to the manufacturer's application guidelines. In some cases, you may want to finish off the final filler application with a glazing and spot putty. This is much thinner, goes on easier, and sands off with little effort. Try to get most of your work done with body filler and only use the spot putty for finite details that were missed. Spot putty shrinks considerably, so you do not want to lay it on very thick. This is a very time-consuming process. However, taking your time here to make sure you do it right will pay in the end, giving you a very smooth finish on your frame and parts and in return excellent visual finish results.

Primer on Parts and Pieces

Once all your sanding has been completed and has cured thoroughly per the manufacturer's specifications, apply a coat of primer over all your pieces. Again, talk with your paint supplier and purchase the product that best suits your particular needs. After the primer has cured, you will want to wet sand it smooth just prior to your paint application. You may have to do more than one coat of primer and wet sand process before you are ready to apply the paint. Since most types of painting will require expensive guns, you may want to leave this step to your local painter, although you need to check with them first because some painters will not apply paint over someone else's work while still offering a warranty.

If you will be applying the chassis paint or having your painter apply it, use of a semigloss black is recommended, as this will closely match what was originally applied. If you are doing a driver or Restomod, then you may want to use a glossier black or even another color to suit your needs or to compliment the body color.

Gloss Differences on Upper and Lower Control Arms

The front upper and lower control arms are painted a little more gloss than what you painted the frame. The cross shafts on the upper control arms should be a natural cast iron. Before painting the upper and lower control arms, mask off the bushings and cross shaft, as these should not be primed or painted.

On the rear trailing arms, it will depend on what you decide as far as natural or painted. Many Chevelles have been documented with several combinations: painted differentials with natural trailing arms and vice versa, everything painted, or all-natural steel. Here is where you will need to decide how you want to do yours. The one exception is, if painting them black, the upper trailing arms were typically a flat black while the lowers were a semigloss. All four have been seen natural as well.

Just like you did for the front control arms, mask off the bushing before you prime and paint. The same goes for the two rear stiffener arms that are mounted on some cars. These were mounted from the front of the lower trailing arms and at the top of the rear crossmember. Normally, if the rear differential is natural, all four trailing arms and rear stiffener arms are natural; if the rear differential is painted, the arms usually are as well.

Front and Rear Sway Bar

Front and rear sway bars have been found in both a natural cast-iron finish and in a semigloss black painted finish. Either way would be considered correct. If you intend to paint yours natural, use a cast-iron colored paint.

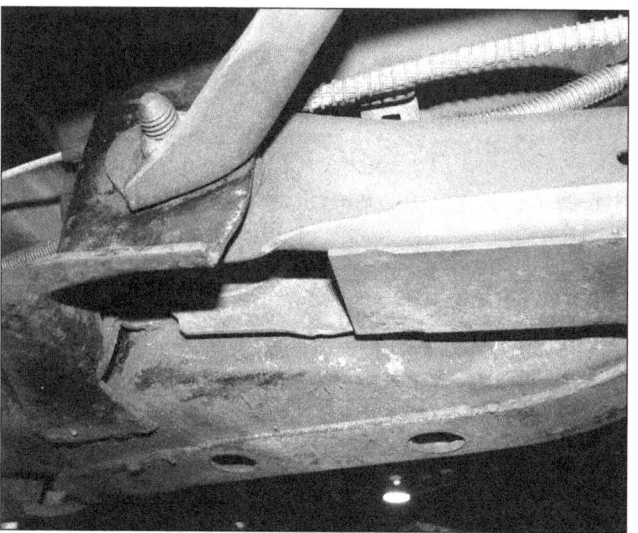

On this particular survivor Arlington LS6, you can clearly see the semigloss black paint as well as the natural-steel lower trailing arm and frame stiffener arm. Attaching bolts are black phosphate while the lock nuts are dull zinc or galvanized. Semigloss black is also correct for the arms.

This is an example of an upper trailing arm that was left natural steel by the supplier to General Motors. On this particular car, all of the trailing arms, stiffener arms, and rear differential were left natural. Also notice the two-digit code ink stamped onto the arm. (Photo Courtesy Brian Henderson)

CHASSIS, SUSPENSION, AND BRAKE WORK

Transmission Crossmembers

Transmission crossmembers have also been found in both natural steel as well as semigloss black. If going for the natural look, use a stainless steel–colored paint.

Natural Steel Coil Springs

Coil springs front and rear were left natural steel and should be painted as such unless you again go for the black or cast-iron look.

Seldom seen is the natural steel transmission crossmember. Typically, they are painted semigloss black to match the frame. Also note that on unpainted crossmembers the welding process has left a bluing color to the metal in the area around the welds from the heat.

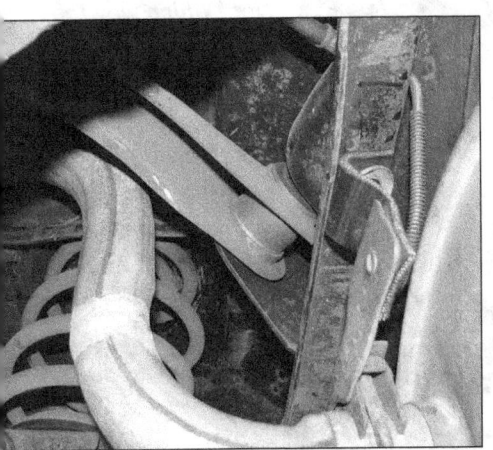

Powdercoating is another good way to paint these, though care must be taken to not get the paint too thick because it may crack when the spring flexes. After painting, you can attach the appropriate spring code decals.

Chassis Reassembly

Now that you have all of your components painted, it is time to assemble the entire frame and all the suspension components. Completely clean your work area so that you have nothing that does not belong there. If possible, put a roll of cheap indoor short-knap carpet on the floor that is at least as large as the frame is long and a little wider than the width of the frame. This will allow you to place your freshly restored parts out in the general area that they will be restored and on something soft so they will not get scratched or otherwise damaged.

Set your frame on floor jacks in an area that will not be in your way as you try and reassemble the frame, and allow enough height to swing the lower control arms down during the assembly process. You will also need to allow room for the placement of a floor jack underneath the control arm; the longest part of the side framerails and at the corners are the best places for the jack stand. Lay all of your front suspension components near the front of the frame and your rear components near the rear. This will include all the

Laying all of your component parts and frame on a piece of carpet will greatly aid in the reassembly step, allowing your parts to be positioned in the area they will go as well as helping to keep them from getting damaged.

Many things can be seen in this photo of a low-mileage survivor Chevelle: the semigloss black frame, natural-metal differential, natural-steel upper trailing arm, natural-steel coil spring, and gray shocks.

mounting hardware, nuts, clips, lines, etc. This is where your previously tagged and bagged hardware will become much easier to install since it will be organized.

Fuel Lines

Start by inserting your single or dual fuel lines into the frame. Insert them one at a time in the oval hole located in the inboard front passenger-side framerail midway through the bend. After inserting them one at a time, guide the front of the lines into the framerail and then out the hole on the front side of the engine crossmember where it meets the framerail. It is very helpful to have a helper guide the rear of the fuel lines and help feed them as well as keeping them from scratching the frame.

Once fully inserted, install the restored fuel line clips back into their original locations and securely fasten them with the same bolts that you removed. You may need to reposition the wrapped spring to allow the clamps to be installed where they are supposed to be and fit that part of the line.

Brake Lines

Move to the brake lines and install the distribution valve onto the framerail near the front. Attach the long brake line that runs along the driver-side framerail using the same clamps you previously removed. Thread the line into the distribution valve but do not tighten it at this time.

Just as on the fuel lines, you may have to reposition the coil springs wrapped on the line to allow the clamps to fit in their locations. If your car is equipped with disc brakes, mount the hold-off valve to the rear crossmember and loosely attach the

The disc brake hold-off valve allows the rear brakes to be applied slightly before the front brakes to ward off a frontal dive that would happen during normal brake application without it. Loosely attach the lines to this valve during the initial assembly process.

brake line to it. Attach the short V-shaped brake line to the hold-off valve and to where it will eventually be attached to the rear flex brake line on the other end.

Moving to the front of the car, loosely attach the cross-over brake line and clips across the rear portion of the engine crossmember and to the distribution valve with their associated brake line clips. In the disassembly process, you removed an L-bracket from either side of the frame where the hard brake lines met the flex lines. Install those back onto the left and right sides of the frame at this time.

On the driver's side, you will have a short brake line that runs from the distribution valve to the L-bracket that is mounted on the same side. Loosely attach this line. Attach the flex lines on both sides of the frame where the L-brackets are. Loosely attach them to the hard line and then insert the flat U-shaped clamp on both sides to lock the lines to the L-bracket. With fuel and brake lines partially attached, we can now move on to the suspension.

Engine Mounts

Before attaching the front control arms, it is time to replace the frame-mounted engine mounts. They can easily be accessed without the control arms in the way. Refer to your photo documentation when

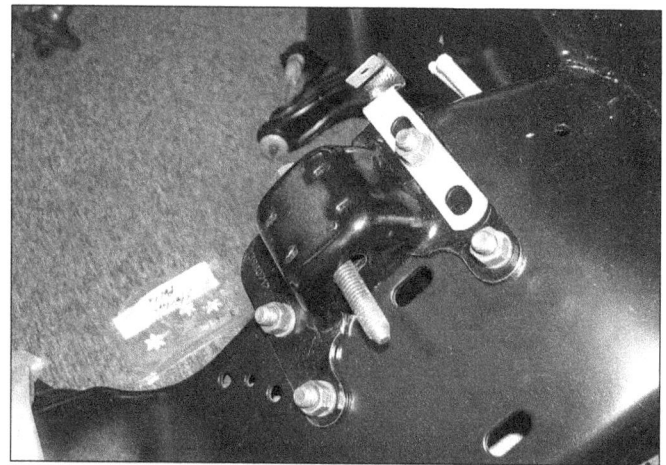

Note which way the motor mount bolts are facing. This will vary by plant and assembly date. Even-part-numbered items or those labeled with an R will always go on the passenger's side. Note how the battery cable bracket is mounted as well.

CHASSIS, SUSPENSION, AND BRAKE WORK

you disassembled the frame and attach the brackets back to the frame on the same sides they came off of and with the mounting bolts orientated as you found them. Even part numbers or items labeled with an R always go on the passenger side.

Do not forget to add the battery cable bracket during this installation process. It will be mounted on the front outside bolt of the passenger-side motor mount and with the battery cable loop hanging down.

Control Arm Bumpers

Before installing the upper control arms, it is imperative that you remember to install the control arm bumper onto the frame at the point where the upper control arm contacts the frame when it is at full lift. Once the front suspension is fully installed, it will be very difficult at best to install it. Place some white lithium grease on the nipple of the bumper, and using a twisting motion, install it into the hole at the top of the frame.

Upper Control Arms

Insert the fully restored upper control arms back onto the frame mounts, making sure you install the correct one on the correct side. Sometimes slight alignment help will be needed to get the cross shaft to start on the bolts. Ever so gently, use a rubber mallet to tap the bolts in the direction needed to align them with the holes on the cross shaft. Lightly tap the cross shaft all the way onto the bolts and thread on the new stop nuts (and lock washers) if yours originally had them. For now, gently snug them up.

Install new bushing compression washers, lock washers, and bolts back onto your cross shaft. Again, only snug them up at this time. Do the same for the other side.

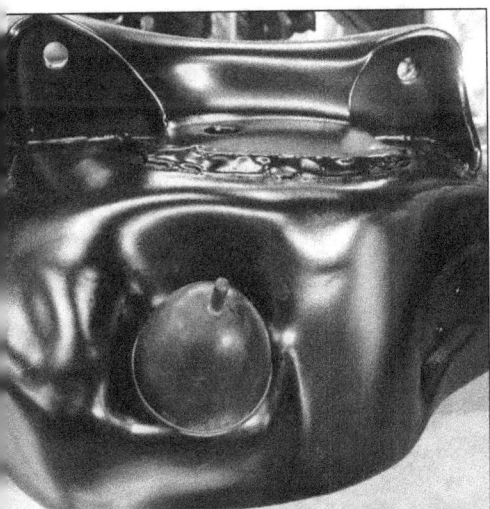

Before installing the upper control arms, it is vitally important to remember to install this small upper bumper. Not doing so now will make for a complete headache later when it will be nearly impossible to install.

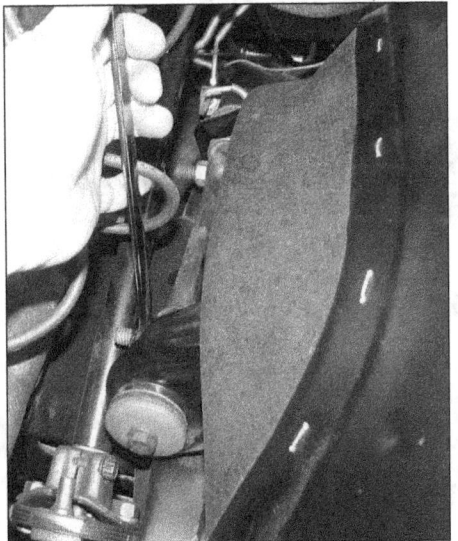

Install the upper control arms onto their studs and only slightly tighten the lock nuts at this time. Also note the bushing compression washers, lock nuts, and bolts are installed into the cross shafts. Only slightly tighten them at this time. A completed chassis was used here for visual purposes only.

Bump Stops and Lower Control Arms

Install new bump stops onto each lower control arm, and then install the control arm into the lower mounts. Again, make sure you install the correct arm on the correct side. An easy way to remember is that the hole for the bump stop will be on the front side of the control arm. Installing the arms can be somewhat difficult if the mounting flanges are bent or compressed in any way. Putting a little white lithium grease on the ends of the bushings will also aid in installing them. It helps to have an extra set of hands here, so if you have anyone available, ask them to help for a bit.

Start by wiggling the control arm into place. Use of a large rubber mallet may also help in the installation. Once the bushings get close, you can often insert a small pin punch or driver through the bolt hole to help align them as well as keep them in place. Once both bushing holes are lined up in the frame mounts, insert new bolts through the holes facing them toward the rear of the car in both the front and rear holes. Slight tapping of the bolts may be required. Finish by threading on new stop nuts onto the bolts but again only snug them up.

Repeat for the other side. After they are both installed, put your spindles onto the lower ball-joint stud and thread the castle nut all the way on, but do not tighten it yet.

Coil Spring Reinstallation

The interesting part comes now with the installation of the coil springs. Use the same method you used when you removed them but in reverse. Again, an extra set of hands will come in very handy and make it much safer.

CHEVELLE RESTORATION AND AUTHENTICITY GUIDE: 1970–1972   69

Make sure the upper part of the coil spring (the flat side) is fully seated around the spring flange up inside the framerail. Also check the bottom coil of the spring and make sure that the coil end will seat into the pocket formed into the lower control arm. Not seating it correctly—on either the top or bottom—will cause severe issues later, so take your time and do it right. Once you have the coil spring in place, start to compress it using your spring compressor.

After applying some compression to the spring, attach a ratchet strap that is of adequate strength about two to three coils from the bottom and diagonally across to the opposite-side framerail and slightly rearward. This will help you keep the spring in alignment with the lower control arm spring perch to aid in assembly. It is a good idea to apply a liberal amount of wide masking tape around the perch area to help protect from any scratches that the coil spring may cause during assembly. However, you want to be sure you have it high enough on the perch that the tape can be removed around the soon-to-be-seated coil spring. As you compress the coil spring, ratchet the strap as needed to pull the spring inward and backward enough to seat it. As always, be sure and wear hand and eye protection.

Proceed to compress the coil spring just enough to be able to raise the lower control arm and spindle up to get the spindle attached to the upper control arm upper ball-joint stud. Once you insert the stud through the spindle, attach the upper castle nut and use this to pull the control arm the rest of the way while the spring compressor stays in place for safety reasons.

Before removing the spring compressor, make double sure that the upper coil is seated around the upper flange correctly and the lower coil end is sitting within its pocket on the lower control arm. If not, your car will never sit level. Once you have verified all is correct, then carefully remove the ratchet strap and spring compressor and repeat all the steps for the other side. Once completed, the hard and potentially dangerous part is now behind you.

Miscellaneous Spindle Attachments

You can now attach the dust seal, caliper bracket, backing plate, and steering arm onto the spindle, making sure the steering arms face forward. On drum brakes, simply install the dust seal, fully assembled backing plate, brake hardware, and steering arm onto the spindle.

Once tightened, install the freshly rebuilt or replacement rotor with repacked or replacement bearings, races, and seals onto the spindle. Now, attach the new or rebuilt caliper onto the rotor using two brake mounting bolts per caliper and lubricated with anti-seize, thereby holding the calipers in place on the caliper brackets.

Complete the opposite side just as you had done previously. Install

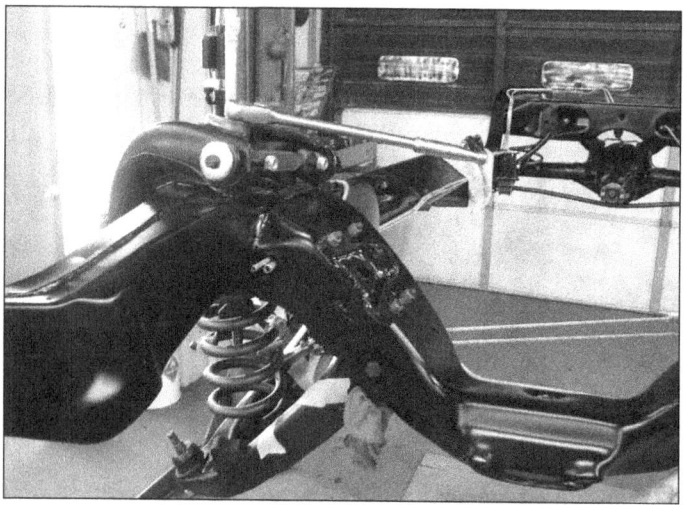

There are several items to note here: the coil spring is clocked to match the spring pocket in the lower control arm, liberal amounts of tape have been applied to protect your paint, and a ratchet strap has been attached diagonally to the opposite framerail to aid in keeping the spring in line with its perch.

Once the control arms and coil springs have been firmly attached, start assembling the spindle and brake hardware. Often forgotten is this dust and grease seal that needs to be placed on the spindle before any more items are added.

CHASSIS, SUSPENSION, AND BRAKE WORK

Install the brake caliper bracket, backing plates, and steering arms onto the spindle. Tighten all bolts and lock nuts to specifications. Once completed, the assembled rotor (or brake drum) and bearings can be installed onto the spindle.

Install the steering box with the three mounting bolts. Both will install in a similar manner onto the frame. From that point, install all the front steering control hardware onto the steering arms, idler arm, and pitman arm.

the manual or power steering box onto the frame and tighten the three mounting bolts. Install the pitman arm onto the steering box. Once completed, install the center link as well as the tie-rods and sleeves onto the front suspension steering arms and snug down the castle nuts.

Install one end of the center link onto the pitman arm and snug down the castle nut. Now, mount the idler arm onto the other end of the center link and again attach the castle nut.

Once done, install the idler arm and tighten to the frame with the two mounting bolts, washers, and stop nuts. Once all is in place, go back and tighten all the castle nuts firmly down with the cotter pin holes exposed.

Install the appropriate-sized cotter pin into its location and bend one end over the nut and the other at a 90-degree bend downward. Trim as necessary to fit. Your front suspension is now complete. Add your wheels and tires onto the frame so that it will be mobile for you to move around in anticipation of mounting the body onto the frame.

Engine and Transmission Installation, Body On/Off

You can install the engine and transmission onto the frame at this time if you choose. Use the opposite procedures as when removing them, or you can install them after you lower the body onto the frame. There are pros and cons to both, so do whichever works best for you.

Before installing the body onto the frame, place all the emergency brake cables in place. Starting with the primary cable, run this through the front frame access hole and out the backside using a Mickey Mouse clip to keep it in place. Make sure the cable runs below the transmission crossmember. Install the intermediate brake cable and saddle onto the primary cable and thread on two fine-threaded nuts a few threads onto the end of the primary cable to hold the saddle and secondary cable in place. Place the large, several-inch-long C-hook into the hole on the crossmember and onto the intermediate cable.

At this point, run each end of the intermediate cable to the rear and attach them to the rear emergency cables using the smaller C cable holders, one per side. The last parts to install are the cable-tensioner S-hooks, one per side. These can be attached now or after the body has been lowered onto the frame. One end will hook around the intermediate cable, while the other end will hook into the bottom of the car.

Tighten all brake line fittings at this time using a flare wrench. Once

 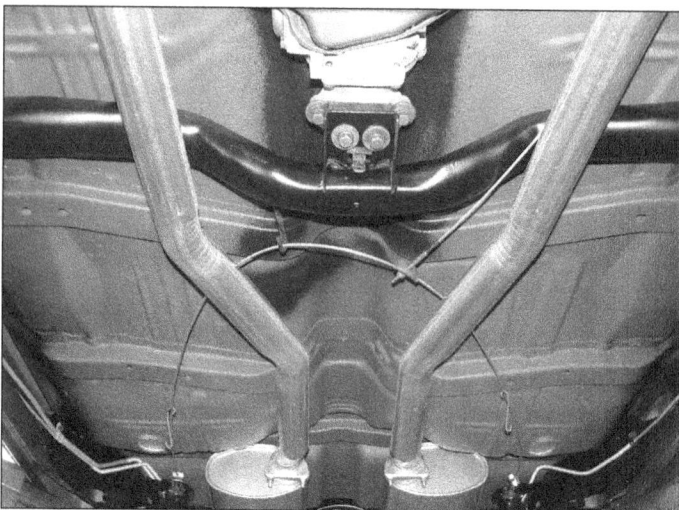

The primary emergency brake cable can now be installed onto the frame in anticipation of lowering the body onto the frame. Use of a Mickey Mouse clip here will hold the cable in place. Once the body is being lowered onto the frame, the front end of the cable will be fed through the hole in the body and attached to the emergency brake pedal.

The entire emergency brake cable assembly can be seen here. The primary cable is attached to the intermediate cable with the use of a saddle and two nuts to hold it on as well as apply tension. The large S-hook is attached to the crossmember, and two small S-clamps hold the intermediate cable to the rear cables. The small S-hooks will be attached once the body is lowered onto the car.

the body has been lowered on the frame and is completely assembled, you can then tighten all the front and rear suspension lock nuts on all of your bushings. The car must be on the ground with full weight on it before you tighten them. A common reminder is to write on a piece of tape and attach to the firewall or windshield with reminders of what steps need to be taken once the body has been lowered and assembled on the frame. You will also need to align the front suspension, but this will need to be one of the last things you do when completing the car's restoration.

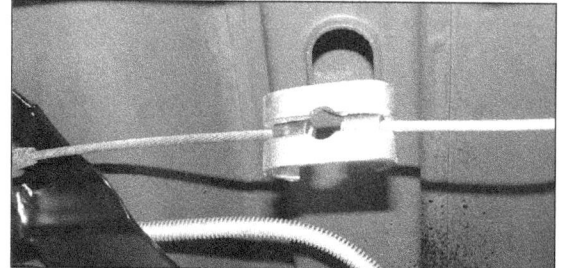

This small C-clamp will couple the intermediate cable with the rear cable and is mounted at the front end of the rear cables. Slip the ends of the cables through the access hole in the C-clamp and pull tight.

Whether you choose to install the engine, transmission, driveshaft, and exhaust now or wait till you have lowered the body onto the frame will be your decision. As was said earlier, there are pros and cons to both. Regardless of which you choose, things will really start getting exciting now.

Your finished rolling chassis will surely get your heart pumping. Just seeing the progress you have made will give you added momentum to finish the balance of the project. Once the body is completed and painted, it can be mounted back on the frame, and things will start to come together rapidly.

CHAPTER 5

ENGINE AND DRIVELINE

All 1970–1972 Chevelles came with either a 250-ci 6-cylinder engine or one of several V-8 engines. Some are desirable from a collector-car standpoint, and some are not so desirable. While there is nothing inherently wrong with the 6-cylinder engine, the 307-ci V-8, or either of the two 350-ci V-8 engines, they are not particularly sought after from a collector or value standpoint in today's market.

The 1970 Malibu-series Chevelles with one of the three small-block V-8s will cost you just about the same to fully restore as one of the two SS Equipment–optioned (SS396 or SS454) Malibu series in all areas except possibly the engine. Machine work required for any engine is going to be comparable, but the small-block V-8s may be less expensive to rebuild in the long run due to the large number of them built compared to either of the 396/402 or 454-ci engines.

It should be pointed out that in 1970 there were three 396/402-ci engines. The RPO L34 and RPO L78 engines actually displaced 402 ci but are referred to as a 396 since that's the way General Motors marketed them. The third 402-ci engine was introduced under RPO LS3 and was rated at 330 hp. This engine was available in all 1970 Chevelles except those with the Z25 SS Equipment option, and it was referred to as 400 Turbo Jet or 400-4 in many repair manuals. This engine was the same 402 ci as the venerable 396 ci, just marketed differently. The L34 was dropped for the 1971 and 1972 model years in favor of the LS3. The Z25 SS396 option was dropped in 1971, and the Z15 SS option was no longer engine specific.

Both 350 Turbo Fire V-8s and the LS3 400 Turbo Jet could be ordered with or without the Z15 option in 1971 and 1972.

Your return on investment just isn't there to restore a small-block Malibu to the same extent as a

An unrestored 1970 L48 350-ci engine shows the PCV valve in the front of the driver-side rocker cover that releases crankcase pressure to the base of the carburetor. Note this engine is equipped with the Transmission Controlled Spark (TCS) relay on the wiring gutter and has a heat tube from the exhaust manifold to the air cleaner housing.

396/402-optioned Malibu or LS5/LS6-optioned one. If the car holds a sentimental value to you—maybe your parents or even grandparents purchased the car new, and it has been in your family for almost 50 years—it could definitely be worth holding on to. If you are not going for a complete frame-off concours-quality restoration and your end goal is a nice weekend cruiser or daily driver, it would make sense to not invest the $70,000 to $100,000 to fully restore it to concours-quality condition. Instead, freshen up the engine, replace those worn suspension pieces, install new brakes, maybe replace that worn carpeting, and buy a set of inexpensive seat covers. It can do wonders without draining your children's college fund. Any needed bodywork, detailing, and personal touches can be done as time and funds allow.

Generally, the same can be said for particular bodystyles. Comparable convertibles will bring more money in today's marketplace than a sport coupe or El Camino bodystyle; as the saying goes, "When the top goes down, the price goes up." That is just the nature of the marketplace.

Naturally, from a purely value and collector standpoint, the king of the hill has to be the 1970 RPO LS6 454-ci 450-hp engine in a convertible. Arguably, the RPO L78 396-ci 375-hp engine of early 1970 would be a close second; not so much because of the L78's horsepower rating but more due to the short production run of the engine before it was phased out in favor of the RPO Z15 SS454 Equipment option in the November/December 1969 time frame of the 1970 production year. Only 2,144 L78 engines found their way into 1970 Chevelles and only 18 of those were additionally optioned with Chevrolet's RPO L89 aluminum head option.

For 1971 and 1972 Chevelles, it is a bit of a different story. The SS Equipment option (RPO Z15) became

This is one of only 18 RPO L78 engines additionally optioned with RPO L89 aluminum heads in 1970, making this a rare find today. It is shown with the optional ZL2 Special Ducted Hood Air System. GM's Air Injection Reactor smog system was mandatory with the L78 engine. (Photo Courtesy L78 Registry)

The 1971 model year would be the last year Chevrolet used the cubic inch/horsepower rating stickers on the air cleaner lid. Note the Turbo-Jet 400/300 horsepower sticker on this 402-ci example. (Photo Courtesy Malibu SS Registry)

ENGINE AND DRIVELINE

In 1972, Chevrolet did not indicate engine identification with cubic inch/horsepower stickers on the air cleaner lid. The LS3 402-ci engine could be ordered in any SS Equipment optioned Malibu as well as any other 1972 Chevelle and, like 1971, did not include any chrome dress-up items. (Photo Courtesy Malibu SS Registry)

This 1972 LS5 is optioned with RPO ZL2 Special Ducted Hood Air System and equipped with GM's Air Injection Reactor smog system. Neither the 1971 nor 1972 SS option included provisions for any underhood chrome dress up. (Photo Courtesy LS5 Registry)

more of a dress-up option than a performance-oriented one. Any optional V-8 engine and optional transmission (meaning no 307 V-8 engine and no standard manual 3-speed transmission) were the only requirements to check off the now single RPO Z15 SS Equipment option box on the order form. The SS option in 1971 and 1972 gave you a few items that could not be ordered on any other Chevelle Malibu, such as the domed hood (now with hood pins standard), black-finished grille, remote driver-side sport mirror, SS badging, the 15x7-inch SS wheels with F60x15 white-lettered tires, and the round-pod dash with speedometer and fuel-level gauge over the linear speedometer of the non-SS-optioned Malibu. While power disc/drum brakes were also part of the SS option, those were available on a non-SS-optioned Malibu as well under RPO JL2 and J50. The same is true for the hood and deck stripes on sport coupes and convertibles (and hood stripes on the El Camino); these were optional on SS- and non-SS-optioned Malibus.

The optional Special Ducted Hood (RPO ZL2) was an SS-only option and was only available with the LS3 402-ci engine and the LS5 454-ci engine. Neither 350-ci V-8 engine could be ordered with the RPO ZL2 Special Ducted Hood option.

Only the optional LS5 454-ci engine required the SS option in both 1971 and 1972. The other three optional V-8 engines could be ordered with or without the SS option. I am sure much of this you may already know, but the idea here is to help you decide what your final goal in the restoration is going to be and to hopefully help you decide how to spend your time and money based on that goal. In 1972, General Motors began putting the engine size and horsepower rating in the VIN. The LS5 engine is coded with the letter "W." This is the only 1969 through 1972 VIN that will prove the car was ordered with the SS option. Even though the LS5 required the SS option in 1971 as well, the engine size is not coded in the VIN. (See Appendix C for engine codes.)

Engine Restoration

When doing a concours restoration, I suggest leaving the engine and transmission rebuild for the end of the process. Your restoration will undoubtedly take some time, depending on the depth of your restoration, your finances, acquisition of parts, and work you may have to farm out. There is no point to having your freshly rebuilt/restored engine and transmission sitting on an engine stand and storage pallet for months on end gathering dust and drying out. However, if there are original or date-coded pieces missing—such as the distributor, carburetor, starter, alternator, pulleys, air cleaner, etc.—that have been changed or replaced over the years, now would be a good time to make a list and start chasing those parts down because many of those pieces may be very hard (not to mention expensive) to come by.

When the time does come, you should have already decided at this point which route your restoration is going to take: a full-on concours restoration and show car that will not see street driving for a few years, a nicely restored/rebuilt weekend cruiser and local car show participant, or a daily driver where reliability is key.

Concours-Quality Engine

For the purpose of this book, we are going to assume your goal is a concours-quality restoration for show purposes in many instances. Other restoration or rebuild levels will, naturally, be less strict on engine appearance or modifications you may choose to make. This means the outward appearance of the engine components is paramount. Correct casting numbers, correct part numbers, acceptable casting dates, markings, and, above all, correct finishes on the numerous pieces are what judges and critics will be looking at.

If you are lucky enough to have acquired a solid survivor car that never had the engine or transmission rebuilt, you are ahead of the game here. You may only need to acquire original equipment manufacturer (OEM) pieces that would have been replaced over the years due to normal maintenance.

Items such as inline fuel filters, air filter elements, and ignition pieces including the distributor cap, spark-plug wires, and spark plugs are readily available in the aftermarket, and you may even be lucky enough to find quality, new-old stock (NOS) replacements.

Plug Wires

Spark plug wires were date coded according to the quarter and year. This date coding was for internal quality control and may be significantly earlier than the car they were installed on. There was generally quite a lead time between 4 to 12 months from the date the wires were produced and the time they reached the assembly line. A typical example would be 2-Q-69 for second quarter, 1969, meaning this wire may not get to an engine on the assembly line until the third or fourth quarter of production and could easily be correct for 1970 models.

First quarter — January, February, and March

Second quarter — April, May, and June

Third quarter — July, August, and September

Fourth quarter — October, November, and December

According to GM specifications, all small-block Chevrolet V-8 engines (283, 302, 307, 327, 350, and 400) have 90-degree spark-plug terminals and 180-degree terminals on the distributor and ignition coil. When the 396-ci V-8 was introduced in 1965, a new type of wire was used with improved insulation to better cope with the higher exhaust manifold and underhood temperatures since (except in 1965) there were no heat shields between the exhaust manifold and the spark plug itself. In addition to the new insulation, a new silicone spark-plug terminal boot was introduced and is gray, as opposed to black used on L6 and small-block V-8s. All spark-plug terminals were-135 degrees with the exception of the number-7 plug, which received a 90 degree terminal due to clearance issues, while the distributor and ignition coil continued to use 180-degree terminals.

Plumbing and Clamps

Quality reproductions of upper/lower radiator hoses, heater hoses, vacuum hoses, clamps, and such are available in the aftermarket with correct markings. Chances are if your car has ever had any of these hoses replaced, the original spring clamps or tower clamps were replaced with

ENGINE AND DRIVELINE

There were several types of hose clamps that were used depending on their particular use. These hose clamps are often replaced with worm gear–type clamps that are not correct for a restoration.

The upper radiator hose shows part number 3942453 and broadcast code SV. Two upper hoses were used for 1970 with broadcast codes SV or KY. While the SV-coded hose has a distinctive S shape to clear the air-conditioning compressor, it has been found on numerous, documented, non-air-conditioned 1970 Chevelles as well with Heavy Duty Cooling. This was also normally found on the LS6 with the Heavy Duty Cooling option and 4.10:1 rear end. Shown here with LS6 engine. (Photo Courtesy LS5 Registry)

common worm gear–style clamps. Do a little research now to see what type of clamps you will need for your application. Also note engine paint overspray. The basic engine assembly was painted at the Tonawanda engine plant, and while some care was taken to not paint things like hoses, aluminum intake manifolds, and chrome rocker covers (1970 only), overspray was inevitable.

The top radiator hose for 1970 396-ci and 454-ci engine Chevelles will most often depend on other equipment ordered. Two top radiator hoses were used on 1970 SS-optioned Chevelles with either broadcast code SV or KY. Their use most often depended on other equipment but not always.

The SV-coded hose has a pronounced S-shape designed to clear the air-conditioning compressor on air-conditioning-optioned Chevelles. However, this same SV-coded hose has been documented on build sheets for Chevelles without the air-conditioning option as well.

Radiator, Thermostat, and Pressure Cap

Let us begin by clearing up some terminology. It seems to be popular to misname various automobile parts for one reason or another. Some terms just seem to roll off the tongue easier than others, and sometimes it is just a matter of, "That's what everyone calls it."

Concerning radiators in Chevelles (and most other automobiles), radiators have one core. There is no such animal as a two-, three-, or four-core radiator. Radiators have two, three, or four rows of cooling tubes but only one core. The particular engine, transmission, and air conditioner play a big part in the factory's selection of the proper radiator for that application. For example, automatic transmission fluid is cooled by passing through a tank built into the radiator, so an automatic transmission car needs the connections for the transmission cooling lines where a manual transmission car does not.

A car equipped with a factory air conditioner will generally get a larger radiator with more cooling rows than the same car without an air conditioner.

There are different radiators based on the engine size, transmission type, and whether the car was ordered with an air conditioner or not. In 1970, neither the L78 396-ci 375-hp engine nor the LS6 454-ci 450-hp engine could be ordered with an air conditioner. These two engines received the same heavy-duty radiators as the L34 396-ci 350-hp and LS5 454-ci 360-hp engine when those were ordered with an air conditioner. The same heavy-duty air-conditioning radiator could be ordered as an option on any L34 or LS5 without an air conditioner through RPO V01.

Many aftermarket aluminum radiators will have larger cooling tubes than factory radiator units. A two-row aluminum radiator with 1-inch cooling tubes can often do the same job as a three-row brass radiator with smaller cooling tubes. This book will not get into the discussion of which is better, aluminum or brass, as each has their camp of followers and their own data showing their material is better than the other. If you are restoring your Chevelle, then a correct brass radiator is the way to go; if you are rebuilding your Chevelle and wish to change to an aluminum radiator, that is up to you.

Fan Shrouds

The same holds true for fan shrouds and fan clutches versus solid-blade fans versus electric fans. When doing a factory-correct restoration, use what the factory used. Fan shrouds perform a valuable service by helping direct airflow through the entire surface area of the radiator. Using a fan by itself will only direct air through the radiator that is equivalent to the surface area of the fan itself. To some extent, fan shrouds also help reduce underhood engine noise by reducing turbulence created by the fan.

As a rule of thumb, your fan blade should be about half in and half out of the fan shroud. Putting the fan as close to the radiator as possible is not necessary when using a fan shroud. A fan shroud can also assist in safety by reducing the chance of getting your hands, shift sleeve, etc. caught by the fan as well as keep foreign debris from entering the fan's path and causing damage. Many aftermarket parts suppliers sell "CAUTION FAN" sticker decals to put on your fan shroud, but Chevrolet did not use these. I suppose if one needs to be reminded not to put their hands in a moving fan these decals can serve a purpose; if you are correctly restoring your Chevelle, leave it off.

Thermostat

The cooling system's thermostat is another subject with a lot of misconceptions about its use and purpose. Thermostats come in various temperature settings: 160°F, 180°F, and 192°F to 198°F. What do these degree ranges mean? The temperature indicates when the thermostat begins to open to allow coolant to flow through the cooling system. A cooler thermostat will not make your car run cooler; a cooler thermostat will only open sooner than a hotter thermostat. When the engine is cold, the thermostat's job is to allow the engine to warm up to a desired operating temperature.

Chevrolet engines of this era were equipped with 192°F to 198°F thermostats for a reason: the car's cooling system, ignition timing, and other parts were designed around these temperature range parameters for normal operations.

A small cylinder is located vertically in the center of the thermostat and is filled with a wax that begins to melt at the designated temperature of the thermostat. A plunger connected to a valve presses into this wax as it melts, pushing the plunger into the wax and opening the valve to allow water to circulate. When the engine is shut off or at least cools down below the operating point of the thermostat, the wax begins to solidify and pushes the plunger back up via the spring and closes the valve.

Some people like to drill a couple of 1/8-inch holes in the valve to allow coolant to circulate into the radiator before the coolant has had a chance to get warm enough to open the thermostat. While this works in a warm climate where it doesn't take the engine long to produce enough heat to open the thermostat, it might not be such a good idea in a cooler climate. It'll take longer for the engine to warm up and take longer for the thermostat to open to give you heat through your heater or warm enough air to use your defroster.

There is debate by many people who believe if they remove the thermostat they will be able to solve hard-to-find overheating problems. This couldn't be further from the truth. Removing the thermostat will allow uncontrolled circulation of the coolant throughout the system. It is possible for the coolant to move so fast that it will not be properly cooled as it races through the radiator, which can make the engine can run even hotter than before under certain conditions. Other times, the engine will never reach its operating temperature. On computer-controlled vehicles, the computer monitors engine temperatures and regulates fuel usage based on that temperature. If the engine never reaches operating temperatures, fuel economy and performance will suffer considerably.

There are also many Chevelle owners who remove the water-bypass system on a Mark IV engine by simply plugging the hole in the front of the intake manifold and the top of the water pump. Some state they've done this for years with no ill effects. While it may clean up the top and front of the engine, it's not always a good option to choose. The Mark IV engine was designed to have this bypass system to allow coolant to flow throughout the engine block and cylinder heads to regulate the temperature of the coolant until the thermostat opens and begins to stabilize the coolant temperature in the system.

The small-block Chevrolet engine has this coolant-bypass system incorporated into the water pump itself, but it is just not as readily apparent. Ever notice when you replace a water pump on a small-block engine that the water-pump-to-block gaskets have what appears to be three mounting holes but only two bolts per side? One of those mounting holes is actually for the coolant-bypass system on the passenger's side of the engine block.

Radiator Pressure Cap

Another variable in engine cooling is the radiator pressure cap. Most people know that water begins to boil at 212°F at normal atmospheric pressure (14.7 pounds per square inch) at sea level. With a 50-50 mixture of water and antifreeze, it goes up to about 225°F or so. As you increase altitude from sea level, the atmospheric pressure decreases and, therefore, lowers the boiling point of water. Not much, but it does. For example, Denver, Colorado, is about 12 pounds per square inch and lowers the boiling point of water to 202°F. With a 192°F to 198°F thermostat in place, that does not give much room for error. However, water under pressure will actually raise its boiling point. Chevrolets of this era were equipped with a 15-pound pressure cap, effectively raising the atmospheric pressure to the equivalent of 30 pounds per square inch and thereby the boiling point of water to 250°F. Antifreeze will also lower the temperature water will freeze. Pure water will freeze at 32°F where a 50-50 mixture of water and antifreeze will lower that to about -35°F. Different mixtures will, naturally, give you different temperatures of freezing or boiling.

Something to be cautious of is that the coolant in your system will increase in temperature when you shut the engine off since it is not being circulated through its cooling cycle. Expect the coolant temperature to increase by 20 to 30 degrees if not more, depending on the outside air temperature. If your water temperature gauge is reading too high or your temperature-warning lamp comes on, find a place to pull off the road and let the engine cool down by itself. Do not attempt to remove the radiator cap until the engine has cooled down, and pass up the temptation to pour cool water over the radiator to cool the engine down.

Engine Emissions Controls

Air quality and exhaust emissions began to be recognized by General Motors as an issue in the early 1960s. Various methods were used through 1972 beginning with the positive crankcase ventilation (PCV) valve in 1961, the air injection reactor (A.I.R.) in 1966, controlled combustion system (CCS) in 1968, and finally the transmission controlled spark (TCS) in 1970.

Positive Crankcase Ventilation

Since the 1961 model year, several methods have been used by Chevrolet to control/reduce emissions. California led the way with a requirement for the PCV valve methodology. A PCV valve system was designed to reduce blowby emissions caused by gasses that get past the piston rings and enter the crankcase causing pressure. Before the advent of the PCV valve, this blowby was simply vented to outside air through what is often called a road draft tube that ran from the rear of the engine block down toward the ground on V-8 Chevrolet engines. When the car is moving, airflow around the road draft tube would create a draft that essentially sucked the pressured air from the crankcase.

With the introduction of the PCV valve system, this pressure and buildup of gasses was now rerouted

All 1970–1972 V-8 engines use CV736C PCV valves, GM part number 6423695, except the 1970 L78 and LS6 engines, which use CV746C, GM part number 6484525. The CV736C PCV valve is used in a multitude of GM models and years prior as well. The CV746C unit can be expensive to find today, and often drivers will use whatever PCV valve happens to fit the grommet on the rocker arm cover.

CHAPTER 5

Positive crankcase ventilation (PCV) valves have been used by General Motors since 1961 on every automotive engine. On all Mark IV V-8 engines, the PCV valve is located on the front portion of the driver-side rocker cover, as shown on this 1970 L78 engine. (Photo Courtesy L78 Registry)

Upper radiator hose markings with part number 3917227 and broadcast code KY were printed onto the hoses. While the SV-coded hose has a distinctive S shape to clear the air-conditioning compressor, the KY-coded hose is much more straightforward with just enough bend to clear the power-steering reservoir on Chevelles so equipped. And, no, the PCV hose should not be routed through the engine lift. (Photo Courtesy LS5 Registry)

back through the base of the carburetor to be reburned. The PCV valve is typically placed as far away from the crankcase air inlet as possible and normally in one of the two rocker covers of a V-8 engine or toward the front of an L6 engine rocker cover.

If you find an excessive amount of engine gasses blowby on your rocker cover or a rough idling engine, chances are your PCV valve is in need of replacement.

Air Injection Reactor

The air injection reactor (A.I.R.) system was introduced on California-destined cars for the 1966 model year. It was designed as an exhaust emission control system to assist in the burning of the unburned portion of the exhaust gases, thereby reducing hydrocarbon and the carbon monoxide content of the exhaust. When the exhaust gases enter the exhaust manifold, they are still hot enough to ignite. When supplied with oxygen, these gases will burn; the A.I.R. system supplies the oxygen.

The A.I.R. system is comprised of an air pump, a diverter valve (a mixture-control valve), check valves, combustion pipes, and various hoses and fittings. Simply put, outside air is drawn into the air pump where it is compressed. This compressed air is fed out of the pump through the diverter valve and check valve into the combustion-pipe assemblies and routed to the exhaust manifold resulting in additional combustion. As a result, the hydrocarbons and carbon monoxide emissions are reduced.

Not all Chevrolet engines required the use of the A.I.R. system, but for our purposes, all L78 and all LS6 engines for the 1970 model year do.

ENGINE AND DRIVELINE

An early attempt at reducing emissions was devised with the controlled combustion system (CCS) introduced in 1968. Note the heat tube running from the passenger-side exhaust manifold to introduce warm air to the air filter snorkel. Also visible on the firewall is the TCS relay on this 1970 Chevelle.

Controlled Combustion System

The controlled combustion system (CCS) was introduced in 1968. It was composed of a specially calibrated carburetor, distributor settings, higher engine operating temperatures, and a thermostatically controlled air cleaner.

Carburetors for CCS-equipped engines have an idle fuel-limiting feature that controls fuel mixture even if the idle mixture is turned out too far. The vacuum for distributor ignition timing advance is taken above the throttle plates of the carburetor where no vacuum is created at idle, and as a result, ignition timing is retarded. Cooling systems, or to be specific, the thermostat's opening temperature was raised from 180 to 195°F to increase engine heat and help reduce emissions.

Transmission Controlled Spark System

In 1970, the transmission controlled spark system (TCS) was introduced on some engines in an attempt to assist in meeting the emission standards. Oddly, the TCS system was renamed combined emission control (CEC) in 1971 but was changed back to TCS in 1972.

The TCS system is designed to regulate the distributor's vacuum advance, allowing vacuum to be applied only at cold start-up, high gear operation, and in some cases, a hot override. The electrical components of the TCS system are further detailed in chapter 7.

Several transmission controlled spark systems were used from 1970 through 1972 depending on the application and transmission type. Be sure to get the correct unit and pieces for your application based on the information on the tables on the following pages.

3-Speed					
Year	Model	Part Number	Qty	Price	Item Description
1970–1971	All	3961567	1	1.69	Trans. control spark
1972	All	3996286	1	1.69	Trans. control spark
1970–1972	Nova, Chevelle, Camaro	3983960	1	0.10	Clip, trans. control (3/4 x 1 5/16 x 1/2-inch hole)
1972	All	3929530	1	0.25	Gasket, trans. control spark switch
1970	All				
1971	Chevelle	3961573	1	1.90	Relay assembly, trans. control spark
1971	All	3990842	1	1.90	Relay assembly, control switch reversing
1971	All	3990843	1	1.90	Relay assembly, control switch delay
1971	All with C.A.C.	6273301	1	5.05	Relay assembly, anti-dieseling
1971–1972	Passenger Chevelle with C.A.C.	3996204	1	1.90	Relay assembly, anti-dieseling blocking
1972	All 8-cylinder, except 402, 454	3996297	1	1.90	Relay assembly, control vacuum advance delay
1972	All 6-cylinder	3996296	1	1.90	Relay assembly, control spark delay (20 seconds)

4-Speed

Year	Model	Part Number	Qty	Price	Item Description
1970	All	3961567	1	1.69	Trans. control spark
1972	All	3996286	1	1.69	Control spark
1970–1972	Nova, Chevelle, Camaro	3983960	1	0.10	Clip, trans. control (3/4 x 1 9/16 x 1/2-inch hole)
1970	All	3961573	1	1.90	Relay assembly, trans. control spark
1971	All	3990842	1	1.90	Relay assembly, trans. control switch reversing
1972	All (307, 350, 400)	3996297	1	1.90	Relay assembly, trans. control spark
1972	All 6-cylinder	3996296	1	1.90	Relay assembly, trans. control vacuum advance

Automatic

Year	Model	Part Number	Qty	Price	Item Description
1970–1971	All with TH400	6462286	1	1.79	Trans. control spark
1970–1971	All with A.T., except TH400				
1972	Nova with TH350	6462549	1	1.58	Trans. control spark
1972	Passenger Chevelle, Camaro with TH350	3996287	1	1.69	Control spark
1972	All with TH400	8627332	1	5.30	Control spark
1972	Nova, Chevelle, Camaro with TH400				
1972	Passenger with TH400 (454)	8623766	1	0.15	Clip, trans. control spark wire lead
1970	Passenger Camaro with TH400, except 396				
1971–1972	All with TH400	8626426	1	1.27	Wire assembly with connection, control spark switch to case connection
1970	All	3961573	1	1.90	Relay assembly, trans. control spark
1971	All	3990842	1	1.90	Relay assembly, trans. control switch reversing
1972	All 8-cylinder, except 402, 454	3996297	1	1.90	Relay assembly, control vacuum advance delay (60 seconds)
1972	All 6-cylinder	3996296	1	1.90	Relay assembly, control spark delay (20 seconds)

Vacuum Advance Solenoid

Year	Model	Part Number	Qty	Price	Item Description
1970–1971	All with A.T., except TH400				
1972	All with P.G.				
1972	Nova with TH350	6462549	1	1.58	Trans. spark control (4.075)
1970–1971	All, except A.T.	3961567	1	1.69	Trans. spark control (4.075)
1970–1971	All with TH400	6462286	1	1.79	Trans. spark control (4.075)
1972	Passenger Chevelle, Camaro with TH350	3996287	1	1.69	Trans. spark control (4.075)
1972	All with TH400	8627332	1	5.30	Trans. spark control (4.075)
1972	All, except A.T.	3996286	1	1.69	Trans. spark control (4.075)
1970–1971	All 8-cylinder	3824400	1	0.20	Clamp, spark control sol. (3.405)
1970–1972	Nova, Chevelle, Camaro, except A.T.	3983960	1	0.10	Clip, trans. control spark (3/4 x 1 5/16 x 1/2-inch hole) (4.075)
1970–1972	Passenger Camaro with TH400 (exc. 396)	8626597	1	2.18	Connector, trans. control spark
1970–1972	Passenger Camaro with TH400 (exc. 396)	8626426	1	1.27	Lead assembly, with connecting trans. control spark switch (4.075)
1970	All				
1971	Chevelle	3961573	1	1.90	Relay assembly, trans. spark control (4.075)
1971*	All	3990842	1	1.90	Relay assembly, trans. control switch reversing (4.075)
1971*	All	3990843	1	1.90	Relay assembly, trans. control switch delay (4.075)
1970	All 6-cylinder	1114431	1	6.75	Solenoid assembly, spark control
1970	All 8-cylinder (exc. 396, 400, 454 with 4BC)	1114432	1	6.85	Solenoid assembly, spark control
1970	All (396, 400, 454, with 4BC)	1114434	1	6.95	Solenoid assembly, spark control
1971	All				
1972	All 6-cylinder	1114444	1	10.50	Solenoid assembly, spark control
1972*	All with NB2 (307, 350, 400)	1114451	1	7.35	Solenoid assembly, spark control
1972*	All (402, 454)	1114453	1	7.65	Solenoid assembly, spark control

ENGINE AND DRIVELINE

Temp Switch – 1.150

Year	Model	Part Number	Qty	Price	Item Description
1970	Monte Carlo with C.A.C., P.G., TH350 (exc. gauges, 400 with 2BC)				
1970	Passenger with C.A.C., P.G., TH350 (350 with 2BC)				
1970	Chevelle, Camaro (396, 400 with 4BC) (exc. gauges)				
1970	Passenger with A.T. (exc. 350 with 2BC)				
1970	Monte Carlo with TH350 (400 with 2BC) (exc. gauges)	1993369	1	3.47	Switch assembly, sending unit (stamped 369) (248 degrees) (Note 1)
1970–1972	All 6-cylinder	6489903	1	5.20	Switch assembly (stamped AC-82B-276M)
1970	Passenger 8-cylinder (exc. C.A.C., gauges, 396)				
1970	Nova 8-cylinder (exc. C.A.C., gauges, 396)				
1970	Chevelle, Camaro (exc. C.A.C., gauges, 396, 400 with 4BC, 454)				
1971	All 8-cylinder (exc. 400 with 4BC, 454)				
1972	All (307, 350, 400)	6489600	1	3.65	Switch assembly (stamped A.C.-63B-257M on shell) (Note 3)
1970	Passenger with TH400 (400, 454) (2nd design)				
1970	Nova (396) (exc. front comp. console instrument cluster)				
1970	Chevelle 8-cylinder (2nd design) (exc. 307, 350, instrument panel gauges),				
1970	Camaro with high-performance (396) (2nd design) (exc. instrument panel gauges)				
1970	Camaro with special high-performance (396) (exc. instrument panel gauges)	1994095	1	3.25	Switch assembly (stamped .095)
1970	Nova, Chevelle with C.A.C., P.G., TH350 (exc. gauges, Monte Carlo)				
1970	Camaro (C.A.C. with A.T.)				
1970	Monte Carlo with C.A.C., P.G., TH350 (exc. gauges, 400 with 2BC)				
1970	Passenger with C.A.C., P.G. TH350 (350 with 2BC)				
1970	Chevelle, Camaro (396, 400 with 4BC) (exc. gauges)				
1970	Passenger with A.T. (exc. 350 with 2BC)				
1970	Monte Carlo with TH350 (400 with 2BC) (exc. gauges)				
1971	Camaro with C.A.C. (400)	6489785	1	4.59	Switch assembly (stamped A.C.-82V-232M)
1971–1972	All (400 with 4BC, 402, 454) (exc. gauges)	6490094	1	5.00	Switch assembly (two terminals stamped A.C.-82B-269M) (Note 2)
1962–1965	Chevy				
1964	Chevelle	5644602	1	0.24	Insulator (2.515)

Note 1: Part number 1993409, 1993369 cannot be used in place of each other due to critical temp range.
Note 2: This switch is located on the right bank of the engine and used with 1993369 on the left bank.
Note 3: These switches are located on the left bank of the engine with no other switch required on the right bank.

CHAPTER 5

Evaporation Control System

The evaporation control system (ECS) was introduced in 1970 for vehicles originally sold in California. The federal government required all passenger cars and light trucks with a gross vehicle weight of less than 6,000 pounds to be equipped with some form of ECS beginning in 1971.

Since liquids—gasoline in this instance—have a tendency to vaporize as temperatures increase, they release unburned hydrocarbons into the air. When exposed to sunlight, a secondary reaction causes the unburned hydrocarbons to be converted into a photochemical smog. ECS is designed to minimize the loss of vaporized gasoline.

Since the fuel tank is a part of the ECS, the fuel level was reduced by lowering the filler neck from the highest point of the tank by about 1 inch. This allows more room for expansion and vapor collection on top of the gasoline. A vapor separator assembly would send the vapor back to the engine compartment via a check and relief valve to a vapor storage canister containing approximately 1.5 pounds of charcoal.

The second part of the ECS is the canister (lower left) located behind the radiator support on the driver's side of the engine compartment. Note the PCV valve has two connections: one to the carburetor and one to the ECS canister. (Photo Courtesy Mark Wilson)

The various assembly plants had their own standard operating procedure about how emission equipment was shown on their respective build sheets in 1972. The Baltimore, Maryland, and Kansas City, Missouri, final assembly plants would indicate the broadcast numbers as fuel lines on the various fuel pipes and describe the A.I.R. system as "K19 EXH EMISSIONS" on their 402 and 454-ci engines.

The Van Nuys, California, plant listed the particular broadcast information as "SMOG SYSTEM" and described the A.I.R. system as "K19 AIR INJ REACT" on their 402 and 454-ci engines.

The Arlington, Texas, assembly plant did not highlight the specific fuel pipes by name and did not show the K19 A.I.R. assembly but did note

Part of the evaporation control system (ECS) introduced in 1970 for cars sold in California is the separator assembly located just above the fuel tank. On a Van Nuys build sheet, this is listed as NA9. Although this car was built at the Arlington, Texas, final assembly plant, it was destined for a California dealer. (Photo Courtesy Mark Wilson)

An evaporation control system (ECS) canister is shown here on a 1972 Monte Carlo. Also note the correct lack of any engine size and horsepower rating decal on the air cleaner lid.

ENGINE AND DRIVELINE

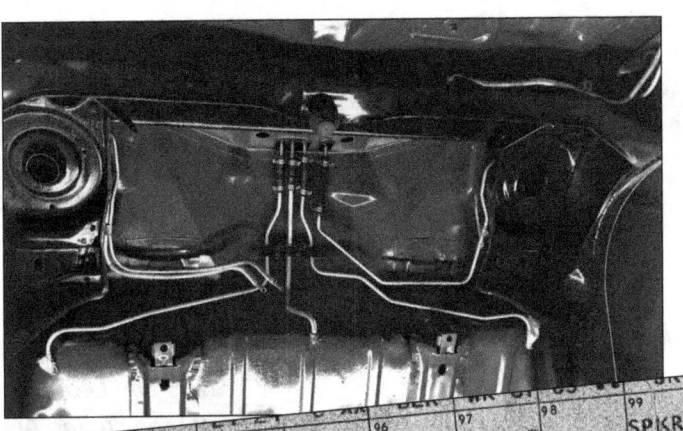

The routing of the numerous fuel and vapor lines on this 1972 Chevelle for the evaporation control system can be a challenge to get correct. The red oxide paint color for the underside of the body is common for Arlington-built Chevelles. (Photo Courtesy Manny Bustillo)

The lower section of 1972 build sheet from the Baltimore, Maryland, final assembly plant for the LS3 engine shows "K19 EXH EMISSION" verbiage. It also includes the three fuel pipes needed for the ECS and the gross vehicle weight to show the car is in compliance with federal regulations.

The lower section of 1972 build sheet from the Kansas City, Missouri, final assembly plant for LS3 engine shows "K19 EXH EMISSION" verbiage. It also has the three fuel pipes needed for the ECS and the gross vehicle weight to show the car is in compliance with federal regulations.

The lower section of 1972 build sheet from the Van Nuys, California, final assembly plant for LS5 engine shows "K19 AIR INJ REACT" verbiage. The three fuel pipes needed for the ECS are replaced with "SMOG SYSTEM 62 79 CH-48," and gross vehicle weight is included to show the car is in compliance with federal regulations.

CHAPTER 5

Shown is the lower section of 1972 build sheet from the Arlington, Texas, final assembly plant for L65 engine showing "L08 ENG EMSSN CHT" applicable for the L65. The two 350-ci engines (L65 and L48) did not require the Air Injection Reactor emissions system. Also note gross weight is not shown on 1972 Arlington build sheets.

"L08 ENG EMSSN CHT" for the specific tune-up sticker applied to the radiator support.

Engine, Transmission, and Rear End Overhaul

This book will not cover the technical aspect of an engine, transmission, or rear end rebuild. There are hundreds of books on the market about how to rebuild and/or hot rod your engine and transmission. Odds are pretty good you will want to freshen up these major components and replace gaskets, seals, etc. and inspect and replace internal components as necessary for reliability. I do not mean to imply that internal pieces such as the crankshaft, connecting rods, pistons, piston rings, camshaft, etc. are not important in an engine rebuild, but those components are not going to be seen by judges or your peers.

I suggest specialty engine rebuilding books such as *How to Rebuild the Small-Block Chevrolet* by Larry Schreib and Larry Atherton for your small-block V-8 or *How to Rebuild the Big-Block Chevrolet* by Tony E. Huntimer; both are available CarTech publications.

If your engine block needs to be bored due to cylinder wall wear, so be it. Nobody is going to see a +0.030 bored cylinder and +0.030 oversize pistons and rings. Same for the crankshaft or camshaft; if either needs to be replaced or the crankshaft turned due to wear, neither are visible once the engine is assembled. I am not saying to skimp on components, but searching for that NOS L78 or LS6 mechanical lifter camshaft is not something one really needs to do, even for a concours restoration.

Original Stamping Preservation

One thing you should alert your machine shop about is the importance of the engine-assembly plant stamp on the engine pad and possibly of the partial VIN stamp if it is on the engine pad. If your engine block needs to have the deck surfaced to fix any warpage or wear, the engine pad must, at all costs, be spared this machining. When you are working with an original-to-the-car engine, it is the only engine that car came with and these identifying numbers/letters are your only real proof the engine is original to the car. It may seem extreme to some, after all, an engine is just an engine, right? For your daily driver or weekend cruiser, that may be. But in the concours restoration world having the original engine can mean, literally, thousands of dollars in the car's value.

If your selected machine shop cannot deck the engine block without obliterating these stamps, find another machine shop. Resist the urge to give in and let them restamp the engine pad. Chances are very slim they will have the correct fonts on their stamp dies for both the Tonawanda engine stamp information plus the correct, and different, stamp dies for the particular final assembly plant and the partial VIN information. If the machinist messes up the restamping, and most will not survive good scrutiny, your car will forever be suspected of having a restamped engine pad, and that could cost you not only in judging but most certainly in resale value should you ever decide to sell the car.

Chevrolet engines were built at the Flint, Michigan, and Tonawanda, New York, engine assembly plants by the thousands each year. While quality control was present, it is

ENGINE AND DRIVELINE

This is a sample engine plant stamp from the Tonawanda engine assembly plant showing the engine plant's letter designation, assembly date, and three-letter suffix code identifying the horsepower rating of the engine and the transmission type. The second stamping is from the final assembly plant, indicating the sequence number of the car the engine was installed in. (Photo Courtesy LS6 Registry)

Engine blocks often have their intended suffix code painted on them in one or more locations at the Tonawanda engine assembly plant. The "CRV" here indicates an LS6 engine to be equipped with the manual 4-speed transmission.

An original, unrestored LS6 engine shows the "CRV" suffix code marking on the rear of the block. These paint markings are found in various locations on the engine block; this one just above the block's casting date of C23 70, indicating the block was cast on March 23. Ensure the casting date precedes the assembly date of your car to help identify a restamped engine block.

important to remember these engines were built for the masses and, to a certain degree, reliability and a long life. Engine blocks were stamped with the engine-assembly-plant letter "T" for the Tonawanda engine plant or "V" for the Flint engine plant (Flint V-8 engines built before 1967 used the letter "F"), a four-digit assembly date depicting the month and date (such as 1025 for October 25 or 0123 for January 23, etc.), and a one-, two-, or three-letter suffix code to identify the advertised engine's horsepower rating and the transmission type.

The basic engine assembly and components themselves were the same regardless of transmission type but would be fitted with either a flywheel and manual-transmission pilot bushing in the crankshaft or with a flexplate for an automatic-transmission car. The final assembly plant also used the transmission information to determine which components they would install on the engine such as the carburetor.

In some years, even the Chevrolet car line made a difference in the suffix code. A 1969 396-ci (402) engine with manual transmission destined for a Chevelle has a different suffix code (JC) than the same engine/transmission combination destined for a Camaro/Nova (JF). In 1970, the 402-ci engine with a manual transmission destined for Chevelles and Novas received the suffix code CTX, while the Camaro received the suffix code CJF. Why is this important? If your original engine is long gone or beyond repair, finding a period-correct replacement is an alternative, and the suffix code can assist you in getting the correct engine for your Chevelle.

CHAPTER 5

Buyer Beware!

Be cautious of engine stamps. There are two schools of thought here, maybe more. One is that it is okay to restamp your original engine block with the same information it was born with in the event the stamps are destroyed during machining. The problem is there is no way to prove or disprove whether the original engine block was restamped or if the restamp was done on a date-correct engine block. A second thought is it is okay to stamp an engine with anything you want (or need) to make it appear correct. This second one I still cannot get my head around. The engine obviously is not original to the car, and any attempt such as this is tantamount to fraud. Whether you inform a potential buyer or not is beside the point; what is that potential buyer going to tell the next buyer?

Often people will use engine-assembly-plant marks on the engine pad, more commonly known as broach marks, as a clue to the engine being original (not decked and restamped). A broach cutter is a toothed tool used to remove rough casting material. Two broach cutters were used during the engine cleanup after casting. One cutter broaches (machines) the oil pan rail and upper half of the main bearing bores. Another is a *V* shape and is used to machine the engine deck and top horizontal surface of the engine block. As these cutters wore, they would leave slight front-to-back scores in the engine block that are visible on the engine pad called broach marks. Fresh blades in the tool left hardly any broach marks at all; as the blade wore, the broach marks became more visible until the blades needed to be changed. Most machine shops will use a rotary grinder to resurface the engine block's deck area. These will leave a swirl mark on the engine pad, making it pretty easy to identify if the engine block has been resurfaced this way.

Warranty Replacement

An alternative to the original engine is a warranty replacement engine. These were used in either short-block or long-block form, depending on the amount of damage to the original engine. Warranty engines are not uncommon today, and there is no shame in using one, but it still may affect the overall perceived value of the car unless you happen to have paperwork showing that engine with its serial number was, indeed, used to replace the original engine in your car.

A Chevrolet warranty engine will have its own serial number stamped on the engine pad. This will begin with the letters "CE" meaning Chevrolet and Engine. Following the CE is a six-digit number identifying when it was used and the serial number of the engine itself. Take CE173169 for example. "C" is Chevrolet, "E" is engine, "1" is the calendar year the engine was assembled (1971), and 73169 is the engine serial number. The Tonawanda engine plant was assigned the number range of 50000 to 79999 for each calendar year; the Flint V-8 engine plant was assigned the number range of 20000 to 49999. In the event more replacement engines were required, the letter "A" was added to "CE," and numbering started over at the beginning (such as CE0A50001). Warranty engines will also normally have a stamp on the starter mounting pad with the engine plant letter and the date, such as T099 for Tonawanda engine plant, September 9 (099). Naturally, if you find a warranty engine block, it should be dated after your car's build date. One cannot have a warranty engine dated 1970 for a 1971 or 1972 Chevelle and have it appear to be legitimate.

Component Stamp and Casting Dates

Another thing to look for is the casting stamped date of the components if you are looking for replacements. All major components have a casting date, or the date of manufacture is stamped on the piece. The engine block, cylinder heads, exhaust manifolds, etc. would not all be cast on the same day and fitted to a particular engine. Each piece would be cast in their respective areas, machined separately, and joined at some assembly point. Some components assembled at the engine assembly plants would come from outside sources (water pumps, starters, distributors, etc.) and would typically have earlier assembly dates than the assembled engine itself. See Appendix C for a more detailed look at this aspect.

Casting dates are generally in the format of a letter for the month (A through L for January through December), a one- or two-digit number for the day of the month, followed by a one- or two-digit number for the year. Many pieces use "70" for 1970 so it is not confused with "7" for 1967. Other components, like distributors, starters, etc., with a stamped assembly date use the letters from A through M, omitting the letter "I" as it can be confused with the number "1."

Normally, all the peripheral components assembled at the engine plants should be dated *before* the engine build date. Components

ENGINE AND DRIVELINE

The starter housing is stamped with the part number and date of its build. Here "0D22" indicates 1970, April 22 (D22). The 1108418 starter housing was used on all 1970 350, 402, and 454 engines with a manual transmission.

An open-element air cleaner assembly was found on most 1970 Chevelles; 402- and 454-ci Chevelles were not equipped with the ZL2 Special Ducted Air System hood option.

used at the final assembly plant to complete the engine may be dated later than the engine build date since they come from a different supplier, but it is not very common and should not be a lengthy time. Items such as starters, A.I.R. equipment, carburetors, and the like may be a few days later than the engine build date but certainly not weeks or months later.

The same can be said for the engine itself and major driveline components. They should all be dated prior to the car's build date. How much prior? Anything from a few days to a couple of weeks typically is not questioned, but some have been documented to be as much as three or four months prior to the car's build date.

Air Cleaners

A variety of air cleaner housings were used from 1970 through 1972. The 1970 model year would be the last year for the open-element air cleaner used on the SS396 and SS454 engines without the ZL2 Special Ducted Air System (also known as cowl induction) hood. The 307-ci engine, both 350-ci engines, and the LS3 402 used the A348C air filter and closed air cleaner housings with a

This 1971 LS5 engine shows the chrome-plated lid on a dual-snorkel air filter housing. This engine is from an exported 1971 Chevelle and as such did not need to meet US emission standards, so it is not equipped with GM's Air Injection Reactor system. (Photo Courtesy Arne Skog)

single snorkel for the air intake. Some SS454 engines were equipped with a dual-snorkel air cleaner in both 1970 and 1971. The 307-ci engine, both 350-ci engines, and the LS3 402 used

Engine size and horsepower rating stickers were not on the 1972 air filter housing as this L48 350-ci 4-barrel engine shows. The only sticker was on the side of the housing showing the air filter replacement requirement. (Photo Courtesy Dave Castine)

This 1971 L65 350-ci engine features a Rochester 2-barrel carburetor with the engine horsepower rating sticker. Note the three grille grates in front of the windshield; these were not installed as original equipment, but many owners and possibly many dealers installed these to keep debris out of openings.

A Rochester Quadrajet 4-barrel carburetor and RPO ZL2 Special Ducted Air System hood option are featured on this 1971 LS5 454-ci engine. Note the painted rocker covers; chrome rocker covers were no longer part of any SS-optioned engine. (Photo Courtesy Domenick Scorziello)

This 1970 LS5 454-ci engine has a Rochester Quadrajet 4-barrel carburetor and RPO ZL2 Special Ducted Air System hood option. Note that 396-ci engines and both 454-ci engines were outfitted with chrome rocker covers; 1970 would be the last year for chrome rocker covers.

ENGINE AND DRIVELINE

Found on several plants' LS6 Chevelles, this dual-snorkel air cleaner housing was used in lieu of the "normal" open element air cleaner housing. These will have "CO" coded on the build sheet. Why is anybody's guess.

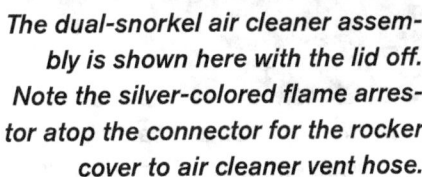

The dual-snorkel air cleaner assembly is shown here with the lid off. Note the silver-colored flame arrestor atop the connector for the rocker cover to air cleaner vent hose.

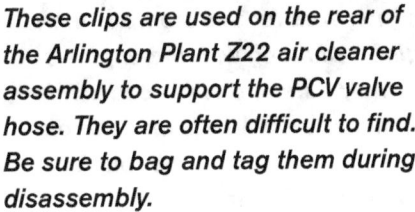

These clips are used on the rear of the Arlington Plant Z22 air cleaner assembly to support the PCV valve hose. They are often difficult to find. Be sure to bag and tag them during disassembly.

the A348C air filter and closed air cleaner housings with a single snorkel for air intake.

Dual Snorkel

The dual-snorkel air cleaner found on some 1970 LS6-engine-optioned Chevelles is not the most common air cleaner assembly found on LS6 Chevelles. There does not seem to be a rhyme or reason for its use over the typical open-element air cleaner. It is primarily found on Baltimore-built LS6 Chevelles but has been seen on Arlington, Atlanta, Kansas City, and Van Nuys build sheets.

Air Filters 1971 and 1972

The 1971 model year saw all engines using the A348C air filter, except the ZL2 Special Ducted Air System-equipped 454-ci engine continued to use the A212CW air filter.

The 1972 model year saw the 307-ci engine and both 350-ci engines with the A348C air filter, while the 454-ci engine used A329C without the ZL2 Special Ducted Air System and A212CW with the ZL2 Special Ducted Air System.

Air Shocks

A relatively rare RPO G67 Rear Shock Absorber Level Control option was introduced with the 1970 Monte Carlo and would remain available as an option on the Monte Carlo through the 1972 model year, but it was not available on any Chevelle. This option allowed the driver to set a specific air pressure in the rear air shocks to keep a stable ride regardless of the load or lack of one. As more weight was added to the back of the car, the air canister would inflate the rear air shocks to keep the

This 1972 Monte Carlo features an LS5 engine and relatively rare RPO G67 Rear Shock Absorber Level Control. Only 621 out of 180,819 1972 Monte Carlos were equipped with this option, down from almost 4,000 when introduced in 1970 and 2,297 in 1971.

This is an electrical harness support clip found on a 1970 LS6 Chevelle. Details like this are very important on a concours restoration and not readily available in the aftermarket, so be careful during disassembly to photograph its location and bag it.

ride level constant, and an air pump would automatically keep the compressed air in the canister ready.

Partial VIN Stampings

A partial VIN should be stamped on the engine block. The location will vary; the most common area is next to the Tonawanda or Flint engine plant assembly date and engine identification stamp. There are a few oddities. In 1970, the Leeds plant at Kansas City happened to stamp the partial VIN upside down on the engine pad. Both Baltimore and Van Nuys plants would sometimes stamp the partial VIN on the engine pad and sometimes on the rough cast area by the oil filter.

When it gets close to engine installation time in the restoration process and you've selected a machine shop to do any work needed to the

The partial VIN stamp locations vary on Chevelle engines, often within the same model year and plant. The most common area for this stamp is the engine pad along with the engine's assembly date and suffix code. This Baltimore partial VIN is an example of the stamp found on the rough cast area by the oil filter.

Note the marking and correct star washer on the negative battery cable connector. Various original equipment manufacturers supplied bolts to General Motors, but it is important to document and photograph what is on your car.

ENGINE AND DRIVELINE

The positive battery cable was secured to this clip on the engine stand on all V-8 1970–1972 Chevelles. Some early 1970 Chevelles continued to use a positive battery cable clip attached to the frame near the idler arm, but it's not known when the change was made.

The front crankshaft/alternator pulley is also a candidate for OEM bolts. It is important to document and photograph what is on your car. The center bolt and washer reinforcement was used on all 350/396/454 engines to help secure the pulley to the crankshaft.

Like all bolts and washers, be sure to document their location, bag, and tag them. It is easy enough to just toss them in a can but you'll wind up with a can of various bolts and washers and might not remember where they go.

manifold bolts with intake manifold bolts come reassembly time. Be sure to bag and note any small clips and photograph their location on the engine block. Also take note and photograph various markings on the bolt heads.

The same holds true for items like water pump bolts, starter bolts, pulley bolts, and especially any washers used.

Pay particular attention to vacuum hose markings and the routing of the hoses as well as wiring connections, especially if your Chevelle is equipped with RPO ZL2 Special Ducted Hood system and the TCS solenoid.

If your carburetor and/or distributor needs to be refreshed or have a complete overhaul, now would be the time to consider having it done. While it might only need a cleaning and gasket kit that can be done in an evening, if your carburetor needs repair parts or missing parts, a carburetor specialist may be needed, and they may require some lead time to fit your job into their schedule.

If you feel confident enough to assemble the engine yourself and install the crankshaft, pistons, piston rings, camshaft, etc., set your engine block on an engine stand and get started. As an alternative, if you are not that confident in the basic engine assembly process, you can ask your machine shop if they can assemble the valves and springs in the cylinder heads and install the rotating assembly of the engine block, so all you need to do is bolt the larger pieces together.

You should always try to reuse as much original equipment from the engine as possible before going to aftermarket or even NOS or OEM parts. Even Chevrolet NOS parts are

cylinder block and/or cylinder heads, you can begin the engine tear-down procedure. Depending on what ancillary pieces you've pulled from the engine to remove it will naturally depend on how much work will be required to tear down the engine. As usual, bag and tag all the small parts and note where they came from. It is easy to confuse items such as exhaust

often service replacement items and may not have the correct markings needed for a concours, judge-ready restoration.

Fuel Pumps

Two fuel pumps were used in 1970: the 40727 fuel pump with no vapor-return line and the 40768 fuel pump with the vapor-return line. All L78 engines and early LS6 engines use the 40727 fuel pump. All L34 and LS5 engines use the 40768 fuel pump. The LS6 engine initially used the 40727 fuel pump but changed to the 40768 fuel pump. The change is dependent on the final assembly plant. Research shows the Atlanta plant changed between 03-25 and 03-31, the Baltimore plant changed on 02-13, the Kansas City plant changed between 02-13 and 02-16, and the Van Nuys plant changed between 04-06 and 04-21. The correct fuel pump for your application is noted on the build sheet in box 33 with either 727 or 768. If you do not have your build sheet, simply check to see if there is one line or two in the fuel pump.

All RPO L78 and 1970 LS6 engines came with a Holley 4-barrel carburetor and aluminum intake manifold. Unlike earlier L78 intake manifolds, the 1970 L78/LS6 intake manifold was low profile due to hood clearance. The 1970 model year would be the last year an aluminum intake manifold or Holley carburetor would be used. All L34 and LS5 engines continued to use the cast-iron intake manifold and Rochester Quadra-Jet carburetor. The cast-iron intake manifolds were low profile, similar to their aluminum counterparts.

Clips and Bolts

There are numerous clips under the hood to help route hoses and wiring away from areas that could cause damage. Many bolts have OEM markings on the head. I can't stress enough to photograph and document the location of these various clips and which bolts came from where. Not only will this information be a valuable resource when reassembling the engine, transmission, and other assemblies, many are just not available in the aftermarket world, and knowing exactly what you are looking for will help in your search if you get lost or just can't remember where it came from.

Transmission

Transmissions are date coded just like most major components. The format of the build dates vary depending on the transmission type and where it was built.

Muncie 4-Speed

The Muncie manual 4-speed went through three date variations from 1963 through 1972. From 1963 through 1966, the Muncie date included only the month and day such as P0110, where P is the code for Muncie and 0110 is January 10. In 1967 and 1968, the date code had

Of interest here is the battery cable covering and frame-mounted clip to keep it out of harm's way. Two fuel pumps were used on SS-optioned 1970 Chevelles: the 727 and 768 fuel pump. The 727 pump does not have a return line where the 768 fuel pump does.

All 1970 L78 and LS6 engines were equipped with an aluminum intake manifold and Holley 4-barrel carburetor. The intake was supplied by the Winters foundry and can be identified by the snowflake cast into the manifold. Four different Holley carburetors were used dependent on the transmission type and whether EEC-equipped or not. The 1970 model year would be the last year for both the aluminum intake and Holley carburetor.

ENGINE AND DRIVELINE

A Muncie RPO M22 manual transmission is being inspected for chipped or broken teeth. Now would be a good time to order any necessary seals, gaskets, synchronizers, and (if needed) gears. Just when you decide to refurbish the transmission is up to your timeline, but it should be done as chassis work is being completed.

After refurbishing and painting, the Muncie 4-speed transmission mounting assembly and shifter assembly is ready to be reinstalled on the transmission.

A Muncie 4-speed transmission shifter assembly is disassembled for cleaning and refurbishing. It's recommended to rebuild this in one setting because there are many small parts that could get lost or their locations forgotten over time.

A Muncie 4-speed transmission shifter assembly is reassembled on the transmission and bolted to the chassis after cleaning. Note the extra transmission-to-chassis support to combat engine torque.

a year designator and a letter designator for the month such as P8A01, meaning 1968 (8), January (A) 1st (01). Note that a Muncie dated with a September to December build date was actually built the prior calendar year. An example would be the date code P8T13, meaning 1968 (8), December (T), 13. The transmission was assembled December 13, 1967, for the 1968 model year. Likewise, a P8S28 stamp means 1968 (8), September (S), day 28 of the calendar year 1967 for a 1968 Chevelle.

The 1969-and-later Muncie date stamps included a suffix letter A, B, or C noted the specific type. The letter A represents the M20 wide-ratio version, the letter B represents the standard-duty M21 close-ratio version, and the letter C represents the heavy-duty M22 close-ratio version. A sample might be P0C25B for Muncie (P), 1970 (0), March (C) 25, M21 (B). Muncie month letters are not sequential for some reason; instead, it skips letters. In addition, a partial

CHEVELLE RESTORATION AND AUTHENTICITY GUIDE: 1970–1972

CHAPTER 5

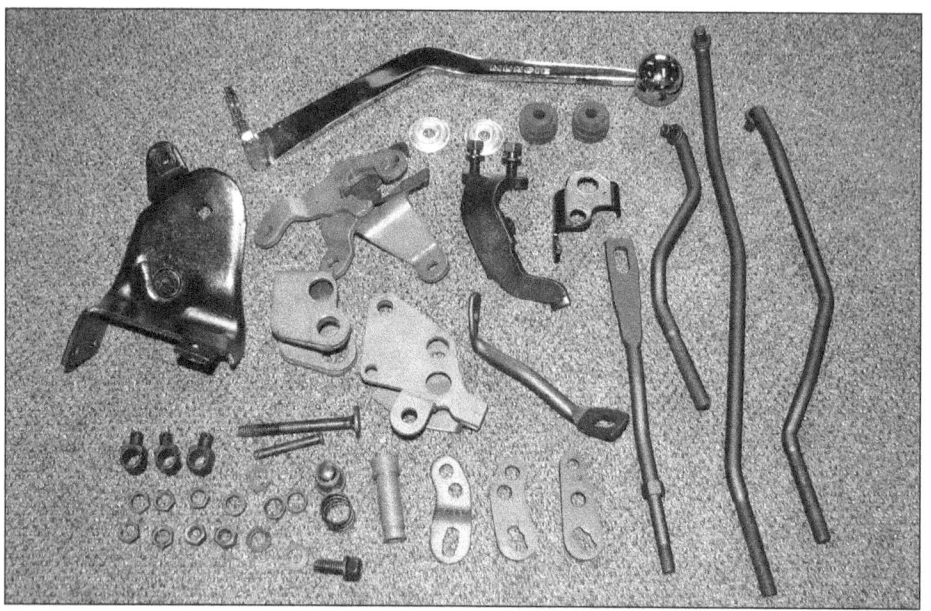

These disassembled components of the manual 4-speed transmission shifter assembly have been cleaned and are ready to assemble. Refer to your photos of the unit when it was disassembled to put it back together correctly.

Broadcast code "WO" is stamped on RPO M22 Muncie 4-speed manual transmissions. This WO code is found on the build sheet in box 28.

Each TH400 automatic transmission has an identification tag riveted to its case. The letters ("CY" in this instance) depict particular application for the transmission. The transmission's assembly date and serial number are found on this identification tag, and tags are color coded for their intended use.

Muncie Date Codes

A - January	B - February	C - March	D - April
E - May	H - June	K - July	M - August
P - September	R - October	S - November	T - December

VIN is stamped on the transmission to identify the car in which the transmission was originally installed, and the broadcast code is ink-stamped on the case.

A Muncie shifter assembly is one item you may not pay much attention to, but judges certainly will.

Turbo-Hydramatic 400

The Turbo-Hydramatic 400 (TH400) has a metal plate riveted to the side of the transmission case to identify its assembly date, its application, and its serial number. Different TH400 transmissions were used based on the horsepower rating of the engine: the lighter-duty L34 and LS5 engines would get a lighter-duty transmission than the L78 and LS6. The date is in Julian calendar format. The Julian date is for a calendar year and not the particular model year, so it is not uncommon to see dates in the 500 to 570 range. For example, a Julian date stamp on a 1970 model-year transmission like 413 means the 413th day counting from January 1, 1969 (February 17, 1970), along with the transmission's assigned serial number.

The TH400 was only used with the 396-, 402-, and 454-ci engines. The 1971 and 1972 350-ci engine SS-optioned Chevelles used the RPO M38 TH350 for their automatic transmission choice.

A partial VIN stamp is also found on the transmission just above the oil-pan rail on the passenger's side to identify the car in which the transmission was originally installed. Another variation on the TH400 is the oil pan

ENGINE AND DRIVELINE

This is an early 1967 TH400 Turbo-HydraMatic automatic transmission oil pan. Note the difference in the dimples on the pan; both the number and locations. This should not be used on later TH400 transmissions as the oil filter and screen are different than later-model TH400 transmissions. (Photo Courtesy Ed Fisher)

The transmission oil pan for the M40 TH400 Turbo-Hydramatic automatic transmission is left neutral and not painted. Note the number and location of the two dimples in the oil pan itself.

and the associated transmission filter. Early 1967 TH400 transmission oil pans have a heel mark, a bump, and three dimples. A *Chevrolet Service News Bulletin* around July 1967 indicates a change in the design that eliminated the heel mark, the bump, and reduced the dimples from three to two.

Various plate colors and prefix codes were used for TH400 applications. These codes and colors have been found so far:

Turbo-Hydramatic 350

The Turbo-Hydramatic 350 (TH350) was introduced in 1969 and was used in SS Equipment in 1971 and 1972 (as well as non-SS Equipment) Chevelles. The TH350 was built at two transmission plant facilities in the United States: Cleveland, Ohio, and Toledo, Ohio. Cleveland-built TH350 transmissions are identified with the letter *B*, and Toledo-built TH350 transmissions are identified with the letter *Y* on owner Protect-O-Plate warranty cards. GM of Canada TH350 transmissions from McKinnon Industries in St. Catharines use the letter *E* on warranty cards. These are dated in the format of the plant letter, the model year, a letter for the month, and a two-digit date such as "Y1K25" for Toledo-built TH350 (Y), 1971 (1), July 27 (K27). Like the Muncie 4-speed manual transmissions, month letters are not sequential for some reason; it skips letters.

An orange paint daub indicates the shifter is assembled and ready. The stenciled date "2 17 70" on this Muncie 4-speed manual transmission shifter housing indicates the date of assembly.

Broadcast Code	Engine	Year	Horsepower
CC	396/402	1967–1969	325 hp
CD	396/402	1968	350 hp
		1970	330 hp (LS3)
		1971	300 hp
		1972	240 hp
CE	396/402	1969	350 hp
CF	402/454	1970	350 hp
		1971	365 hp
		1972	240 hp
CR	454	1970	360 hp*
CS	454	1970	360 hp
CW	402	1970	375 hp
CX	396	1969	375 hp**
CY	454	1970	450 hp

* Found on Van Nuys LS5s prior to at least 01-14
** Also reported on 1969 427 COPO

CHAPTER 5

Whether you are restoring a car with an automatic or manual transmission, now is a good time to refurbish that shift linkage.

Rear Axle Housing

The rear axle housing does not have a partial VIN stamped on it. It does, however, have a center-section casting number and casting date along with a stamped rear-axle gear ratio on the axle tube.

10-bolt Casting Number	Year
3969277	1970–1972

12-bolt Casting Number	Year
3969278	1970–1972

The center-section casting number and casting date are located in the webbing. The casting date is in the format of a letter for the month, a one- or two-digit number for the date, and a single digit for the year. For example, "A 8 0" would be for January 8, 1970, and "E 11 0" would be for May 11, 1970. Letters A through L are used for the months January through December.

The 1964 through 1969 rear end assembly and ratio codes generally follow the format of a two-letter prefix code for the ratio, a one- or two-digit number for the month, a one- or two-digit number for the day of the month, and the rear axle assembly plant code letter. The stamped letters and/or numbers were individually stamped and not often very deep and certainly not very neat. Sometimes the letter "E" was stamped to indicate Eaton Positraction and sometimes not, depending on the person stamping the axle housing. Since the two-letter prefix code would identify a positraction over an open rear end, it may have been considered redundant by the person at the time.

The 1970 model year saw the introduction of a third letter to the ratio code. This third letter is the letter C for Chevrolet, so a 1970 ratio code might read CCF where CF is the ratio code. A 1970 example would be something like "CCF 0821B" for a Chevrolet Positraction 3.31:1 built August 21 at the Buffalo, New York, axle assembly plant. Whether the

The same yellow paint daub was applied to the rear end housing in several areas, such as this where the axle tubes meet the center section.

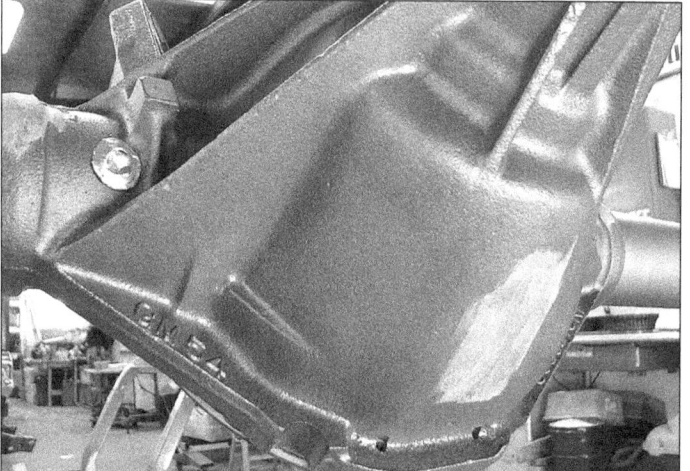

The yellow paint daub found on the underside of the rear end center section indicated the rear end housing was ready for installation and use.

A white paint daub is found on rear shock mount, and a blue paint daub is on the brake line clip. The exact significance of the white "Z" or "2" is not known but could be the inspector's identification mark.

The rear end assembly is restored and ready to be installed in the chassis. Note various colors of paint daubs to indicate they passed inspection at their respective assembly/inspection stations.

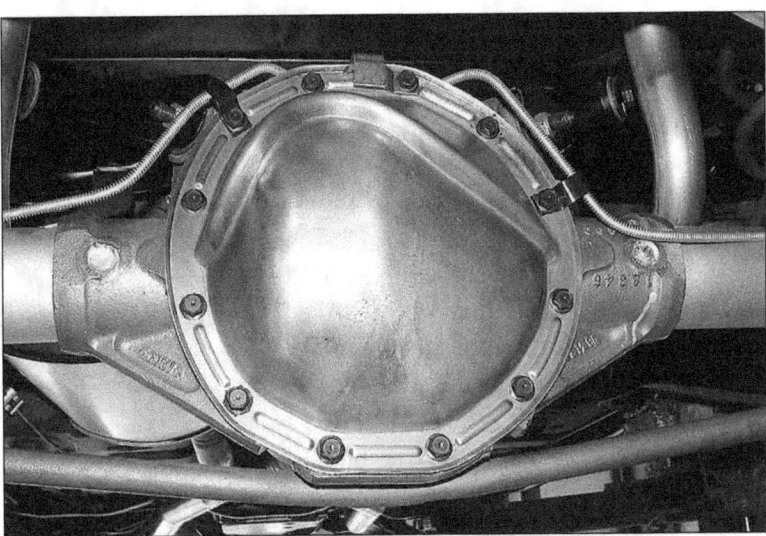
Often the entire rear end assembly was left its natural metal color instead of being painted black. There does not seem to be a reason for one over the other.

This is the original rear end housing brake line distribution block. The single center hose is a rubber composite to allow for flexibility, while the two lines to the rear brake cylinders are hard lines.

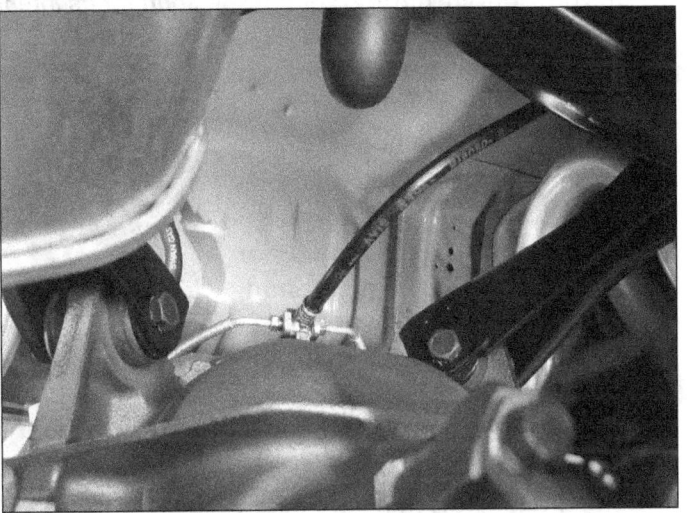
The restored rear end assembly has been installed in the chassis. The replacement of hoses and hard lines are not only show-quality restorations but a good idea from a safety standpoint after almost 50 years of use.

plant changed its standard operating procedure or not is not clear, but most Buffalo assembly plant stamps beginning in October have either a trailing 1 or 2 indicating the plant shift number such as "CRU 1020B1" or "CRV 1205B2."

The 1971 model year saw a slight change in the scheme of the ratio and date stamping. The axle assembly plant code letter was moved from the last position to the third position, such as "CF C" in the example. The two-letter ratio code and plant letter may be stamped together or may be separated by a noticeable space like "CFC" or "CF C." There were no hard-and-fast rules on this. The date format was changed from the previous month/day format to a Julian date code of the calendar year that the assembly was built. Since the 1971 model year was introduced in September 1970, any 1971 Chevelles built in calendar year 1970 would have a rather large Julian date. Some early calendar-year Chevelles would also have a 1970-calendar-year rear end date as supplies were exhausted. The 1972-model-year

Chevelle would follow the same theme as 1971-model-year Chevelles. A rather large Julian date would mean a late-1971-calendar-year rear end assembly would have gone into early model-year 1972 Chevelles. For example, "RVC 320 2E," would mean a positraction 3.31:1 from Buffalo on November 26, 1971, second shift would be for a 1972-model-year Chevelle. The rear axle assembly-plant code is a single letter with "C" indicating the Buffalo, New York, axle assembly plant; "G" indicating Chevrolet Gear & Axle; "W" indicating Warren, Michigan; and "K" indicating McKinnon Industries in St. Catharines, Ontario.

If you noticed during your test drive any unusual noises coming from the rear end, that issue needs to be addressed.

Original rear-axle housings have been found painted black, and some were unpainted. Be sure to photograph any factory paint marks on the rear-axle housing before cleaning and rebuilding if needed.

Propeller Shaft and Universal Joints

The driveshaft is more accurately known as a propeller shaft, and that is how it will be referred to in this book. Typically, a propeller shaft was left a neutral color and not painted. When restoring your propeller shaft, take note of the identifying stripes and colors if they are still visible.

The width of the paint colors and the location of the stripes will vary depending on the person painting the propeller shaft stripes. In these two examples, both have orange, pink, and blue stripe colors. But note the difference in the distances between the various colors, particu-

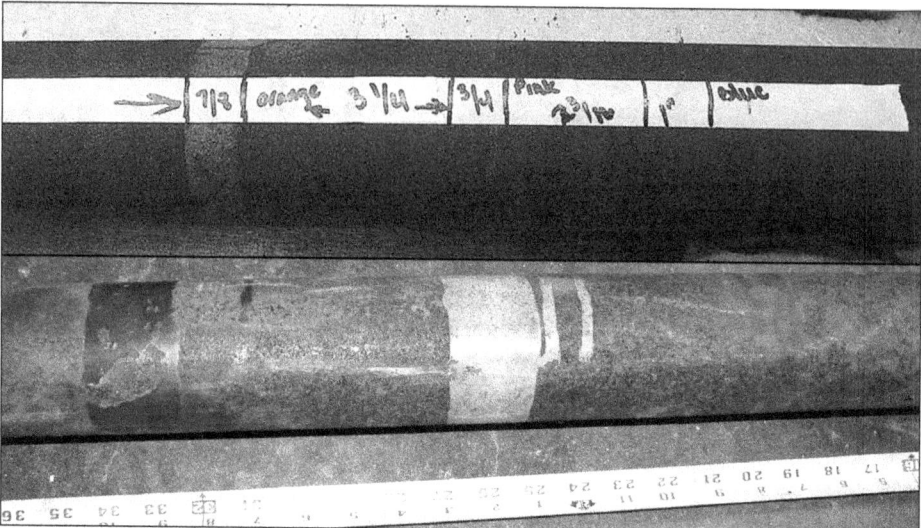

Before refurbishing your propeller shaft, take care to mark the location and width of the color-coded stripes if they are still visible. The position and width of these color stripes will vary depending on the person marking the propeller shaft for its intended use. (See Appendix D.)

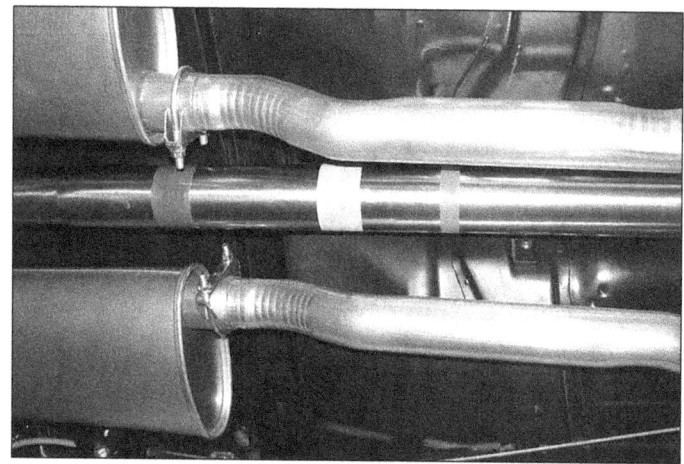

A refurbished propeller shaft can be cleaned and appropriate color stripes reapplied in their original positions and original widths. The propeller shafts are left natural but can be clearcoated to help combat rust on your restoration.

larly the pink and blue color stripes.

Different applications have different-colored stripe schemes. Assembly plants even differed on how they depicted the propeller shaft colors on their build sheets. For example, for the 1970 model year, the Baltimore assembly plant used a two-letter code for its propeller shaft colors such as "GO" for green and orange, while Arlington, Atlanta, Kansas City, and Van Nuys used two two-letter codes such as "GR-OR" for the same green and orange. A manual-transmission propeller shaft was a different color-code than one destined for an automatic transmission, and SS396-engine (both L34 and L78) propeller shafts were different than those destined for SS454 (both LS5 and LS6) engines. Due to the frame being longer with the El Camino bodystyle, those color codes were different than those for the sport coupe and convertible.

Why were the propeller shafts color coded with different stripes? Simply so the assembly-line worker

ENGINE AND DRIVELINE

Often aftermarket universal joints use this type of C-clip retainer since using the correct plastic injection method was hard to duplicate and not many shops offered the service.

This is a close-up photo of the original plastic-injection method of retaining the universal joint on both LS5 and LS6 Chevelles. Replacement universal joints available at your local auto parts store may not be of this type as they require more work to install correctly.

Paint daub colors can vary from plant to plant. Here the rear yoke has blue paint daubed on the pinion yoke and an orange paint daub on the universal joint itself.

The front universal joints are assembled with the same injected plastic as the fronts with the 454-ci engines. Note the daubs of paint on the pinion yoke, signifying it has been inspected and installed to specifications.

This rear yoke has a yellow paint daub, indicating it is assembled and ready. Note the rear universal joint in this instance is held in place by two straps with bolts when used with the 9210 pinion flange found on LS5 and LS6 Chevelles instead of other engines that used a smaller universal joint and a U-bolt/nut arrangement.

could look at the code on the build sheet and get the correct propeller shaft off the shelf for a particular engine/transmission/bodystyle application. (See Appendix D for more information.)

Universal joint installation methods varied over the years. Some will use an E-clip set into a groove on the outer ears of the propeller-shaft yoke, some use a C-clip on the inner portion of the universal joint, and all 1970 454-ci engine-equipped Chevelles use a plastic injection, although you'll find many that have been replaced with an inner C-clip style. It is always a good idea to replace these whether they look worn or not. Now is a good time while everything is apart and readily accessible. Rear U-joints have

This restored and completed rolling chassis is ready for the restored body and interior to be installed. Only a few ancillary items like the fan remain and are installed after mating the rolling chassis to its body.

If you or your shop has the ability to remove the body, now is the time to mate the body back on the completed, restored rolling chassis with the engine and transmission installed.

two methods of bolting to the rear end pinion yoke. One is with two U-bolts and nuts, and the second is with straps and bolts.

Once you are satisfied with the driveline/chassis restoration, it is time to mate the rolling chassis with the body. How the body is mated with the rolling chassis will depend on the equipment you or your shop has. A hydraulic or electric lift of sufficient lifting capacity certainly makes it easier to marry the two than having 8 to 10 of your friends try to manhandle the body into position.

Finishes

Components may have different finishes depending on the plant and/or time of production, and miscellaneous variations may even have escaped our detection.

Engine Block/Heads Paint: Chevrolet orange in a semigloss paint is correct.

Starter Housing: It was semigloss black. On manual-transmission cars with the cast-iron nose, the starter was painted as a unit. On automatic cars with the aluminum nose, only the main starter housing was painted semigloss black.

Distributor Housing Paint Daubs: Distributor housings are natural aluminum. Paint daubs were applied to the main body of the distributor around the area that the arm of the vacuum advance fit into the housing. The color of those paint marks depended on the application. Other paint markings have been found around the base of the housing where it meets the block as well as the shaft area; but again, these depend on the application.

Brackets and Braces/Master Cylinder: Either natural cast-iron or a light coating of semigloss black is correct. The machined areas were done after the paint was applied.

Brake Lines: Natural steel color is correct.

Distribution Block: These were either left natural brass or in the case of the cast-iron units have been found in both natural bare cast iron and semigloss black.

Power Brake Booster: It was gold cadmium.

Hood Hinges and Springs: It was dark gray phosphate.

Alternator Housing: Bare aluminum is correct. Stampings depended on the application: "CW" was found on 1970 and early 1971 Chevelles with 37-amp units, "DK" on late 1971 37-amp units, and "EC" on 1972 37-amp units. 1970 L78 and LS6 engines have "CZ" due to the deep groove pulley. Air-conditioning-optioned 1971 and 1972 Chevelles have an "NF" stamp, while 1972 air-conditioning-optioned Chevelles have "YM" for their 61-amp unit.

When optioned with RPO K85, the optional 63-amp unit, 1970 L48 and L65 engines are stamped "NK," while the 1970 L34 and LS5 engines are stamped "NJ." 1971 K85 units are stamped "RA," while 1972 K85 units are stamped "YN." The extra characters found on 1971 and 1972 build sheets such as the asterisks, dashes, and dots would not appear on the unit stamp itself.

Plants varied on how the broadcast code is shown on the build sheet.

Exhaust Manifolds: They were

ENGINE AND DRIVELINE

Alternator Part Number/Amperage/Broadcast Codes

Application	Part Number	Amp	Arlington	Atlanta	Baltimore	Kansas City	Van Nuys
1970							
307/350/402/454	1100834	37	CW	CW	CW	CW	CW
L78/LS6 (deep groove pulley)	1100837	37	CZ	CZ	CZ	CZ	CZ
AC optioned	1100843	61	NF	NF	NF	NF	NF
L34/LS5 with K85	1100847	63	***	NJ	NJ	NJ	***
L48/L65 with K85	1100847	63	***	***	NK	***	***
1971							
Standard V-8 (early)	1100566	37	CW**	n/a	CW	CW	CW---
Standard V-8 (late)	1100566	37	DK**	n/a	DK	DK	DK---
AC optioned	1100843	61	NF**	n/a	NF	NF	NF---
K85	1100847	63	***	n/a	***	RA	***
1972							
307/350 V-8	1102440	37	EC**	n/a	EC--	EC	EC--
402/454	1102454	37	EC**	n/a	EC--	EC	EC--
AC optioned	1102463	61	YM**	n/a	YM--	YM	YM--
K85	1100917	63	***	n/a	***	YN	YN--

Notes:
1. Broadcast codes above are from build sheets in the database. Those marked with three asterisks (***) indicate no build sheets for that year/plant/alternator. One can only assume those codes would be the same as other plants for the year.
2. Early and late dates in 1971 are hard to pin down; "CW" seems to appear through at least 12–30 and "DK" from at least 01–07, but there is not enough data to qualify that for every plant.
3. Atlanta did not build Chevelles after 1970.

1970 Propshaft Stripe Color Broadcast Codes

Plant	L34 manual	L34 automatic	L78 manual	L78 automatic	LS5 manual	LS5 automatic	LS6 manual	LS6 automatic
Arlington								
HT/Conv	PK-OR	BL-BK	***	***	PK-BL	***	PK-BL	GR-OR
Atlanta								
HT	BL-YE (1)	BL-BK	BL-YE	BL-BK	PK-BL	GR-OR	PK-BL	GR-OR
HT	PK-OR (1)							
Baltimore								
HT/Conv	TG (2)	TK	TG (2)	***	PB	GO	PB	GO
HT/Conv	DL (2)		DL (2)					
El Camino		TJ	***	***	***	***	PW	GO
Kansas City								
HT/Conv	BL-YE (3)	BL-BK	BL-YE (3)	BL-BK	PK-BL	GR-OR	PK-BL	GR-OR
HT/Conv	PK-OR (3)		PK-OR (3)					
El Camino	BL-YE (3)	BR-OR	OR-BL	***	PK-WH	GR-YE	PK-WH	GR-YE
El Camino	PK-OR (3)							
Van Nuys								
HT/Conv	BL-YE (3)	BL-BK	BL-YE (3)	BL-BK	PK-BL	GR-OR	PK-BL	GR-OR
HT/Conv	PK-OR (3)		PK-OR (3)					
El Camino	***	BR-OR	***	***	***	***	***	***

Notes:
1. BL-YE through 11-07, PK-OR from 11-11
2. TG through 11-10, DL from 11-14
3. BL-YE through 10-27, PK-OR from 10-29
*** No data to determine

1971 Propshaft Stripe Color Broadcast Codes

Plant	LS3 manual	LS3 automatic	LS5 manual	LS5 automatic	L48 manual	L48 automatic	L65 manual	L65 automatic
Arlington								
HT/Conv	***	***	PI-BL	GR-OR	***	PI-OR	***	***
Baltimore								
HT/Conv	BL-BL	BL-BK	PK-BL	GR-OR	BR-PK	***	***	GR-OR
El Camino	***	***	***	***	***	***	***	OR-OR
Kansas City								
HT/Conv	BL-BL	***	PK-BL	GR-OR	BR-PK	PK-OR	PK-BR	PK-BR
El Camino	***	BR-OR	***	***	***	***	***	***
Van Nuys								
HT/Conv	***	***	PK-BL	GR-OR	***	PK-OR	***	BR-PK
El Camino	***	***	***	BR---	***	***	***	***

Notes:
*** There is no data to determine, but it appears the same broadcast codes were used in 1971 and 1972 at the respective plants. So, without further documentation, one might assume those missing from one year but found in the other would be applicable.

1972 Propshaft Stripe Color Broadcast Codes

Plant	LS3 manual	LS3 automatic	LS5 manual	LS5 automatic	L48 manual	L48 automatic	L65 manual	L65 automatic
Arlington								
HT/Conv	***	***	***	***	***	***	***	***
Baltimore								
HT/Conv	BL-BL	***	PK-BL	GR-OR	***	PK-OR	BR-PK	***
El Camino	***	***	***	***	***	***	***	***
Kansas City								
HT/Conv	BL-BL	BL-BK	PK-BL	GR-OR	BR-PK	PK-OR	PK-BR	PK-BR
El Camino	***	***	***	***	***	OR-YE	***	PK-OR
Van Nuys								
HT/Conv	***	***	PK-BL	GR-OR	GR-OR	PK-OR	BK-PK	BR-PK
El Camino	WT-GR	BR-OR	***	***	***	OR-YE	OR-OR (1)	PK-OR

Notes:
1. OR-OR appears on 1972 13639 and 13669 four-door sedans. These have the same wheelbase as the El Camino.
*** There is no data to determine, but it appears the same broadcast codes were used in 1971 and 1972 at the respective plants. So, without further documentation, one might assume those missing from one year but found in the other would be applicable.

bare cast iron with Chevrolet orange. These were painted almost entirely orange when the engine was painted as an assembly, but most of the paint burned off. Many survivors that have been documented still have orange overspray on the flange area around the area where it bolts to the head as well as where the exhaust pipe bolts onto them.

Transmission and Shifter Assembly: Natural aluminum or natural white metal is correct. Muncie shifters are normally plated in a dark gray phosphate.

Propeller Shaft: The propeller shafts were made from cold-rolled and welded steel and were left natural. There are usually three colored bands painted on the shaft, depending on application.

U-joints: They were natural cast iron with various-color paint daubs on the front slip yoke and rear pinion flange based on applications.

Rear-end Housing (natural and black): This is a tricky area. Some plants (Arlington and Atlanta normally) left the rear differential natural in color, while other plants painted them a semigloss paint. Others can be found with a spray out of semigloss black on the rear portion of the differential only. More often than not, this was done at the dealership to ward off any surface rust so that it would not look bad while on the lot.

Numerous Engine Clips: This is another tricky area. Brake-line clips are normally olive drab or semi-transparent metallic green, while fuel lines were normally a semi-transparent metallic blue. However, there can be and are variations of this from plant to plant and supplier to supplier, so use this only as a guide and try to determine what

ENGINE AND DRIVELINE

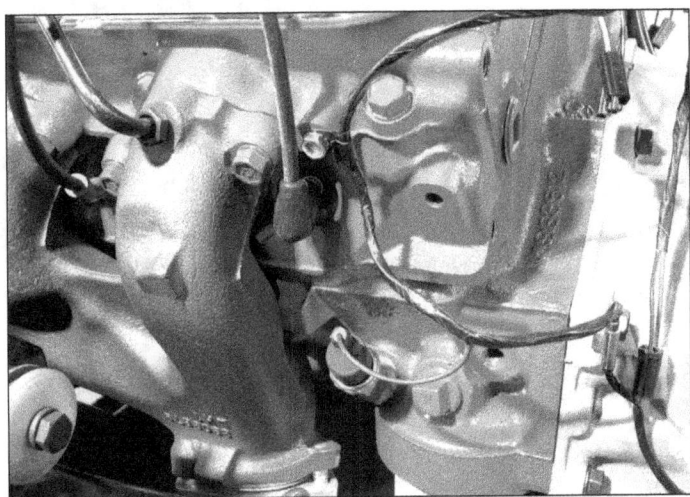

The wiring clip on the driver's side of the engine block retains the oil pressure wiring. It is important to document the location of these various clips.

This 1971 RPO L65 350-ci 245-hp engine shows the last year the engine size and horsepower rating decal was applied to the air cleaner lid. Note the heat tube directing warm air from exhaust manifold to the thermostatically controlled air cleaner; a necessity for a correctly restored 1970 L65 engine. It is hard to find if yours is missing.

your originals were. Spreading open the clamp and examining the original finish is helpful.

Engine Tune-Up Labels

An engine tune-up label is affixed to the radiator support, typically on the driver's side of the car. The label is specific for the particular model year and engine size. Normally the engine tune-up label will have information on it for both a manual and automatic transmission. One oddity is the 1970 L34 SS396 engine tune-up label: different broadcast codes were used for an L34 with a manual transmission and an L34 with an automatic transmission even though both labels contain information for both transmissions. To add confusion, plants used one broadcast code on L34 engines with an automatic transmission through March 10 and then changed the broadcast code for the tune-up label from March 11 on. See chapter 9 for more details.

Additional Underhood Labels

An engine coolant label was introduced with the 1970 model year and was used for 1971 and 1972 as well. This label, part number 3979912, was affixed to the passenger side of the radiator support as per the factory assembly instruction manuals for those three years. But, since a human was responsible for placing these labels, any location is possible. If yours is not in the correct location and it is original, as with other details, be sure to photograph and document its location to show future viewers if they inquire about it.

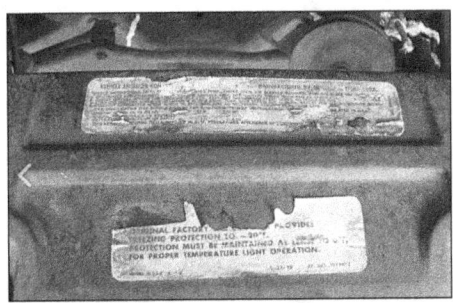

This is the only 1970 Chevelle I have had in the shop in 15 years that was outside the norm and was restored almost 10 years ago. It just goes to show the importance of documenting the details before restoration as the two tune-up and coolant stickers are not placed according to the assembly instruction manual; never say never.

Models from 1970 have a separate emissions sticker when NA9 (evaporation emission control, part number 3980217) is called for (California-built or California-destined), along with the engine cooling-system label (part number 3979912). However, I have no good, original images of the emission-control label. When used, the Assembly Instruction Manual (AIM) shows its placement in the center with the engine tune-up label on the driver's side with cooling-system label on the passenger's side.

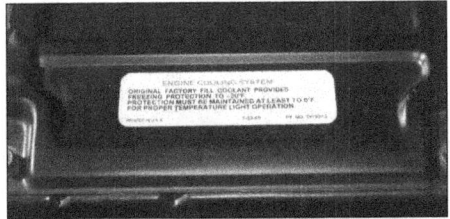

The engine coolant label was affixed to the radiator support along with the engine tune-up label. The location could vary depending on who put the label on the car. It is shown here on the correct passenger's side, but originals have been found centered on the support on rare occasions. It all depended on the human applying the labels.

CHAPTER 5

CHAPTER 6

BODY AND PAINT WORK
TEXT AND PHOTOS BY JAMIE COOPER

Before you get started on the metal fabricating and body repair, it is important to photograph and document many areas of the project, both before you get started and while you are disassembling the car. Whether you are using the original sheet metal or if you plan on replacing some of it, it is important to photograph how everything fit prior to disassembly. Hood-to-fender gaps, fender-to-door gaps, and the gap where the doors and trunk lid meet the quarter panels are very important to achieve a good-looking and correct restoration. These photos will be a good reference to fall back on when realigning the original panels or replacing them with new. If you are restoring the Chevelle for a customer, it will also document what you started with, what had to be done to correct it, and why. Photo document any factory defects such as paint runs, sloppy welds, color application, etc., especially if you intend to restore the car exactly as it was built.

Clean Up, Pressure Wash, and/or Degree

Before you move forward, it is best to clean the body thoroughly so you can document what you find. If

Once the body has been completely stripped, it is a very good idea to gently pressure wash the entire body with a high-pressure soap and water solution to remove 45-plus years of grunge while you are photo documenting. Be careful not to remove factory undercoating, inspection marks, or details you may need.

Once you have the entire body thoroughly cleaned, photograph every square inch to document caulking and primer applications, overspray areas, primer colors, as well as any inspection marks you may find.

BODY AND PAINT WORK

you are looking to find some of the original inspection marking or even the colors of the primers and undercoats, cleaning and degreasing your floors may help you uncover it if it was there to begin with. Years of road grime, dirt, and debris seem to build up everywhere. If you have your body on a rotisserie or have access to one, pressure washing the floors is a good way to get it cleaned up. This will allow you to turn the body and pressure wash the floors inside and out. It will also dry much easier if you are able to rotate the body to get rid of the water.

Another way is to take wax and grease remover, spray a 2x2-foot area, and wipe clean with a dry rag. This way will take a little more time but will produce the same results. Be sure to photograph all of the color overspray patterns and inspection markings for placement, size, and color that you find. If you are planning on doing an assembly-line correct restoration, these photos will once again come in handy when you get to that point.

Seam Sealer Application

Take photos of all the areas that have seam sealer. This will help you document areas it was applied to, the amount that was applied, and the color that was used. You may also want to make note of when it was applied (i.e., over the primer, over bare steel, if it has body-color overspray on the sealer, etc.). You need to remember that seam sealer was applied by human assembly-line workers (not a machine), so Chevelles may vary from one to the next and have been applied differently. Whether it was applied lighter, heavier, or just not applied at all may

Take note of seam application and color if you are attempting to reproduce a factory-original restoration. Note that there may be different colors of sealer that were factory applied.

The floor plugs were held in with caulking once the car had been primed. These are most often white in color, though they may appear to be off-white due to age. Green has also been found depending on the plant and assembly date.

The Atlanta plant used a greenish-grey primer followed by a thin blackout paint applied to the dash area. Also note the application of the caulking on all the seams, which would also include many areas where brackets were welding to the floor, such as bucket seat mounts.

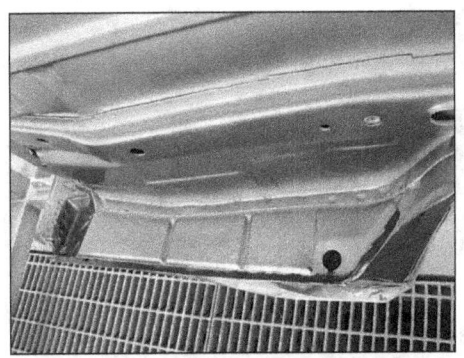

The trunk drop-down panel was originally stamped from galvanized steel and often had little primer sprayed on them. Caulking was also applied to the seam where the drop downs and quarter panel met.

vary from car to car and manufacturing plant. Also, how neat or sloppy it is will also vary from car to car. Here is where that Monday or Friday build comment comes into play.

Original Primer and Paint Application

Document what color the original primer was because this varied from plant to plant and from year to year. Make note of any blackout paint that covered the primer on the floor and firewall if the plant your car was built at did that. Look for any paint drips on the belly pan and firewall. Investigate to see if your firewall was painted prior to the body color being painted or after based on overspray patterns because this also varies from plant to plant. How far did the body color overspray cover the primer or blacked-out areas? Is the paint coverage in the door, hood, and decklid jamb areas thinner than the main body? How was any sound deadener applied and to what areas?

Look for any areas of the body that may still retain original factory-applied paint. Areas such as under the decklid surface, on the cowl ends, under the door or decklid weatherstripping, or under the upper roof-rail weatherstripping are good places as many times these areas were unmolested during a repaint. This will give you a very close example of what color paint was originally applied to the car. Using paint chips, you should then be able to determine the original color. In the case of special-order painted cars (on the trim tag), finding these original-painted areas will not only give you a color example, but it may be used as proof of its origin. Photographing all of these areas will help immensely in the paint restoration and documentation process. If you choose to restore your car exactly how it was built, all of this will give you photographic proof of where and how things were done.

Removing Seam Sealers and Undercoating

The seam sealer that was used in the floors was black in color and will scrape out with a putty knife rather easily. On occasion, using a heat source such as a heat gun will aid in the removal. The problem is it will leave behind an oily residue that will need to be cleaned up. PPG's DX330 or DX440 is a good wax and grease remover to use for this. Both are great products; DX440 is a little stronger than DX330, and both can be obtained from most auto-body paint suppliers. You will need to spray it on and wipe it dry several times to get it cleaned up. You may also notice the oily residue creeping back from beneath the pinch weld of the two panels where it was applied. Be sure to get it all cleaned up before sanding or media blasting.

The seam sealer used in the floor area was usually black in color and had a greasy look and feel to it. Lord Fusor 805HD is a great sealer that can be used to duplicate the rich black factory look. These sealers were brushed on (so you will also find brush marks) and can be purchased from any automotive paint and body supply stores.

Virtually every plant sprayed sound deadener in the rear wheel-tub area as well as behind the tires for rock-noise reduction, so look for that during your cleanup process. If you find a floor that was completely undercoated, it is very likely that was done at the dealership or later.

Undercoating may be a little more challenging to remove, depending on the type that was used. Some of it may flake off while pressure washing or

BODY AND PAINT WORK

After cleaning, make special note and photo document how the factory sound deadener was applied so that it can be restored the same way. This application varied from plant to plant and the assembly line worker doing the actual spraying.

A common area for the Chevelle to rust out is the lower side of the cowl. This is made up of two panels: the inner and the outer cowl side panel. Depending on how bad yours is, if at all, you may consider sectioning in the lower half rather than replacing the complete cowl side panel.

even by using the putty knife to scrape it. If that process is taking too long or if it's too difficult to remove, you can try a little heat. Or, if you have oxy-acetylene torch or even a handheld propane torch, you can wave the flame over the panel, being careful to not apply too much heat because it may catch fire and burn. Keeping a distance of 8-or-so inches away from the panel, slightly warm up the undercoating and loosen it. This will allow you to scrape it off much easier and not risk warping the panel.

Common Rust Areas

Depending on where and how your Chevelle was used or stored will determine the amount of metal fabrication or rust repair your project will need. Repairing these areas properly is vital to ensuring the longevity of your restoration and the value of it. Some of the common areas of rust that you may encounter are: cowl side panels, toe boards,

This type of damage rust is very common on these cars and is often missed when casually looking over the car. It can also be very costly to repair. Expect and plan for the worst when budgeting for your restoration.

The area where the front side of the cowl rolls down and meets the floor or toe board is another area that can have a common rust problem and will take extra care, time, and money to repair.

CHEVELLE RESTORATION AND AUTHENTICITY GUIDE: 1970–1972

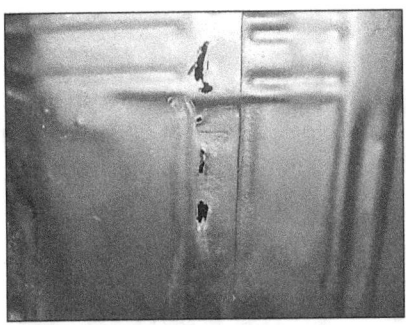

These two panels are lapped over top of each other: the cowl is on the bottom, the floor panel sits on top of it, and both are welded together with a spot weld. At the very least, these areas will often need to be separated, cleaned, sealed, and spot-welded back in place.

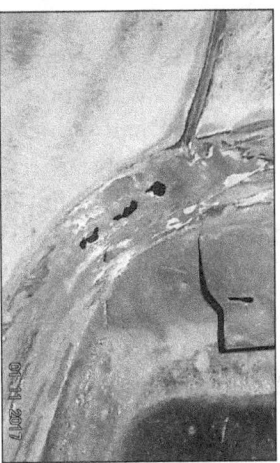

If there is an area around the windshield or the back window that is rusted through, most of the time it can be repaired by grafting in a small patch. Be sure to cut the area of rust out and graft in a new piece of metal using a butt weld. It is important that you fit the glass and window molding up to the repair area after welding. Do not use body filler to try and make that area fit the contour of your window trim.

The section of the floor under the back seat tends to get soft over time due to rear-glass leakage. Whether you choose to section in a small piece of floor or you need to replace the entire main floor, make sure to compare the stamped impressions in the metal, especially if you are restoring your car to the concours level.

If you are replacing a quarter panel because of rust in the wheel opening, there is a good chance that the outer wheelhouse will be rusted out as well. Even as likely is the trunk floor extension or drop off panel. Be sure the new quarter panels fit and are aligned on the car before welding in the replacement wheelhouse.

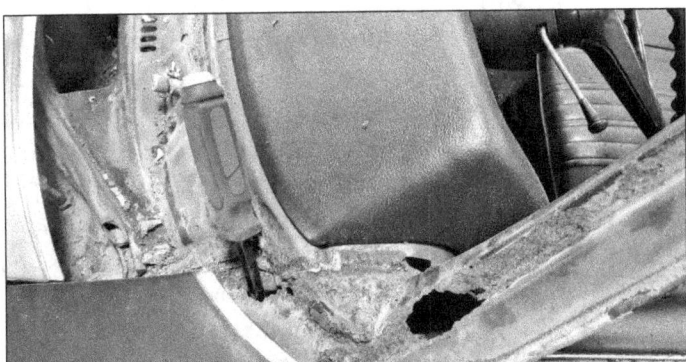

A very common area for rust through is in the front and rear glass channel, where water often sits for extended periods of time, causing extensive damage. These areas need to be completely cut out and replaced. Replacement channels can be purchased from companies such as beldonspeed.com and make for a much-easier repair.

Other issues that you will likely encounter if you find rust in the quarter panel are the inner wheelhouse to trunk floor-pan seam. This pinch-welded area also held moisture and will likely need addressing.

floorpans, the windshield, roof pillars, and outer rear wheelhouses besides the most common areas, such as fender bottoms, door corners, and quarter-panel wheel openings.

Checking for Original Body Color Match

No matter what paint manufacturer you or your body shop may be using, you will want to verify the correct color match before you start stripping the paint off of your car. Just because your paint jobber has a formula available to mix the color does not mean it will be a correct match. There are different types of base coats and single-stage paint products that could give you a different shade of the color. It is very important that you do a spray out of the color with the paint line you intend on using and compare it to an area on your car that is still in original paint.

Remember that more often than not, these cars have been repainted over the years, and just because it appears to look like the correct color does not necessarily mean that it is. A lot of times once you have removed the fenders from the car, the side of the cowl will give you a good look at the original color. Because that area has not been exposed to the sun, you should be able to polish it up and have a good sample of the original color to match your spray. Underneath your door panels and seals is another place you could possibly find original paint to compare your color spray-out card. This is a step that is easily forgotten and will be too late once the body is stripped.

Paint Removal

There are several ways to remove the old paint finish from the outer body and sheet metal. No matter which method you use, start by wiping down the area with the appropriate PPG cleaners. DX330 is a great cleaner specifically designed to remove wax, grease, silicones, road tar, and other contaminants. This process is done to avoid driving any contaminants down into the metal surface.

Finding out how many times the panels have been painted, how thick the paint products are, or even what type of paint products were used may help you decide what will work best. Your budget may also weigh in on how you proceed with stripping the paint. And you have to decide whether or not you are able to do it yourself or if you would need to pay a professional to do it. Remember that there are pros and cons to each and every method that you choose, so consider all options. If you are doing your own work, make sure to wear all the proper protection items, such as a face shield, goggles or safety glasses, face mask or breathing apparatus, and gloves.

Machine Sanding

Sanding the old paint and body filler from outer surfaces of the body and sheet metal is a big job and is very time consuming. Most sanders are dual action and can be used as an orbital sander or can be used in a grinding mode. Using a dual-action sander in a grinding mode will cut faster, but it will create more heat. If you are not very careful, you could possibly warp or distort the panel.

Using a dual-action sander as an orbital sander will work, but it can also be time consuming, as it does not remove material as fast as it does in the grind mode. Keep the sander flat on the surface and be careful not to tilt it at an angle. Tilting the sander will not only wear out the outside edge of the paper but will also create heat and may causing the panel to distort or warp.

The safest way to machine sand is to use 80-grit dual-action paper. Keeping the sander flat on the panel and using light downward pressure, run the sander slowly back on forth over the painted surface, removing one layer of paint at a time. This will cut the fastest, get you the longest life out of your sandpaper, and create less heat. Be careful not to apply too much downward pressure to the sander. This could generate heat and could warp the outer panel. Using light pressure will

Many times the side of a cowl panel can offer up good original paint samples. If you take some wax and grease remover and rub the side panel and buff it with a heavy cutting compound, you will normally be able to get it clean enough to see the correct tone of the original color as well as have a large enough area to apply a color-match camera called a spectrophotometer. Many body shops and most paint-supply stores have this available and can be used or rented to give you your paint match.

CHAPTER 6

What appeared to be original body panels during the inspection turned out to have lots of bodywork done to it. Be careful not to underestimate what type of work has been done at some point.

Once the body is stripped, it can reveal previous body damage that was missed during your initial assessment. Depending on how well the repair was originally made, it might require additional work and drive up the cost of the restoration. Here, you see a previous repair that was made. Fortunately, this will not require too much additional work due to the quality of the patch, while in other cases, it can get rather expensive.

not only cut better, it will prolong the life of the sandpaper. Forty-grit sandpaper can also be used, but remember, the more aggressive papers will cut faster and create more heat. If you're not careful, you will put too deep of a scratch in the metal. The pros to machine sanding are that it's a safe way to remove the paint, and it will not pit or abrade the metal. The cons are that machine sanding will not remove the rust.

Chemical Stripping

There are a couple methods that can be used to chemically strip the paint products from your project. You can use chemical strippers that can be applied with a paintbrush, or you may opt to bring your car to a business that specializes in chemical stripping. These types of business will take all your sheet metal and body core and lower it into a large tank to chemically remove the paint. This process will not remove rust, seam sealers, or body filler, so keep that in mind when pricing it out. This is usually not terribly expensive and takes only a short time, but clean up here is the key to success; improper cleaning and prep can lead to major paint issues later on.

Brush-On Stripper

Using brush-on stripper is messy and a slow process, but it is an effective way to remove the old paint. Because of the harmful vapors, this will need to be done in a well-ventilated area and away from any flame source. There are many different products on the market, and before starting, make sure you read the directions and the safety instructions on the label of the product you choose. It would also be a good idea to read up on the Material Safety Data Sheet that is supplied by request, so you know what you are working with and how to treat yourself in case of an accident. Be sure to protect your eyes and hands with solvent-resistant gloves and goggles.

Pour the paint remover into a metal container and brush on a thick

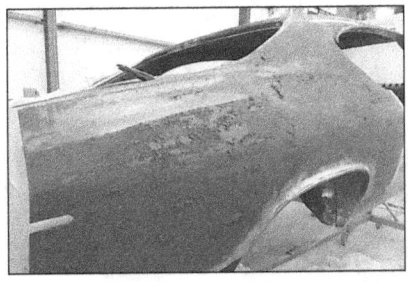

Chemical strippers are an effective but messy way to remove the paint and primer from the exterior panels, especially when you are stripping off older lacquers and enamels. Some of the newer urethane products may need to be stripped a couple of times to get all of the paint products removed.

BODY AND PAINT WORK

What you hope to find underneath after chemical stripping is virgin sheet metal requiring minimal repairs, but that is seldom the case. Make sure these areas are thoroughly acid washed and rinsed to get all chemicals out of the steel before proceeding with any bodywork or priming.

All of the structural adhesives that are between the inner and outer panels as well as any panel caulking will have been softened and lost during the acid-tanking process. Be sure to reapply those adhesives and caulking where they are needed before painting.

coat with a chemical-resistant brush. Start by working a 9-square-foot area, brushing the stripper in one direction. Generally, it will take 10 to 15 minutes for the paint to soften or blister. The paint can then be removed with a flexible plastic scrapper. Be sure to neutralize the chemical based on the manufacturer's specifications and dispose of chemicals as instructed on the label. The pros to using a chemical paint removal are that it works best on original paint. The cons are that it's a messy job, leaves the metal smooth, does not remove rust, is slow for cars with multiple paint jobs, and does not remove body filler.

Acid Dipping

Sending your project to a facility that can acid dip is a great way to get the entire body and sheet metal stripped to the bare metal. Most have large dip tanks of safe chemicals that they can submerge an entire body into and remove the paint, rust, primer, and sealers. These chemicals will strip the paint and remove the rust from the entire project. On the downside, it will also remove any panel bond and seam sealer, so areas such as the hood and decklid will need to be addressed because the factory bonding material will be removed. This will need to be replaced to keep the sheet metal bonded to the inner structure. One such stripping business is Maintenance Equipment Chemicals in Nanty Glo, Pennsylvania. MEC uses a water-based rust inhibitor to keep the steel parts from re-rusting for up to 60 days when stored under roof. For more information on acid dipping, visit their web site at mecchemicals.com.

If you chose to have your panels acid tanked, all of the undercoating, seam sealer, and paint materials will be stripped off, and you will be left with a bare steel panel. This will require immediate priming to keep the panels from flash rusting unless they are properly stored for up to 90 days.

Media Blasting

There are many different types of media blasting available. A good rule of thumb to use when media blasting is to use the mildest abrasive possible with the least amount of air pressure needed to get the job done. We will only touch on the abrasives that are most commonly used in the automotive world and are widely available around the country. These media types include aluminum oxide, silica sand, crushed glass grit or glass beads, and biodegradable abrasives, such as walnut shells and baking soda. One of the latest newcomers to the paint removal world is the dustless waterborne abrasive removal system. All have pros and cons, so you need to consider everything before deciding which one to use. Read up on each type thoroughly before deciding which one will work best for your particular application.

You may also consider using more than one type of abrasive paint removal method, depending on what it is you intend to blast or have blasted due to each of their potential positive aspects or downfalls. In the case of most all of the abrasive methods, you will need to immediately treat the metal to ward off flash rusting that will occur, so be prepared ahead of time. You also need to understand that some media will remove rust and body filler, while others are not coarse enough to remove either. In all cases, you must check your local codes and ordinances as well as thoroughly investigate the products' dangers before using any of them if you are not contracting this part out.

Aluminum Oxide: Aluminum oxide is one of the hardest sandblasting medias available. In fact, only diamond media is a harder than aluminum oxide. Aluminum oxide is very abrasive, so it cuts through metals quickly. It also creates very little dust, making it a safe choice when working on hard metal surfaces. When used on metal surfaces, it creates a matte-looking finish to the metal surface and will often require follow-up preparation of the metal to finish off the etching that the aluminum oxide has created. However, in some cases, such as on a chassis, the results will give you a good adhesion base for the paint. Because the abrasive is very fine, it will also get into every nook and crevice, and great

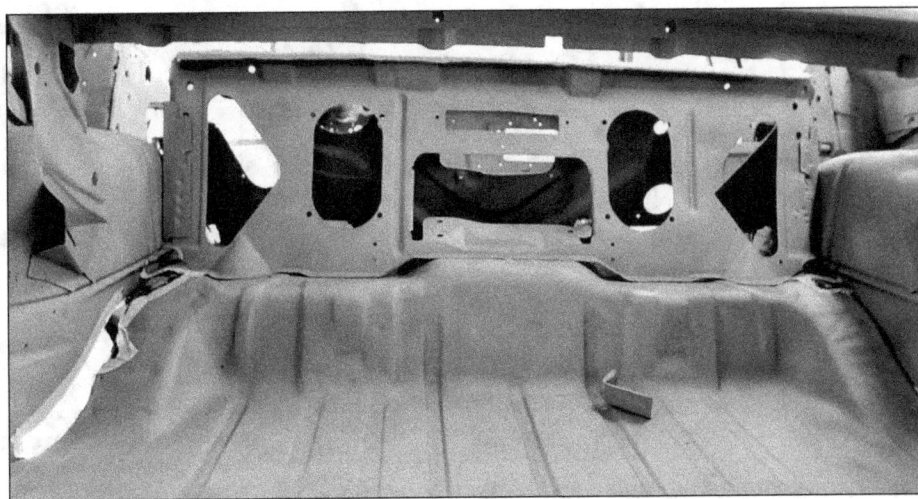

Sandblasting works great for removing the paint and primer from the floors and inner structural parts of the body because these panels have many strengthening areas and will not warp as easily as a flat body panel. It may also expose much more damage than you originally thought.

care will be needed to remove it all before you start you painting process.

Silica Sandblasting: Silica sandblasting is yet another way to remove paint and rust from most of the panels. Because of the heat that is created from sandblasting due to extreme air pressures, it is not recommended that sandblasting be used on the flat outside panels of the car, such as the roof, quarter panels, fenders, doors, hood, decklid, etc. Sandblasting works great when removing the paint and rust from areas like your floors, rockers, pinch welds, and jambs. It also gets into those hard-to-reach areas, such as the cracks and crevices. Sandblasting the inside of a door shell is a great way to remove the paint and rust, but be careful not to abrade the outside of the door skin. The profile left behind in the metal from sandblasting will also leave a good adhesion for primer.

Sandblasting works great for pitted rusty areas and will remove body filler as well. This method is perfect for spot blasting small areas of rust that will need metal and fabricating work. Sandblasting also works great on frames and heavier-gauge metal. The cons are it has severe potential for warping or distorting the panel and has the most potential for damage to the vehicle due to the heat generated during the blasting process.

Silica sand is among the most popular media-blasting methods that are used in the automotive restoration industries. Although it is inexpensive and effective, it also creates a significant amount of dust and can be very dangerous. It requires an extreme amount of air pressure and volume to work correctly.

Besides the mess involved with the large amount of dust, it has also been proven to cause lung disease in some users. Sandblasting with silica sand also requires the use of an air-supplied hood to allow the user to breathe clean non-contaminated fresh air. Care must also be taken to blast upwind of the item you are working on, and all others should be kept away from your work area. Using this coarse sandblasting method will likely expose many very thin areas in

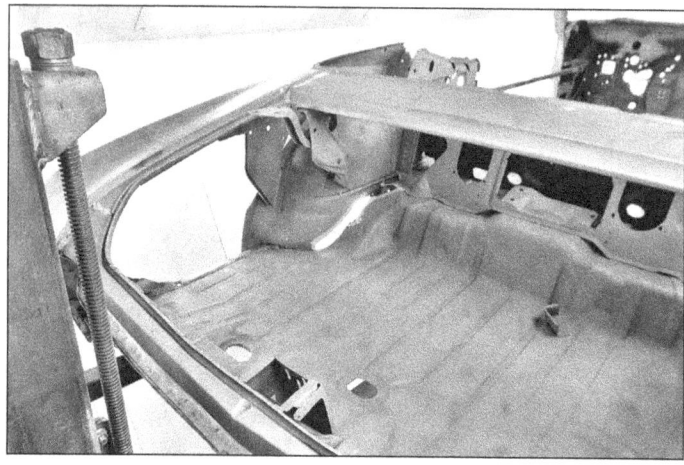

If you are planning on replacing the quarter panels, it is best to do the sandblasting before welding the new one on. This will make removing the sand much easier. If you were able to retain the original quarter panels on the car, be careful and just puff over them to ensure they do not warp, and be sure to clean the sand up from all the cracks and crevices.

Sandblasting may also open up many pinholes or soft spots in the metal that up until now would have gone unnoticed. Once you see how much damage is present, you will need to decide whether to do many small repairs or replace the entire floor panel.

After blasting, the use of painter's masking tape will greatly aid you in marking the trouble areas so that you can focus your attention at repairing these areas or deciding to replace the entire panel before moving on.

the metal, such as pinholes. This will give you a better idea of the condition of your floors and substructures, and you will then have to decide whether to repair or replace those areas.

Glass Media: Crushed glass grit or glass beads are also effective types of blasting media and are somewhat recyclable, making them rather economical. As a general rule of thumb, the smaller the glass pieces, the smoother the surface will be. Glass media is generally going to be used on smaller pieces of your project, such as brackets, clips, retainers, etc. Any small items that do not have heavy pitting or rust are good candidates. Another good use for it is for aluminum items, such as intakes, distributor housings, transmission cases, and thermostat housings. This will require a cabinet built or sold for the sole purpose of blasting because you will need to retain the media to reuse it, and it will require a vacuum system to remove fine dust that will inhibit you to see what you are blasting. There are a variety of cabinets that can be purchased online or through tool stores.

It is very important that you thoroughly clean the part before using glass media because this will not only contaminate the media and cabinet but will also hold the media within the item you are blasting. After blasting, pressure wash or thoroughly blow the item to get all of the glass media off, especially when used on an intake manifold as this could damage the internal engine parts.

Plastic Media: There is an alternative to both sandblasting and chemical stripping your Chevelle. Plastic media blasting has become one of the most popular, economical, and accepted methods of paint removal. Plastic media is mainly used for the sheet metal portions of your Chevelle. This method uses small plastic granules that are harder than paint but softer than the substrate. Using a low pressure, high-volume process, the media will cut, shear, and lift the paint without affecting the metal surface.

Since it is a dry non-water-borne process, there is no flash rust after stripping, and most importantly, the plastic won't warp or pit the metal. It's noncorrosive and safe for all metal, stainless steel, fiberglass, plastic, and aluminum. Like some of the other medias, it won't remove rust, so other methods of blasting may have to be used in those areas. It is best used on a body that is very solid and for the most part rust free.

Biodegradable Medias: The gentlest, least expensive, and most environmentally friendly types of media include corncobs, walnut shells, and baking soda.

Corncob grit will clean areas affected by smoke damage and absorb grease or other substances. It can also be used to clean, deburr, or polish thin metals engine parts or springs.

Walnut shells are used to make a biodegradable blasting media grit. This type of grit is somewhat inexpensive and is effective in cleaning and polishing sensitive items that you do not want to leave an abrasive finish on or one that leaves a film behind. It is fairly inexpensive but can usually only be found in larger cities. It can be purchased and used in blasting cabinets on smaller parts.

Baking soda is also biodegradable and somewhat easy to contract out in most areas. It is an excellent product to use on automotive bodies, although it will not remove rust and most body fillers because it is just too soft and uses low pressure. Soda will remove paint, oil, mold, carbon, grease, grime, and many other difficult-to-remove soils and paints without damaging the underlying material and is an excellent method to use on most car bodies. It is also water soluble, nontoxic, nonhazardous, and safe for the environment. The down side is that soda needs to be neutralized, and since it is water soluble, it needs to be rinsed thoroughly with a vinegar and hot water mix. The fact that you are now working with bare steel and water, oxidation will set in immediately. Though inexpensive to use, the cleanup and prep will raise the costs and make soda blasting an option that should be considered last.

With any of the media options available, be sure and check with your painter and paint manufacturer for their warranties and liabilities before deciding which media to use.

Panel Replacement

When to repair and when to replace is the question. When restoring your Chevelle, more than likely you will come across areas that have rust and will need some metal and fabricating to repair the damage. In most cases, it is best to try to keep as much of the original panels as possible for integrity as well as originality. You will need to make a judgment call on what is most cost effective: repairing or replacing. Keep in mind that a lot of times reproduction panels and even NOS may be slightly different from the original assembly-line part. Even though they may be NOS, due to their age and the age of the tooling, it may not fit as nicely as you would have hoped. Although they will fit up and appear to be correct, there may be subtle differences in style lines or the stamped impressions in the metal. If it's important to you that your project appears to be assembly-line correct, you may want to take the extra effort and expense in repairing the part.

Using an original donor panel off another car may also be a good alternative to an NOS one. There are several manufacturers that reproduce complete replacement and partial repair panels. Depending on how bad your panel is, this will help you decide what is best used. If there is only a small area of rust or a little hole, grafting a small piece of a partial replacement panel would be best, easiest, and least expensive. If only the area around the actual wheel opening is rusted and originality is key, then butt welding in a repair panel will still allow you to claim

If the damage to the particular body panel is minimal, it is both cheaper and easier to do a patch repair. These can often be bought as well as made, and they make for a simple repair while still maintaining the original sheet metal for the car.

BODY AND PAINT WORK

Many times, the damage to a panel is so severe that the only remedy is to replace the whole panel with an NOS or a quality replacement reproduction panel. You will need to decide which one is a better fix on your particular application and budget.

Moisture gets between the two pieces of metal, causing them to rust from the inside out. Weld-through primers are generally a zinc-based product applied to the inside of the two panels prior to welding. When the weld is performed, the zinc liquefies and flows between the two pieces of metal, helping to protect from corrosion.

Resistance spot welds (RSW) are the most common welds used on your outer body and inner structure. These welds are used to join overlapping pieces of metal by applying pressure and electric current. There are two electrodes opposite of each other that squeeze the metal using roughly 600 pounds of pressure and a large amount of electric current. The force of the weld tip will deform the metal and form a small dent or puddle as the metal gets hot, making a spot weld. The size of the electrode and the amount of current used will determine the size of the spot weld. Most welders have different arms or attachments that will allow you to weld in those hard-to-reach areas. If you are replacing your quarter panels and are concerned with the

your car has original sheet metal. There are several manufacturers, such as Auto Metal Direct (AMD), Goodmark, and Dynacorn, that are able to supply you with most of all the panels you will need, and all have made good panels.

Metal Welding and Fabricating

When getting started with the metal and fabricating part of your restoration, keep in mind that this will be the foundation that your bodywork is done on top of. Like every other process, how well you perform this task will determine how easy or difficult the next step will be. If you are doing this part of the restoration yourself, having expensive equipment (such as inverter-resistant spot welders) is probably out of the question. In that case, a plug weld will need to be used. Keep in mind that no matter what type of weld you plan on using, always consider using weld-through primer between the flanges. Panels that are welded together are notorious for rusting.

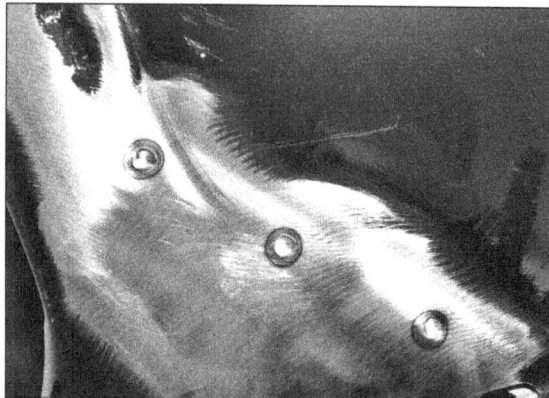

If you are doing a concours-correct restoration and will be replacing your quarter panels, make sure to use a resistant spot weld (RSW) to install them. RSW will replicate the appearance of what was originally done at the factory.

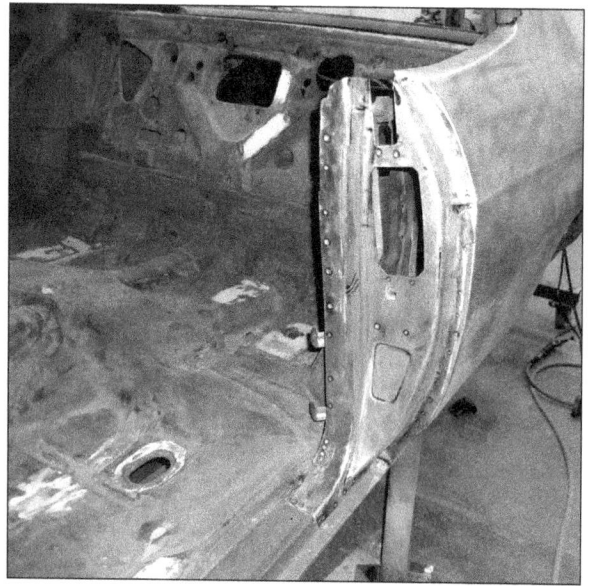

Make sure you document the location and how many welds were present in that area. It is important to try to duplicate how the original panel was installed. Also, the size of the spot weld can vary depending on which panel you are replacing.

CHAPTER 6

appearance of the spot welds, you may want to outsource this to your local body shop if they have the equipment.

Plug Welding

If using a resistance spot welder is not an option, the alternative would be a plug weld. A plug weld is done by drilling a 5/16- or 3/8-inch hole in one of the two pieces of metal, clamping the two pieces of metal together tightly, and welding the hole up with a metal inert gas (MIG) welder. Make sure the two pieces of metal fit together nicely and that there are no odd gaps between them. If you have to use a clamp or Vise-Grips to get them to fit flush, be careful not to bend or deform one or the other of the two pieces of metal. This will make for a difficult body repair. Also, be careful not to weld for too long in the same area. Plug welding will create a lot of heat and could warp the panel. It is best to rotate around the panel, welding in different areas, and you can use a blow gun to help cool the plug weld when finished.

Once you have finished with the plug weld, it is time to grind and dress up the weld. What usually works best is an angle die grinder with a 2-inch flap disk. These disks can be purchased in several different grits, but I recommend using 60 or 80 grit for this task. When dressing the weld up, be careful to grind the weld and not the material around it; this would cause the metal that you are welding through to be thin and brittle.

If you are looking to duplicate the look of the RSW, there are some tricks that you can use, but remember that they are not perfect and can usually be detected by professionals in this trade. Once you have smoothed up the plug

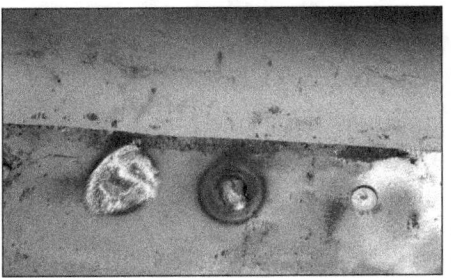

If you do not own or have access to a resistant spot welder, or if your spot welder is not able to reach an area that needs to be welded, the plug weld is a great alternative to it. Although it will not give the exact impression of the spot weld, it will give you a strong weld.

welds and grinder marks with either body filler or primer filler, you can take the same angle grinder and install a carbide die grinder burr. These can be purchased from local tool dealer or venders such as Eastwood. There are several styles of burrs, so choose one that will cut on the end. These are called ball burrs or radius-end burrs. When doing this, be careful not to burr too deep in the metal. I recommend putting a small divot in the body filler or the primer surfacer.

Butt Welds

Butt welds are generally done when sectioning or grafting in a piece of metal to repair a small area rather than replacing the entire panel. This weld is done to keep the panels parallel without overlapping the metal. When repairing an area that is visible, it will help avoid a thick overlapping weld that will need body filler to smooth over the overlapping metal. The butt weld will also help cut down on corrosion that can be caused by moisture trapped between the panels.

When sectioning in a repair panel, it is best to cut out the area that is bad and remove all of the dam-

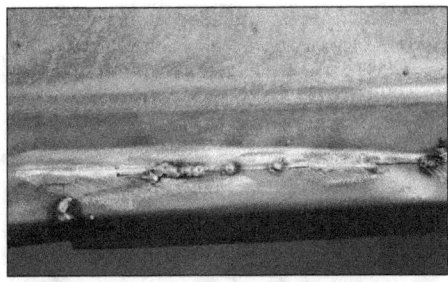

Butt welds are a good way to section or graft in a partial panel or patch panel. When done correctly and ground smooth, the two panels will be perfectly flush and the weld will be undetectable from the outside. With careful grinding on the inside, this weld will be undetectable.

aged or rotten metal. Cut the replacement panel, leaving it roughly 1 inch bigger than the area that you cut out. Basically, you will be lapping the new panel over the top of the repair area by roughly 1 inch. This can be accomplished by drilling a series of holes throughout the entire length of the seam where they overlap and inserting screws or rivets to hold the two metal panels together to keep them from moving during the welding process. Clamps can also be used in those areas where you can get the clamps into.

At this point, you will be ready to take a small air reciprocating saw that uses a thin metal blade to cut through both pieces of metal. As you cut through both panels, peel away the excess metal and tack weld the two panels flush together, creating a butt weld. Work your way around the entire panel to be installed, tack welding it every inch or so as you go. Once the panel is tacked into place and all of the excess metal is removed, you can finish butt welding it into place. Be careful not to weld too much area at one time, as this will create a lot of heat, which

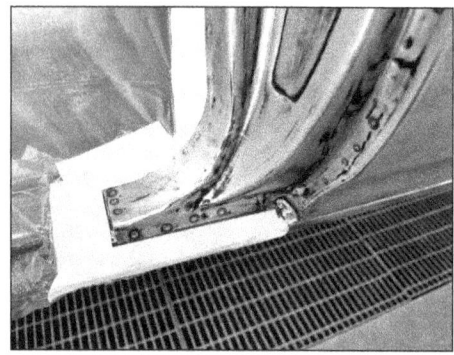

Brazing is a good way to hold the quarter panel in place before welding it up permanently. Once the quarter is fit on the body and all of the panel gaps are correct, you can braze the front side of the quarter panel where it meets the rocker on the inside jam. This is the way it was done at the manufacturing plant and will ensure that the quarter panel is flush to the rocker panel.

will warp and distort the panel. It is best to make welds 1/2-inch long and cool it with a blow gun. As you weld, moving from one end of the panel to the other will also to reduce the heat from welding.

Braze Welding

Brazing is a metal-joining process that is used to join two pieces of metal together by flowing a filler metal such as brass between the panels. This is not a process that should be used to repair or replace any panels. Brazing was used to attach the bottom front side of the quarter panel to the rocker panel, keeping them flush prior to spot welding the quarter panels on permanently.

Panel Removal

Removing panels that are welded on is a very tedious process. When doing so, be careful not to damage the panel that is attached to the panel you are removing. Clean up the pinch weld or the area that will need the spot weld removed. Use an angle die grinder with an 80-grit flap disk to run over the spot weld area. Also, using 80-grit sandpaper to sand the spot weld area will help to locate and enhance the welds. Once you have located the spot weld, use a center punch to mark the center of the weld. It is very important when it comes time to drill out the spot weld that you have marked the center of the weld and not offset it a little because it may cause the panels to not totally separate from each other.

There are several types of spot-weld cutters on the market, and most all will do the job; just make sure that you use one with a 3/8-inch cutter head. Place the centering pin on the cutter in the divot that you made with the center punch earlier in the chapter. When drilling, be careful not to drill too deep. Drilling only through the first panel will give you a nice clean surface on the inner panel to attach the replacement panel to.

As you continue to drill out the spot weld, take a spot-weld chisel to help you separate the panels. If you have not completely drilled around the outside of the spot weld, the chisel will help you cut through part of the spot weld that is still attached, but be careful not to tear the inner panel. If you took the time to mark the center of the spot weld with a centering punch and are careful not to drill too deep into the panel, you will be able to remove the panel much easier and will save yourself a lot of work once the panel is removed. Once the panel is removed, you will need to clean up the metal debris that was left behind on the inner panel. Using an angle die grinder with a flap disk will work best.

Aligning Sheet Metal

Typically, the outer-body gaps or the gaps between the sheet metal panels were less than perfect from the factory; the same could typically be said of any bodywork done to the car in previous years. We have talked previously about restoring a car exactly how the factory built it. Paint and panel fitment are two areas that most restorers will improve on over the factory, and both are areas that are widely accepted by the judges. Fewer and fewer people want to see orange peel in the paint or poor gaps, so keep that in mind.

Door Gaps

Whether you are using the original sheet metal or replacing it, some massaging and welding may be needed to get the desired panel gaps. When aligning the sheet metal, it is best to start with the doors. The rocker panels in most cases are a panel that will not need replacing. Usually at worst it will only need minor repair. If that is the case on your project, aligning the door to the rocker panel is usually where you will start. Leave the front edge of the door approximately 1/8- to 3/16-inch back from the front edge of the rocker. This will help give you a nice door-to-fender gap and leave a very narrow gap between the bottom of the fender and the rocker panel.

You will want to make sure that the horizontal door-to-rocker panel gap and the vertical gap from the rear of the door to the quarter panel is even from top to bottom. Double-check the wear in the door pins and bushings by picking up the rear of the door and feeling for movement or play in the hinge area. If there is any movement in the

CHAPTER 6

Leaving the front edge of the door slightly back from the front edge of the rocker panel is a good place to start when mocking up the door. This will allow a nice fender-to-door gap that will be slightly wider than the gap between the fender and the rocker panel. Not doing this will cause a large and unsightly fender to rocker gap.

The gap between the bottom of the door and the rocker panel should be roughly 1/4 inch and needs to be even from the front to the back. An uneven gap along the bottom of the door will throw off the fender and quarter panel gaps where they meet the door. It is also a good idea to simulate the weight of the glass and hardware so as to take up any sag these will cause when installed.

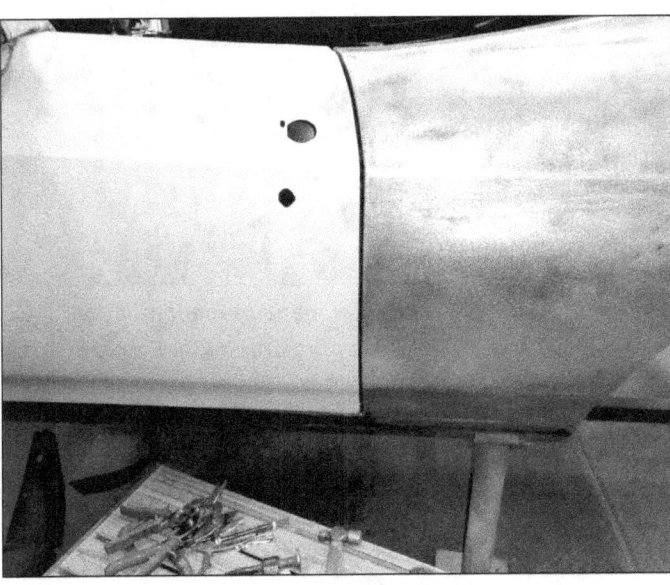

Once you are comfortable with your door placement, you can then proceed to align the rear quarter panel to the door, making sure your gaps are equidistant from top to bottom and that the beltline seam lines up correctly as well.

door, then replacing the door pins and bushings should be done first. On a full restoration, now would be the time to replace the pins or hinges even if they are not showing excessive wear.

Always align the doors first, even if the plan is to replace the quarter panels. This will help you get the replacement quarter panels close. There will be a little wiggle room in the quarter panel, which will help in getting the desired gaps.

Decklid Gaps

From there, installing the decklid is next. The fit of the decklid at the back side was usually not perfect on Chevelles. It is often a good idea to straighten the bumper and hang it on the car at this time to use as a guide to align the decklid lip so that it follows the contour of the bumper. Now would also be the time to massage the quarter panels to meet the decklid lip along the rear so that it

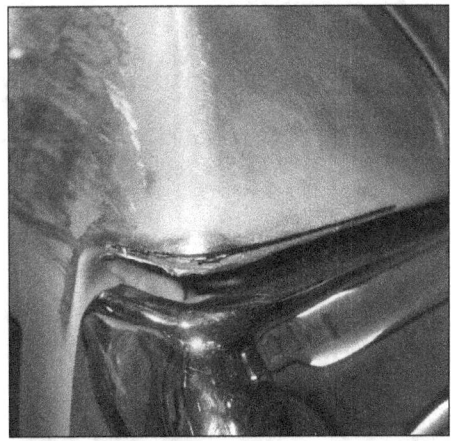

While aligning the rear quarters to the body, it is imperative to make sure the taillight extensions are parallel with the top of the bumper. If not, now is the time to cut and weld them in order to make the gap the same from the left side of the car to the right between the bumper, taillight extensions, and decklid.

BODY AND PAINT WORK

flows evenly from one side of the car to the other. Check to ensure that the rear quarter panel extensions run in the same plane horizontally to the decklid lip just above the bumper.

Quarter and Valance Fitment

Before finishing the welding on your quarter panel, you must also mount the rear valance and the bumper onto the body to ensure that they all fit together as a unit with no unsightly gaps. Make sure the rear lower valance panel fits evenly with the quarter panels on both sides. If the rear, lower half of the quarter panels are pulled in too far or not far enough, the valance panel will not fit flush, and you will either have unsightly gaps or not enough room to fit the valance between the quarter panels.

Fender and Hood Gaps

Once you are satisfied with the alignment on the back half of the car, it is time to move forward with the fenders and the hood. Many times, Chevelle doors do not follow the contour of the front fender where the two meet, especially above the body line and more so on the passenger-side door. This should be addressed many times by welding onto the face of the door to change the contour where it meets the fender. A common trick is to take a thin piece of paper or card stock and slowly open the door while sliding the paper up and down the joint. If the door at any point grabs the paper, the gaps need to be slightly widened. Otherwise, it will chip the paint later after it has been applied. For the most part, there is plenty of adjustment in the fenders to give you the needed gaps.

Once you are happy with the rough gaps in the jamb area, you then want to check the front clip to ensure it is square. Find the same location on the front and the rear of each fender and use that same starting point. Use a tape measure to measure diagonally across from the front of the fender on one side to the rear of the fender on the opposite side at the top. Once you get that measurement, do the same procedure on the other side and compare measurements. These need to be the same to within about an 1/8 inch. If it measures more, you will have alignment issues with not only the hood but also the front bumper and headlight extensions. This will also not allow the fenders to be in the same plane as the rest of the body when looking down the side from front to rear.

After you have the front sheet metal square, pay close attention to the hood-to-fender gaps. Make sure there is plenty of clearance between the fenders and the hood and that they are completely parallel from the nose to the rear with as tight of a gap as possible without the hood hitting the fenders when opening and closing. When closing the hood, be sure to do it slowly and watch the back side of the hood where it meets the fender. If the fenders are pulled in too close, the hood can scratch the rear of the fender when you open

Another common area that is missed during a restoration is the fitment of the valance to the quarter panels on both sides as well as to the bumper. Your finished panels should fit flush on both sides without gaps or being skewed. Fix this area before you finish weld or bodywork.

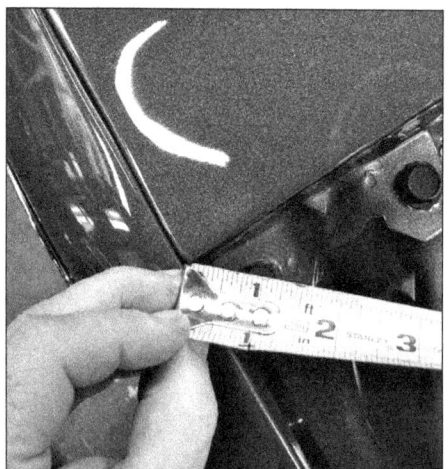

It is imperative that you take a diagonal measurement from one fender's front corner to the opposite fender's rear corner. Pick a common point on both fenders and repeat the measurement side to side.

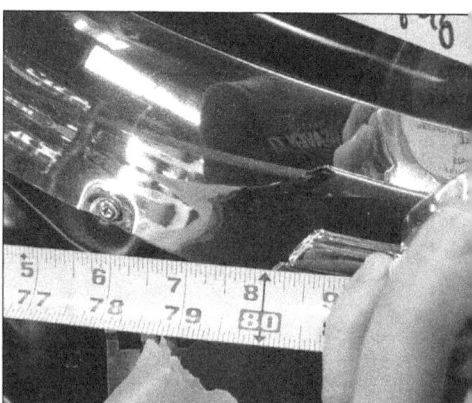

The total measurement must be within approximately 1/8 inch of each other, otherwise you will not be able to align the hood, fenders, bumper, or headlight extensions. Make sure you measure from the exact same points on both fenders to get an accurate measurement.

CHAPTER 6

If great care is taken during the bodywork phase of the restoration, it will pay dividends when the car is completed, and you have perfect gaps on every panel. This is the difference between a driver-quality car and one that much time was spent on making it perfect and therefore is much more valuable.

The roof laps over the top of the quarter panel, leaving a shallow cavity in an area called the sail panel. This area originally had a few stitch welds in it and then was leaded over. It is recommended that you weld the entire lap joint from one end to the other and grind it smooth before moving forward with leading the seam back in.

Leading (60 percent lead and 40 percent tin) is somewhat of a learned art and takes a lot of practice using a paddle and heat to get it to flow into your work area correctly. It is also dangerous to work with due to it being lead, though lead-free solder can be used as well. Care must be taken not to warp the surrounding steel during the melting process.

or close it. The front-end alignment steps need to be performed before the major bodywork is completed and again when permanently mounting the finished and painted parts to the chassis.

Body Repair

Before starting the bodywork or any body repair, all of the metal and fabricating work should have been completed, and the bare metal should have been sprayed with epoxy primer. Applying body fillers over the top of the epoxy primer will provide you with the maximum corrosion protection, but be sure the epoxy has had a chance to dry overnight before starting. For maximum adhesion, apply fillers within seven days of spraying the epoxy. If you have exceeded the seven-day window, scuff the primer with P120- to P180-grit paper, but be sure not to break through to bare metal. There are several different types of products that will be used when doing the bodywork. Knowing where to use them and how to apply them will help give you a quality repair and ensure the longevity of the restoration.

Start by the Windshield Pillar Seams

A great place to start when working on the body is at the seams where the top of the windshield pillar meets the front of the roof and where the rear sail panel on the quarter meets the rear of the roof. These seams will have a slight indentation where the panels meet and are recessed as well as originally having been filled with lead. If you removed the lead to gain access to the weld seam when you replaced a quarter panel or removed it because of corrosion beneath the lead, you will have an indentation that will need to be filled. Reapplying lead is great way to bridge that seam, but it takes experience in that process to do it correctly and can be dangerous if you mishandle the lead.

If that is not an option for you, using a product by USC called All-Metal will work great. All-Metal is an aluminum-filled automotive compound that spreads and sands like a typical body filler. Its excellent adhesion and the fact that it is waterproof makes it ideal for restoration. It also should be used over the top of any weld seam you have ground smooth when repairing a panel or grafting in a patch. All-Metal has a liquid hardener that uses 15 drops per golf-ball size of the filler. Use a plastic spreader and apply firm pressure to spread a thin layer of the filler to the surface. It will start to set in about 3 minutes, so be sure to work quickly. In 15 minutes, it should be fully cured and ready to sand using P80- to P120-grit sandpaper. If needed, additional layers can be applied for up to a 1/4 inch of film build.

Body Filler

Whether you are repairing the waves in the metal left behind from straightening damage or just skimming the outer surface with filler to block it straight, body filler will be needed to get razor-straight panels. Keep in mind that body fillers were not designed to fill deep dents and dings, so be sure you have done the metal work needed to pull the dents and straighten the panels before you get started. Lightly blocking over the epoxy primer that was sprayed on the panels will not only promote good body filler adhesion, it will help you identify high and low spots in the metal. There are several manufacturers of sanding blocks to choose from when doing the bodywork. Dura-Block is just one of them that makes a nice seven-piece set that is affordable and will give you different shapes and sizes for flat or contoured surfaces.

Using P150-grit paper on a flat sanding block, lightly sand the epoxy primer on the surface. This will help you identify the high and lower surfaces on the panel. Apply a thin, light coat of premium lightweight body filler rather than thick, loose coats. When doing large panels, it is best to cover a larger area rather than several small spots. Using a premium

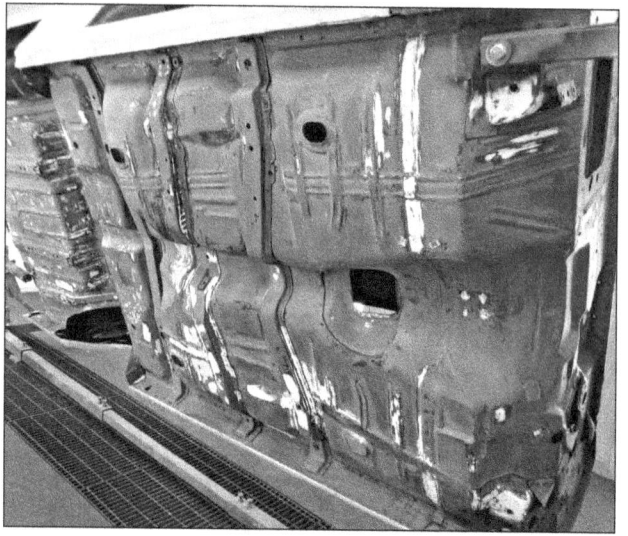

Whether you are doing a driver-quality or a concours restoration, there are areas of the car that can require hundreds of repair hours fixing the dents and pitting left behind from the rust and road damage. This is very common due to its continual exposure to the road debris.

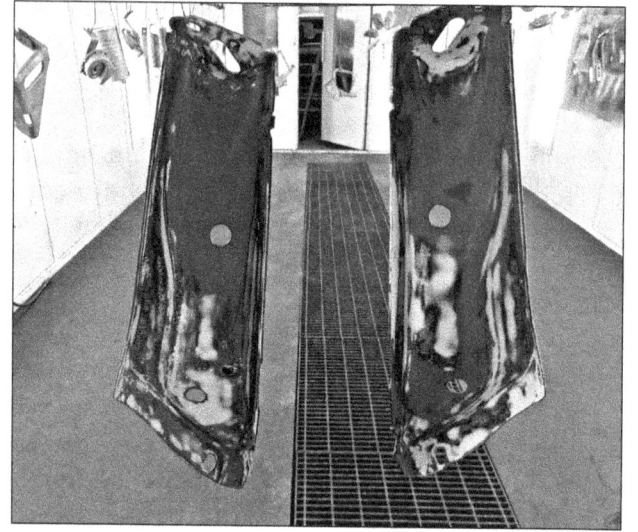

Here is a good example of many hours spent on the small miscellaneous parts, such as bumper brackets. By the time you bead blast, prime, hand sand, and repair the pitting in them, you could easily spend days, but when it comes time to reassemble the car, you will be glad you put the effort into them.

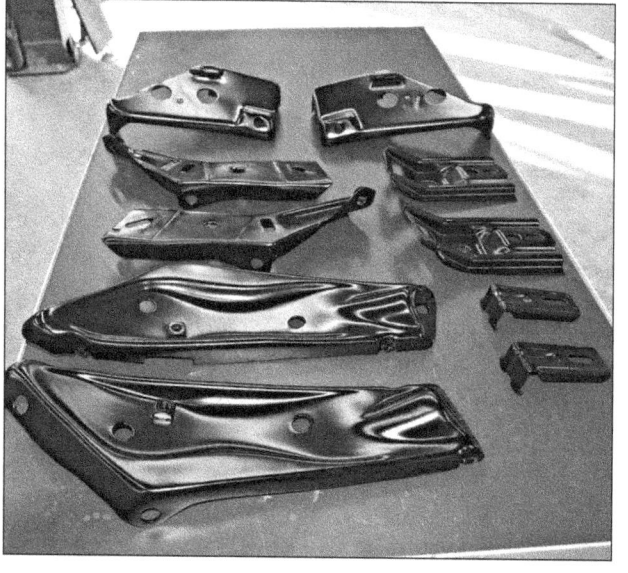

Too often, restorers do not put the effort into these small pieces because they feel they are hidden and won't be noticed. This could not be further from the truth and again sets the professionals apart from the amateurs. You should always put the same effort into items that are not readily seen as to those that are readily seen for a top-quality restoration.

lightweight body filler, such as Evercoat Rage Ultra, will extend the life of the sandpaper and allow you to start blocking with P80 grit rather than courser grits, such as P40 grit. The courser-grit sandpapers will put a deeper V in the scratch that will need to be sanded out. Applying 3M dry guide coat to the filler before you start sanding will help you identify the low areas.

Finish sanding the body filler until the guide coat is gone. If low spots in the body filler still exist, spread another coat of filler and block sand again. When you have finished sanding with P80 grit and are confident that the panel has been blocked straight, you will need to continue sanding the filler with finer-grit paper. Apply guide coat to the filler sanded with P80 and continue blocking with P150 until the guide coat lying in the bottom V of the scratch is gone. This will ensure that all of the P80-grit scratches have been sanded out and only P150-grit scratches remain.

Once you are confident that the panel has been blocked straight and all of the low spots are gone, you can then move forward with spreading a thin layer of polyester putty. Polyester putties are used as a finishing coat over body fillers. Spread a thin layer of the mixed material using firm pressure across the body filler. This will help fill scratches and pinholes that were left behind. Evercoat Metal Glaze Ultra is a good product to use and has great sanding qualities.

Block sand the polyester putty starting with P180 grit, and if an additional thin coat is needed, it can be applied. When finished, apply a dry guide coat and continue sanding with P220 grit. When the dry guide coat has been sanded off and gone from the V of the scratch, you should be ready for primer.

Always remember, the amount of time and detail you put into your project up to this point will show in the end. If you cut corners now, you will pay for them later. Many restorers will not spend the appropriate time on the belly pan, small brackets, or floors of a car because they do not think they can be easily seen. To someone wanting to buy the car in the future, this can be the difference between a quick sale and a stagnant one, not to mention the amount of the total sale.

Temperatures and Dry Times

Today's products require heat to help them dry and cure properly. Paint dry times and cure times are based on sheet metal temperatures that are between 68°F and 70°F. Keep in mind that the sheet metal temperatures will often be less than the actual air ambient temperature. Using an infrared thermometer laser gun will give you the actual sheet metal temperature, and they are inexpensive to purchase.

Two-component products or products that are catalyzed could slow down significantly or even stop curing in temperatures below 60°F. Although they may appear to be dry, these conditions could result in reduced durability or gloss level and may not repair easily. This is due to the products never reaching a fully cured state. The worst thing you can do at the end of the day when you are finished working on your project is to turn the heat back on the thermostat. It is critical to maintain metal temperatures of 68 to 70 degrees Fahrenheit. To explain how import standard temperatures are and how they can

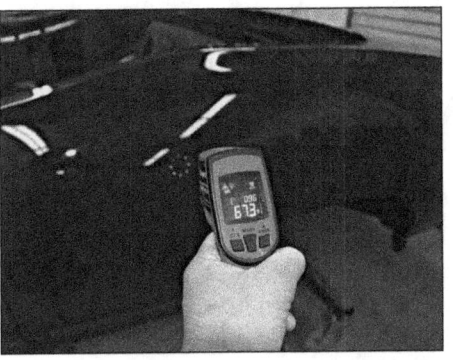

An infrared laser gun can serve many purposes throughout the restoration process, not only allowing you to make sure that you are at a minimum of 70°F before you start but also allowing you to make sure that your paint has returned to its original minimum temperature before recoating.

affect dry times and pot life is what is known as the 15-degree rule. For every 15-degree increase in temperatures above standard conditions, a product's dry time and pot life can be reduced by half. For every 15 degree decrease in temperatures below standard conditions, a product's dry time and pot life may double.

Clean Dry Compressed Air

Another very important factor that is often overlooked is the quality of the air that comes from the compressor. First, make sure your compressor is big enough for the job and you have filtered it to produce clean, dry air. The humidity in the air lines should be less than 10 percent. A 5-hp 20-cfm compressor will provide you with enough volume of air and will not overwork the compressor.

As your compressor works to generate compressed air, it also generates heat, creating contaminations and condensation. These contaminates will need to be filtered before the air can be used. If not, they will be forced through the air tools and onto the panels as you blow them off as well as through the spray gun as you are priming and painting. Shops will filter the air just before it is piped into the spray booth, and that is important, but don't forget about the shop air. As you are sanding body filler and primers through the body process, you will be using that air to blow off the dust and debris from the panels as you work on them. It is equally important that your shop air is as clean and free of contamination as your paint-booth air. There are several types of line dryers on the market, ranging from several hundred to several thousand dollars. Choose one that fits your budget and be sure to maintain it per the manufacturers specifications.

Primers

The cost of restoring a car seems to increase year after year. That can be caused by the condition of the car you are starting with, which directly reflects the amount of hours it takes to restore it. Another is the cost of paint materials and the process it takes to give you that show-quality finish. To go through the restoration process—whether you are doing it yourself or paying a professional to do it for you—and not end up with the quality you expected would be unacceptable and extremely disappointing.

There will be four different types of undercoats or primers used in the refinishing process, each having specific characteristics and roles. These undercoats are used to create corrosion protection, fill scratches and imperfections in the bodywork, and be the foundation of all your repairs. These products will give you a flat, uniform bed to spray your topcoats over. Knowing how and when to use them will be critical when looking to achieve a show-quality finish.

If you have not followed the correct process from the ground up, the best painter out there will not be able to give you the look that you want, and the longevity of the restoration will not be there. Today's paint products are so different from what they were in years past, and they continue to change as new products are introduced. Whether it is because of the lack of demand for the product or different regulations, paint manufacturers will introduce new products and phase out some that you may be accustomed to using. The state you work in and regulations the paint companies are required to comply with determine what type of paint and solvents you are able to buy or even use.

The purpose of the solvents (also known as reducers or thinners) is to reduce the viscosity of the paint materials you are mixing it with so it can be sprayed and to change the speed of drying and flash-off time. There are basically three different types of solvents that make up the reducers or thinners in the refinishing process. They are what we call front-end solvents, middle solvents, and tail solvents.

The front end or frontal solvents reduce the materials and allow them to be sprayed through your paint guns. These solvents are designed to evaporate and leave the material quickly. The purpose of the middle solvents is to help the paint materials start to flow and level out on the panel. The tail solvents allow the paint materials to finish flowing and stay open to promote adhesion. These solvents require time and standard temperatures of at least 70°F to evaporate from the paint materials. Force baking as per the material products sheet will speed up the drying process and will ensure that the materials as fully cured.

Epoxy Primer

It is extremely important to start with the best foundation possible. When used properly, epoxy primers will give you the best foundation possible to work off of. It will provide you with excellent corrosion protection and adhesion to many types of properly prepared metal, aluminum, and fiberglass substrates, as well plastic fillers. Epoxy primers come in several different colors, although DP90 is more commonly used because of its rich black color. This will give you a good visual of how straight your panels are and will help you identify the high and low spots before starting any of the bodywork.

Polyester Primer Filler

Primer fillers, such as VP2100 polyester primer, are used to help level and fill minor imperfections such as pinholes and sanding scratches

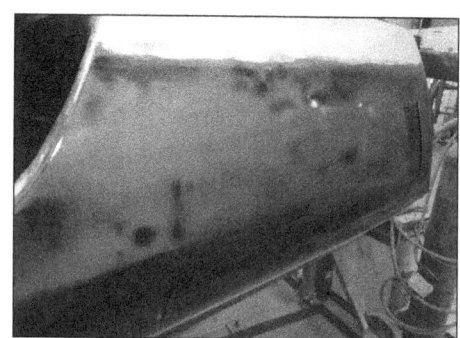

Black epoxy primer, such as DP90, serves two purposes. It provides you with great corrosion protection when sprayed over properly prepared bare metal and when it is blocked it gives you a great visual of the high and low spots in the panel.

in your body filler. Polyester primer also locks up harder than a urethane primer surfacer and will provide you with an even and consistent sanding surface. Up to three consecutive coats of polyester primer can be applied at one time, but be cautious not to exceed a total of six mils in total thickness. Polyester primers are considered porous and should be dry sanded rather than wet sanded. This primer is too porous to be painted over directly and should be primed over with a urethane primer surfacer.

Urethane Primer Surfacer

Once you have sprayed urethane primer surfacer, it could be considered the final prime if you are not planning on using a primer sealer. This urethane primer is designed to fill in the sand scratches left behind from sanding the polyester prime. If you are not planning on spraying a primer sealer prior to painting, urethane primer (when sanded correctly) will give you an acceptable bed of urethane primer to paint your color directly over.

If you are not using a primer sealer prior to painting, make sure to use the correct shade of primer surfacer to give the best coverage for the color of the topcoat you intend to use. Whether you or your painter are mixing the color on an in-house mixing station or you are purchasing it from a particular vender, they should be able to tell you what shade of primer is recommended based on the color of the topcoat you are planning on painting your project.

Urethane Primer Sealer

If using primer sealers, this should be considered the last primer that you use. Primer sealers have a higher level of resin than a primer surfacer, resulting in a harder surface for your topcoats to be sprayed over. PPG sealer also offers seven different shades of sealers to give you the best color match and help you to achieve the best coverage for the final body color that you are using. Primer sealers can be topcoated over without sanding, although you must follow recommended dry times. Keep in mind that if you are not sanding it could leave more texture or orange peel in your finish. If you are planning on sanding the sealer, be sure to spray two coats and finish sanding using the grits that are recommended for the topcoat that you are using.

Manufacturing Plants and Primer Colors

While on the topic of primers, and if you intend to restore your Chevelle back to factory correct, you may also want to finish prime your Chevelle in the same primer colors that the original assembly plants used. The shades can vary from plant to plant and month to month since they were only a primer and not a topcoat and did not follow the same stringent paint color specs that the finish body color would have. Also keep in mind that for the most part the bodies were assembled and painted in the Fischer Body section of the plant, whereas the front sheet metal was manufactured, primed, and painted in the assembly-plant area. The front sheet metal was painted in a black e-coat, whereas the Fischer Body plant used its own colored-primer process.

Spray versus Dipping (Arlington)

Most Fischer Body plants sprayed the primer coats onto the cars with the exception of the Arlington plant, which dipped the bodies in a large tank of liquid red oxide primer. This would completely cover the entire main car body in primer, including areas that a paint gun could not reach. The only exception would be in places where air pockets could form, although these areas were very limited. This assembly plant did not topcoat this primer with anything else color wise other than the chosen body color and only blacked out the face of the firewall in a semigloss black. As with all plants, the floor drain plugs were not installed until all priming had taken place.

Primer by Plant

Primer was slightly different at the Kansas, Flint, and Baltimore plants. These plants used different shades of what we refer to as a Rosette colored primer, and though similar they were in fact different shades. This primer step was followed by a black washout color coat on the belly pan and firewall. This washout black was very thin and was just enough to barely cover the colored primer.

Arlington dipped the bodies in a tank of red oxide primer, completely covering virtually every square inch of the sheet metal. They did not apply and blackout paint over the top of the primer. Also seen is the overspray of the Forrest Green color on the doors and edges of the floor pans.

1970 Chevelle Primer by Plant

Below is a list of the most common primer colors found on the 1970 Chevelle. Please note, these *can* and *will* vary by plant and dates due to changes in the assembly-line process, the mixing of the paint, suppliers, who painted it, etc. These were also just primers, so the shade of the primer can and will change throughout the year. General Motors was also known to have used leftover paint that was collected and then used as a primer on the belly pans of these cars, so as you can imagine, that color would vary dramatically.

Another note to keep in mind, these cars were sprayed with a lacquer paint and many times the overspray of the body color onto the primer will visually change or tint the color of the primer to make it appear something other than what it was originally. That being said, it is better to find a primer sample color in an area that has little or no body color overspray.

Atlanta Commonly used a greenish gray primer
Arlington Commonly used a red oxide primer
Baltimore Commonly used a rosette colored primer
Flint Commonly used a washed out semigloss black
Kansas City Commonly used a rosette colored primer
Van Nuys Commonly used a washed out semigloss black
Oshawa Commonly used black primer

More often than not you can still see the original primer color on the back sides of stiffener braces or other areas where the spray gun and applicator missed while spraying the washout black.

The Atlanta plant typically used a greenish gray primer also carried over into the interior and with no topcoat. Van Nuys and Oshawa often used a semigloss black primer.

These individual plant primer colors were also used throughout the interior and not topcoated with blackout paint other than in designated areas, such as around the dash, while leaving the rest of the inner floorpans primered in their respective colors. Body color overspray was then cast over much of the perimeter of the inside door structure, sills, package tray, and the tops of the rear inner door structures and was similarly applied at all the plants. For interior restoration purposes, the bodies were first primered, then the caulking was applied, followed by installing the floor drain plugs. Once completed, the body was then sprayed the body color, and this color oversprayed onto those areas.

In all cases, the bodies were primed first, then sprayed with their respective colored paint choice. The paint was oversprayed onto the bottom of the belly, around the rear bumper areas, wheel tubs, and the outer edges of the firewall. Some plants sprayed the blackout paint onto the firewall, then the body color while others did the opposite, so good detective work prior to paint stripping will help you determine how yours was done.

Primer by Location at the Plant

The front sheet metal was manufactured and painted in the assembly-plant area. These pieces were covered in an e-coat primer and would not match the rest of the body's primer, which was done in the Fischer Body plant. When painted with the chosen body color, the edges of the fenders and hood will have body-colored overspray on the backsides of them. This, like any

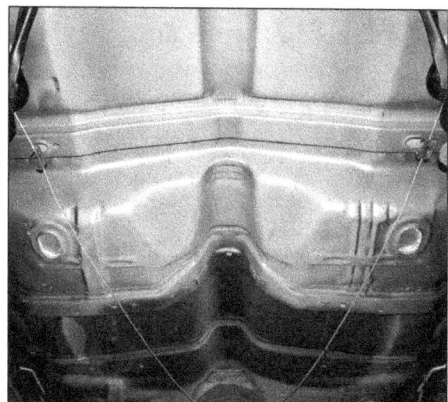

This is a good example of an Atlanta floorpan where the plant used a greenish gray primer. Also seen here is the body-color overspray, in this case Fathom Blue, as well as the assembly-line-sprayed sound deadener. This varied on every car because they were sprayed by humans within a limited amount of time between cars.

All plants were fairly careless with the paint application with regard to oversprays. This will carry over onto areas such as the rocker floor area, the tail panel, wheelhouses, and firewall ends. How much if any that you apply will be strictly up to you or your restorer.

CHAPTER 6

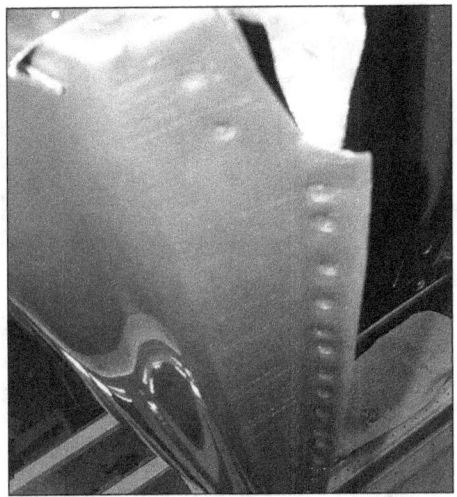

When originally painted at the factory, the painter seldom concentrated on getting paint into areas that were not readily seen or easily accessible by the applicator's spray gun, so these areas will be thin, such as the bottom side of the rockers, that were replicated during the restoration.

Another area that was often missed by heavy paint application was the doorjamb area around the hinges. Due to the limited amount of time a painter had between cars, they would concentrate on the outer body while skimping on areas that were not easily seen. It is up to you how or if you want to replicate this area.

other part of the car, can vary dramatically from car to car and plant to plant. Many people do not like this overspray when restoring their cars and will choose to leave it off. The same holds true for the belly pan and interior pan overspray. If you choose not to use this overspray method, it can save you both time and money but will not be restored to how the car was originally built.

While on the subject and before you spray the body color onto your car, you may also want to determine how accurately you want to restore your car compared to how it was originally sprayed. The paint applicators had a very limited amount of time between cars to get them sprayed. Therefore, they concentrated on getting a nice paint application to the main body while concentrating less on how nice it was in areas such as the rocker bottoms, tail panel, the bottoms of the quarter panels, and the doorjamb. These more often than not will have little paint on them from the factory, and the primer color will instead be seen. Many owners do not like this look and therefore may choose to put a full-coverage color coat on their cars, while others want to replicate exactly how their cars were built. The choice is completely up to you. More often than not, a high-end muscle car will go the authentic route while the lower-end cars will be restored with full paint coverage.

Solvent and Waterborne Basecoats

The two-stage paint system, or what is more commonly known as basecoat clear coat, was introduced in the 1980s. Prior to that, there were single-stage paints such as acrylic enamels and lacquer. These products performed two roles, both color and gloss in the same application. Although single-stage paints are still around, the technology has changed immensely. Today's acrylic urethane single-stage paints use a stronger resin. This helps with what is called color hold, or the resistance to fading. They are more durable than the older technology.

When it comes to basecoat, there are a couple of options. You can use solvent basecoat or waterborne basecoat. When used correctly, both products will give you the look that you want, but making the decision on which to use may fall on the environment that your car will be sprayed in. Will you or your painter be spraying the car in a controlled environment (a heated paint booth) or will you be spraying it in one of the bays in your garage? The sheet metal temperature and the amount

A good example of the bottom side of a hood that was oversprayed at the factory during the paint process and replicated during the restoration. The amount of overspray can vary from little if any to almost full coverage of the bottom of the hood.

of airflow that moves over your car while painting will be important to achieve a show-quality finish.

Solvent Basecoat

Solvent basecoat such as PPG's Deltron 2000 (DBC) is a premium-quality basecoat that will work well in different shop conditions and spraying environments. Although it is best to spray in a controlled environment, that may not be an option for those who choose to paint their project themselves. This basecoat gives you the option of choosing a solvent to reduce the color according to the temperature in the environment in which the car is being painted in. There are five different DT reducers to choose from ranging from cooler temperatures of 60°F to warmer temperatures of 95°F. Keep in mind that when reading the product sheet, the dry time, flash time, and pot life are based on a sheet metal temperature of 70°F.

Every coat of basecoat applied should leave you with 0.4 mils of dry film build. The number of coats that you will need to spray may be determined by the amount needed to achieve proper coverage and hiding. Some colors are more transparent than others and may need additional coats to cover. It is recommended that you spray a test panel, such as a spray out card, prior to painting anything on your car. This step should have been taken earlier in the restoration when verifying the correct color match. This will give you a good idea of how many coats of color will be needed before you begin spraying the car.

Waterborne Basecoat

The latest technology in basecoats are the waterborne products. Although waterborne paint technology was first introduced to the OEM assembly plants in 1986, the PPG version that we use today is Envirobase High Performance (EHP). This basecoat was introduced to paint shops in 2006. As of 2013, there were more than 28,000 body shops worldwide using this basecoat. With its latest technology, it is the most advanced basecoat available today.

Some of the advantages to using EHP are less odor and improved air quality. EHP also gives you better metallic control over solvent basecoat all the while using less product to achieve coverage. Where solvent basecoats are said to leave you with roughly 0.4 mils of film build per coat, waterborne basecoats are half that, leaving you with a smoother, flatter surface to apply clear coat. This product was engineered to reduce volatile organic compounds (VOC) and is environmentally friendly.

Waterborne basecoats are much different than solvent; they require a dedicated waterborne equipment, such as a paint gun, and the process in which the basecoat dries is totally different than solvent. The flash times are enhanced by creating turbulent airflow across the wet waterborne basecoat. Do not use your spray gun as an air dryer. It will cause the basecoat to dry up and plug the fluid tip in the gun.

There are many different options out there for air-dry equipment and with a wide range in prices. The least expensive are the handheld paint drying gun. This handheld gun attaches into the spray-line air hose in your paint booth and is used to direct turbulent air across the painted surface, speeding up the flash time and the dry time. Thinning this product so that it can be sprayed through a paint gun is also much different

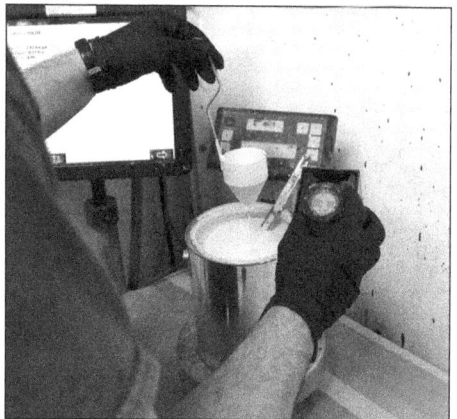

When spraying waterborne basecoat, the spray viscosity of it is very important for correct color match, dry times, and even how the waterborne basecoat will lay down. Depending on the temperature and the humidity, the spray viscosity can change from day to day, so be sure to check it every time you spray.

than solvent basecoats. For example, where solvent basecoats will use a mixing ratio such as one part color to one part solvent, waterborne basecoats are thinned using deionized water and a viscosity cup. This is a cup with a small hole or orifice in the bottom that permits the flow of the basecoat through it. Just submerge the cup in the paint, lift it out, and time how long it takes to drain the cup. It cannot be emphasized more as to how important it is to check the viscosity of the basecoat every time you spray. The product sheet for EHP states that the sprayable viscosity range is between 23 and 28 seconds.

It has been found that most colors spray best at 23 seconds. Temperature, humidity, air movement, and film buildup will affect the dry time of the waterborne basecoats. Spraying in a controlled environment with adequate airflow is very important with this product. Waterborne basecoats will also give you better metallic control and color matching over solvent basecoats. Keep in mind that waterborne basecoats cannot be wiped down with any solvent or waterborne cleaners before clear coating. Doing so will remove the color from the panel. If you are not spraying in a controlled environment, use of waterborne basecoats is not recommended.

Sanding Your Primer

If you are sanding your primer sealer prior to spraying color, keep in mind that because of the minimum film build, waterborne basecoats are only able to fill an 800-grit sand scratch or finer. If you sand your sealer with anything courser than 800 grit, the scratch could show up in the basecoat. Sanding with an interface pad on an orbital (DA) sander will work best. Because the film build per coat of waterborne basecoat is much less than solvent basecoat, it will need a finer scratch to cover them up.

Clear Coat

By now you should have an idea of what look you are expecting from the final finish on the car. By that I mean, "Are you looking for a totally flat, slicked down, show-quality finish or are you wanting a more factory look that will have some texture or what is known as orange peel in the clear?" Depending on how aggressively you are planning on blocking the clear coat, the sanding and buffing process could remove a couple of mils of clear. You will need to make sure enough clear coat has been sprayed to compensate for the sanding and buffing process. The selection of a buffing system is very important. They are not all the same; therefore, a complete system should be used as well as a sanding system. Clears should be fully cured before sanding and buffing. This will depend on your spraying conditions. The longer the clear dries, the better.

Clear Coat Choices

There are many different clears to choose from. For the most part, they are all designed to give you the look that you want, but not all of them will perform or spray the same. Some clear coats are higher in solid content, which makes them thicker or higher in viscosity. The speed which a clear dries and cures is also important, especially depending on your spraying conditions. Normally, a slow-drying clear works best for restoration to help the flow and appearance of the clear.

When fully cured, some clears will be softer than others. The softer clear coats will sand and buff much easier and faster than the harder ones. The down side to using a softer clear coat is that they will mar and scratch easier than clear coats that are harder. Where the harder clears are more mar and scratch resistant, they will also require more effort and take longer to get sanded and buffed. They must also be final sanded with a finer-grit paper.

The spray conditions in which the car is being painted will make a difference when choosing which clear to use. Are you painting the car in a manufactured paint booth or a homemade designated spray area? The amount of air that flows over the vehicle during the paint process will change the flash time between coats and the overall dry time. Is the paint booth heated and/or is it a bake booth? Heat and dry time are very important for the clear coat to reach a full cure.

Even though they are dry to the touch and seem to sand easily, this does not mean that they are fully cured. Sanding and buffing before they have reached a full cure means that there are still solvents trapped in the clear coat and may cause the shine to die back over time. Bake cycles from your paint booth and keeping the sheet metal temperatures at 70°F or above for an extended period of time are what is needed to drive the solvents out speeding up the cure time. If baking is not an option for you, pulling the painted body and sheet metal outside on a sunny day works great. Have you ever touched a car outside on a sunny day? That can easily get the sheet metal temperatures up to 120°F, and best of all it costs you nothing.

Sand and Buff

As much as we like to give credit to the painter for the awesome-looking finish, as a painter I must be honest with you. That show-quality finish comes from countless hours of wet sanding after the clear coat has fully cured. When your car rolls out of the paint booth, there is still much more work to be done. The wet sanding and buffing process can easily take 100 to 125 hours to achieve that totally flat show-quality finish. That look is what we call "slicked," and that may be one of the hardest, most time-consuming, tedious jobs you will tackle on this restoration. Not to mention you have to be very careful not to sand through the clear into the basecoat, especially on the corners, edges, and body lines.

Sanding too much clear coat from the panel will also cause the gloss level to fade and will leave you with a less-durable finish. What grit sandpaper you start with and what type of sanding block you use makes a difference in how flat of a finish you will end up with. If you are planning on a slicked down show-quality finish, you will need to start blocking with P600-grit wet sandpaper, and you will need to use hard blocks. Different shapes and sizes are available for cutting the flat areas and for fitting in the curves and contours of the panels.

Using P600 grit will block the panel the flattest, sanding away the texture and the orange in the clear coat. Sand only till the orange peel is gone, removing only what is necessary to flatten the panel. Be sure to stay off of the corners and edges of the panels with the coarser grit because they are the easiest to sand through. Now that there is a 600-grit sand scratch in the clear coat, you can apply graphite guide coat to an application pad and rub it over the sanded clear. 3M Dry Guide Coat is used in the dry primer sanding process to identify surface imperfections, such as pinholes and deep scratches in primer.

When sanding polyester filler, it ensures the filler is flat with no ripples and that the body-styling lines and contours are straight and correct. It also ensures the total primed area is sanded prior to topcoating. You will repeat this process using P800-, P1000-, and P1200-grit sandpaper with the harder sanding blocks. As you go to the finer grit of P1500, P2000, and 2500, you can use softer-block-style sanding blocks.

The reason for using the softer pads at this point is that you are finished with the flattening process and are only sanding to remove the scratch left behind from the previous courser grit. You will notice that every time you move to a finer grit the sanding process will take you longer than the previous one. I recommend only using the guide coat up to the P2000-grit sandpaper. The reason for this is that we have noticed that a dry guide coat can be coarser than the finishing grits of 2500, 3000, and finally 5000 and can put a stray scratch back into the clear coat. The 3000- and 5000-grit papers can also be done by hand, using a soft pad, but another option is to machine sand by using a 3/8 orbit DA sander with an interface pad.

You will notice as you sand through the finer grits that each step will add more and more shine back to the clear coat. If you are wanting more of a factory-looking finish with a bit of orange peel, you will want to use the same process, but start with P1500 sandpaper. After your first initial cut using P600 grit or whatever grit you decide to start wet sanding with, I recommend that you run the body and sheet metal through another bake cycle. Sanding reopens that skimmed-over surface of the clear coat, and baking helps drive any solvents that are still remaining. If baking is not an option, remember you can move the car outside on a nice sunny day using the heat from the sun to do the same job.

How Much Does My Paint Job Cost?

Often you will hear someone ask the question, "How much did that paint job cost?" or "How much would it cost to give my car a paint job?" A paint job may have been something that you got years ago, but nowadays when restoring your car, there is so much more that goes into the refinishing process for it to be called a paint job. You need to ask yourself what quality of refinish job do I want: daily driver, high-quality restoration, or high-end show quality? Not only do you need to know which paint materials to use, you need to know how and when to use them.

Knowing what it takes to make them perform and dry properly is important, as is knowing what spray

This is the normal appearance of a hood just after it was painted. As you can see, there is some orange peel in the finish. This would be more of an original factory-looking finish, although this is not normally what you or your customer may want to replicate.

The same hood is shown after it was wet sanded and polished as well as having the stripes applied. As can be seen, this will give you a much deeper-looking finish. It should also be noted that the stripes should always be painted on a correct restoration. They should also be sprayed on top of the clear so that you can feel them and they do not meld into the color coat.

gun to use and what size of fluid tip should be installed, how many coats to apply and the amount of film build or mils per coat that is recommended, the flash time between each coat, and total time needed at 70°F for that particular product to dry and cure properly. Does the product you are using desire a force dry from a bake booth or heat lamp, or is air drying acceptable? At 70°F, it may take weeks or months to completely cure depending on air movement, temperature, humidity, and film build.

Using a heat lamp or bake booth greatly speeds up the curing process. Your product needs to be completely cured before moving on to the next step to get the best results. Not doing so or rushing will cause you nothing but headaches and issues down the road. What are the compatible surfaces that you can spray a certain product over, and what is the proper surface preparation before you do? Because today's paint materials are so sophisticated, it is important to follow the guidelines on the product sheet to ensure that you get the best results.

Have you ever looked at a restoration a few years after it was completed and noticed that there were sand scratches that appeared or maybe the gloss level on the car had died back a little? Often, that is caused by poor surface preparation, misuse of the paint materials, and less-than-standard shop conditions. The PPG custom restoration guide states that "standard conditions are temperatures, humidity and air flow data, and are used to determine a paint product's dry time, cure time, pot life and all general performance characteristics." Using anything less than standard conditions could cause a less-than-acceptable restoration.

Conclusion

Whether you choose to hire out the bodywork and paint or attempt to do it yourself, you must come to terms with the cost, efforts, and time it takes to complete your project. Out of the entire restoration, the paint and body will be the most scrutinized and first-seen part of your Chevelle that everyone who comes in contact with it will judge. Mess this part up, and the rest of the car will not pass muster. This is one area where you cannot skimp, and the only way to do it right regardless of which avenue you choose is to budget the money for the work. You do not want to stop this part of the project due to running out of funds. Doing so will most assuredly end the progress of the project, and it will never get completed.

If you hire out a professional to do the body and paint, make sure you are both on the same page before a wrench is ever turned. Get an estimate in writing as well as how long the project will take. Most anyone will tell you they cannot give you a carved-in-stone estimate until first removing the paint from the car and seeing what is under it. That being said, anyone who has worked on a number of Chevelles will still have a good idea what it will cost and how long it will take as well as pad the estimate to cover some unforeseen issues.

Have the money to complete the project set aside; do not use it for anything other than the bodywork and paint, and never miss or be late on a payment because your car will then go to the rear of the shop and become just another body-shop hostage. It is a good idea to stay on the good side of your painter and be there when he or she needs you as well as stop by periodically to check on progress and that you are satisfied with their work. If you live out of state, communicate no less than bimonthly. Communication is key here. Have your painter send lots of photos to you every month. If they do not take photos, find another shop.

Catching issues early on is as much of a key to making this a successful marriage as having something go wrong down the road will be a sure sign of divorce. If this part of the restoration turns into a nightmare, rest assured that the entire project will turn into the same. If you and your painter work well together, at or under budget, in a timely manner, and the project comes back to you looking better than you could ever expect, the rest of the restoration will seem fairly easy and exciting.

Your project is done. Take a deep breath, stand back, and take it all in. You can now understand why not cutting corners at this stage of the project will pay dividends when it is completed.

CHAPTER 7

ELECTRICAL

Charging into your electrical wiring system (pun intended) can strike fear into the bravest souls. With a myriad of wires, connectors, circuit breakers, fuses, and electrical devices from lights, horns, starter systems, electric windows, wipers, etc., you can see your electrical system plays a vital role in keeping our Chevelles running and operating properly.

The most meticulous $150,000-plus concours restoration can be frustrating if the car won't start when you turn the ignition key or some electrical accessory does not work. It never ceases to amaze seeing a very-high-dollar Chevelle go across an auction block only to see a brake light not working.

If your wiring is suspect and/or has been extensively modified by a previous owner, it would be a better choice to replace what you have with a quality aftermarket reproduction than repair what you have. Choosing either a factory-style replacement or a more modern wiring and fuse box system would be dependent on your overall intention for the car.

Before you do, and if you are not an electrical guru, document and photograph all your electrical connections. Note the component you are removing the harness from and the wiring colors. Aftermarket universal wiring kits and even some original equipment replacement wiring kits may have different connectors. It is good to know what the connector and wires it contains is supposed to have.

A Checklist of What Works and What Doesn't

There are a number of books and guides explaining automotive electrical systems on the market today along with many aftermarket suppliers of wiring kits. Before you tear all that old wiring out of your Chevelle, it is a good idea to ensure, as much as you can, that your current electrical system and all electrical components are working beforehand. If your project is in any drivable condition at all, any small items that need attention should be attended to first.

- Are there any apparent fixes or upgrades by previous owners, such as an aftermarket radio/speakers or auxiliary gauges added?
- Do these appear to be working?
- Does the car start and stay running?

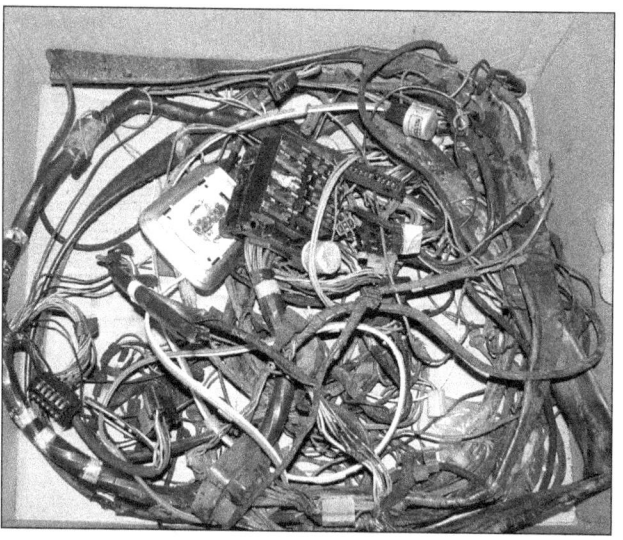

This is a typical 1970 through 1972 interior wiring bundle. Unless you are thoroughly familiar with the particular year you are restoring or rebuilding, be sure to tag all the wiring connections before doing this. Even if you are planning to replace everything electrical, it is good to know what the original connections and harness looks like.

CHEVELLE RESTORATION AND AUTHENTICITY GUIDE: 1970–1972

CHAPTER 7

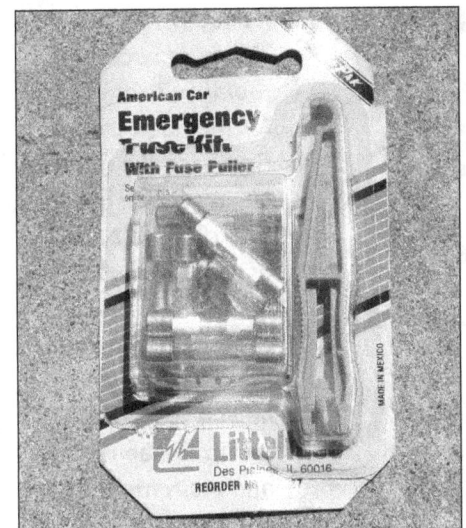

Glass fuses are what one typically finds in cars of this era. These come in various lengths and amp ratings. Your fuse box has the amp ratings and major component silk screened by each fuse. This emergency kit has several fuses with different amp ratings. The fuse puller is a very handy item to have on hand.

- Do all bulbs and switches for headlamps, taillamps, parking lamps, turn signal, and brake lamps work as expected?
- Does the horn work?
- If equipped with electric windows and/or an electric convertible top, do they work?
- Do the current gauges—such as fuel level, water temperature, clock (if equipped), ammeter, etc.—work? To be honest here, clocks in a 40-plus-year-old Chevelle seldom work anymore, so that issue may deserve a pass.
- Do dash lamps, glove-compartment lamp, dome or under-dash/underhood/trunk (if equipped) courtesy lamps work?
- Does a circuit continue to blow fuses? Do you have spares on hand to help find the culprit?

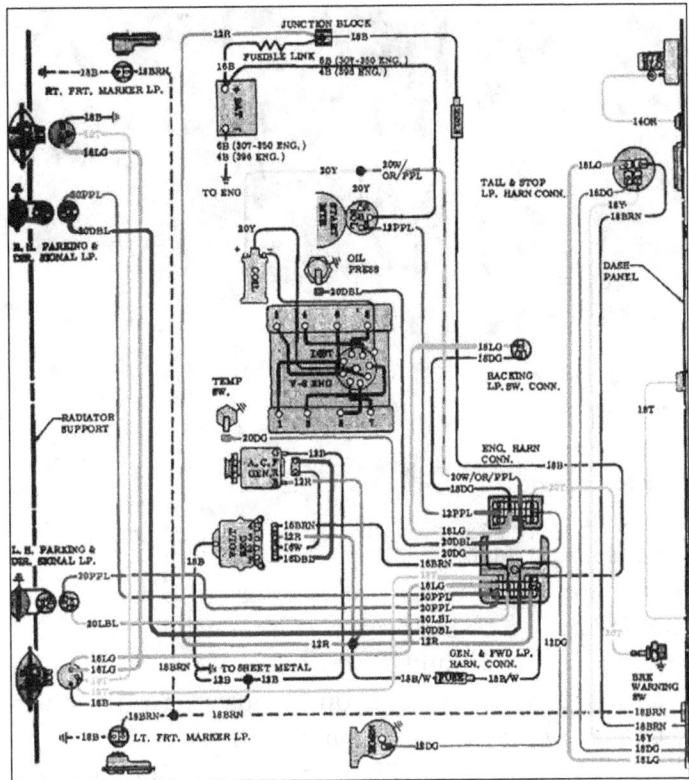

The basic engine compartment and front-end wiring harness schematic shows wiring to such under-the-hood items as the starter, ignition coil, headlamps, parking lamps, side markers, generator, and regulator. This example is colored, and the gauge of the wire is noted such as 20PPL is a purple 20-gauge wire.

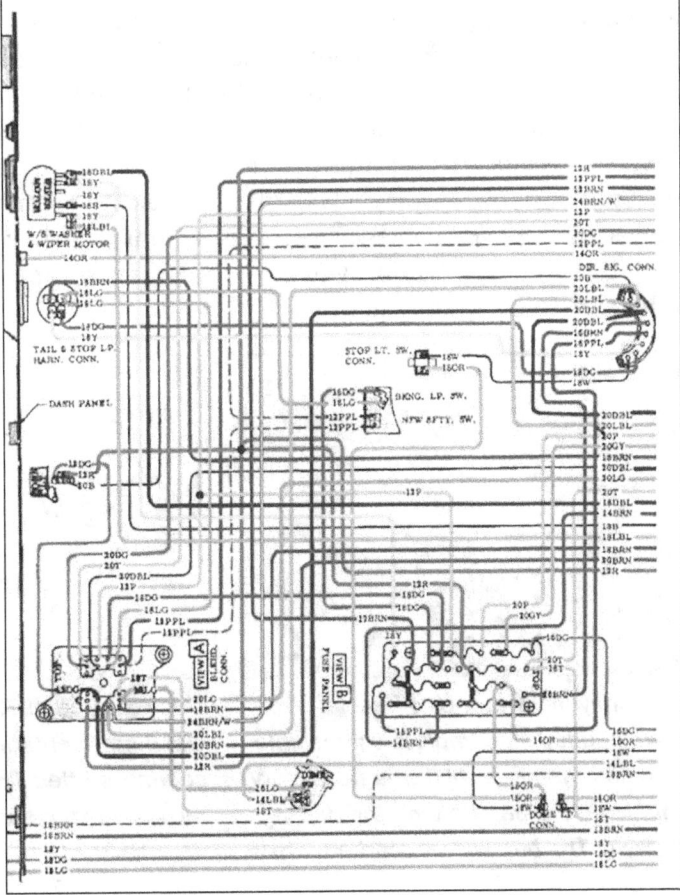

Like the basic engine compartment and front-end wiring harness schematic, this fuse block schematic shows the routing of wiring for basic components along with wire color and gauge. This example is colored, and the gauge of the wire is noted such as 12R for a red 12-gauge wire.

ELECTRICAL

Printed circuit board configurations vary with their use: a gauge-optioned dash will have a different printed circuit board than one with warning lamps. Note all the dash lamps (the round black sockets) are fed from the circuit board as opposed to the old method of a wire to each lamp.

It is easy to see how a printed circuit replaces a lot of wiring for the dash cluster. Compare the relatively clean printed circuit board with a mass of wires and connectors used for other components behind the dash; imagine having individual wiring to each gauge and instrument-panel lamp.

If the answer to any of these is no, now is a good time to inspect the switches, bulbs, fuses, etc. to see if it is a simple fix or something possibly more serious that will need to be addressed in the future.

Since there are so many variations of components and options, we can't possibly cover every possibility within the restraints of this book. However, we will cover the most common areas and popular options. There are some aftermarket companies that make general wiring schematics for your model-year Chevelle, and even the factory assembly instruction manuals have basic wiring diagrams in their books.

Since your classic Chevelle does not have on-board computers, you should not have to worry about electronic control modules (ECM) unless you are converting to some sort of electronic fuel injection system in the future. If that may be the case, worry about that when the time comes. Their instructions generally assume you have a factory wiring system to begin with.

Circuits

The 1970 through 1972 Chevelle gauge clusters are outfitted with printed circuits instead of individual wiring for gauges and lamps. This was more cost effective for General Motors and it saved space and reduced weight. Not to mention, it eliminates a lot of extra wiring. On the positive side, if something goes bad, you can simply replace the printed circuit. On the negative side, if one thing goes bad, you have to replace the entire printed circuit. Unlike printed circuit boards in

This 1970 LS6-optioned Chevelle with a U14 Special Instrumentation dash was pulled as complete as possible to keep major components together until it was necessary to disassemble the unit. Note the bag holding the dash assembly mounting screws. The bag will be marked later when the dash is taken apart.

This restored 1970 LS6 dash cluster features U14 Special Instrumentation. Note this particular carrier is for a column-shifted TH400-transmission car with the shift pattern below the speedometer. This carrier is easily identified as a 1970 as the numbers, words, and tic marks are white. Those for 1971 and 1972 are a light green.

CHAPTER 7

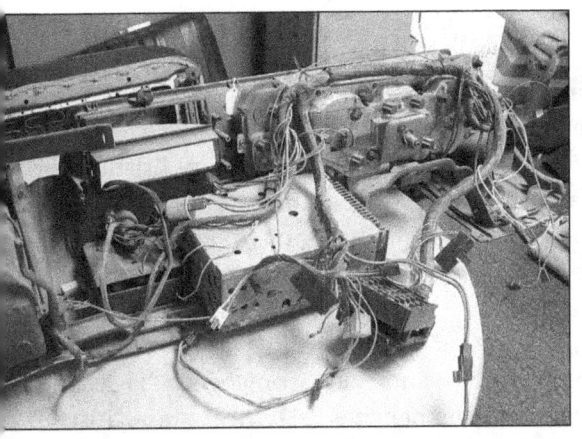

Quite a number of special connectors, different wiring colors, etc., are shown here. Unless you have done a number of these, be sure to take good notes (and photos if possible) so you can remember where everything goes down the road when it all goes back together.

The electrical relay used for the Transmission Controlled Spark (TCS) switch (part number 3961573) is typically mounted to the wiring gutter, although its placement on the gutter can vary from plant to plant. It was often mounted in the center of the gutter (as shown here) but has also been found on the passenger's side of the gutter.

If your Chevelle is optioned with RPO ZL2 Special Ducted Air Hood System, this relay (part number 4540898) comes into play. The relay is typically mounted on the firewall just behind the distributor, but the exact position can vary from plant to plant. This example happens to be a 1970 Arlington-built Chevelle.

An alternate mounting position for the relay (part number 4540898) is mounted at an angle just to the passenger's side of the windshield washer pump. This example happens to be a 1970 Kansas City-built Chevelle but has been found on Arlington-built Chevelles as well.

computers or many computer-controlled devices, these printed circuits are flexible plastic with conductive copper circuits embedded in them.

It is easy to see why a printed circuit replaced a lot of wiring.

Switches

Electrical switches and components eventually wear out and/or get corroded connections over time; now is a good time to find out what switches or components are in need of replacement, such as the headlamp switch, ignition switch, windshield washer/wiper motors, heater/air-conditioning switches, brake light switches, voltage regulators, etc. If you are doing a concours restoration or just want the security of knowing your various switches are new, it is a good idea to determine if the current ones are working; there may be electrical gremlins elsewhere that could cause them to appear inoperative.

Transmission Controlled Spark

A Transmission Controlled Spark (TCS) system was one of GM's ideas to combat emissions. The intent was to limit the advanced timing by way of vacuum advance to the distributor only when it was needed in the hopes of reducing emission output. It's a three-piece system: the TCS relay is mounted on the wiring gutter, the solenoid is mounted on the right front side of the intake manifold, and a switch is in the side of the transmission. Control of the distributor's vacuum advance is accomplished by the two-position, solenoid-operated valve. The relay is used for both hot and cold override conditions. When the engine's coolant temperature is below 63°F or above 232°F, the relay de-energizes the solenoid and allows full vacuum to the distributor.

There are wire harnesses that extend to the trunk area for such components such as the tail/stop/turn lamps, trunk lamp, license-plate lamps, and fuel-level gauge. This harness, often called a ribbon cable, runs along the floor under the carpeting and is flat to avoid chaffing. It is held in place by clips that simply hold the cable against the floor to keep it from shifting position.

On sport coupes, sedans, station wagons, and El Caminos, the

ELECTRICAL

Often referred to as a ribbon cable since the wiring harness is flat, this assembly takes power to all electrical components in the rear of the car: tail/stop lamps, backup lamps, trunk lamp (if equipped), fuel tank sending unit, and license-plate lamps. Welded-in clips keep the cable from shifting.

This photo before a restoration shows the routing of the standard ribbon cable and additional accessory wiring in the lower portion of the image for additional options such as rear speakers, rear defogger, etc. The red oxide primer indicates this is an Arlington-built Chevelle.

The dome-light wiring of this sport coupe is one place you may want to consider leaving the wiring as is. Attempting to reroute it between the top's frame and roof panel may be a bit of a challenge. Be cautious of the plastic clips retaining the two wires because they become brittle over time and can easily be broken.

dome-lamp wiring runs inside the roof panel, so care should be taken when servicing this area. The clips holding the wiring in place are plastic and can become very brittle over time. Convertibles do not have a dome lamp for obvious reasons.

Test Equipment

There are some very basic and inexpensive electrical test instruments that will greatly assist you in troubleshooting and tracking down those electrical gremlins.

Jumper Wires

Jumper wires are primarily used to find an open electrical circuit. An open circuit can be the result of a wire internally corroded and not readily visible, corroded connections, or simply a blown fuse or burned-out bulb. Jumper wires are typically fabricated from various lengths of standard automotive wire with some type of connector at each end (a male or female spade connector, alligator clip, or pin connector). A well-equipped toolbox will have several of these in various lengths, wire sizes, and connectors to help troubleshoot any number of problems.

If you are working around other electrical components, insulated spade connectors and alligator clips should be seriously considered to prevent accidental grounding or sparks that cause more problems or an electrical fire. Continuity tests on hot wiring circuits are often necessary; caution is the concern here due to the possibility of a fire.

Speaking of fires, a good fire extinguisher is always a handy thing to have close by when working on your Chevelle. Never use water, foam spray, or wet chemicals on an electrical fire; ABC powder or carbon dioxide are the preferred methods to extinguish an electrical fire.

Naturally, when conducting a continuity test on a negative circuit, fire is not so much an issue, and disconnecting the negative battery cable is advisable. Always use safety glasses when disconnecting or connecting cables to the battery. An acid-based battery can explode, causing severe burns or blindness if acid gets in your eyes.

12-Volt Test Light

A 12-volt test light is used to check circuits with current flowing through them and is used for voltage and ground tests. A variety of 12-volt test lights are available, but they typically have three main components: a ground clip, a probe, and a lamp. Many look like a typical screwdriver with a wire lead coming out of one end and a pointed metal probe with a lamp of some kind internal to the handle. These can range from under $10 to $100 for ones with all the bells and whistles with 20-foot leads and various connectors.

Connect the ground clip to a good, bare-metal ground and use the pointed end to touch the suspect connector, or prick a wire's covering. If the lamp lights, you have good electrical current flow through the wiring. If your test lamp does not illuminate, you know you have no power up to that point and the circuit is open. Move the test closer to the power source until the lamp illuminates. When it does, you know the open circuit is somewhere between that point and the last point tested where no connectivity was indicated.

The 12-volt test lamp does not mean that 12 volts are present, only that *some* voltage is present. A 12-volt test lamp should never be used to test electronic ignition spark plug or coil wires.

Self-Powered Test Light

A self-powered test light has its own power source, typically a 1.5-volt battery, and works the same as a 12-volt test lamp, except it does not require the Chevelle's battery to be connected. For this reason, your Chevelle's battery should be disconnected when using a self-powered test light. The same type of open-circuit or short-circuit testing can be performed. Never use a self-powered test lamp with the Chevelle's battery connected. A 12-volt circuit can easily burn out the 1.5-volt test lamp.

Open-Circuit Testing

Use a self-powered test light to check for open circuits. Before testing for open circuits, disconnect the battery or wiring-harness connector. If something simple like one taillamp is not working, it may just be a burned-out bulb. If both taillamps and the brake lamp are not working, it may still be the bulb, but it could also mean an open circuit. Connect the test light to a good ground and start probing sections of the circuit. If the test lamp does not light, the circuit is open. Keep probing along the circuit until the test lamp illuminates.

Short-Circuit Testing

Using a self-powered test light, you can check for shorts in a circuit by isolating the circuit from both power and ground. Connect the test-light clip to a good ground and probe along the circuit. If the light comes on, there is a short somewhere in the circuit. Keep probing the circuit until the light fails to illuminate.

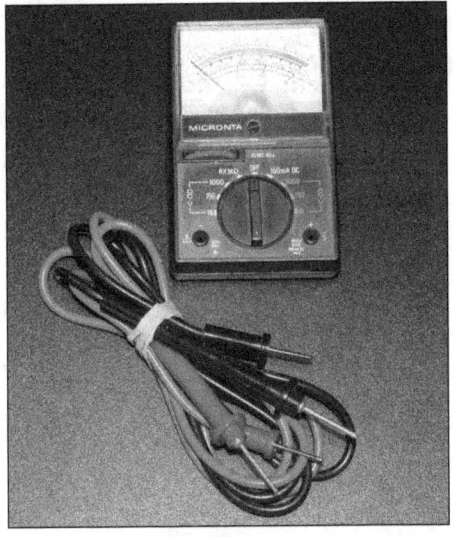

Multimeters range from very basic units like this one that reads in analog format to a digital readout. These can range from a few dollars ($8 to $10) to hundreds of dollars for heavy-duty industrial-strength units, depending on their range and intended use.

The battery in a self-powered test light does not provide much current. You can check the battery in the self-powered test light by touching the ground clip to the probe to see if the lamp lights up.

Voltmeter

A voltmeter is used to, wait for it, measure voltage at any point in a circuit. A voltmeter can also be used to test the voltage and continuity in a circuit indicating current flow from one end of the circuit to another. Voltmeters have various scales and a dial to select various ranges of voltage. Small, handheld voltmeters are typically powered by a 9-volt battery and have two leads for testing. The black lead is the negative (–) lead and should be connected to the negative side of the circuit. The red lead is the positive (+) lead and should be connected to the positive side of the circuit.

A voltmeter can be connected in parallel or in series in a circuit. When using a voltmeter in parallel, only a small current will flow through the voltmeter's current path, the rest will flow through the normal circuit, and the circuit will work normally. When connected in series, only a small amount of current will flow through the voltmeter's current path. The overall circuit may not work correctly, but the voltmeter will show if the circuit is complete or not. Voltmeters are almost always used in parallel since a voltmeter has a very high resistance to current flow.

Handheld voltmeter devices are often found in what is called a VOM (or DVOM for digital readout) volt-ohm-millimeter multimeter, meaning three measuring instruments on one device. These are available in analog or digital readout formats.

What Is Normal Voltage?

That question depends on what you are measuring. If you are looking to measure your battery's voltage, it should register 12.5 volts or more when not under any load, close to 12 volts under normal load, and even less under heavy load. Set your voltmeter's selector switch to its range of 15 volts or higher (different voltmeters will have different range choices). Setting the selector to too high of a voltage reading will be hard to read on an analog scale.

With the positive lead connected to the positive side of the battery, turn the ignition switch to the ON position (do not start the car). Briefly touch the negative lead to the negative side of the battery and read the scale. A charged battery should read 12.5 volts or a bit higher. If the meter reads below 12 volts, the battery may not be able to operate the electrical system properly.

Aftermarket voltmeter gauges are quickly overcoming ammeters. The hookup on a voltmeter is very simple: one wire to ground and one wire to an ignition hot (when ignition switch is on and/or the car is running) 12-volt source. A voltmeter only requires an 18-gauge wire. For obvious safety reasons, the battery's negative cable should be disconnected when wiring a voltmeter. When your Chevelle's battery is fully charged, a voltmeter should read about 12.5 volts. When the engine is running, the charging system of the car should get the voltmeter reading to anywhere from 13.8 to around 14.5 if there is no load on the charging system.

Your electric windshield wipers, heater/defroster, radio/stereo systems, etc. will cause a lower reading when in use. If the voltage runs under 14 volts for an extended period of time, it could run down the charge in your battery. If it runs under 14 volts with no load accessories running for very long, you should have your charging system checked. The same is true when indicated voltage goes above 15 volts, which is a good indication the voltage regulator may be causing a problem by allowing your charging system to overcharge, which can be harmful as well.

Chevelles equipped with RPO U14 Special Instrumentation or Instrument Panel Gauges (verbiage depends on the year of the option) include an ammeter. An ammeter requires a larger-gauge wire, typically 10 gauge or larger, and runs between the positive side of the battery and the alternator's charging wire. For obvious safety reasons, the battery's negative cable should be disconnected when wiring an ammeter.

Ammeter

The ammeter measures the amount of current flowing through a circuit in units of amperes (or amps). To get a bit technical, Ohm's law states the current flow in a circuit is equal to the circuit voltage divided by the total circuit resistance. Simply put, the more resistance (in ohms) a circuit has, the greater voltage required to achieve the same result. When you start your Chevelle, the starter solenoid requires voltage to engage and turn the starter causing an ammeter to show a temporary discharge from the battery.

After your Chevelle starts, voltage is supplied back to the battery via the alternator, so your ammeter will show a positive charge. If it does not, one of several things could be the culprit. The battery may not be capable of accepting the charge, the alternator may not be capable of producing the charge, or the voltage regulator may be bad (either not allowing the alternator to recharge the battery or, if the voltage regulator is burned out, by continually charging the battery and causing eventual damage to the battery).

An ammeter will also show a short negative reading when operating some accessories, such as headlamps, air conditioner, and even aftermarket stereo systems. A short negative reading is normal when the accessory is first turned on followed by a short positive reading if the alternator is capable of charging the battery again.

If your ammeter does not show a positive charge after starting or after turning on a high-load accessory, your alternator may not be up to the challenge of keeping your battery charged. An ammeter is always installed in series with the circuit so all current flowing through the circuit must also flow through the ammeter. Excessive current can blow fuses, trip circuit breakers, and damage a battery, while a reduced current can cause lights to be dim or motors such as the heater/air-conditioner blower, wipers, etc. to run slow.

Ohmmeter

An ohmmeter is designed to read the resistance of a circuit or component in ohms when there is no voltage applied to the circuit, and any voltage present can burn out an ohmmeter; be sure there is no voltage in the circuit being tested. Since an ohmmeter is self-powered (typically by a 9-volt battery), it can also be used as a circuit-continuity check for open or shorted circuits. The ohmmeter in a multimeter tool should have a selector switch for multiplication of the meter reading, such as 10, 100, 1000, and 10,000, and a calibration knob to be set to zero simply by touching the two multimeter leads together and setting the reading to zero. The internal battery can weaken with age; zeroing the meter will compensate for this. If in doubt, change your multimeter's internal battery.

The ohmmeter's internal resistance and voltage are known values, so the reading of the meter is the result of resistance of the circuit or component being tested. An internally corroded wire can cause abnormal resistance and thereby cause a larger amount of voltage to flow through the wiring and possibly overload the capability of the wiring itself.

Electrical Terms

We've been discussing various electrical terms such as voltage, amperage, and ohms, but what do they all mean? Think of your electrical system as a water system. Voltage is like water pressure. A garden hose has no pressure if the water source is turned off. Like the garden hose that is turned off, you have no voltage if your electrical system is turned off. Turn the water source on and it fills the garden hose with water under pressure; how much pressure depends on the size of the hose and the force of the water source. Too much pressure, or voltage, can be just as harmful as too little pressure.

An ammeter measures the volume of electricity in a circuit or water going through the garden hose. As you increase the pressure, more water will flow through a given-size garden hose just as more electricity will flow through a given-wire size. An ammeter should use an 8- or 10-gauge wire. A smaller-gauge wire will not be able to withstand the pressure of the electrical circuit and will burn up just as too much pressure through a small garden hose would cause it to burst.

Aftermarket automotive ammeters are typically ranged from –60 to +60 and should only be used on vehicles with alternators rated at 60 amps or less. Chevelle's optional gauges have a visible range of –40 to +40. An ammeter will read negative amperage when the battery is providing most of the current, such as when you first start your Chevelle. It should immediately switch to a positive amperage as the car's charging system replenishes the battery, and the gauge should eventually return to the centered zero (0) mark or slightly on the positive side of zero within a few minutes. Naturally, any load on the electrical system, such as the heater/defroster, wipers, etc., running continually will take a bit more time to recharge the battery. Any continually high reading in the 10- to 20-amp range with no accessories running is a sign of an electrical issue or you may have a weak battery that will not hold a charge.

Ohms are simply resistance to the flow of electricity. Just how much resistance there is in a circuit depends, naturally, on the circuit. Typically, an ohm meter is used to detect breaks in a circuit as discussed earlier. An ohmmeter can also be helpful in determining the resistance of electrical parts, such as spark-plug wires. The less resistance a spark-plug wire has, the more electrical energy it can supply to the spark plug. A spark-plug wire with an excessive resistance can cause misfires and a rough-running engine.

If you are running aftermarket spark-plug wires, you should check with the manufacturer of the wire set to see what the resistance should be for those wires. Resistance on spark-plug wires is generally measured per foot of spark-plug wire. Aftermarket spark-plug wire kits often come packaged as universal kits and typically have one of three spark-plug ends: 90-degree, 45-degree, or 135-degree ends. The distributor ends of the wires are left without a terminal end and requires they be cut to proper length. Instructions supplied with the spark-plug wiring kit explain how to strip the wire and crimp the terminal ends, and the wires are precut to various lengths. The spark-plug wires should be measured, cut, and terminated so they are long enough to reach from the spark plug to the distributor with very little extra spark-plug wire. First, it not only looks sloppy to have a 4-foot wire looped around your master cylinder when a 2-foot wire will do the job, you are adding extra resistance in the longer-than-needed wire. Original equipment replacement wires are generally assembled for a specific engine-size application and should not need to be modified.

Spark-plug wires should never, I repeat *never*, be taped or zip-tied together in a bundle. Spark-plug wire dividers/separators are used by Chevrolet for a reason. Often original wire separators get old and brittle, and you may find one or more has been broken. It can be difficult to find original equipment replacements. During inspection or tear down of your car, it's a good time to begin the search for original-type replacements. Spark-plug wire dividers/separators keep two or more wires from chafing against each other as well as parts of your engine, such as valve covers and exhaust manifolds. Separators will also keep two spark-plug wires from arcing and misfiring.

In the aftermarket world, there are literally dozens of choices available for dressing up your spark-plug wire routing as well as a great variety of colors, sizes, and materials for your spark-plug wire replacement.

Multimeters

As noted previously, one type of multimeter reads volts/amps/ohms, but there are certainly other meters with more than one purpose such as a tachometer/dwell meter to assist in setting the correct ignition points gap and engine RPM. Multimeters come in both analog and digital versions and can be small enough to hold in your hand or part of larger test-equipment station.

Wire Gauges

Automotive wire comes in many colors, both single solid and multiple colors, and many gauges or thicknesses. Their use will dictate the gauge, and the manufacturer of the wiring harness (the collection of wiring) will determine the colors they will use for a particular application. It's easier to trace a wire of a certain color and gauge through a wire loom from one point to another. Imagine having a bundle of black wires running from under the dash to the engine compartment and how much time would be wasted trying to find one that isn't completing its circuit.

Automotive wiring is measured by American Wire Gauge (AWG) standards. Typically, the gauges of wire in a Chevelle can run from 4 to 20 gauge with the larger-gauge number being a smaller wire in overall diameter, resistance, and capacity to handle amperage. While a 4-gauge wire (cable) might be appropriate for a battery cable, it wouldn't be applicable to a water-temperature sending unit or wiring your headlamps. As the cross section of the conductor decreases, the resistance increases along with the gauge size number. A wire with a higher gauge number will carry less current than a wire with a lower gauge number. A wire that is too small for the circuit you are using it on will add extra resistance plus an additional voltage drop to the circuit.

The wire size gauge refers to the size of the conductor itself, not the physical size of the wire with its covering; two wires may be the same gauge but have different diameters due to the thicker insulation on one relative to the other. Wires come on one of two forms for automotive use: single-strand and multi-strand.

As the name implies, a single-strand wire is one wire and typically found in components such as alternators, electric motors, and other devices not typically exposed to the elements. Multi-strand wires are made up of, wait for it, multiple wires in a single-covered conductor and may be individually routed or routed as part of a harness.

Factory assembly instruction manuals and numerous vehicle-specific how-to and shop repair manuals will have general wiring schematics for a given car with the gauge and colors often noted. In certain instances, printed circuit boards have replaced individual wiring in many Chevelle components—in particular the instrument panel, where space behind the dash is limited. A wiring harness will plug into the circuit board at a single point. Main power distribution circuits often use 10- or 12-gauge wire, such as primary alternator wire or wiring from the positive side of the battery to a junction block where other accessories get individual power. As wiring length increases, so does resistance in that wire. For example, an 18-gauge wire can carry a 10-amp load for about 10 feet with an acceptable voltage drop, but if that same load is needed over a longer distance, say 15 feet, the same load would need a heavier 16-gauge wire.

Luckily for most of us, the electrical engineers at General Motors figured all that out a long time ago, and standard wiring harnesses will work just fine. It's when you begin adding accessories such as aftermarket power windows, power seats, larger sound systems, etc., that these factors come into play. When buying aftermarket gauges or accessories, their instructions will typically tell you not only where to connect the required wires to but also what gauge wire to use.

If you are not going for a concours restoration and plan to add accessories, you might consider an

CHAPTER 7

aftermarket wiring kit from any number of suppliers in the market today, such as Painless Performance Products. Many times, these kits are

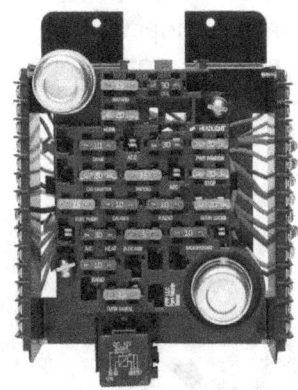

One aftermarket alternative to your wiring solution is a modern fuse box with blade fuses. This unit from Painless Performance includes hazard and turn flashers, a horn relay, and wiring for most major components needed for the 1970–1972 round-pod dash assembly complete with an instruction manual and lots of photos. (Photo Courtesy Painless Performance)

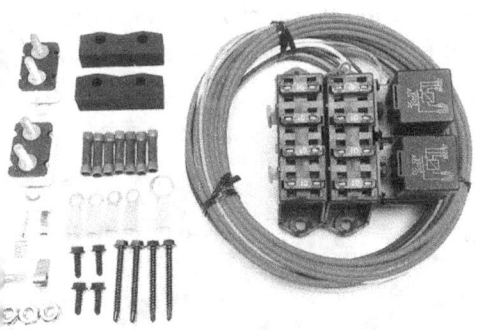

If you are adding additional electrical devices to your Chevelle, this CirKit accessory can come in very handy. Several variations are offered; shown here is an auxiliary fuse block with three always hot and four ignition hot circuits. A single wire to the battery and a single wire to an ignition hot connection on your fuse block is all that's required. (Photo Courtesy Painless Performance)

designed for multiple years of cars, such as 1968 through 1972 Chevelle/Malibu, and use more modern blade-type fuses rather than the old glass style and often have options for additional accessories on multiple circuits. If you plan on using extra electrical items like electric fans or an electric fuel pump, a good relay kit may be in order to absorb the shock of the sudden surge in power requirement from Painless. Another alternative is an add-on accessory such as the CirKit Boss from Painless Performance Products. Several variations are available; my favorite has always been their part-number-70217 version with three 20-amp constant hot and four ignition hot circuits. This unit has a single connection to the battery through a 50-amp circuit breaker and one connection to any ignition hot fuse in the fuse block.

Wiring Diagrams

Wiring diagrams, or schematics, show the wiring path from point to point. These are often rather generic in their depiction, such as *front-engine harness* or *dash harness*, and may or may not take into account accessories including instrument panel gauges, air conditioner, etc. Some companies offer laminated copies of these schematics with actual colors of the wires themselves along with the wire gauge size. Black and white schematics will show essentially the same thing, but colors are abbreviated, such as DG for dark green, Y for yellow, or BRN/W for a brown wire cover with white stripe. The various wires do not depict how they are routed or grouped into a harness; they are simply the point-to-point connection.

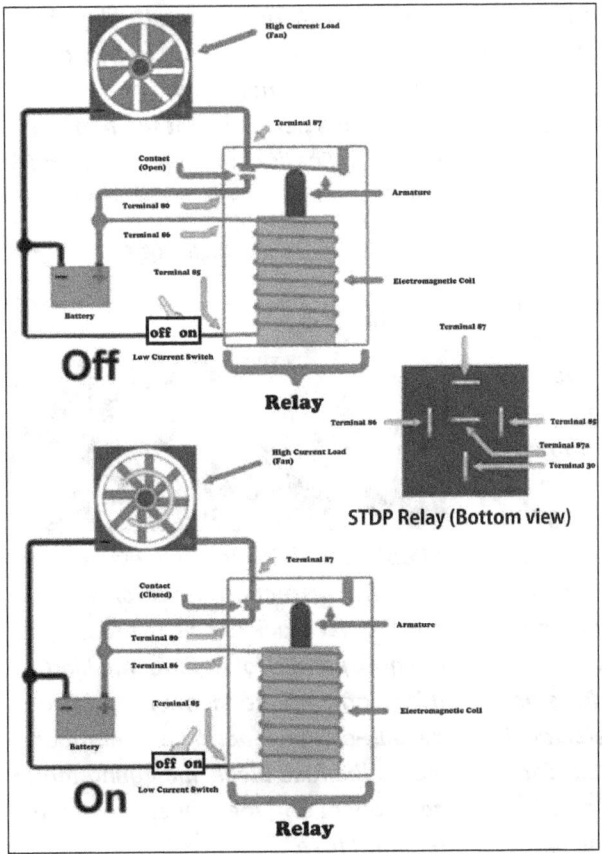

A breakdown of just how a Bosch-type 30 amp relay works. The internals of the relay include the various contacts, the armature, and the electromagnetic coil used to energize the contacts to close. Wiring for each terminal is shown, and an electric fan is depicted as the attached device. (Photo Courtesy Painless Performance)

ELECTRICAL

The majority of ready-made, specific-application wiring kits come with correct connectors, including a ring connector for a screw or nut/bolt, a male or female spade connector, or a multi-wire connector used for a collection of wires in a harness. There may be occasions to change or add a wiring terminal. A quality wire stripper and crimper should always be used along with the proper terminal end for the intended use. It is also advisable in a case like this for the wire to be soldered to the terminal end if possible before being crimped and given a gentle tug to ensure the connection is stable.

There are typically two categories of terminal ends: those with an insulator of sorts covering the crimp area and those with no insulator. A terminal end with an insulator can be a challenge to solder since the insulator itself can get in the way. When soldering a non-insulated terminal, it is advisable to use a heat-shrink tube to cover the soldered area. An ohm meter or self-powered test lamp can be used to test for continuity of the wire itself.

Fuses, Bulbs, and Circuit Breakers

Whether building a concours-quality restoration or a weekend-enjoyment driver, using the correctly rated fuses and circuit breakers is without question a necessity. Replacing old bulbs and sockets where applicable can save hours of troubleshooting when that right turn-signal blinker or a brake light on one side doesn't work; a bulb or socket is often the culprit. If your project car was in any kind of drivable condition before you started, many of these electrical issues would, hopefully, have been discovered and noted for repair or replacement as needed. Normally I am from the school of "If it isn't broken, don't fix it." But, if you are doing

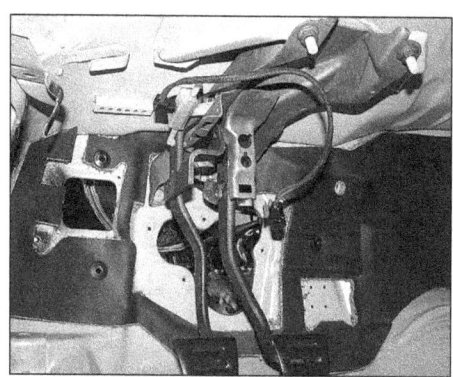

This is the same car before the fuse block and associated wiring harness are installed. The same attention to detail with what appears to be no attention to detail is evident here as well. It's certainly not the neatest paint application, but it is accurate for the car.

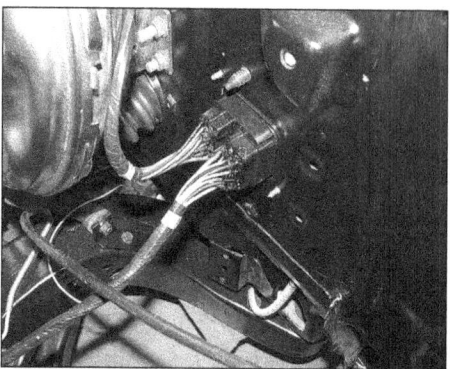

This is the engine side of the firewall fuse block assembly. Not only are the pair of wire bundles done correctly with non-adhesive wiring tape but the bundles have the correct color-coded label indicating their specific use. While it is tempting to use standard electrical tape, it's not correct for a restoration.

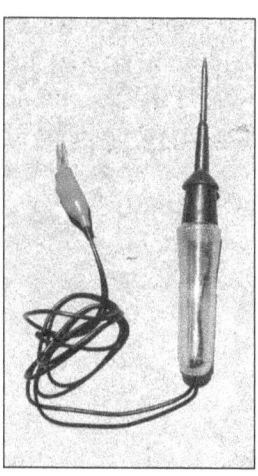

Test lamps range from simple units like this example that can cost as little as $6 to $8 to over $100, depending on its intended use. This model is not self-powered and requires electrical flow in the circuit being tested. The clip goes to a good ground, and the probe is used to complete the circuit.

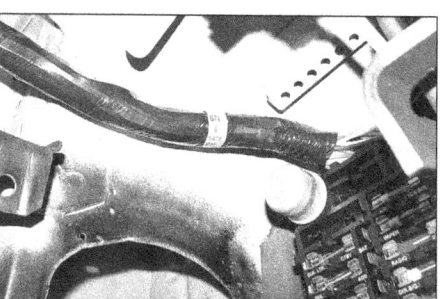

Attention to detail is again evident here. The correct primer color with applied flat black shows the factory did not spend a lot of time masking things off to make them pretty. Note the silk-screen lettering and numbering on the fuse block, indicating the component and the amperage of the required fuse.

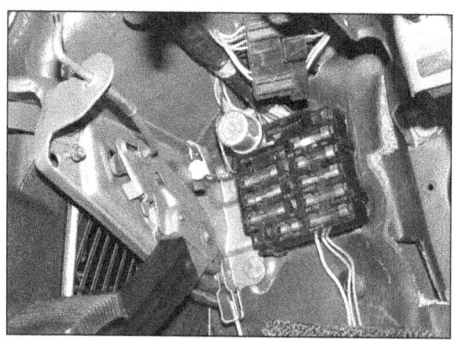

An excellent example of a properly restored to concours standard fuse block and wiring harness. Note the red oxide primer coating indicating this is an Arlington-built 1970 Chevelle. While a flat black might seem more appropriate, correct coloring of components is a necessity when doing a concours restoration.

CHAPTER 7

Electric fans draw a lot of current, and the relay and circuit breaker in the kit absorb that initial electrical requirement. This kit comes complete with wiring, a relay, a circuit breaker, various connectors, and a water-temperature thermostat to turn fans on when the water temperature gets to 200°F. (Photo Courtesy Painless Performance)

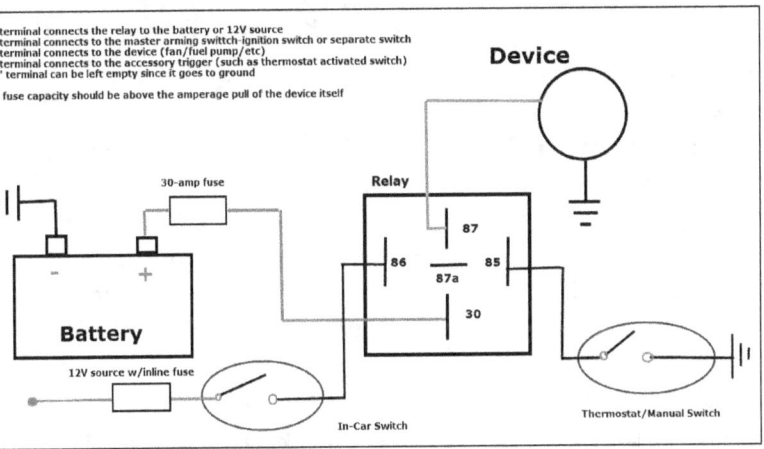

If you are adding an electrical device to your Chevelle's system and would like to include a relay and wire it yourself, this basic schematic shows the pin assignments for a typical Bosch-type 30-amp relay.

a concours restoration, you are most certainly going to be replacing wiring harnesses and connectors anyway, so why not the bulbs and fuses as well? Even for a driver-quality car, ensuring your electrical components are up to the task is highly desirable and is pretty cheap insurance.

Most lamp bulbs are in the dash, in the console (if equipped), or otherwise pretty well hidden or so inaccessible that even a concours judge isn't going to be sticking his or her hands under your dash to unplug a lamp or radio to see if it has correct markings or the correct replacement bulb. A judge may ask you to turn equipment on to ensure that said equipment is in working order though. So, if you have clear parking lamp/turn signal lenses that require an amber bulb, it might be a good idea to use an amber bulb. Other lamps and bulbs, such as headlamps, are readily visible; the original-equipment type are almost mandatory for a concours restoration. Even local/regional show judges will notice if you have two, three, or four different brands of headlamps.

Wiring harnesses should be as correct as possible when being replaced for a high-level concours restoration; everything from the fuse block to labeling, the bulkhead connector, wiring colors, etc.

If you are rebuilding your Chevelle for your pleasure, and the wiring could stand to be replaced, you might consider an aftermarket assembly with modern blade-type fuses and extra circuits to add a larger sound system or power seats, windows, etc. These are typically plug-and-play direct replacement kits with modern components, such as kits sold by Painless Performance and others.

If you are adding additional electrical components such as an electric fuel pump, electric fans, aftermarket gauges, etc., these all need a power source. An alternative to tapping into existing wiring and possibly overloading a circuit, Painless Performance offers several styles of auxiliary fuse block kits to handle these accessories, such as their CirKit Boss series. This particular kit has three 20-amp constant hot and four ignition hot circuits. All it takes is one wire to the hot side of any ignition hot fuse in your fuse box and one wire to the battery protected by a circuit breaker. Up to seven accessories can then be wired into your system and have their own fused protection.

Electrical components that will draw an initial high current, such as electric fans and fuel pumps, should have a relay, such as a Bosch-type 30A unit, to absorb the shock. There are numerous kits on the market with relay, wiring, fuses, etc. included for everything including the headlamps, electric fan(s), electric fuel pump, electric water pumps, etc.

Tools

Specialty tools can speed up any wiring project. Tools such as wire strippers, connection crimpers, etc. will make any wiring task much easier than trying to strip wiring ends with a pocket knife and crimping the ends with a pair of pliers.

Wire Stripper/Cutter

There are several types of wire strippers on the market, so your choices are many. Personally, I like the dedicated wire stripper. Simply insert the wire to be stripped until

ELECTRICAL

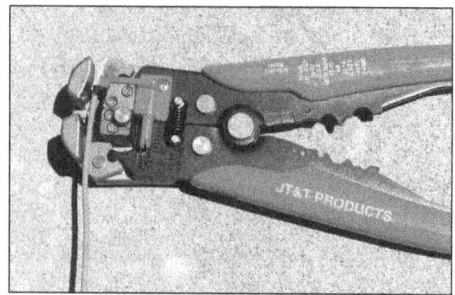

To use this type of wire stripper properly, simply place the wire's end to be stripped against the stop in the jaw as shown here. Squeeze the handle, and the jaws will clamp the wire in place and strip approximately 1/2-inch of insulation off the end.

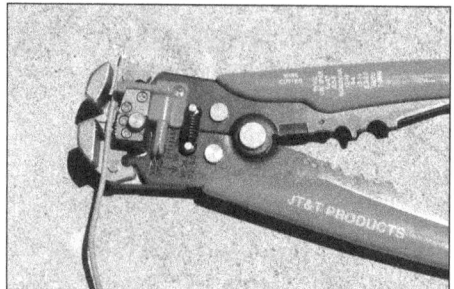

This shows a nice clean cut of the wire's insulation and the resulting stranded wire that is ready for a terminal. This unit runs around $30, and they are often sold by vendors at trade shows, car shows, etc. They will save you the headache of a less-expensive wire stripper that may tend to cut off the wire instead of strip it.

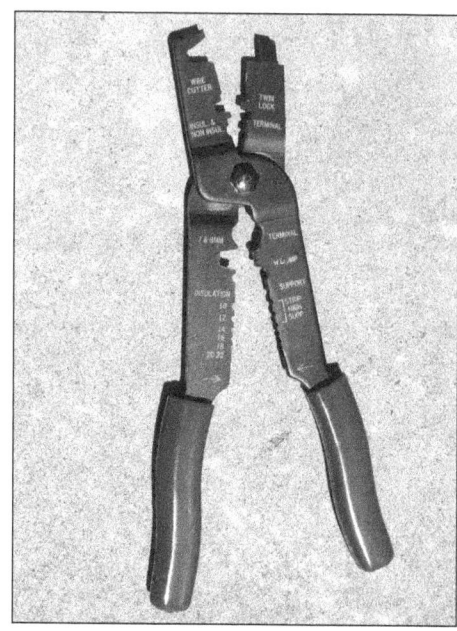

A combination wire stripper, cutter, and terminal crimper like this has been around for years. This all-in-one tool is handy for the occasional user. The stripper section has separate cutouts for the wire gauges, here 10-gauge to 22-gauge are supported. A wire cutter at the top, a terminal crimper, and even spark-plug wire terminals can be handled easily.

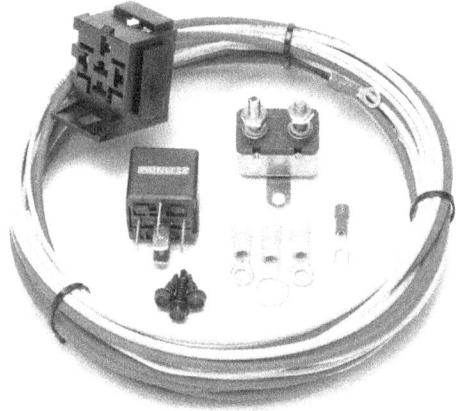

Similar to electric fans, electric fuel pumps draw a lot of initial current. The kit not only absorbs that initial electrical requirement, it is designed to prevent voltage drops at the fuel pump to maintain constant fuel-pump pressure and prevent amperage overload to your Chevelle's electrical system. (Photo Courtesy Painless Performance)

it hits the stop and squeeze the handle. The jaws will grip the wire and strip off about 3/8-inch of the insulation.

A second type incorporates a wire cutter, wire stripper, and connector-crimper all in one. This type of tool has graduated cutters for 10-gauge wire down to 20–22-gauge wire. Simply put the wire in the correct-gauge jaw, squeeze, and rotate or twist the tool, and it will cut through the insulation. You also have more control over the amount of insulation is to be stripped. As you can see, there is a wire cutter on the very end as well as a terminal crimper for both insulated and non-insulated terminal ends. This tool is also capable of installing spark plug ends in both 7- and 8-mm sizes.

Terminal Ends

Terminals and butt connectors come in a wide variety of configurations, and the insulated terminals/butt connectors like these are color coded for the particular wire gauge they can accommodate. Red insulated terminals are for 22–16-gauge wire, blue insulated terminals for 16–14-gauge wire, and yellow insulated terminals for 12–10-gauge wire. Wires larger than 10-gauge generally require a non-insulated terminal, such as battery-to-starter or ground cables. Terminal ends can vary from ring style—for a particular screw size, and even those can be numerous for

A good selection of insulated terminals and various connectors are almost essential for any weekend mechanic and certainly a necessity for a professional. Terminals come color coded for the gauge of wire and have almost every imaginable end available from ring to male/female, spade connections, butt connectors, etc.

CHEVELLE RESTORATION AND AUTHENTICITY GUIDE: 1970–1972

CHAPTER 7

each wire gauge size—to fork style and male/female blade terminals.

Butt connectors can be used to temporarily fix a broken connection but probably should not be used for a permanent connection if it can be avoided. It can lead to corrosion and make a dead system difficult to troubleshoot. If at all possible, use a single-wire run or use heat-shrink tubing and solder the wires together.

Soldering Tool

There are a variety of soldering guns/irons on the market. A soldering tool can range from an inexpensive soldering iron with no temperature control to a soldering-iron station that includes a holder stand for the soldering gun, variable temperature range settings, a solder roll holder, and even a sleep timer that shuts the power off to the soldering iron if you are gone too long or forget to unplug it. My preference is a soldering gun. It can be left plugged in indefinitely and is only activated when the trigger is pulled.

Most soldering irons and soldering guns have replaceable tips because they do burn out and become contaminated over time. If being cordless is your thing (sometimes it is very convenient to not be tied to an electrical plug), there are soldering irons that operate on butane gas and even lithium batteries. The down side of these, naturally, is you must replenish the butane fuel and/or recharge the batteries as needed.

Soldering Paste

Soldering paste is powder metal solder suspended in flux, a medium that acts as a temporary adhesive until the solder melts to make the connection and prevent oxidation. You can solder without flux, but it's not advisable for copper electrical connections. There are two basic types of flux: acid core and rosin core. Acid core is used for plumbing and rosin core is used to electronics; your obvious choice here is resin core. Most electrical solder has a rosin core inside the solder wire.

There are typically two types of solder as well. Lead-based solder is a mixture of tin and lead, usually a 60/40 tin/lead mix that melts around 180 to 190 degrees. Manufacturers are moving away from lead-based solder for health concerns, but unless you are in an industry where soldering is an ongoing venture, your exposure is pretty limited. The smoke you see is from the rosin flux, not from the solder melting. Of course, the smoke could be from some combustible material nearby; always make sure there are no combustibles when working with a soldering iron or gun. Lead-free solder is, as its name implies, solder without lead. Lead-free solder has a higher melting point, so it's a little harder to work with.

Solder comes in spools with different thicknesses for different types of work. If you are soldering battery cable connections with large stranded wires, a thick roll of solder such as 0.062 inch will be necessary. Two other sizes of solder rolls, such as 0.032 inch and 0.020 inch, will be sufficient for most automotive electrical wiring soldering needs. The larger of these two would be suitable for wires ranging from 10 to 14 gauge or 16 gauge, while the smaller might work best for 18- to 22-gauge wiring connections.

In a real emergency, a product that hit the market a few years ago is a simple three-piece connector that lets you connect two (or more) wires together with no soldering and no crimping required. Like most connectors, these are color-coded for wire-gauge size. Unlike other connectors, these require no crimping or soldering.

Simply strip back a portion of the wiring, unscrew each end of the connector, insert the stripped portion of the wire into the ends, and screw it back together. The metal contacts on each end secure the wire inside for a clean, quick connection.

Connectors

Of course, there are literally hundreds of specialty connectors for wiring you may need to make removable for any number of reasons. Quick connectors and weather packs require a bit more work to initially assemble, but they allow you to make up modular wiring harnesses

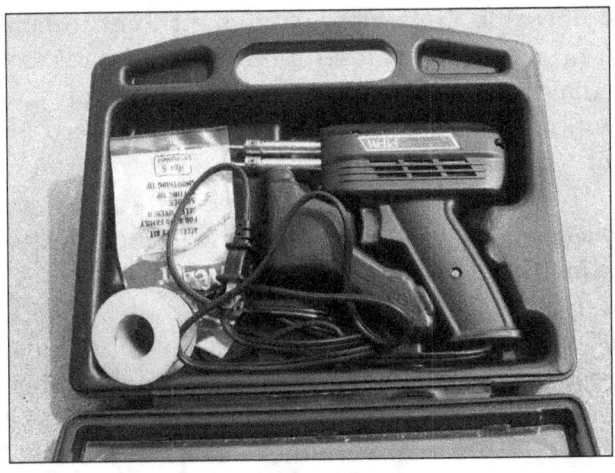

When making permanent electrical connections, a good soldering iron or soldering gun is needed. While a soldering iron may work well at the workbench, if you need to do some solder work under the dash or under the hood, the soldering gun is much easier to use; it only heats up when you pull the trigger.

ELECTRICAL

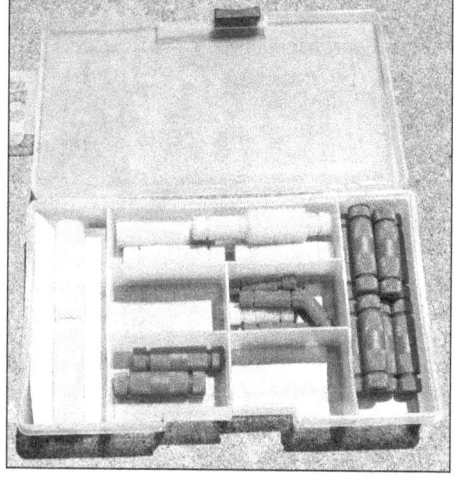

Posi-Lock connectors have been around for several years and offer several advantages over typical butt connectors. These come in a variety of sizes and are color coded for the gauge of wire the unit supports. They are easy to install and do not require any wire crimping.

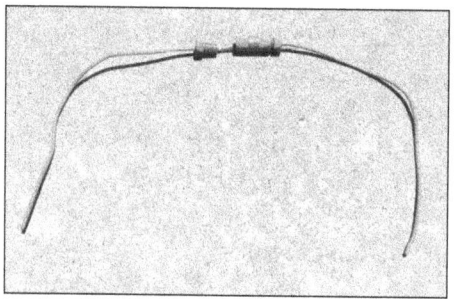

The connector is composed of three pieces: two matching end pieces, the wire to be spliced together, and the center piece that makes the connection. The wires to be connected are stripped to expose the stranded wire and fed through the matching ends, which are then threaded to the center piece.

The center piece of the connector contains an electrical-conducting core with tapered ends. When the end pieces are threaded into the center piece, the wires are snugged down to this center core, completing the electrical circuit. They are handy to have in an emergency, and they are reusable.

that may need to be unplugged occasionally for service or accessibility for such things as aftermarket gauges/tachometer, electric window circuits, or circuits with relays (electric fans or electric fuel pumps), where a quick disconnect can come in handy.

These connectors come in male and female pairs as well as male and female terminals. The wiring can be crimped and soldered to the terminals without the need for any protective covering since the connector itself provides protection against the terminals coming in contact with a ground source.

Relay

If you are adding your own relay in a circuit, these can be purchased as female connectors and terminals to mate with the male terminals on the relay. Some individuals prefer

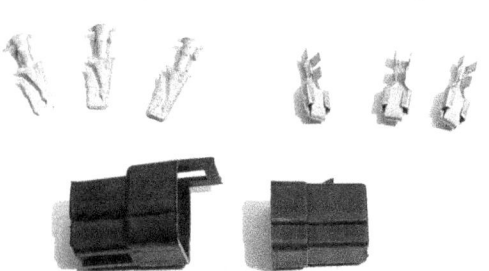

to buy their relays in kit form with the female terminal already wired so they can simply splice into the circuit, while others prefer to do their own where they get to determine the wiring color and can determine the length of the wiring itself. Some relays have a mounting tab where the female connector does not.

Many relay kits will have the female plug with a mounting tab, and the relay itself does not. There is

When you need to connect multiple wires in a bundle and need a method to disconnect them if necessary, male and female terminals as well as male and female connectors are readily available. These come in a wide variety of configurations.

no difference; it is just a preference in mounting the unit. A relay with a mounting tab will (or should) still fit in a female plug.

Fuse Block

If you are retaining your factory fuse block, you might want to note what fuses control what devices and keep spares handy. If you are upgrading your wiring with a modern kit with blade fuses, check the stock-fuse capacity for specific systems, so you will know what fuse to use with the new system.

As with glass fuses, it is a good idea to carry a variety of blade fuses around the shop and especially when traveling. Blade fuses are color coded to match the amperage they will

Want to wire your own Bosch-type relay? Individual relays, female connectors, and appropriate terminals are your solution. Connectors such as these are much cheaper when purchased in small quantities rather than one or two at a time. Note that the terminal ends often come in break-apart sets of 10 or more.

CHAPTER 7

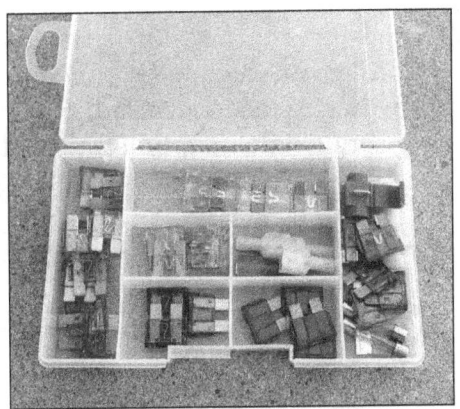

Like their glass fuse counterpart, blade fuses come in a wide selection of amperage capacities. When updating your electrical system to a more modern blade fuse box, a selection of various fuses is a good thing to consider keeping on hand and in that emergency travel box.

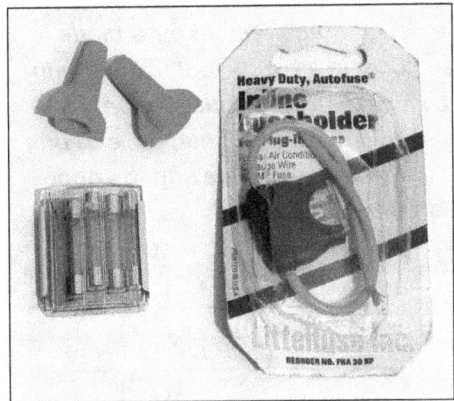

If your needs are minor, an inline blade fuse holder may be your solution along with a selection of glass fuses for your older wiring system. Never use the wire connectors shown here in orange. These are designed for home electrical connections and not for any connection that may be exposed to damp or wet conditions.

Amperage and Body Color for Blade Fuses	
Amperage	Body Color
500mA	Dark Blue
1A	Black
2A	Gray
3A	Violet
4A	Pink
5A	Tan
7.5A	Brown
10A	Red
15A	Blue
20A	Yellow
25A	Clear
30A	Green
35A	Blue Green
40A	Orange/Amber

handle, plus they have the amperage number in large numbers on the fuse making them easy to identify.

There have been variations found in some amperage colors, but even if you find a variation in color, the amperage is always labeled on the fuse itself.

Blade fuses come in a variety of sizes, and depending on the supplier, they will have different names such as medium, small, and mini. What one manufacturer might label as a small fuse, another will label as a mini; be sure to check the physical size of the fuse your system requires. Typically, blade fuse kits come with a puller to make it easier to extract the fuse. Regardless of their size and name, they all come in various current amp ratings and are generally color coded for the ratings the same.

Blade fuses come in many other varieties for any number of specific applications. Be sure to match what you have or, in the case of an aftermarket kit of some kind, what that manufacturer supplied in their kit.

Blade fuses are just as susceptible to blowing as any glass fuse. If you are constantly blowing a particular fuse, either the fuse is not rated high

Blade fuses are color coded for their amperage rating, and most manufacturers will have the rating imprinted on the fuse where it is easily readable. This is the larger-style blade fuse used in most aftermarket replacement wiring kits today.

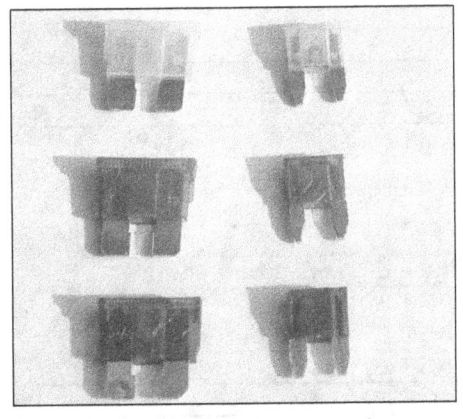

Here is a side-by-side comparison of the medium and mini/small blade fuses. The larger of the two typically measures 18.8 mm in height and 14.5 mm in width, and the smaller measures 16.3 mm in height and 10.9 mm in width. Here the yellow fuse is rated at 20 amp, the blue at 15 amp, and the red at 10 amp.

A mixture of medium and mini/small blade fuses is in an organizer. As you can see, regardless of the physical size and blade type, the colors are consistent with the amperage rating. In the left compartment is a fuse puller; it just happens to be orange and its color is not significant.

ELECTRICAL

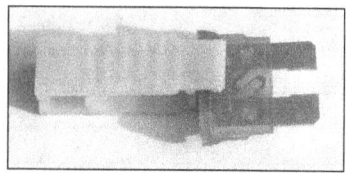

While not a definite requirement for a blade fuse, a fuse puller is a handy tool to have with your fuse collection. It works just the opposite of typical household tweezers. Open the end that clamps on to the fuse by squeezing the opposite ends together. The fuse is grabbed below its lip and is easily extracted.

enough in amperage for the application, or you many have a short in the wiring to the particular electrical accessory device or a problem with the accessory device itself.

1970 Bulbs and Lamps

Bulbs and Lamps	Number Required	Trade Number	Candle Power per Lamp
Automatic transmission quadrant	Column 1	194	2
Automatic transmission position pattern	Floor console, 2	1445	1
Backup	2	1156	32
Brake warning	1	194	2
Courtesy – Instrument panel	2	631	6
Courtesy – Seat separator	1	212	6
Directional signal indicators	2	194	2
Dome	1	211	12
Generator indicator	1	194	2
Glove compartment	1	1895	2
Headlamp – Outer	2	4002	High – 37.5 W, Low – 55.0 W
Headlamp – Inner	2	4001	High – 37.5W
Headlamp – High-beam indicator	1	194	2
Heater controls	1	1445	1
Instrument cluster	10	194	2
License plate – Rear	1	67	4
Luggage compartment	1	1003	15
Oil pressure indicator	1	194	2
Parking	2	1157 1157A (SS optioned)	3 2
Turn			32
Radio	1	1893	2
Side marker – Front	2	194	2
Side marker – Rear	2	194	2
Tail	2	1157	3
Stop and turn	2		32
Temperature indicator	1	194	2
Underhood	1	93	15

1970 Fuses and Circuit Breakers

Circuit	Type of Protection	Location and Circuit*
Air conditioner	AGC 25 fuse	In line
	AGC 25 fuse	Fuse panel (a)
Automatic transmission quadrant lamp	AGC 20 fuse	Fuse panel (c)
Backup lamps	AGC 20 fuse	Fuse panel (d)
Cigarette lighter	AGC 20 fuse	Fuse panel (b)
Clock	AGC 20 fuse	Fuse panel (b)
Clock lamp (with tach)	AGC 4 fuse	Fuse panel (c)
Courtesy lamps	AGC 20 fuse	Fuse panel (b)
Defogging unit	AGC 20 fuse	Fuse panel (d)
Directional signal indicator	AGC 20 fuse	Fuse panel (c)
Dome lamp	AGC 20 fuse	Fuse panel (b)
Folding top motor	40-amp CB	Hinge pillar
Fuel gauge	AGC 10 fuse	Fuse panel (d)
Generator indicator lamp	AGC 10 fuse	Fuse panel (d)

CHAPTER 7

1970 Fuses and Circuit Breakers

Glove compartment lamp	AGC 20 fuse	Fuse panel (b)
Headlamps	15-amp CB	Light switch
Headlamps – High-beam indicator	15-amp CB	Light switch
Heater blower motor	AGC 10 fuse	Fuse panel (g)
Heater controls lamp	AGC 4 fuse	Fuse panel (c)
Instrument cluster lamps	AGC 4 fuse	Fuse panel (c)
License plate lamp – Rear	AGC 20 fuse	Fuse panel (b)
Luggage compartment lamp	AGC 20 fuse	Fuse panel (b)
Oil pressure indicator lamp	AGC 10 fuse	Fuse panel (d)
Brake indicator lamp	AGC 10 fuse	Fuse panel (d)
Parking lamps	20-amp CB	Light switch
Power seats	40-amp CB	Hinge pillar
Power windows	40-amp CB	Hinge pillar
Radio and radio lamp	AGC 10 fuse	Fuse panel (c)
Side marker – Front	AGC 20 fuse	Light switch
Side marker – Rear	AGC 20 fuse	Light switch
Tachometer	AGC 10 fuse	Fuse panel (d)
Tail, stop, and turn lamps	AGC 20 fuse	Fuse panel (b)
Tailgate window motor	40-amp CB	Hinge pillar
Temperature indicator lamp	AGC 10 fuse	Fuse panel (d)
Traffic hazard indicator	AGC 20 fuse	Fuse panel (b)
Underhood lamp	SAE 20 fuse	In line
Windshield wiper	SAE 20 fuse / 14-amp CB	Fuse panel (f) / Switch

* Letter suffix indicates circuit.

1971 Bulbs and Lamps

Bulbs and Lamps	Number Required	Trade Number	Candle Power per Lamp
Automatic transmission quadrant	Column 1	194	2
Automatic transmission position pattern	Floor console, 2	1445	1
Backup	2	1156	32
Brake warning	1	194	2
Courtesy – Instrument panel	2	631	6
Courtesy – Seat separator	1	212	6
Directional signal indicators	2	194	2
Dome	1	211	12
Generator indicator	1	194	2
Glove compartment	1	1893	2
Headlamp	2	6014	High – 60 W / Low – 50 W
Headlamp – High-beam indicator	1	194	2
Heater controls	1	1445	1
Instrument cluster	5	194	2
License plate – Rear	1	67	4
Luggage compartment		1-1003	15
Oil pressure indicator	1	194	2
Parking	2	1157	3
Turn	2		32
Radio	1	1816	3
Side marker – Front	2	194	2
Side marker – Rear	2	194	2
Tail	2	1157	3
Stop and turn	2		32
Temperature indicator	1	194	2
Underhood	1	93	15

1971 Fuses and Circuit Breakers

The headlamp circuit is protected by a circuit breaker in the headlamp switch. An overload on the breaker will cause the lamps to flicker on and off. If this condition develops, have your headlamp wiring checked immediately. Also, a special circuit breaker mounted on the firewall protects the power window, power seat, and power top circuits if vehicle is so equipped. Where current load is too heavy, the circuit breaker intermittently opens and closes, protecting the circuit until the cause is found and eliminated.

Fuse Use	Fuse Rating
Radio, TCS, rear defogger, Hydramatic downshift	10 amp
Windshield wiper	25 amp
Stop lamps, hazard flasher	20 amp
Heater, air conditioner	25 amp
Directional signal, backup lamps, side marker lamps, blocking relay (air conditioner)	20 amp
Instrument lamps, floor shift lamps	04 amp
Gauges, instrument panel warning	10 amp
Clock, courtesy, lighter, glove box, and dome lamp	25 amp
Taillamps, license plate (rear), side marker lamps	20 amp
Air-conditioner high blower speed fuse (inline)	30 amp
Fusible Links are incorporated into the wiring system. These are wires of such a gauge that they will fuse (or melt) before damage occurs to an entire wiring harness in the event of an electrical overload.	

1972 Bulbs and Lamps

Bulbs and Lamps	Number Required	Trade Number	Candle Power per Lamp
Automatic transmission quadrant	Column 1	-194	2
Automatic transmission position pattern	Floor console, 2	-1445	1
Backup	2	1156	32
Brake warning	1	194	2
Courtesy – Instrument panel	2	631	6
Courtesy – Seat separator	1	212	6
Directional signal indicators	2	194	2
Dome	1	211	12
Generator indicator	1	194	2
Glove compartment	1	1893	2
Headlamp	2	6014	High – 60 W Low – 50 W
Headlamp – High-beam indicator	1	194	2
Heater controls	1	1445	1
Instrument cluster	5	194	2
License plate – Rear	1	67	4
Luggage compartment	1	1003	15
Oil pressure indicator	1	194	2
Parking	2	1157	3
Turn	2		32
Radio	1	1816	3
Side marker – Front	2	194	2
Side marker – Rear	2	194	2
Tail	2	1157	3
Stop and turn	2		32
Temperature indicator	1	194	2
Underhood	1	93	15
Map light (mirror)	1	563	4
Seat belt warning	1	194	2

1972 Fuses and Circuit Breakers

Circuit	Type of Protection	Location and Circuit*
Air conditioner	AGC 230 fuse AGC 25 fuse	In line Fuse panel (g)
Automatic transmission quadrant lamp	AGC 4 fuse	Fuse panel (c)
Backup lamps	AGC 20 fuse	Fuse panel (d)
Cigarette lighter	AGC 25 fuse	Fuse panel (b)
Clock	AGC 25 fuse	Fuse panel (b)
Clock lamp (with tach)	AGC 4 fuse	Fuse panel (c)
Courtesy lamps	AGC 25 fuse	Fuse panel (b)
Defogging unit	AGC 10 fuse	Fuse panel (d)
Directional signal indicator	AGC 20 fuse	Fuse panel (c)
Dome lamp	AGC 25 fuse	Fuse panel (b)
Folding top motor	30-amp fuse	Firewall
Fuel gauge	AGC 10 fuse	Fuse panel (d)
Generator indicator lamp	AGC 10 fuse	Fuse panel (d)
Glove compartment lamp	AGC 25 fuse	Fuse panel (b)
Headlamps	CB	Light switch
Headlamps – High-beam indicator	CB	Light switch
Heater blower motor	AGC 25 fuse	Fuse panel (g)
Heater controls lamp	AGC 4 fuse	Fuse panel (c)
Instrument cluster lamps	AGC 4 fuse	Fuse panel (c)
License plate lamp – Rear	AGC 20 fuse	Fuse panel (b)
Luggage compartment lamp	AGC 20 fuse	Fuse panel (b)
Oil pressure indicator lamp	AGC 10 fuse	Fuse panel (d)
Brake indicator lamp	AGC 10 fuse	Fuse panel (d)
Parking lamps	20-amp fuse	Fuse panel
Power seats	30-amp CB	Firewall
Power windows	30-amp CB	Firewall
Radio and radio lamp	AGC 10 fuse	Fuse panel (c)
Side marker – Front	AGC 20 fuse	Fuse panel
Side marker – Rear	AGC 20 fuse	Fuse panel
Tachometer	AGC 10 fuse	Fuse panel (d)
Tail, stop, and turn lamps	AGC 20 fuse	Fuse panel (b)
Tailgate window motor	30-amp CB	Firewall
Temperature indicator lamp	AGC 10 fuse	Fuse panel (d)
Traffic hazard indicator	AGC 20 fuse	Fuse panel (b)
Underhood lamp	SAE 15 fuse	In line
Windshield wiper – Two speed	SAE 25 fuse	Fuse panel (f)
Seat belt warning lamp	AGC 10 fuse	Fuse panel

* Letter suffix indicates circuit.

Battery

ACDelco is a subsidiary of General Motors most notably identified with electrical components such as batteries, relays, starters, etc. Numerous ACDelco batteries were used over the years, depending on the particular application. Often the options sold on a particular Chevelle, such as air-conditioning, required a more robust battery and was either part of that option or GM mandated it be ordered. Your build sheet will show which battery your Chevelle had installed at the assembly plant. For 1970, the battery's broadcast code can be found in box 49; for 1971 and 1972, the broadcast code is found in box 47. The corresponding positive and negative battery cable broadcast codes are found in boxes 50 and 51 for 1970 and box 48 for the 1971 and 1972 model years.

ACDelco batteries used in 1970 for various applications include Y55, R59, R59S, R79, R79W, and R89W; in 1971, batteries used are Y87, R89, and R89W; in 1972, only R89 and R89W have been found.

ELECTRICAL

Various ACDelco batteries were used from 1970 through 1972, depending on the particular application. The RPO code T60 was used each year to designate the heavy-duty battery for that particular model year and not a specific ACDelco battery type, such as R59, R79W, etc.

Chances are your starter could use a quality rebuild at this point. As long as you have the starter apart, it is a good time to inspect the insides and have it rebuilt by a professional. Be sure to retain or tell your rebuilder to keep the original case with the correct part number and date on it.

Delco batteries have one push-in cap with a clear tube reaching down into the battery acid in a cell. This infamous Delco Eye was intended to allow service personnel to look at the cap and see if the cell was low on battery acid or not. In reality, the acid level is hard to see in the best of conditions, and only one cell on a battery ever received this. I remember working various auto parts stores in the late 1960s and early 1970s and selling a ton of these batteries, often to dealers to replace under warranty. We would stock the dry battery and the battery acid was separate. I would use the Delco Eye cap to punch the six cell's protective cap and fill the battery. I don't know if it was just habit or using original batteries as an example, but the Delco Eye cap was always the second cap from the left with the remaining push-in caps for the other five cells.

If the particular ACDelco battery is designated as a heavy-duty battery, that will be noted in box 107, where all the options are listed as T60 HD BATTERY. It should be noted that RPO T60, the heavy-duty battery, is not a single ACDelco battery type but is simply the heavy-duty battery for the application and year. For the 1970 model year, the heavy-duty battery was the ACDelco R79W battery, although at least two very late Kansas City–assembly-plant Chevelles in July 1970 show the ACDelco R89W, and at least two very early Kansas City–assembly-plant Chevelles in September 1969 show the ACDelco R79. Two other ACDelco battery types were used in 1970 for SS-optioned Chevelles: R59 and R59S. Non-SS-optioned 1970 Chevelles typically received the R59, but an L6 or base 307-ci V-8 came standard with a Y55 battery.

Many dealers in the northern United States requested a heavy-duty

Often dealers in the northern United States would order their dealer-stock Chevelles with a heavy-duty battery due to severe weather conditions. This 1970 Greenbrier station wagon with the base 307-ci V-8 engine dealer invoice for Minnesota is one example.

Two typical V-8 starters for Chevelles are shown. Note the starter on the right is a low-torque starter used primarily in low horsepower V-8s and has an overall shorter case than the high-torque starter on the left and, as such, does not require the copper spacer for the field connection. (Photo Courtesy Ray McAvoy of Ray's Chevy Restoration)

battery for their dealer stock due to harsh weather conditions in the winter and would probably highly recommend the current heavy-duty battery to any customer ordering a car with their requirements.

Starter Motor

There are basically two classes of starter motors: low- and high-torque models. The low-torque design is shorter in overall length, and the field connection to the starter solenoid does not have a spacer. The high-torque starter has a longer case and requires a spacer between the field connection and the starter solenoid. The starter solenoid itself is the same for both starter motors. The Delco Remy part number for all starter solenoids, or switches as GM calls them, is D981 with GM part number 1114458.

Typically, there are only three wire or cable connections to the starter switch. The larger top center post is for the battery's positive cable; the left or outside post marked "R" is typically a 20-gauge yellow wire and is used to bypass the resistance wire from the coil for a hotter spark during engine cranking. The third, inside post is marked "S" and is wired to the ignition switch often through a clutch safety switch on a manual-transmission car or neutral safety switch on an automatic-transmission car.

As a general rule, small-block V-8 engines (307 ci and 350 ci) use a 153-tooth flexplate or flywheel and starter bolts are in line with each other, while the big-block V-8 engines (396, 402, and 454 ci) use a 168-tooth flexplate or flywheel and starter bolts are offset.

Starter cases have an identifying number stamped on them along

Starter motors varied for V-8 engines depending on the engine size and transmission type. This particular 1970 RPO LS6 starter motor is used in conjunction with the TH400 automatic transmission. Note the spacer between the solenoid and field connection used on all high-torque starters. Low-torque starters do not typically have this spacer.

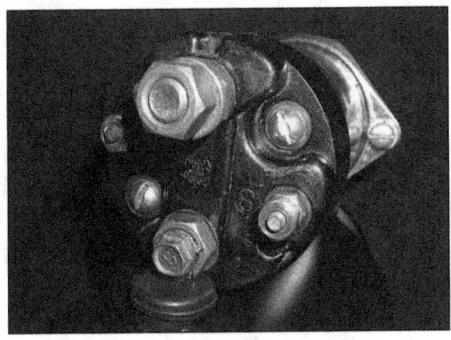

All V-8 engines use the same starter switch, more commonly known as the starter solenoid, whether you have a low-torque or high-torque starter. Most aftermarket starter switches come with the high-torque copper spacer for use with a high-torque starter. Since this a low-torque starter, the spacer is not used. (Photo Courtesy Ray McAvoy of Ray's Chevy Restoration)

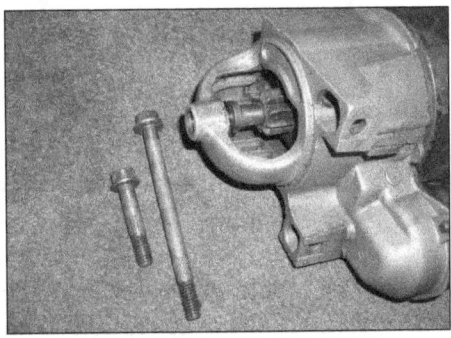

The starter nose for a 153-tooth flywheel/flexplate is shown. The longer, knurled shank bolt is used in the hole closest to the engine block and is 3/8-16 thread and 4-5/8 inch in length. The shorter bolt is the same 3/8-16 thread but 1-7/8-inch in length and uses the hole to the outside of the engine block. (Photo Courtesy Ray McAvoy of Ray's Chevy Restoration)

This is the starter nose for a 168-tooth flywheel/flexplate. Both of the knurled shank bolts are 3/8-16 thread and 4-5/8-inch in length. Also shown here is a sample shim that may be necessary to give the proper clearance between the flywheel/flexplate and the pinion gear in the starter. (Photo Courtesy Ray McAvoy of Ray's Chevy Restoration)

Starter motors have provisions for a front brace that aids in supporting the starter motor's weight. This brace bolts onto an extended stud on the top of the starter front and to the engine block itself. These are often discarded when the starter and/or solenoid are replaced, and they can be difficult to find today.

with the date. The date stamped is in the format of a single digit for the year, a letter for the month, and a two-digit number for the day of the month, such as "9L14," identifying it as being manufactured in 1969 on November 14. The month letters range from A for January to M for December with the letter I not being used so as not to confuse the letter with the number 1.

Starter Numbers by Year	
1970	
Number	**Application**
1108367	307 automatic and manual
1108427	L65 automatic transmission*
1108338	L65 manual transmission
1108430	L48, L34, L78, LS5, LS6 automatic transmission
1108418	L48, L34, L78, LS5, LS6 manual transmission
1971/1972	
Number	**Application**
1108512	307-ci V-8
1108430	L48, L65, LS3, LS6 automatic transmission
1108418	L48, L65, LS3, LS6 manual transmission
* The 1108427 and 1108430 starters were used in 1970 on both the L65 and L48 engines at one point. The L65 engine changed from the 1108427 to 1108430 starter sometime between 04-10 and 05-06, while the L48 engine changed from the 1108427 to 1108430 starter between 12-03 and 12-11, depending on the final assembly plant.	

The last three digits of the starter number are shown as the broadcast code on your Chevelle's build sheet. They could be 367, 427, 338, 418, 430, or 512.

Chevrolet starter motors also have a brace on the front that bolts to the engine block for support. Many times this brace is discarded when the starter and/or solenoid is replaced by service shops or previous owners. The Chevrolet service replacement part numbers for this brace are 3965588 for all 1970–1972 402-ci and 454-ci engines and 3965589 for 1970–1972 350-ci engines. All 1969-and-later 396/402/427/454-ci engines also use a heat shield for the solenoid. Originally, this shield (part number 3954224) was stainless steel, but a service replacement has been available with a galvanized finish (part number 361443). There are aftermarket stainless steel units available.

Automatic transmission starters typically have aluminum noses and are left natural. Manual transmission starters typically have cast-iron noses and were painted with the rest of the housing.

Alternator

The Delco alternator (GM documentation refers to it as a generator) is more specifically a Decotron generator. Because most people today call the current device an alternator, that's the term that will be used here to avoid confusion with older-model-year generators.

Just what is an alternator and why is it important? The alternator produces electricity by converting mechanical energy to electrical energy to maintain the charge of your battery and provide the primary source of electrical requirements of your engine and accessories while it is running. If an alternator is not up to the task of keeping the battery charged, you'll soon wind up with a dead battery. An alternator, unlike a generator, cannot charge a dead battery.

An alternator is a generator that produces alternating current (AC) that is converted to direct current (DC) for your Chevelle. A second piece of the circuitry is the voltage regulator. Its job is to regulate the output voltage to between 13.5 and 14.5 volts.

In a non-gauge-optioned Chevelle, you will have a warning lamp labeled GEN to alert you when there is an issue with your charging system. If the lamp lights during operation, it indicates a problem with your charging system, and the alternator is typically the culprit. People often refer to this warning lamp as an idiot light for some reason. Maybe that's because they like real gauges and think only idiots need a warning lamp to alert them of potential problems. While gauges are nice, a bright red warning lamp will typically get your attention quicker than a gauge will.

In a gauge-optioned Chevelle, you will have an ammeter mounted in the upper-left dash pod, replacing the generator warning lamp on SS-optioned Chevelles. The ammeter measures amps flowing from the charging circuit to the battery and is connected in series between the two, meaning the connections are always in a hot (live) state. The ammeter on gauge-optioned Chevelles have a –60 amp to +60 amp range. Immediately after starting your Chevelle, the ammeter should show a slight charge as electricity is supplied back to the battery. If the meter is in the negative range while driving, it means your charging system is failing or your system is not sufficient to handle the current load. The same can be said if your amp gauge is always showing a positive charge; something is amiss in your charging circuit.

Accessories such as the air conditioner, radio, windshield wipers, and headlamps will typically cause a spike in requirements, and your ammeter should show this with a positive charge reading. A continual 10- or 20-amp charge can mean a problem.

CHAPTER 7

Alternator Numbers by Year

1970

Number	Amps	Application
1100834	37	All standard V-8 without air-conditioning
1100837	37	RPO L78 and RPO LS6 with deep pulley
1108843	61	All with air-conditioning
1100847	63	Optional

1971

Number	Amps	Application
1100566	37	All standard V-8 without air-conditioning
1108843	61	All with air-conditioning
1100917	63	Optional

1972

Number	Amps	Application
1102440	37	307- and 350-ci V-8 without air-conditioning
1102454	37	402- and 454-ci V-8 without air-conditioning
1102463	61	All with air-conditioning
1102464	63	Optional

Alternator Broadcast Code by Year

1970

Code	Application
CW	V-8 without air-conditioning
CZ	RPO L78 and RPO LS6 engine with deep pulley
NF	V-8 with air-conditioning
NJ	Optional RPO K85 63-amp alternator

1971

Code	Application
CW	V-8 without air-conditioning through December
DK	V-8 without air-conditioning beginning January
NF	V-8 with air-conditioning
RA	Optional RPO K85 63-amp alternator

1972

Code	Application
EC	V-8 without air-conditioning
YM	V-8 with air-conditioning
YN	Optional RPO K85 63-amp alternator

With the advent of very-high-output aftermarket alternators, a 100-amp alternator would be typical to allow the use of high-end stereo systems; the old standby –60 to +60 amp gauges are not up to the task. Many people today prefer to use a voltmeter instead of an ammeter to measure the voltage of the battery. Voltmeters are considered safer, they give a more accurate account of your battery's condition, and they are only hot when the car is running. Many aftermarket-wiring-kit suppliers today do not include wiring for an ammeter in their wiring kits for safety reasons, so you may wish to take that into account if converting your wiring harness to a modern system.

An alternator has two major components: a rotor and a stator. The rotor is essentially a number of electromagnets that spin inside the stator. The stator is mounted to the case of the alternator and is a stationary group of wiring. The stator has three sets of wires with numerous loops evenly distributed to form a three-phase system.

The 1970–1972 alternators are rated in amps they can supply: 37 amps for standard, non-air-conditioning-optioned Chevelles; 61 amps for air-conditioning-optioned Chevelles; and an optional 63 amp alternator. The particular engine size is not relevant to which alternator the Chevelle would receive.

Alternator cases have an identifying number stamped on them along with the date. The date stamped is in the format of a single digit for the year, a letter for the month, and a two-digit number for the day of the month. For example, "1J22" identifies it as being manufactured in 1971 on September 22. The month letters range from A for January to M for December. The letter I was not used so as not to confuse the letter with the number 1.

Alternator broadcast codes are

All 1970–1972 Chevelles use the same voltage regulator (part number 1119515). Service replacement units have part number 1119519. The regulator cover is secured with silver-cadmium-plated, non-slotted screws. The capacitor shown here is one of several used on various electrical components to help suppress radio static when any radio is ordered.

found on the build sheet as well since the assembly plant has to know which alternator to use when assembling the engine component. This broadcast code is ink stamped on the alternator case to speed identification by the assembly plant personnel.

The RPO K85 63-amp alternator was a relatively low-option selection with only 2,447 ordered in 1970, 3,620 in 1971, and 4,918 in 1972.

Voltage Regulator

The voltage regulator controls the field current applied to the rotor component of the alternator. When there is no current applied, there is no voltage produced by the alternator. When battery voltage drops below 13.5 volts, the regulator will apply current to the field of the rotor and the alternator will begin charging. When battery voltage reaches 14.5 volts, the regulator will stop supplying current and the alternator will stop charging. Current is regulated by the state of the battery. When the battery is weak, its voltage is not strong enough to keep the alternator from trying to charge it.

Two voltage regulators were used in the 1970–1972 model years: part number 111915 for 37- and 61-amp alternators and part number 1119519 for the 63-amp alternator.

Distributor

The final major component of your electrical system is your ignition distributor and its subcomponents. Without the ignition distributor, spark-plug wires, and spark plugs, all the juice in the battery is not going to do you much good. All 1970–1972 Chevelle ignition distributors were a single-ignition point variety.

While all 1970–1972 Chevelle V-8 distributors will physically interchange, each year and engine will have a variety of correct distributors designed for a specific engine and often transmission. The combinations account for the vacuum advance units as the requirements will vary from engine to engine. It is known that 1970 LS6 distributors were produced with four batch dates: 9H14, 9L11, 9M10, and 0C19. Whether other distributors followed a similar limit of build dates isn't known. Since engines were shipped from Tonawanda or Flint with the distributors installed, it makes sense the distributor date should precede the engine build date.

A distributor's part number and date are stamped on the lower portion of the distributor housing where the electronics are situated. The date is stamped in the format of the calendar year (with a single digit), the month with a letter A through M for January through December, (the letter I is not used). For example, a one- or two-digit day of the month such as "0E25" would decode to 1970 model year on April 25. Note that like most part's assembly dates, the model year

Ignition Distributor Numbers by Year

1970

Number	Application
1112005	307-ci 200-hp with automatic transmission
1111985	307-ci 200-hp with manual transmission
1112002	350-ci 250-hp with automatic transmission
1112001	350-ci 250-hp with manual transmission
1111997	350-ci 300-hp with automatic transmission
1111996	350-ci 300-hp with manual transmission
1111200	402-ci 350-hp with automatic transmission
1111200	402-ci 375-hp all
1111999	402-ci 350-hp with manual transmission
1111998	402-ci 350-hp all
1111963	454-ci 360-hp all
1111437	454-ci 450-hp all

1971

Number	Application
1112039	307-ci 200-hp with automatic transmission
1112005	307-ci 200-hp with manual transmission
1112005	350-ci 245-hp with automatic transmission
1112042	350-ci 245-hp with manual transmission
1112045	350-ci 275-hp with automatic transmission
1112044	350-ci 275-hp with manual transmission
1112057	402-ci 300-hp all
1112052	454-ci 365-hp all

1972

Number	Application
1112039	307-ci 130-hp with automatic transmission (first design)
1112154	307-ci 130-hp with automatic transmission (second design)
1112005	307-ci 130-hp with manual transmission (first design)
1112152	307-ci 130-hp with manual transmission (second design)
1112005	350-ci 165-hp all (first design)
1112314	350-ci 165-hp all (second design)
1112039	350-ci 175-hp all (first design)
1112154	350-ci 175-hp with automatic transmission (second design)
1112152	350-ci 175-hp with manual transmission (second design)
1112057	402-ci 240-hp all
1112052	454-ci 260-hp all

changeover generally started around July/August of the previous calendar year, meaning a distributor destined for a 1971 model-year Chevelle would begin manufacturing in June/July 1970. So, an assembly date of say, "0J11," which decodes to 1970, September 11, would be destined for a 1971 model-year Chevelle.

All 1970–1971 V-8 Chevelle engines use a single-contact-point system and separate condenser. The same contact points and condenser have been used since the 1962 model year, so these ACDelco parts are readily available along with scores of aftermarket suppliers. GM service replacement, as well as aftermarket, contact points come in two basic styles: one where the ignition coil lead and condenser lead connect via a spring-loaded tab, and the second style uses a screw to hold the two leads with ACDelco part numbers of D106P (GM part number 1931988) and D196PS (GM part number 1966289) respectively, where the S means the screw attachment.

High-performance Chevrolet engines use a variation under ACDelco number D112P (GM part number 1966294) that has a stronger spring strap to combat the contacts from not closing at higher RPM. General Motors and the aftermarket came out with a single-piece contact point and condenser set under ACDelco number D1007 (GM part number 1975000 for all V-8 except high-performance applications and 1852572 for high-performance applications). The single-piece unit eliminated the condenser bracket and screw along with the condenser lead to the contact point, making replacement much easier. If you've ever dropped the condenser bracket screw under the ignition plate, you know what I'm talking about.

Back in the day, the difference in $4 for a contact set and around $1.50 for the condenser was cheaper than the $8 or so for the single-piece setup but often worth it in the long run. Today, original D106P or D112P contact points can run $75 to $100 in auctions. So, you have to ask yourself if it is really worth it compared to an aftermarket set of points for $15 to $30 when in all likelihood no judge is going to ask to remove your distributor cap to see what kind of ignition points you have. If your intention for your Chevelle is a daily or weekend driver with an occasional show, who is going to see the contact points, condenser, or rotor to see if they are genuine GM parts with old-school part numbers on them or even an electronic module conversion? Only in the rarest instance would any car show judge ask you to remove your distributor cap and rotor to check which contact point set you have installed. The distributor cap itself should at least give the appearance of being correct—that means using a black distributor cap and not a blue, tan, or other-color aftermarket unit.

Ignition Shield

Corvettes always had to use some sort of ignition shield to suppress radio noise. In 1970, Chevrolet began using a similar shield in Chevelles for the same reason. FM radio stations were coming into vogue for the Chevelle-buying crowd, and buyers wanted less radio static interference. The condenser shield used in Chevelles under service part number 1846216 is located under the distributor cap and covers the contact points and condenser.

The condenser shield was used to combat radio interference. These were often discarded during an ignition contact points change, and research so far indicates they are not being reproduced. Note this is a 1970 Arlington LS6 with the PCV hose routed behind the carburetor.

Spark Plugs, Wires, and Ignition Coil

The spark plugs, spark-plug wires, and ignition coil are three of the items providing spark to ignite the fuel-and-air mixture in the cylinder walls. The ignition coil provides the high voltage to the distributor that in turn sends a high-voltage electrical spark through the spark-plug wires to the spark plugs themselves.

Spark Plugs

Spark plugs are another item that most judges are not going to be looking at, but they just might. Period-correct spark plugs have four green stripes around the white ceramic body ridges and will have the spark-plug identifying number and/or letter if applicable. The number, such as 43, 44, or 45, indicates a specific heat range. A plug number higher than Chevrolet installed as standard equipment is considered a hotter plug, while a lower number is considered a colder plug.

Changing the recommended heat range in a normal application will not affect performance and can actually cause damage in many cases. A hotter plug will transfer heat from the spark plug to the cooling system slower than a colder spark plug. If you do a lot of low-speed or short-trip driving where engine temperatures do not get to (or stay at) normal operating temperature for any length of time, a hotter plug will help prevent plug fouling. A colder plug will tend to foul more easily under light-driving conditions. Just a word of advice, stick with the recommended ACDelco-or-equivalent spark plug and see how your engine reacts.

I remember back in the day, my 396-ci engine would tend to foul spark plugs every couple of weeks and cause sputtering at higher RPM. It just seemed like a fact of life, and with spark plugs costing around $1 to $1.25 each, it wasn't that big of a deal. Later in life when the lead additive was removed from our gas, I went with the advice of many, and when it came time for an engine rebuild, I had hardened exhaust-valve seats installed in the heads. Being cheap, I ran the lowest-octane regular gas, typically 83 or 85, with 10.25:1-compression pistons for a couple of years before I realized I was running the same recommended spark plug and was not experiencing any pinging or stumbles. When I pulled the spark plugs to inspect them, they showed normal wear and color. During good weather, which I see plenty of here in Oklahoma, I'd drive the car to and from work every day, about 10 miles each way, and take off to car shows anywhere from 200 to 800 miles one way and never suffered any consequences whether running a Holley 3310 or Accel/DFI fuel injection. Whether you subscribe to the idea of replacing your exhaust-valve seats with hardened units or not is up to you, and you should seek more than one opinion—especially if you are driving your Chevelle regularly and take into account the type of driving you do.

Spark-Plug Wires

There are basically three different sets: one for L6 engines, one for small-block V-8 engines, and one for big-block V-8 engines. All wires were manufactured by the Packard Electric division of General Motors. The Packard 58404R wire was a TV and radio suppression wire with a non-metallic conductor to reduce noise interference with electrical devices. It has an approximate 4,000 ohms resistance per linear foot. This suppression wire is different from the aftermarket version of the Packard 440 solid-core wire often used in racing at the time.

Spark-plug wires were date coded according to the quarter and year, and this date coding was for internal quality control and may be significantly earlier than the car they were installed on. There was generally quite a lead time: between 4 to 12 months from the date the wires were produced to the time they reached the assembly line. A typical example would be "2-Q-69" for the second quarter. 1969 means this wire may not get to an engine on the assembly line until the third or fourth quarter of production and could easily be correct for 1970 models.

First quarter – January, February, and March

Second quarter – April, May, and June

Third quarter – July, August, and September

Fourth quarter – October, November, and December

The 307- and 350-ci engine spark-plug wire has a 90-degree terminal at the spark plug and a 180-degree terminal at the ignition coil.

The 396/402- and 454-ci engine spark-plug wires have a 135-degree terminal at the spark plug with the exception of spark plug number-7, which has a 90-degree terminal due to clearance issues and a 180-degree terminal at the ignition coil.

All ignition coil-to-distributor wires are 180-degree or straight.

As one would expect, the routing of the spark-plug wires differed between the two engine types: small-block (307/350) and big-block (396/402/454). Due to the proximity of the spark-plug boots to the exhaust manifolds, the small-block engine used heat shields between the spark-plug boots and the exhaust manifolds where the big-block engine did not.

With both V-8 engine types, the distributor cap has a metal opening to allow for the adjustment of the ignition points. The number-1 spark-plug wire should connect to the first terminal to the left (as you face the distributor) of this window. The firing order for both remains the same as it has since the introduction of the 265-ci engine for the 1955 model year: 1-8-4-3-6-5-7-2. Cylinders are numbered 1-3-5-7 on the driver's side of the engine and 2-4-6-8 on the passenger's side of the engine.

ACDelco Spark Plug Numbers and Letters

What do all the numbers and letters mean on an ACDelco spark plug? Glad you asked. Take a spark plug number R46TS as an example.

R – Resistor used to help curb radio frequency interference

4 – Thread size (14 mm)

CHAPTER 7

6 – Heat range. The lower the number (such as 43, 44, or 45) is a colder plug, while a higher number (such as 47 or 48) is a hotter plug

T – Tapered seat with no copper crush washer necessary

S – Extended tip

TS – Tapered seat with extended tip

There are two general categories and five variations of ACDelco spark plugs depending on the use. Note there are several heat ranges available with each spark design/type.

ACDelco Number	Design and Size
R43T	Small plug–tapered seat with 0.460-inch reach and 5/8-inch hex body
R43TS	Same as above but with extended tip
R44	Big plug–gasket seat with 3/8-inch reach and 13/16-inch hex body
R44S	Same as above but with extended tip
44N/44XL	Big plug–gasket seat with 3/4-inch reach and 5/8-inch hex body
44XLS	Same as above but with extended tip

Spark plug recommendations in Chevrolet's AMA Specifications	
1970	
Engine	Recommended ACDelco Spark Plug
307-ci	R45
350-ci	R44
402-ci	R44N/R44T*
454-ci	R43N/R43T*

* GM revised the cylinder head design to change from the 13/16-inch head spark plug to the tapered 5/8-inch head tapered design without a sealing gasket.

1971	
Engine	Recommended ACDelco Spark Plug
307-ci	R46TS
350-ci 245-hp	R45TS
350-ci 270-hp	R44TS
402-ci	R44TS
454-ci	R43TS

1972	
Engine	Recommended ACDelco Spark Plug
All V-8	R44T

Ignition Coil

All 1970 through 1972 V-8 Chevelles use the same ignition coil (GM part number 1115293) and are embossed "293 B-R." GM service replacement coils carried part number 1115238 and are embossed with "238 B-R."

An original 1970 ignition coil shows the numbers "293" and letters "B-R" embossed on the case. Service replacement ignition coils, if you were to go to your Chevy dealer to purchase, are a different part number and have "238" and "B-R" embossed on the case. This later coil is listed as a service replacement for all 1967–1972 V-8 Chevrolets.

At least two styles of lettering have turned up on Chevrolet ignition coils. This example has the letter y in "Delco-Remy" on the same baseline as the rest of the lettering, while the second style found has the letter y as a serif character and "Delco-Rem" are raised from the part line.

Numerous variations of wording on distributor caps have been found. The original 1970 LS6 cap has "Delco-Remy" with a serif letter y, "R," and "PATENT PENDING." The question you should ask yourself here is, "Would any show judge ask you pull the spark plug wires off to inspect the wording?

CHAPTER 8

INTERIOR

With a little effort, you can make the interior of your car just as dazzling as the outside. With little more than a weekend and basic tools, you will change the appearance of your car.

Interior Removal

Once again, keep everything you remove and/or replace until the car is completed, then throw away or sell what you do not need or no longer want. This chapter will be written as if you were going to restore the entire interior. If you intend to only restore parts of it, skip ahead to those sections. The removal steps are written in a way that has worked out best for most, though you may choose to remove your interior in a different order or not remove some of the components at all if all you are going to do is recover the seats or replace the carpeting.

In the Beginning

If you are one of the very lucky ones and have a great interior other than maybe a couple of small tears or holes, you are in luck. These can be easily repaired with kits available at most auto parts retailers. As with any do-it-yourself job, it is recommended that you spend the extra money to buy a quality kit and not the cheapest one you can find.

The Eastwood Company sells a very nice kit for making minor repairs to fix vinyl, plastic, and leather

You have reached that part of the restoration where you will hopefully spend most of your time in the seat behind the wheel. If your car has anything close to the normal amount of mileage that an almost 50-year-old car would have, then it is more than likely that the seats, carpet, door panels, and headliner are in nowhere-near-good condition. The nice part about interior work is that there is very little mechanical work; it is mostly cosmetic work that a normal home mechanic is more than capable of doing other than maybe having the seats recovered and the headliner reinstalled.

CHEVELLE RESTORATION AND AUTHENTICITY GUIDE: 1970-1972

upholstery, as well as padded dashboards. The kit comes with seven different colors and includes everything you need, including the heating iron. With the different colors and some practice, you will be able to mix and match your existing interior color. Just follow the directions that come with the kit. Lesser quality sets can be found at your auto parts retailer.

It is imperative that all surfaces are very clean and especially void of any silicones, as these will inhibit adhesion of most adhesives and all paints. It is pretty much a guarantee that most any classic car has been introduced to ArmorAll or another similar product at least once in its lifetime, and the silicone in that product is your paint's worst nightmare. All surfaces must be thoroughly cleaned with a good cleaning product such as OxiClean, Magic Eraser, or Simple Green to name a few. When you are done cleaning everything, clean it again! Give your interior a good cleaning before you decide what to replace.

If you are one of the more common and unlucky ones, you will need a complete interior makeover. If this is the case, take a complete inventory of every item in the interior that needs attention or replacement. Once you have made a list, purchase replacement items in advance of starting so that by the time you get to the point of being heavily involved in the interior you will have all the new pieces in front of you. Complete interior kits can take four to eight weeks or longer to receive, and it takes at least another two weeks to have someone recover the seats. Having everything on order from the onset will greatly speed the restoration time of the interior and lessen the chance of you putting the interior on hold.

Depending on the severity of your interior damage, your list may be lengthy but is needed to cover all the bases. Items on your list may include carpeting, carpet sound deadener, sill plates, front and rear seat covers, headliner, dome lens and bezel, dome light harness, sail panels, sun visors, rear package tray, rear seat divider and insulation (if used on your particular car), firewall pad, door moisture barriers, window cranks and door handles, under dash insulation, dash pad, lock buttons, seat adjusters, head rest releases, seatback bumpers, replacement headrests, seat releases, bucket seat back and side covers, seat belts, seat belt buckle covers and labels, seat trim and hardware are all likely to need replacing in many cases. In very severely damaged interiors, you may need replacement foam padding, burlap, and sometimes springs. These are normally available from your interior supplier.

All of these can add up to a very expensive interior remodel, so make sure to budget for it in the beginning. If there is one thing that usually holds true and of which you should keep in mind: if the interior looks to be in pretty good shape but the seat covers are worn, replacing them will now make your once acceptable door panels stand out against the new covers and will now need to be replaced. Same goes for the rest of the interior.

As with any item, you get what you pay for. If you want to go cheap, then expect cheap. If you demand the best, then spend a little extra money and buy the best. It is always suggested to buy door panels that are already assembled because the cost savings to buy the unassembled ones are not worth it and rarely look as good when assembled.

Buy name-brand carpet and do not skimp there either. Quality

Well in advance of starting your interior restoration, make a complete list of every item you will need and order them. Think long and hard before deciding that some pieces may be good enough, as they may no longer match the new surroundings of new interior pieces.

brands are heat-formed to the contours of your floors and will normally drop right in with minimal fuss whereas you will spend hours trying to get the cheaper brands to fit the contours of the floors correctly. If your car needs a complete makeover, work with your supplier; most will get you a huge discount when purchasing an entire interior kit including all the small items, plus it all comes packaged in one or more boxes for easy inventory.

Carpet

If you are not too picky, you can trim the carpet to fit the openings. If you want a concours installation, then you will have to do a little more, including cutting the carpet out from under the seats and cutting the flaps for the seat tracks and under the console the way the factory originally did it. This will be expounded on later in the chapter with the complete installation process. Regardless, try to wait until you have the carpet completely fit in the front and rear before making any cuts because once you do so, you own it so you better make sure it is where you wanted it.

Firewall Pads

When it comes to firewall pads, you can buy inexpensive flat-fiber pads or you can buy the heat-formed pads such as those from QuietRide Solutions. These are considerably more expensive but match the factory firewall pad much more closely and also fit a little better. They also look correct where the carpeting tucks under the firewall pad in the footwell area.

Dash and Components

In addition to the interior upholstery, now is the time to decide if your radio, speakers, steering column, wiring harness, dash vents, dash, etc. need attention as well. In all likelihood, they all will.

Dash harnesses are insanely expensive, so if you can clean yours up and repair it, all the better. If some hack was there years ago installing that fancy 8-track player and multiple speakers, chances are you have a major expense to look at. Cutting corners on any wiring harness is not advised because this can lead to possible fires and cancel out all of the hard work you just put into your car.

There are many suppliers of harnesses. It is suggested to buy from the vendor that best suits your needs, be it factory stock or a modern custom-made harness. It is also recommended to replace the gauge panel circuit board because these are just too old and a melted wire in the circuit board can be the beginning of a melted car.

In the beginning of the book, I advised you to give your car a

Always lay in your new carpet and take several measurements before cutting the carpet. Many times the carpet is not manufactured correctly or other issues may cause your carpet to be out of spec. Once you cut the carpet, it will not be returnable, so check it over before cutting.

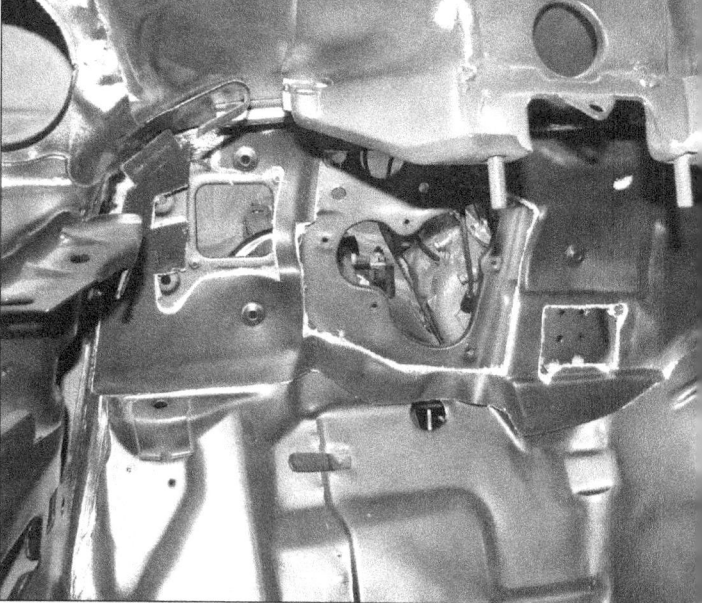

When it comes to firewall pads, there is cheap and there is near exact. Decide early on which one you want, as there is a drastic price difference. For a concours restoration, choose the form-fit pad. The flat pad would be fine for a daily driver.

CHAPTER 8

Anytime you are doing a complete restoration replace the dash's printed circuit. If you are on a budget, at least look it over thoroughly to ensure that it is in perfect condition. An issue here can burn your car to the ground later.

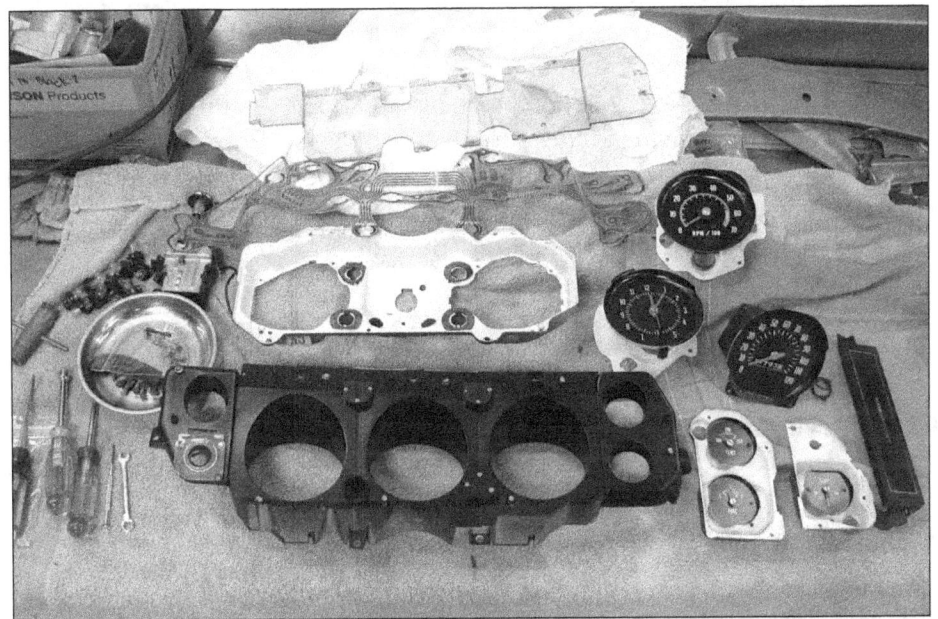

When doing a complete restoration, it is strongly advised to completely rebuild every component with your gauge cluster being no exception. With 50-year-old grease, if it has not failed yet it will. For that reason and the fact that you have the cluster out of the car, now would be the time to go through every gauge.

complete inspection and make a list of which items worked and which did not. Now is a good time to reference back to that. When you have the dash out of your car, check the gauges. Even though your clock and tachometer (if so equipped) may be working, now is a good time to have a professional tear the speedometer and instruments apart, clean them, replace the 50-year-old grease with new modern grease and recalibrate them.

After the dash is back in place and everything has been reinstalled is often when that neglected tachometer or clock decides to stop working. It is doubtful anyone wants to pull a dash apart simply to repair a clock when it could have been done when the dash was already out. You can also modernize your clock to a quartz movement and upgrade your radio to a more modern electronic stereo while still maintaining your original face appearance.

Interior Restoration

You made the list and placed the order for the interior; now let's start removing the current one. As with any part of your restoration, it works best to take a complete photo inventory of what you are starting with before you ever turn a screw in the interior. This will come in handy when ordering parts or trying to describe to someone the appearance of a part you are trying to replace. Once you are done with that, we can start removing components.

As with other parts of the restoration, bag and tag each area of the interior so that you can keep each part of the interior hardware separated. Try and leave the carpet in until most all of the interior has been removed. The carpet will act as a pad for your knees and your back, making for a more comfortable removal of the interior.

Before starting to remove the interior, keep in mind there may be a buried assembly plant build sheet or broadcast sheet somewhere. This is not a for sure thing; it depends on the assembly plant and if the interior has ever been removed or altered in its lifetime. Some places to look for a build sheet include the front and rear seats (both top and bottom), inside the seat springs, wrapped around the main seat structure, behind the

INTERIOR

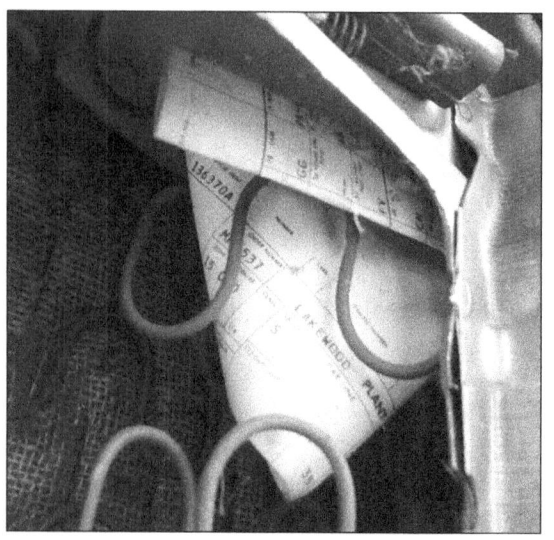

When disassembling the interior, leave no area unchecked when looking for factory documentation or other potential story-telling artifacts. Build sheets and broadcast sheets can be found in many locations within the interior, so take your time and look before tearing anything apart.

Be especially careful when removing the sound deadener, as there may be a build sheet that was laid underneath it. Many times it is nearly impossible to read due to staining. However, all of the important numbers might be legible. This is a very common place to find them in Arlington-built cars.

bucket seat rear cover, inside the bench seat upright, glued to the back of the door panel, under the package tray, inside the headliner, rolled up under the dash pad, stuffed inside the A-pillar, under the carpet, or under the carpet sound deadener. The locations are unlimited but not every car had one.

Flint cars did not come with a build sheet but broadcast sheets have been found in them.

Seat and Console Removal

Exact steps to remove seats may vary depending on the year and model Chevelle you are restoring. The following is applicable to the 1970 Chevelle.

Start by removing the floor sill plates. If yours are in very good condition, removing them will ensure they do not get damaged when taking the seats out. These are unique to each side, so make sure you mark them as passenger's or driver's side.

Move on to the front and rear seats and seat belts. Remove the front seat belts and retractors first to get them out of your way. It is a good idea to photo document the tags on the belts and their respective locations so you can put them back where they were originally. You can also tag them with a piece of masking tape and permanent marker with their respective location. Also pay close attention to which way the tags are showing where they were bolted down, otherwise your buckles may be upside down or the belts twisted when you are done reinstalling them. At the very least, I use the mounting bolts or zip ties to keep the seat and shoulder harness belts together by seat location.

Bucket seat belts are simply unbolted and removed; bench seat belts have to be fished through the bottom seat cushion to get them out. Seat belt retractors are left- and right-handed, so take note of their respective locations. Regardless, the belts should pull up and retract with that part of the retractor closest to the seat they are near.

Bucket Seats

Bucket seats have three nuts and one bolt per seat to hold the seats to the floorpan. Remove those and bag them. Now simply fold the seats

Bucket seats are fairly easy to remove. You should find three bolts and one nut holding the tracks to the floor per seat. Once the seats and console are removed, make note of how the carpet was installed if it is the original carpet. Leave the carpet installed for now to use as a pad while you remove the rest of the interior.

down and carefully lift them out of the interior, taking care not to hit the door panel, jamb, or steering wheel.

Bench Seat

Bench seats can be a little more complicated. It is best to separate the seat backs from the bases for ease of removal as well as storage. This way you can simply lay the seat backs on a storage shelf. Since only one side of the seat back can be folded at a time, the seat would have to be stored in an upright position and take up valuable space on your floor or shelves.

Bench Seat Back Removal

To remove the seat back, remove the plastic cover of the outer hinge arm. There is a metal pin that is pressed into the plastic cover from the rear. Gently pry this pin out to

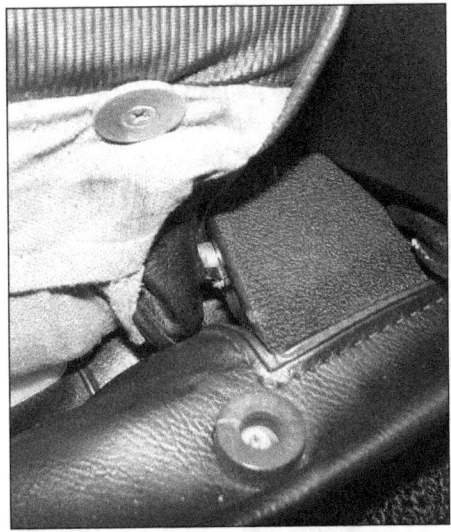

Once the seat hinge arm has been separated from the seat base, lean the seat forward and then pivot the seat back toward the inside while separating the inner pin from the center pivot found in the middle of the seal. Remove these and then the seat bottom for storage.

enable removal of the plastic cover. Once the cover is removed, you will see a metal retainer washer. To remove this washer without breaking it, wedge a couple of flat-bladed screwdrivers underneath the washer and gently rock the washer off.

At this point you will be able to pull the seat back enough to clear the pivot pin. Now that it is free from the pivot pin, fold the seat back forward slightly and tilt upward toward the center to clear the inner holding tang. Repeat these steps for the other side. Put all hardware into a marked bag. Bench seat cars use four bolts to hold them down; two on each side. To make it easier to remove the bolts, move the seat forward and/or backward to gain access to the mounting bolts. Once all the hardware is out of the way, remove the seat bottom and place the hardware in its own bag.

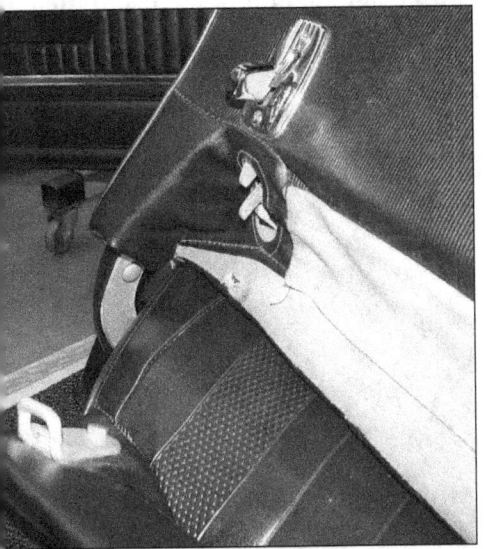

It is easiest to separate the seat backs from the base on a bench seat to ease removal. Starting with the hinge arm, pull the pin that holds the plastic hinge cover, remove the cover, and then remove the retaining washer holding the arm onto the pivot pin. It will be much easier to remove and store the bench seat when separated.

Console Removal

If you had bucket seats, the odds are that you may also have a console. This would be a good time to get that out of your way as well. The automatic and manual consoles are very similar in removal. Start by removing the six screws that hold the top cover plate on.

If your car is a floor-shift automatic, you will have to remove the shift indicator lens first, which is held on by four of those six screws. To make removal of the indicator plate just a little easier, place the automatic shifter in the neutral position. Once loose, lift up slightly and remove the two black/gray wire light sockets from the back of the indicator plate. Now completely remove it and the top plate and place it somewhere safe.

Open the console door and find the two bolts or Phillips screws, whichever yours may have holding the console to the floor at the bottom of the map well. In the shifter cavity, you will find a single bolt holding the center mount to the floor. Remove it. Lastly, move to the front interior of the console and remove two bolts holding the nose of the console to the floor.

In this same area, an electrical connector that connects the console wiring harness to the console pigtail runs under the carpet and up under the dash. Detach the connector from the console base as well as any ground wires and separate the harnesses, leaving the main harness connected to the console assembly.

On automatic cars, you will need to unplug the light green, dark green, and purple wire terminals from the shifter selector at the base of the shifter and the ground wire terminal from the floor. Leave the shifter in place and the wiring harness

INTERIOR

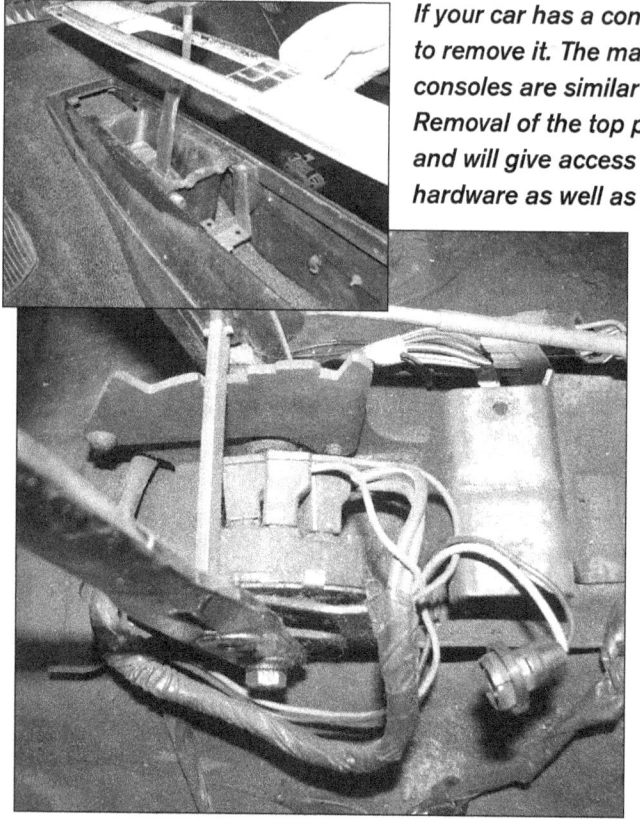

If your car has a console, now is a good time to remove it. The manual and automatic consoles are similar in their removal process. Removal of the top plate is the same on both and will give access to all the other mounting hardware as well as electrical.

Note how the electrical wires are connected on your automatic shifter and take photos. Do not forget to unplug the console pigtail at the nose of the console as well as the ground wire attachment. Once these are removed along with the console mounting bolts (five of them), remove the console, leaving the harness attached to the console.

attached to the console for now.

Four-speed console removals are very similar, though you will need to remove the black plastic shifter filler collar from under the top plate. The collar simply sets in place and can be lifted up over the shifter for removal. With manually shifted cars, there will not be any wires that need to be removed from the shifter, though you will still need to unplug the rear courtesy light connector at the nose of the console.

Your console should now be completely loose. Lift it up to clear the shifter while being careful not to hit the dash with the front of the console. Remove from the car and place safely into storage.

Carpet

If your carpeting is original, now would be a very good time to photograph how it was cut out around the shifter and mounting plate and under the seats and seat tracks for later replication. If original, retain this carpet to use as a template to aid in cutting in the new piece when that time comes.

You will likely also find a manufacturing label attached to the bottom of the carpet on the front section near the driver's side rear part of the carpet. If this is a replacement carpet, simply use it as a knee pad or to lie on to work on the rest of the car, as it will serve little other purpose.

For manual nonconsole cars, pay special attention to how the carpeting is installed under the shifter boot mounting flange. Remove the four trim screws holding the shifter boot bezel from the boot retainer. Next, remove the screws holding the boot retainer to the floor. You can remove the boot later when you remove the shifter.

Four-speed console cars use a rectangular mounting ring. The removal steps are very similar; the only difference is that there are more mounting screws than the square nonconsole version. Again, pay attention to how the carpeting is cut and retained around the ring.

Rear Seat Removal

With your seats and console (if you had one) now removed from the interior, move on to the rear seat. Start by removing the rear seat bottom. The bottom is held on by a hook that is welded to the floor and holds the wire spring frame of the seat. You will find these just to the outside of center of the seat bottom on each side.

With two hands placed on the face of the seat bottom directly over the hook, push back on the seat with a fair amount of force and then

When removing the rear seat bottom, push the base of the seat rearward and pull up at the same time. The objective is to unhook the seat base wire from the floor hook. Once this is done, simply pull the seat base up and out of the car. Take caution to not break the plastic armrests found at either end of the seat.

lift the seat up in the front in one motion. Repeat for the other side. Once both sides are unhooked from the floor hook the seat will simply pull out. Be careful when pulling the seat base out so as to not crack the plastic seat side armrests.

Rear Seat Back Removal

Now move on to the rear upright seatback. You will see two 7/16-inch headed large washer bolts holding the metal ring of the seat back frame to the metal rear seat divider. Remove these two bolts and put them in your bag.

Behind the seatback are three hooks that are welded to the metal seat divider. It works best to start on one side, work to the center, and then on to the other side. Put your shoulder onto the seat directly in front of one of the outboard hooks and push back on the seat with some effort while pulling up on it

Removal of the rear seat is fairly straightforward. Pick one side or the other of the seat and firmly push rearward as you lift the seat up and disengage from the hook. Once disengaged, pull the seat back slightly forward so the hook does not reengage. Next, move to the center and then the opposite end. Once all are separated, remove the rear seat back.

at the same time. You will only be able to pull up on the seat slightly because the other two hooks are still engaged. As you push in and pull up on the seat, you should feel that particular hook disengage. When it does, pull the top of the seat slightly forward so that it will not re-hook. Now move on to the center and finally the other end. Once all three hooks have released the seat, it too can be removed.

Trunk Divider and Seat Belts

You should see a cardboard seat divider behind the seat. Make note of how that was installed to aid you in reinstalling it or finding a replacement piece. Once the rear seat is completely removed, you can remove the rear seat belts. This would be another good time to take a photo of how the seat belts are installed and how they are orientated with regard to what male and or female belt is attached to

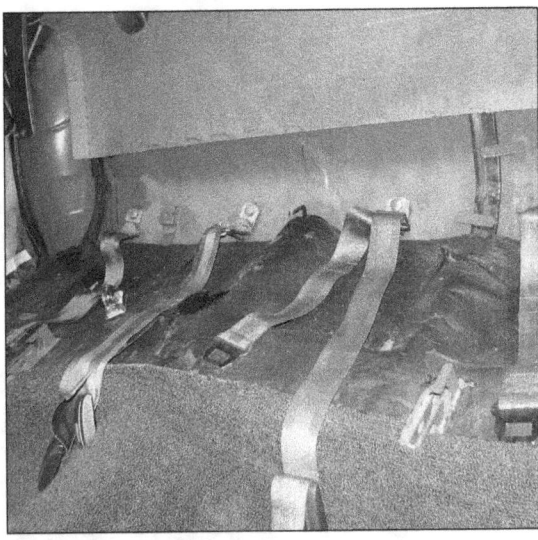
Note and photograph the orientation of the seat belts. Save for later when you are installing them back into the car. Mark them with tape and a permanent marker to note exactly where they were mounted before removal to ensure they are placed back in their same locations.

which bolt. Tag these and put them in their own bag.

Rear Armrests and Panel Removal

With the seats removed, you can now move on to the door panels and rear armrests. Remove the two chrome-finish washer Phillips screws that hold on the plastic or metal rear armrests (depending on coupe or convertible) at the nose of the armrest.

At the top and rear of the armrest is the metal seat filler panel. There should be two screws holding these onto the steel inner structure through the rear inner door panel. Remove those and very carefully take them and the plastic armrest loose from the sides. Make sure to hold on to both of them while removing because the plastic tab on the armrest can break off where the seat filler panel attaches to it. Once loose

Moving on to the rear seat back, look for these two bolts found on the bottom. They are used to retain the seat back to the rear seat divider bulkhead. Remove these and place them in the bag with your other seat hardware.

INTERIOR

Coupes and convertibles are slightly different in their design and the materials they are made from, but they will come apart almost the same. Look carefully to ensure all screws have been removed before pulling any panels away from the inner structure so as to not damage them.

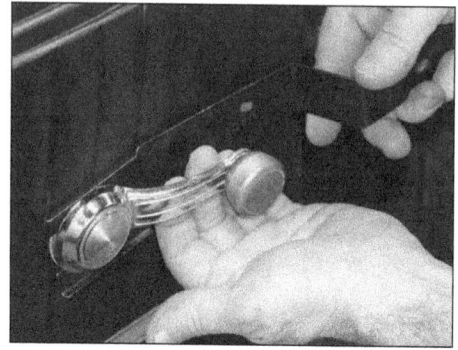

The use of a window crank and door lever tool will greatly aid in the removal of these items. They can be purchased online or from most auto parts stores. They are very simple to use and will not damage your parts or your door panels.

The removal tool is designed to remove the handle retainer clips from the window crank and door levers. Once the clip is removed, the lever may be pulled off. This tool can also aid in putting the retainer clip onto the crank or lever when reinstalling back onto the door.

Though pictured on the front door panel, rear door panels are removed in the same manner. Gently place the panel removal tool between the door structure and the door panel and pry the panel loose, making sure that the tool head is placed around the pin and not just next to it. Not doing so may damage the door panel.

and laid down, remove two more Phillips screws from the base of the filler panel to rear of the armrest on coupes. These will crack easily, so proceed with caution.

Convertible rear armrests are slightly different. They are made from vinyl-covered steel and are held on in a similar fashion to the coupes. The convertible uses a top well cover instead of a seat filler panel, though these are also held on the armrest in a somewhat similar fashion.

After the armrests have been removed, use a window crank removal tool to remove the window crank from the door panel area. Slide the tool toward the center of the crank from directly behind the crank lever. A spare window crank handle without a retainer clip installed will come in handy throughout the interior removal process to raise and lower the windows for removal of the door panels, so have one nearby. The clip slides into the crank through some slotted holes and the ears of the clip will always face the knob of the crank. On some cranks, you can also use the tool to insert the clip onto the handle.

The rear panels are held on by two retainer pins near the face of the panel. Place a flat panel removal tool as close to the pin as possible, gently pry between the door panel and inner door structure, and disengage the retainer pins. Look for any other attaching screws; some plants did use another Phillips screw near the upper rear part of the door panel, though this is not very common. Roll the window all the way down and gently push up and out of the door panel. It should come loose fairly easily.

If your car has power windows, simply unplug them from the harness as the door panel is being removed. It is strongly suggested that you place each door panel's hardware

CHEVELLE RESTORATION AND AUTHENTICITY GUIDE: 1970–1972   169

into its own bag and label accordingly. Repeat for the other side.

Front Door Panel Removal

For the front door panels, start by removing all of the peripherals on the door panel, such as the armrest, door release, window crank, mirror hardware (if any), and lock knob. Remove the three Phillips-head screws holding the armrest to the door panel. With this removed you will have access to the door release handle. Using your door lever tool again, remove the clip locking the handle onto the door release mechanism.

Next, remove the window crank from the window regulator. If your car has a remote mirror, remove the screws holding the adjuster plate onto the door panel. Remove the door lock knob from the top rear of the door panel. Move to the bottom of the panel and remove four or five screws (depending on year) from the bottom of the door panel.

With everything removed, use the pry tool once again to gently pry the door panel from the door structure. Keep the pry tool as close to the panel retainer pin as possible. There are three pins holding the door panel on in the front and three in the rear of the door.

Just like before, if you have power windows, separate the wiring plug from the back of the door panel after you have released the door panel from the door. Repeat for the other side.

Steering Column Removal

Before removing the dash carrier, you will want to remove the steering column. If the wheel needs restoration (and they usually do), it is usually easier to keep the steering wheel attached to the column because you can use the wheel as a stand for storage later. You can also use it as a handle to hold while removing the column, though it may get in your way if the seats are still in the car. Use which ever method you think best for your situation.

Steering Wheel Removal

If the steering wheel is in a good original condition and not needing restoration, you can certainly remove it at this point to get it out of your way and to protect it from damage during removal of the column. On the standard steering wheel there are four Phillips screws that hold the horn shroud onto the steering wheel. They are located on the backside center section. Remove these and put them into a bag large enough to also hold the horn shroud.

Upon removing the four screws, gently let the horn shroud hang from the column by the black and white horn button wires. The end of this wire fits into a white plastic retainer within the face of the steering wheel. Using a very small slotted screwdriver, carefully push in on the wiring terminal going into that plastic retainer and then quickly release it. There is a spring behind this terminal; press and quickly release it to pop the wires and terminal out of the retainer. Keep a hand over the area

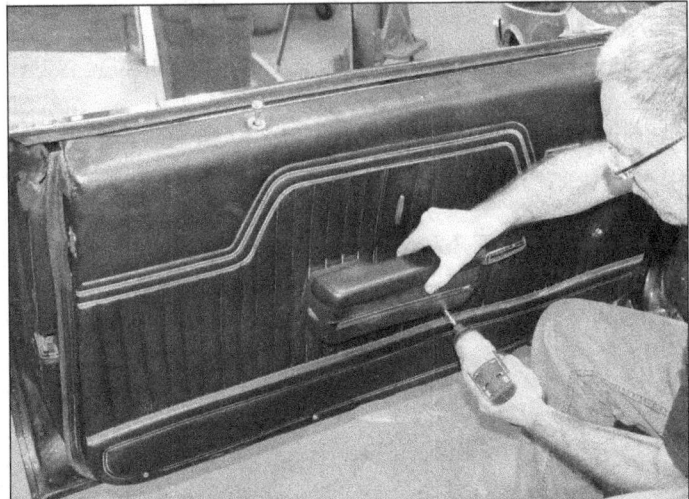

When it comes to the front door panels, start by removing the armrests, window crank, door release lever, door lock knob, remote mirror adjuster cover plate (if optioned), and miscellaneous screws. Gently pry the door panel from the door using your door tool and remove the door panel.

Behind the steering wheel shroud (on standard steering wheels) you will find two wires running to a socket. There is a spring behind this socket that can be removed by pushing in slightly and quickly releasing the insert. Be careful to not lose the spring, as it may fly out.

INTERIOR

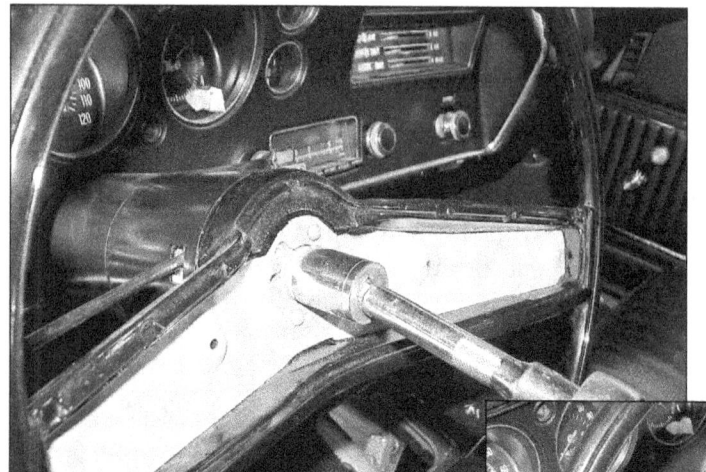

Use of a steering wheel puller helps immensely in removing the steering wheel and will stop you from damaging the wheel. These pullers are inexpensive to purchase or can also be rented at many auto parts stores.

With the steering column locked, carefully remove the center nut holding the steering wheel onto the steering shaft. This must be reinstalled and tightened securely during the restoration process or the steering wheel can fall off.

because the spring will want to jump out and disappear. Tape this spring to the backside of the shroud for later installation.

On cushion rimmed sport wheels, gently pry off the center round horn button. Remove the three screws holding the contact assembly to the steering wheel. Remove the four Phillips screws holding the steering wheel to the hub assembly, and then remove the steering wheel.

In both instances, you will now have access to the center shaft nut. Remove this 7/8-inch headed nut and washer from the shaft. You will thread them back on the shaft in a moment. Using a steering wheel puller (they can be purchased or rented from most any automotive parts retailers), remove the steering wheel or center hub from the sport wheel option. Pull the wheel or hub from the column using the threaded holes provided in both options. For the sport wheel, it is easiest to reassemble the hub, horn contact, and horn button back onto the steering wheel and store it as a unit so the smaller pieces do not get lost.

Air-Conditioning and Ductwork

If your car is equipped with an air conditioner, start by removing any ductwork and vents found on the bottom of the dash carrier. Remove the entire lower vent assembly from one side of the dash bottom to the other at this time and put into safe storage.

Remove the steering column cover panel from the bottom side of the dash carrier by removing the four screws. These are slightly different between a Malibu and an SS car. Place these and the panel in a large bag.

Steering Column Removal and Components

Underneath the dash carrier is a bracket holding the steering column to the dash carrier using two 9/16-inch headed flanged nuts. Remove the passenger-side nut and place it in its bag. Loosen the driver-side nut almost completely for now. This will allow you to drop the column and slightly twist it to access the shift indicator cable found on column shift automatic as well as the column wiring harnesses.

In some rare cases, you may find shims between the column mounting bracket and the column mounting studs. Make note of their placement and return them to their respective location during reassembly. These shims will allow the column to fit evenly in the opening of the dash panel.

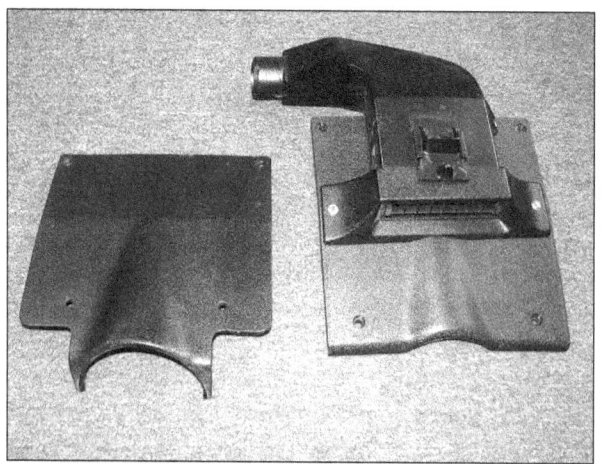

You will find a square plastic cover that has four screws holding it to the dash carrier directly under the steering column where it meets the dash. The one on the left is from a Malibu while the one on the right from an SS Chevelle. You may also find an air-conditioning vent attached to it. These all need to be removed.

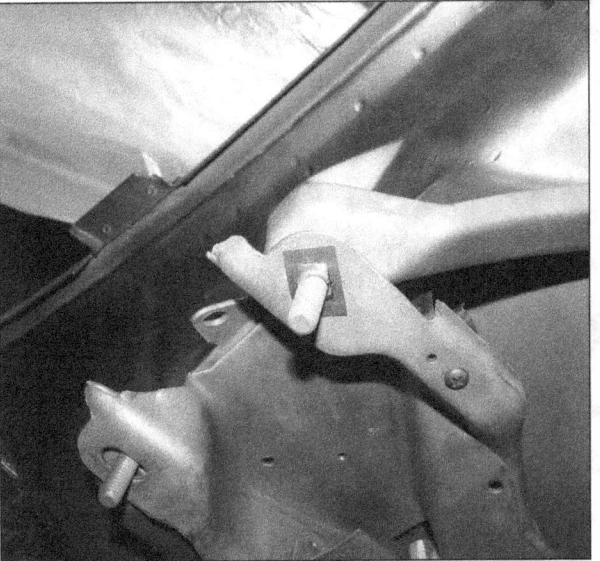

You will first want to remove the kick panel and loosen the column to firewall plate at the firewall. Regardless of whether you are leaving the column in the car or taking it out completely, for the purpose of removing the dash you should at least get it out of your way. Remove the two nuts on either side of the column mounting bracket and drop the column down.

If the column has never been removed, and depending on the assembly plant, you may find a retainer clip used on the assembly line to hold the pedal assembly to the interior of the body structure. It is not mandatory that you replace this, and they are often destroyed when trying to remove them. You will need to remove it if you intend to drop the pedal assembly.

Remove the kick panel from the firewall and tape the two machine bolts to the back of the panel for storage. Behind the kick panel there may or may not be a piece of insulation around the column. Remove it to obtain access to the column to firewall attaching plate.

You may or may not find shim(s) under the mounting bracket. These are used to locate and center the steering column squarely in the opening of the dash. The column mounting bracket, attached by four bolts, can be left attached for the time being.

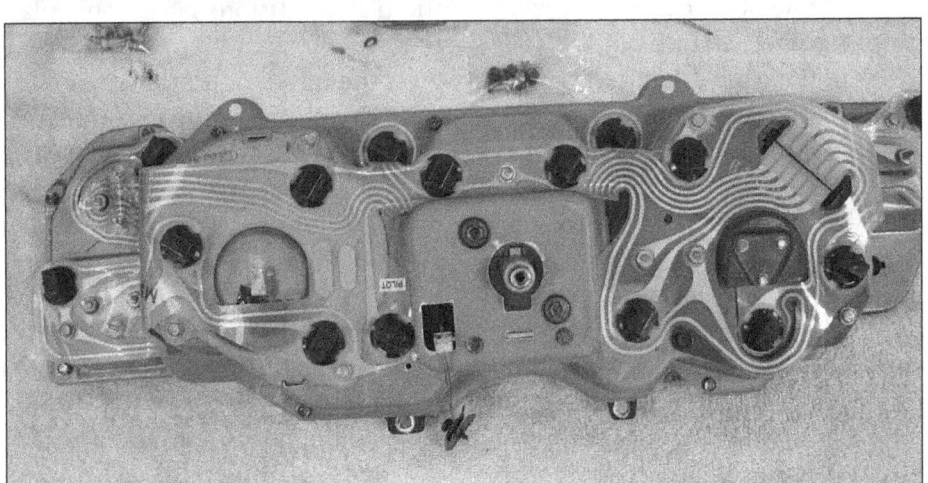

On column-shifted automatic cars, there is a cable that runs from the gauge cluster to the steering column collar and held on by a small machine bolt. This indicates what gear you are in when moving the gear selector on the steering column by way of a small window at the base of the gauges. Lowering the column before removing this will damage the cable and the indicator.

INTERIOR

This harness is for the brake light, emergency flashers, horn, and turn signal circuits. It will also need to be unplugged in order to drop the column. There may be other wires, depending on options such as cruise control. Gently and slightly pry up on the tab in the middle of the two connectors and then gently pull them apart. The harness will stay with the column.

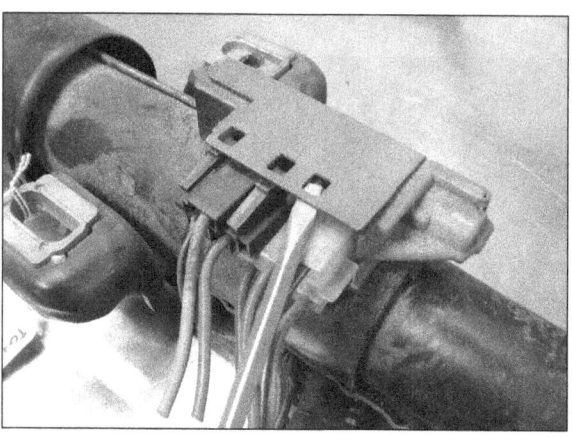

Before removing or dropping the column down completely, these ignition harness plugs need to be removed. Using a screwdriver and starting with the black plug first, depress the locking tabs while gently pulling on the plugs. First the black, then the clear plug.

In some other cases, there will be a spring steel retainer on one of the studs holding the column up. This will have to be removed if you are doing a full restoration and removing the clutch and brake pedal assembly. This does not have to be replaced unless you are restoring to concours condition. It was only used by the factory to aid in the assembly of the brake pedal housing. Spinning it counterclockwise by hand in most cases is all that is needed to remove it. In some instances, it may be necessary to cut it off with a pair of dikes.

Moving to the base of the steering column, remove the two bolts holding the firewall kickplate to the firewall. Tape the bolts to the backside of the plate and store safely. This plate protects the firewall insulation and gives the carpeting a finished look.

On column-shifted automatics, you will have a very small metal cable that runs from the steering column up to the shift position indicator seen just below the speedometer. There is a Phillips screw that holds the cable retainer to the collar. Remove this screw and gently pry the retainer loose from the shifter collar on the steering column and place it out of the way at the point you drop the column.

You will need to unplug the ignition harnesses as well as the steering column harnesses where they both attach to the side of the column to get them out of your way. They will not come out with the steering column. Locate the long, flat electrical plug-in for the steering column wiring harness.

Separate the plug-ins by gently prying up on the single black tab found in the center of the plug-in and separating the two halves. Just above this plug you will find two ignition terminal plugs consisting of one black and one clear plug. Due to their interlocking design, you will have to depress the two tabs on the black connector and remove it first followed by the single tab on the clear connector.

Unplugging the Neutral Safety Switch

Depending on the type of transmission, you will need to unplug the clutch safety (commonly referred to as the neutral safety switch) from the switch mounted on the clutch. You will also need to unplug the brake light harness from the brake switch mounted just in front of the brake pedal.

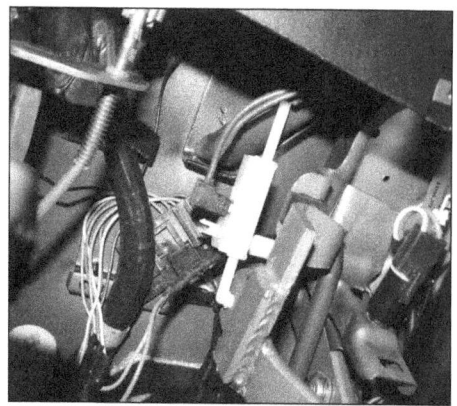

On manual shift cars, you will have a clutch safety switch mounted to the clutch pedal. Gently pull this two-wire plug from the switch. Be very careful here, as these switches are very brittle after nearly 50 years. Once disconnected, you need to fish the two wires back over the top of the clutch/brake pedal assembly.

CHAPTER 8

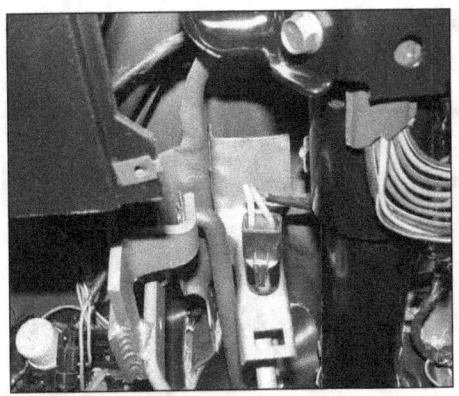

There are two tabs; one on either side of the brake light switch plug. Gently lift up one at a time and pull slightly on the switch to clear the tab. Then move to the other side and do the same. Once both are released, you can pull the harness clear of the car.

Unplugging the Reverse Switch

Moving back down to the base of the column, you will find another switch with either one dual terminal plug or two dual pin plug-ins, depending on the type of column. These terminals are connected to the reverse switch, which has the pink and green plug-in and/or neutral safety switch (on column-shifted automatics only). The neutral safety switch has the two purple wires, one with a white stripe. Photograph and/or tag these wires for later when you need to reattach them.

Helping Hand

From this point on, it would be very beneficial for you to have a helper to help you remove not only the steering column but the dash carrier as well. Use caution when handling any part of the steering column and intermediate shaft. These are designed to collapse in the event of a frontal accident, and the mishandling of either of these components may also cause premature collapsing of them and a lot of extra work on your part.

Remove the nut and cross bolt on the constant velocity (CV) coupler housing located at the top of the intermediate shaft. When pulling the steering column out from the firewall, this coupler housing should be separated from the main shaft.

At the base of the steering column near the firewall, you will find one last plug that will need to be disconnected. Depending on the type of column and transmission, this will vary. Disconnect the plugs that are present and set aside. This completes the column wiring.

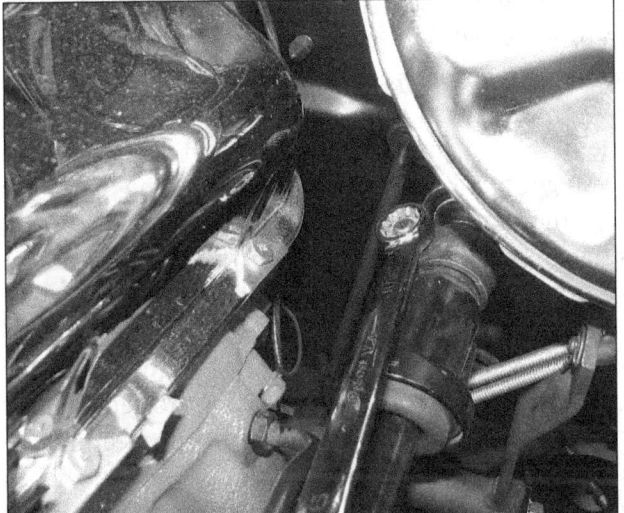

When removing the column, you can either separate from the chassis at the base of the steering column with the CV joint or where it connects to the rag joint. Several different ways are possible, but all will depend on the condition of the parts and the ease of separation. Rust can make it very hard to separate some parts.

Another way to separate the column is at the rag joint. Depending on the type of rag joint, the through bolt can be removed either from the firewall side or the steering gear side of the joint. Use of a 7/16 12-point socket is required. You can also separate the two halves of the rag joint, though that takes a little more effort.

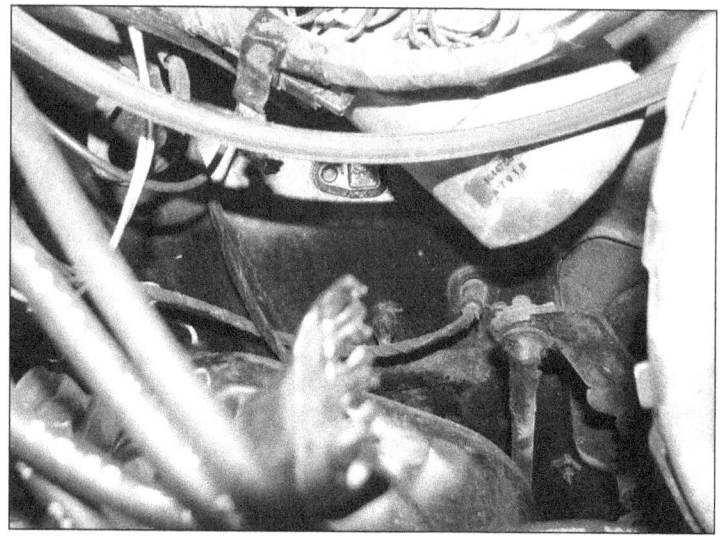

On column automatic shift cars, locate the rod that comes up from the frame and connects to the shift or lockout (depending on transmission type). This is held on by a spring clip and in some cases a washer. Remove the clip and separate the rod from the arm before removing the steering column.

Manual shift lockout rods are held to the column in a similar manner as the automatic cars. Simply remove the spring clip and washer and leave the rod hang for now. Place the clip back into the rod after removal from the lever.

This can sometimes present issues, especially if it is rusty. If you get too aggressive, you may damage the rubber seal or coupling housing. It is recommended to separate the column at the rag joint instead.

If you are having difficulty separating these two at the coupler, remove the two nuts and lock washers from the rag joint and take the entire intermediate shaft along with the column when removing it. Leaving the intermediate shaft attached makes removal of the column a little more cumbersome, but in cases of a rusted CV coupler joint, this will allow you to still be able to remove the column and separate the rusted items on a bench where you can more easily access them.

Big-block cars and small-block cars use a slightly different flange assembly located at the rag joint, but removal is similar. You can also remove the 7/16-inch headed 12-point front through bolt that holds the rag joint onto the steering gear input shaft and pull the complete rag joint along with the intermediate shaft. You will need to decide based on what you find on your car as to which will work best in your case.

Since you are there under the hood, take a moment to remove any rods associated with the steering column removal. On all column-shifted automatics, you will need to remove the spring clip that holds the shift selector/lockout rod to the column. You can find this at the very tail end of the steering column just behind and below the power brake booster and/or master cylinder.

Spring Clip and Z-Bar Lever Disassembly

On floor-shifted manual transmission steering columns, you will need to remove the spring clip from the reverse lockout rod and separate it from the column. Since you are there and it will be in your way shortly anyway, also take this time

If your car is equipped with a manual transmission, remove the spring clip and separate the clutch rod from the Z-bar lever. Replace the clip back into the rod. Note where the two pinched tabs are on the clutch rod in relation to the shift rod boot. Replace the same way you hopefully found them: with the tabs in the engine side of the boot.

to remove the pin from the clutch rod at the clutch Z-bar lever. Leave it loose for now. In the rare instance you have a column-shifted 3-speed

CHAPTER 8

The manual cars have an additional flange and boot for the clutch rod. Loosen and remove four of the five attaching bolts from the plate to allow the bottom end of the steering column to pivot when you detach it from the upper dash end.

Removing both the steering column and dash carrier will go much easier and safer with the aid of another person to help hold and guide parts. The steering column is very susceptible to damage if mishandled, and with help can be safely guided and removed from under the dash. This holds true for reinstallation as well.

manual transmission, you will need to remove the shift rods and lockout rods in the same manner.

At the base of the firewall and steering column, you will see a metal plate that holds the column to the firewall just behind where you removed the plastic kickplate. Depending on if your car has been apart before, there may or may not be a piece of firewall insulation covering this plate. You will have to gently remove this to gain access to the plate and bolts. The plate is held on by five 3/8-inch headed, large integral washered bolts. Remove all of these bolts except the top one, which you will loosen almost completely. Doing this will still hold the base of the column up and not allow it to drop and be damaged.

Clearing the Area

You will see a speedometer cable running from the firewall up under the dash. Gently pull this cable aside so it is not in the way of the metal firewall plate when you remove the steering column. If equipped with a manual transmission, you will need to remove the three bolts holding the clutch rod boot flange to the firewall plate.

Remove the spring clip holding the clutch pushrod to the clutch pedal, and since you have already removed the clip from the engine compartment side, simply pull the rod clear out of the boot. Once removed, replace the spring clip back onto the rod. Before removing, note the location of the two flat tabs on the rod where they meet the clutch rod boot on the engine side. Make sure you assemble them the same way upon reassembly with the tabs forward of the boot. These tabs pull the boot back into the firewall during clutch release. Also note which end of the rod that went to the clutch pedal and which end went to the Z-bar. Label accordingly and bag it.

Almost Done!

You are now ready to completely remove the steering column from the cab of the car. Remove the last remaining bolt that you previously left holding the metal steering column to firewall plate. Bag it with the other ones you previously removed. Remove the last 9/16-inch nut from the steering column to dash carrier and have your helper assist you under the hood to help separate the CV cup connector or rag joint connector, whichever one you choose. Lower the column and pull rearward to remove it from the car, being careful not to hook and damage the intermediate shaft if it is still attached.

You will need to rotate the column slightly to give access for the lever at the base of the column to clear the firewall opening as well as maneuvering the firewall plate around the brake pedal and speedometer cable. Place the steering column and intermediate shaft on your storage shelves.

Dash Removal

It is now time to remove the dash. Again, it will be a lot easier if you have a helper in this process. Start by removing the dash pad. This is held on by four vertical screws underneath the top lip and above the face of the dash where the chrome trim surround is.

Open the glove box and remove two more screws at the top of the glove box doorjamb. Now your pad will be loose from the dash carrier. However, the forward part of the dash pad is held on by six metal tabs that are attached to the bottom side of the dash pad.

Slightly and gently lift the face of the dash pad up at the face of the pad just enough to clear the plastic dash carrier panel. Gently pull the pad toward you, releasing the pad from the dash panel. There are six panel

You will find four screws holding the dash pad onto the dash carrier just above the gauges. They are equally spaced just inside the lip where the carrier meets the pad. Simply remove these and bag. These are unique screws and care must be taken when reinstalling to center them in their existing holes.

Moving to the passenger's side, you will find two more attaching screws just inside the glove box door opening. Though they are similar in appearance to the carrier to pad screws, these are actually shorter. Bag and tag!

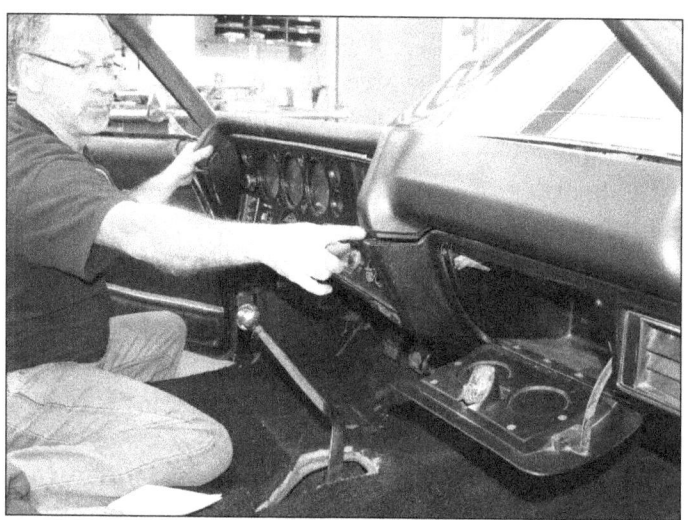

When removing the pad, simply lift up on the face of the pad high enough to clear the plastic dash carrier. This will allow you to gently pull the dash pad toward you without damaging the carrier.

On the front side of the pad, you will find six pad-to-cowl retainer clips. These are simply friction clips and will pull away from the cowl as you pull the dash pad rearward. Make note of where the clips belong in the pad because there are two different types of clips that are unique to their location.

CHAPTER 8

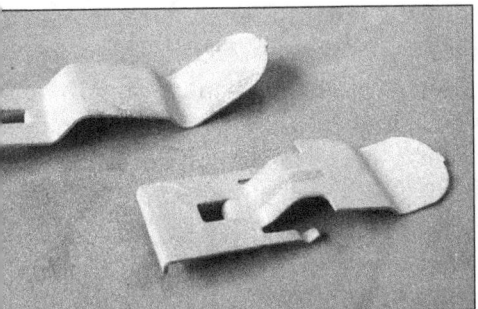

You will note the two different style dash retainer clips. These snap into a recessed notch on the underside of the dash pad. If the pad is original and has not been damaged, these will simply snap back into place. If the dash pad is damaged, you may have to glue the clips back. The outer two clips are on the left while the inner four are on the right of the photo.

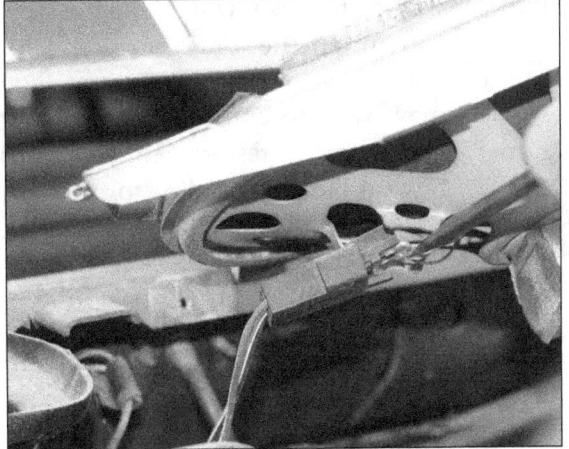

You may elect to remove the dash carrier intact and leave the wiring harness in the cab of the car. It is really a flip of the coin as to which is easier. If you are completely restoring the car then remove the harness. Regardless of which method you use, document the placement of the harness as well as where each plug and ground destination was with several photos.

Regardless of a single or dual dash-mounted speaker, remove the speaker from its mounting bracket and unplug the speaker harness from the speaker or the pigtail, depending on which one you have. Remove the speaker and place in safe keeping.

You may want to consider replacing your old radio with a modern stereo with modern features while still maintaining the OEM face of the original style. They will give you all the modern electronic hook-up features, are considerably lighter, and take up far less room.

As can be seen, the modern stereo will imitate the original almost exactly yet give you all the new up-to-date hookup possibilities, not to mention longevity due to modern electronics.

clips that hold the front of the dash pad to the cowl area. Once you have separated the pad, wiggle it out from between the A-pillars and store it away. It is a good idea to note which dash retainer clips go where on the back side of the dash pad and tape them to their respective location because the outer two clamps are slightly different from the inner four. If any fell during the removal process, find and reattach them or tape them to the underside of the pad.

Dash Speaker Removal

In the very rare instance your car did not come with a radio, disregard the next few paragraphs. Whether your car has two dash stereo speakers or just a mono speaker, remove them at this time for their safety and to help gain access to the rest of the dash carrier.

Center speakers differ not only in size but in how they are attached to the dash carrier. Remove the 5/16 headed sheet metal screws from the brackets and gently lay the speaker aside to gain access to the harness plug and speaker brackets. Find the plug-in at the speaker on the mono speaker, release the locking tab, and gently unplug it.

Generally speaking, the dual speakers will unplug at the end of their respective speaker wire pigtails. Unplug them from the main radio harness at this time. Photograph this for future reference regarding wire

INTERIOR

colors and orientation to help during the reinstallation.

If someone has replaced the speakers with aftermarket ones, you will need to mark which wire goes to which terminal. There is a positive side as well as a negative side of the speaker terminal. If your car does have a stereo, locate the rear speaker harness pigtail behind the dash and firewall pad and unplug the rear speaker harness from the stereo harness. Trace the wires from the back of the stereo to locate this plug-in.

Now remove the speakers and bracket(s) from the dash. The two-speaker arrangement used a bracket with two screws mounted into the cowl and one into a bracket at the dash on either side of the dash. If only equipped with a center mono speaker, it uses two screws into the cowl and two mounted into speaker bracket. Remove the speakers and mounting brackets from the dash carrier and set aside.

As a side note here, the round-gauge dash uses slightly different single and dual speaker brackets than a sweep dash would use, so be aware of that if you need to replace them or they were missing. These brackets are also unique from side to side, so mark them as to which side they were removed from. Remember to take pictures.

This would also be a good time to remove the rear speakers and/or defroster (if so equipped) to keep the entire radio wiring and speakers together. Put them all away in a safe place. The rear speakers used a blue/black and tan/black plug if stereo equipped.

If the speakers need work, now would be the time to either order new ones or send your originals off for re-coning so that you are not waiting for them when it comes time to reinstall them. If you intend for your Chevelle to be driven often, you may want to consider having your radio/speaker restorer convert your 50-year-old AM radio to modern stereo equipment while still retaining the factory appearance of your radio face. You can also buy one of the aftermarket stereos already modernized using an OEM face. Another alternative is to purchase a completely new stereo that already has the OEM face on it but is brand new, has all the modern features, and is considerably lighter than an original.

Emergency Brake Pedal Release Handle Removal

Look under the dash on the driver's side to find your emergency brake pedal release handle. Follow that under the dash and locate where the handle rod connects to the emergency brake pedal assembly relay rod. There is a clip holding the two together where the two rods meet. Gently pry the clamped end off the relay rod and raise the handle rod and clip from the relay rod. Reattach the clip to the relay rod for safekeeping at this time.

Again, this chapter is being written using a Super Sport Chevelle, non-air car as a model, though air-conditioner-equipped cars and Malibus will be somewhat similar. Before you actually drop the dash, you will need to remove some wiring connections, clips, terminals,

Locate the emergency brake pull lever and separate it from the relay rod on the e-brake pedal assembly. There you will find a clip holding the two rods together. First separate the clip from the relay rod by gently prying on the two tabs. Once loose, raise the pull knob rod and clip off the relay rod.

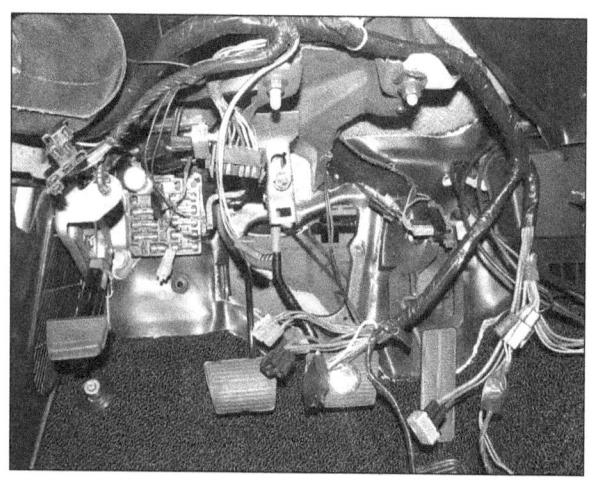

If you are only removing your dash panel assembly and not restoring the entire interior, you may find it easier to disconnect the harness from the dash carrier and leave all else connected at their individual components on the firewall. Take lots of notes and photos of where the leads were connected to the dash carrier assembly.

antennas, ducting, etc. If you are simply removing the dash for restoration or complete replacement, it may be easier to disconnect all the electrical connectors from the dash, leaving them hang for now, and reconnect them upon replacement of the dash. If you are removing the entire interior, it is better to remove the harness along with the dash and leave all the dash connectors intact on the back of the dash so as to better keep track of where they belong.

Air-Conditioning

If your car is equipped with air-conditioning, locate the upper center air vent outlet in the rear center of the dash. Remove the screws holding the outlet to the dash and slide the flexible hose from the base of the outlet. On both A/C- and non-A/C-equipped cars, unplug the terminal and light socket(s) from the heater/air-conditioning control head. Very carefully release the control unit from its place in the dash and make sure it is free from obstructions as the heater or A/C selector panel will remain in the cab during the dash removal. For now, leave it hang behind the dash carrier.

There is also a vacuum plug-in that is attached to the A/C control unit. Make sure the vacuum hoses are also free of any obstructions and that all wiring is clear of these and will not be in the way during dash removal. Unplug the blue/yellow/orange terminal from the top center of the firewall mounted heater box on non-A/C cars and let it hang. Locate the antenna wire at the rear of the radio assembly at this time, gently wiggle it to pull it out from the radio, and let it hang.

You can either leave the radio in the dash or remove it now. Due to the sheer weight of the radio, it is suggested to simply remove it and get it out of the way. Most radios will be very similar in their removal. It is nearly impossible to remove a radio from an air-conditioned car without a lot of finagling and duct removal, so it may be best to take it with the dash or as you are removing the dash.

Radio Removal

Start by removing the two knobs and tuners behind the knobs if so equipped. This will expose the nuts that hold the tuner and volume shafts to the dash carrier. You will normally find two types of nuts: a 5/8 hex nut that can be easily removed with a deep well 5/8 socket or a round nut with opposing slots. The round nut usually requires a special removal tool available at most restoration parts suppliers, or

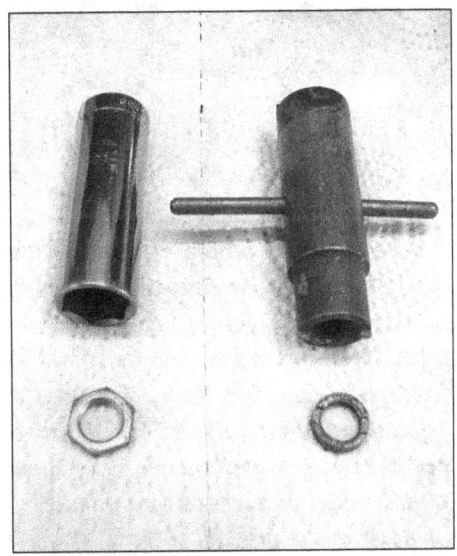

You will generally find two different types of radio shaft lock nuts. One is a 5/8 hex headed nut. The other is a spanner type nut that usually requires a special tool to remove, though gentle turning with a slotted screwdriver can sometimes persuade it to come off.

you can sometimes persuade them to loosen using a slotted screwdriver. Once those are removed, go to the rear of the radio and find the antenna lead as well as the power/speaker harness connector at the rear of the radio and remove both. The last thing to do is remove the rear radio brace that mounts to the carrier frame and to the back of the radio. Carefully persuade the radio from its mounting position and lower it from the carrier.

Miscellaneous Items Left of Brake Pedal

On the firewall area left of the brake pedal, you will find the fuse box assembly. This is held on by two 5/16 headed bolts located on bottom left and top right corners of the fuse panel. Completely loosen these at this time. They may or may not come out of the fuse panel, so do not be alarmed if they do not pull completely out.

The junction plug for the intermediate harness is hanging just above the fuse box. Unplug this harness connector now. Remove the tan emergency brake pedal indicator light wire from the switch mounted at the rear of the e-brake pedal. Gently pull the bullet connector vertically just to the right of the 90 degree terminal. There will normally be a black sheath covering this area. Do not try and pull the silver connector from the rear of the switch because this will damage the switch.

Lastly, locate the dimmer switch. Unplug the three-wire connector from this switch by gently prying on the two plastic tabs on the terminal. Remove the terminal assembly and let it hang freely so it will not get caught on anything during the dash removal.

INTERIOR

If you are removing the dash harness with the dash, separate the fuse panel from the firewall as well as the e-brake indicator light, intermediate harness, and dimmer switch. All of these pigtails will come with the dash harness. Make sure any auxiliary optional wires that are connected to the fuse panel are also noted and removed.

Tachometer Wire

If your car is equipped with a tachometer, remove the tan lead from the ignition coil terminal in the engine compartment at this time. Push the wire and grommet through the face of the firewall and back into the cab area.

Disconnect any accessory terminals at the fuse block, such as the cowl induction or automatic transmission down shift electrical leads. These plugs are unique and most will only fit into the fuse box in their own designated terminal slot. It is still best to photograph and tag their insertion locations into the fuse panel and routing for future reference and then leave hang for now. There are just a few remaining leads left that will have to be removed before we can remove the dash.

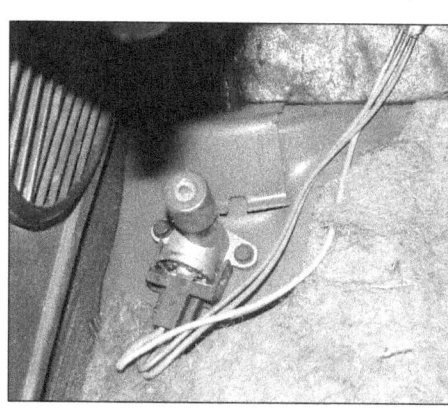

The three-wire pigtail for the dimmer switch is easily removed by simply opening up the tabs on the connector and pulling it free from the switch. Pull out and away and make sure that it does not catch on anything during the dash removal.

Underhood for the Harness/Fuse Panel

You will now need to go back under the hood and locate the main harness plugs just under the brake master cylinder. These engine and light harness plug-ins are held onto the fuse box with a 3/8 headed bolt. Using a long extension and swivel

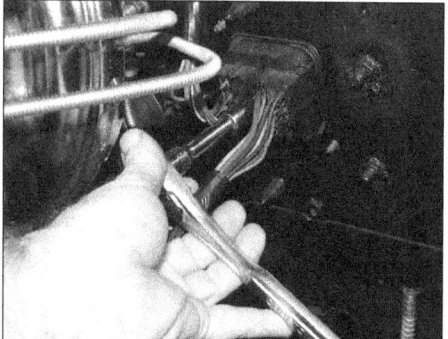

Before you can completely remove the fuse panel from the firewall, you must first separate the inner fuse panel from the outer engine compartment harness connectors. There is a 3/8 headed bolt that holds this to the fuse panel. Loosen but do not remove this bolt. Grasp the harness and pull it away from the firewall.

(if the front clip is still on the car), loosen the bolt completely and pull the two plugs away from the fuse panel as a unit. The attaching bolt is designed to stay with one of the plugs, so do not attempt to remove the bolt completely from the plug in.

Unplug any accessory terminals from the fuse block only after you have documented their locations and routing for the purpose of reinstallation. Most often these terminals can only be placed into certain slots due to their design, but it is best to document them anyway. These harnesses are generally separate from the main dash harness and will not come out with the dash.

CHEVELLE RESTORATION AND AUTHENTICITY GUIDE: 1970–1972

CHAPTER 8

Driver-Side Floor Near Cowl

Locate the two purple wire terminals at the clutch pedal switch (if so equipped and if not already removed) and unplug at this time.

Moving to the emergency brake pedal assembly, locate the single black ground lead just above and behind where the relay rod enters the emergency brake pedal assembly. Using a 5/16 nut driver, remove the screw holding this wire to the bulkhead.

Locate the turn signal flasher mounted in its snap bracket on the top right side of the brake pedal bulkhead assembly and gently pop it from the bracket and let it hang. Malibus will be slightly different in their location or on some cars the flasher will just be hanging free.

Locate the center console pigtail (if so equipped) or you may have previously disconnected at the front of the console. Follow this pigtail up and behind the firewall pad and heater box. Locate the connector where this pigtail attaches to the main dash harness. Unplug this connector from the main dash harness and let it hang.

Unplug any other air-conditioning harnesses and vacuum lines from the dash that run through the firewall.

Dome Light Wiring Removal

Unscrew the dome light switch from the doorjamb, pull the switch out, and disconnect the wires from there. This can be done before you start removing the dash. Using a needle-nose plier, gently pull these wires from the back of the switch. There is a very small locking tab that needs to be released on the connector, which makes them a little difficult to remove. Be very careful to not damage the lead or the switch.

Do the same for the passenger dome light switch in the opposite location. This will only have one white wire and will be a bullet terminal. Gently pull it from the back of the switch. Another way is to remove it while you are taking the dash out. This can be cumbersome to reach and slightly easier as the dash is being removed but locate the two black and white wires running to the driver-side dome light switch just about the side kick panel. Remove the leads in the same manner as previously described.

Unplug the two-wire brake terminal from the brake switch. It can be found threaded into the brake pedal housing assembly just above the

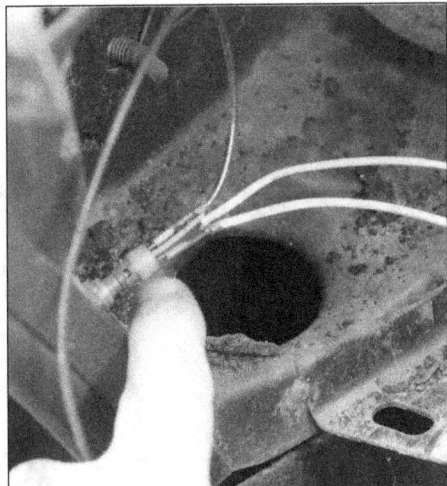

Locate the courtesy light switch on both sides of the cab just above the kickpanels. It is easiest to remove the switch through the doorjamb, being careful to not twist the wires. Be especially careful removing the wires from the driver's side as there is a very small tab that needs to be depressed on the connect in order to remove it. The passenger's side uses a bullet connector and this simply unplugs.

steering column, which you should have already done previously.

Dash Carrier Assembly Removal

You are now ready to remove the dash assembly. This would once again be a good time to solicit the help of a buddy to aid in its removal. Supporting the center of the dash is critical so as to not crack or damage it during removal. It is very heavy on one side and not supporting it correctly could crack it between the main gauge face and glove box area.

There are (normally) seven 7/16 headed machine bolts that hold the dash assembly to the firewall. One upper and lower bolt on the driver's side of the dash, one upper and lower at the far passenger's side, two located

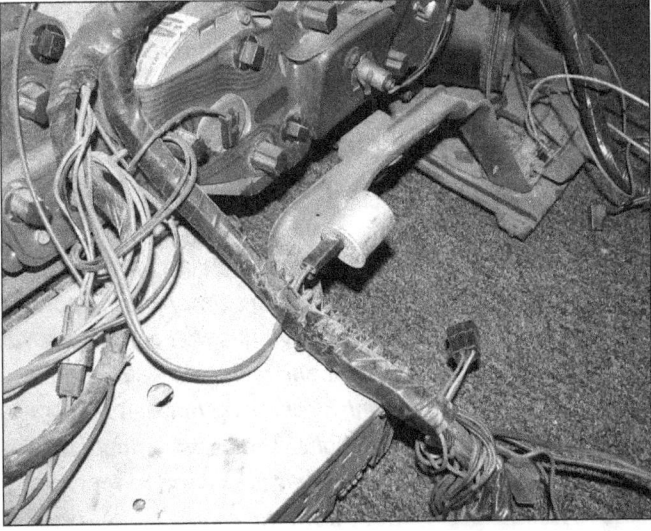

Generally speaking, you will normally find the turn-signal flasher mounted in a snap bracket located on the top passenger's side of the brake/clutch pedal bulkhead just behind the dash. Other years may vary. Pull the flasher from the bracket and leave it hang during the dash removal.

INTERIOR

just right of center behind the dash, and one directly above the steering column mount you just recently removed. It is best to leave the top three bolts across the dash assembly loose but not totally removed until you are completely ready to remove the dash. This way using your helper and one of your free hands, you can support the dash while removing the last three remaining bolts.

Removing the Dash Carrier Assembly

1 Locate the number-1 bolt on the upper left corner of the dash. Loosen completely but do not remove. This will help hold the dash in place till you are ready to take it out.

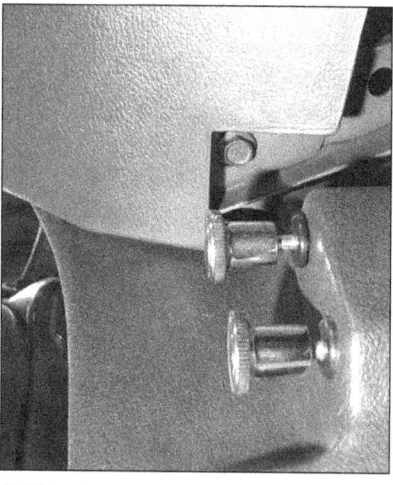

2 Just below that same corner and underneath the dash you will find number-2 bolt facing up vertically. Completely remove this bolt.

3 Moving to the right side of the dash, find the number-3 bolt in the opposite location as you found number-1. Loosen it completely but do not remove it.

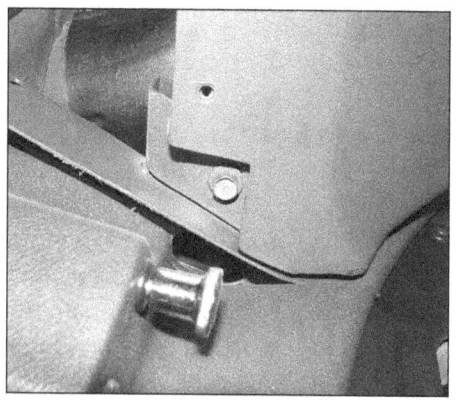

4 Just below that same passenger-side corner and underneath the dash you will find the number-4 bolt facing up vertically. Completely remove this bolt.

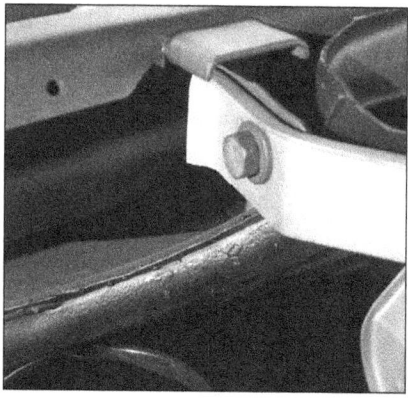

5 Just to the right of center you will find an upper dash bracket attaching the dash carrier to the firewall. Completely loosen the number-5 bolt but do not remove it at this time.

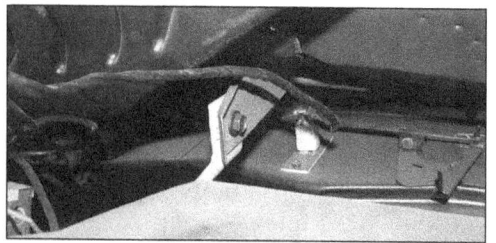

6 Just below and to the right of the number-5 bolt is the number-6 bolt. This bolt can be completely removed.

7 The last bolt is number-7 and is often missing. This is found just above the steering column and can be seen after dropping the column down. Remove this bolt completely. At this point and with your helper, you can finish removing numbers-1, -3, and -5 bolts. The carrier should now be completely loose and ready to remove from the cab.

CHEVELLE RESTORATION AND AUTHENTICITY GUIDE: 1970–1972

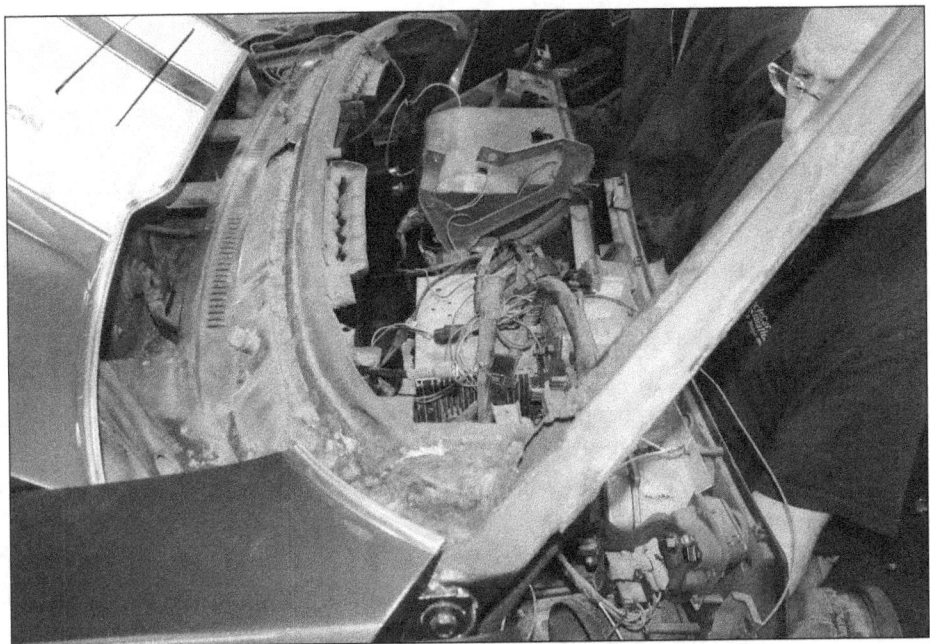

Now that everything is unplugged (except the speedometer cable) and unbolted, you and your helper can gently pull the carrier toward yourselves, paying close attention to any forgotten cables, wires, brackets, etc. If you feel any resistance, stop and determine why before you break anything. If something was forgotten, you can always lay the dash back in and replace bolt numbers-1, -3, and -5 and fix the issue before trying again.

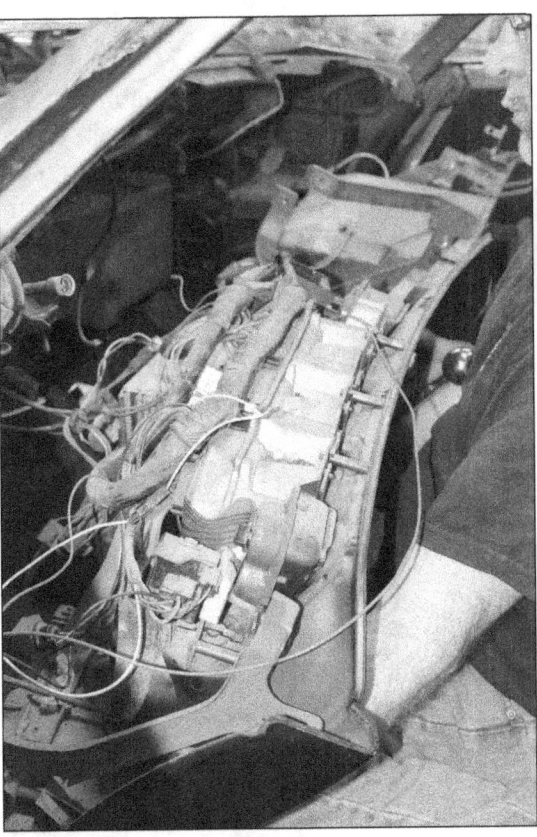

With the dash held firmly by you and your helper, take one last look to make sure everything has been disconnected. If you are satisfied, then continue to remove it from the cab and either set it on a stand or a workbench with the glove box side supported.

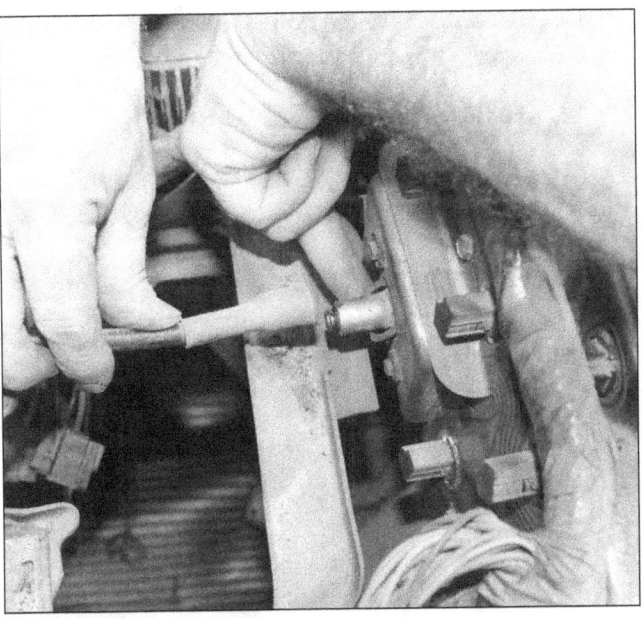

As you are removing the dash carrier, pull it away from the firewall mounts by a couple of inches, just enough to get your hand behind it. Depress the metal retainer holding the speedometer cable to the speedometer and pull the cable free. Make sure that you and your helper work in tandem and do not bend the dash in the center because it may crack.

Very slowly and gently pull the dash toward you and away from the cowl and firewall mounts while still maintaining a visual behind the dash. Make sure nothing is getting caught or that you missed a connector or two, then slowly and gently continue to remove the dash. If you feel any resistance, stop and determine where it is coming from before you proceed. Make sure your heater/air-conditioning selector is clear from the dash and set on the floor.

If you were not able to remove the radio previously, you can do so now or remove it once the dash is on a bench. When you have pulled the dash back an inch or two, look down behind the dash for the speedometer cable. It runs to the rear of the speedometer gauge. Depress the metal tab at the base of the cable and remove the cable from the gauge.

Remove the complete dash and wiring harness assembly from the cab and place on a solid surface such

INTERIOR

as a table top or a carpeted floor. Notice that the glove box area will not be touching the table top, so much caution must be taken to not push down on this area. Placing a small rolled up towel or cardboard box under this part of the dash will help support it and give you an added safety margin.

Interior Firewall Area

Now that the dash carrier assembly is removed and out of the way, you can move on to the last components on the firewall and kick panel area. You should still have a defroster vent, heater box and control, brake/clutch pedal assembly, throttle pedal, dimmer switch, emergency brake pedal assembly, firewall pad, kick panels (if not already removed), and cowl vents. Remove each of these items if you intend to do a full-blown restoration.

Remove the two round ducts that were connected to your dash vents on non-air-conditioned cars and all of the remaining ducting if your car has air-conditioning. The plastic vent tubes simply slide off. Mark which one was the driver's side and which one was the passenger's side. The actual cowl vents are held in place by a small metal clip that slides onto the cowl vent opening. Remove the clip and pull the vents free. If you have not already removed the kick panel vent cables from the upper cowl vents, do so at this time. Photograph how you found these and the vents. The vents are left- and right-handed and need to be orientated correctly in their respective openings.

If you are completely restoring the car, it may be easier to hold off on any more until you have removed the entire front clip, engine, and transmission. This will make the remaining items in the interior firewall area just a little easier, especially if equipped with air-conditioning. If you have already removed the engine then proceed ahead.

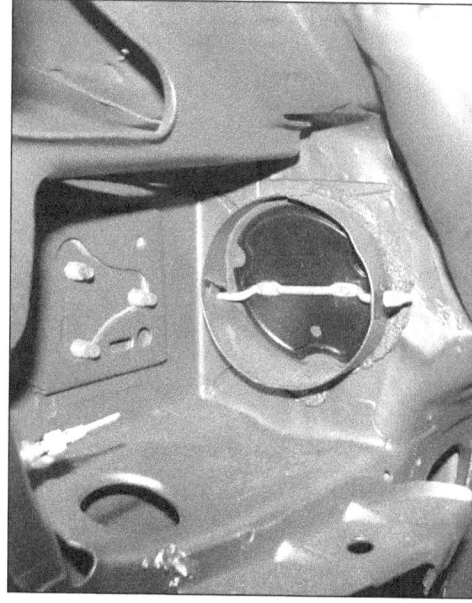

On a complete full restoration, remove the upper cowl vents. Take good photographs of these as they must be put back on the correct side as well as oriented correctly in the vent holes. There is a flat retainer clip that must be removed in order to remove the vent. This can be found near the arm where the cable attaches to it. Slide this clip off and pull the vent free.

Once the dash is completely removed, you can see what remains mounted to the firewall. Remove these items and place them away in a safe spot before proceeding.

The defroster vent is held on by four round washer-headed Phillips screws, two per side in the inside of the upper vent openings. On some cars you may also find a sheet metal screw holding the defroster vent on the right side about midway down. Lastly and only on some Chevelles, you may find a large washer-headed sheet metal bolt holding the base of the vent to the heater box.

CHAPTER 8

Remove the defroster duct from the firewall by unscrewing the four Phillips round-headed screws from just inside the vent opening at the top of the dash. On some cars you may find an additional screw down the right side of the vent tube. You may also find a washered screw holding the base of the duct to the heater box, but not all cars had these. Place all the screws in a bag and tape the bag to the defroster unit.

Heater Core Removal

In a non-air-conditioned car, remove the heater core housing by unbolting the five 7/16 speed nuts from the engine compartment side that holds the heater core cover on. Drain the radiator of anti-freeze/coolant (if not already done), and remove the two heater core coolant lines at the firewall.

It is best to cut the heater hoses off at the end of the inlet/outlet pipe and then carefully slice the remaining rubber pieces lengthwise to remove them from the inlet/outlet. This will eliminate any chance of damaging the heater core or the pipes by attempting to twist the hoses from these connectors and possibly cracking the pipes at their soldered joint at the core.

Now gently wiggle the interior heater box from the firewall. Gently pull it rearward and away from the firewall and let it rest on the floor. If you recall from an earlier step, you disconnected the heater selector and cable assembly from the dash and let it hang. At this time, you can remove the entire heater box, cables, and selector housing from the car as a unit. You can also photo document where the cables were attached and disconnect them from each of their vent arms to get the selector out of your way.

Emergency Brake Pedal

Once you have removed the heater box, you can remove the emergency brake pedal. Start with the pedal in the fully released position and slightly depress the parking brake. This pulls up on the primary cable. Place a locking plier at the base of the cable where it goes through the floorpan and lock it. This will hold the cable and give it some slack. Release the pedal (you may have to pull up on the pedal a little). If present, remove the cable retaining clip from the pivot lever and pull the cable end clear.

You can also detach the primary cable from the intermediate cable by loosening the lock nuts where the two meet under the car. This will also afford you plenty of slack in order to remove the cable end from the e-brake pedal.

Now that you have removed the cable and the brake switch wire,

This is how the complete heater box and control assembly will look when you remove it. Leave the cables and selector attached until its removed and put it on the bench so you can document where the cables run and how they are attached. It is much easier to do it then instead of trying to remove the cables now.

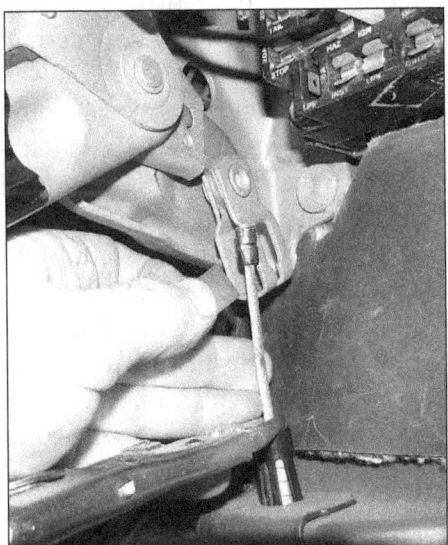

Simply depress the pedal slightly and place locking pliers on the cable where it meets the floor. Release the pedal, remove the retaining clip, and pull the cable free from the pivot assembly. Release the cable and remove the pedal assembly.

INTERIOR

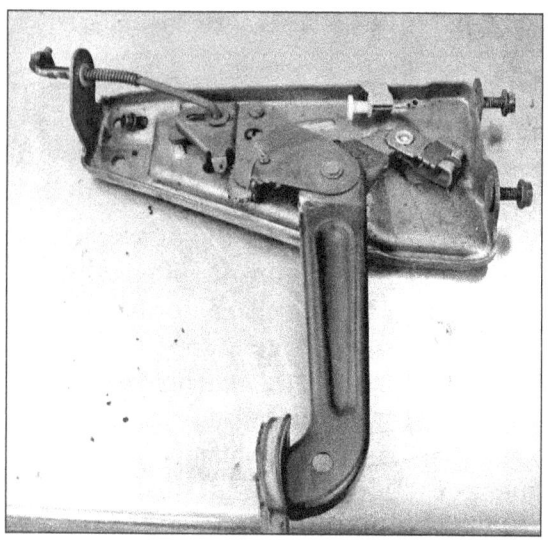

With the pedal assembly on the bench, you can see all of the items in this photo. On the right are the two studs and nut that hold the assembly to the firewall, the cable pivot and retainer clip, the brake light switch, the front attaching bolt, and the relay rod to release handle rod clip.

move to the engine side of the firewall. Remove the two nuts holding the pedal assembly to the firewall. Going back into the cab of the car, remove the sheet metal bolt holding the pedal assembly to the side bulkhead of the cab found near the nose of the assembly. The pedal assembly can now be removed from the cab of the car. Put all the hardware in a bag with the pedal assembly and store.

At this point, you can also remove the primary cable from the body. Simply attach a small worm hose clamp around the cable and tighten snugly around the base where it comes through the floor. Doing so will compress the locking tabs, which will then allow you to gently push the cable back through the hole. Sometimes a light tapping with a small hammer and punch will be needed to help push it through. If it does not want to push through, make sure all the locking ears are completely depressed or you will break them off when trying to force the cable.

Kick Panel Removal

Each of the two side kick panels on non-air-conditioned cars are held on by five hex-head sheet metal screws and caulking found under the snap on vent covers. Start by removing the vent covers by simply inserting a flat screwdriver or similar tool between the edge of the cover and the kick panel. Gently and slowly pry the vent cover off to expose the screws and remove them.

On air-conditioned cars, you will usually find two finish screws holding the kick panel to the interior bulkhead. Remove those. Once all screws

Remove the five 5/16 screws and gently pry the panel loose from the interior bulkhead. Once you feel the caulking has released itself, gently pull rearward slightly to clear the pinch weld in the doorjamb. Twist and wiggle the panel loose from the opening.

are removed, gently and slowly pull the kick panels toward the interior of the car just enough to break loose the caulking that was applied by the factory around the vent opening on the backside. Once you have that loose, pull the kick panels rearward just enough for the finish edge to clear the pinch weld in the doorjamb area. The kick panel has steps on the rear of the panel around the vent opening and with a little twisting and wiggling motion you will get them to clear the opening. Once clear, remove the panel completely.

It is imperative to replace the caulking (or duct seal) on the rear of the panel during installation or you will have a huge water leak inside the cab the next time you wash the car. This caulking can be found at most hardware stores in the electrical department. Once everything is out of the way, vacuum out the vent

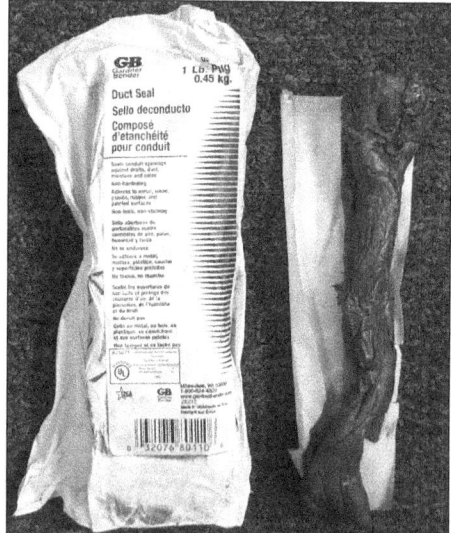

Replacement caulking can be found at your local hardware store and must be replaced on the rear of the kick panel or they will leak water. Make a 1/2-inch diameter round rope after cutting the caulking into strips and apply to the rear of the kick panel to reseal it upon reinstallation.

opening in the body cavity as many leaves, branches, paper, rags, etc. can usually be found there.

Brake Pedal Rod

From inside the cab, locate and remove the locking clip that holds the brake pedal rod to the brake pedal using a small pin. Once removed, push the pin through, move the rod away from the hole, and reassemble them. You will also want to observe the location where you found the pin because they will differ between a manual brake car and a power brake car. Depending on which type of brake you have, you may also find a return spring and clip as well as a brake light switch bracket mounted on the pedal. Document how all of these were found and oriented for later installation.

Locate the pin and retainer clip holding the brake actuating rod to the brake pedal. Remove the clip and pin, slide the rod out of the way, and reinsert the pin and clip for safekeeping. Also make note of any other springs, retainers, and brackets attached to the brake pedal. You can leave them in place for now, but document their location.

Brake Lines and Hardware

If not already removed, the brake lines will contain fluid, so make sure you have a way to catch the fluid as you take them off. Be careful not to drip fluid on any painted surfaces, as the fluid will eat the paint. After removing the master cylinder and brake metering valve (if so equipped), drain them of all fluid, rinse with hot water or solvent, and store them away. Remove the power brake booster bolts (if so equipped) after disconnecting the power brake vacuum line running from the intake manifold to the booster if you have not already done this.

On the back side of the booster you may find a small bracket that holds the two brake lines coming up from the proportioning valve. Remove this and place in a bag along with the attaching bolt and two rubber cushions that are wrapped around the brake lines inside the bracket. Once removed, the booster will be free from the brake pedal and the firewall and can now be removed.

If so equipped, remove the brake metering valve and bracket after first removing the lines from the brake master cylinder and proportioning valve. Be careful not to drip brake fluid on any painted parts. Thoroughly clean, dry, and place in storage before moving on.

Depending on the type of brake system you have, you may or may not have this bracket if your car is not equipped with disc brakes. On drum brake cars, a brake line bracket can be found on the frame. Regardless, document its location before removing and placing in a bag. Regardless of the brake type you will need to remove the four nuts holding the brake pedal assembly to the firewall.

INTERIOR

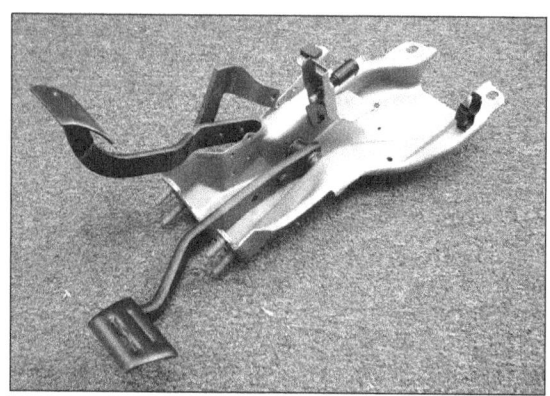

After removing the brake and/or brake and clutch assembly from the interior, place it on a bench and photo document the placement of parts, colors, inspection marks, etc. After you have done that, disassemble, clean, and restore the unit.

Clutch and Brake Pedal Assembly Removal

Next will be the clutch and brake pedal assembly. Depending on the transmission type in your car, you will find either one or two pedals, but the assembly and its removal are much the same. You should still have one of the two nuts that you removed when you removed the steering column from the cab and was lightly threaded back onto the stud (see page 171).

You may now remove that nut, which will then allow you to drop the entire brake/clutch pedal assembly from the cab of the car. Lay the assembly on the bench and document its parts, paint coverage, and any inspection marks. Place aside for later restoration.

Speedometer Cable

If not done already, pull the speedometer cable through the firewall and place it in a safe place. The cable will run through a round rubber grommet held onto the firewall with three small tabs. Carefully pry this loose from the firewall and keep with the speedometer cable. These are generally in poor condition and will have to be replaced. There will likely be other clips spot welded to the body that also hold the cable up away from the exhaust. Gently pry these open and pull the cable clear.

Accelerator Pedal Assembly Removal

Remove the accelerator pedal assembly. This will vary slightly based on if it is a cowl-induction or an automatic-equipped car. If so equipped, unplug the wiring to the cowl/downshift switch located near the top of the pedal rod. Remove the switch that is attached by one sheet metal bolt and place in a bag.

You have likely already disconnected the accelerator cable from the carburetor but not from the accelerator pedal yet, so now is a good time to do so. You should find a very small black plastic cable retainer at the top of the pedal rod with the cable threaded through it. Push this out of the rod along with the cable and then separate the cable from the plastic retainer. Put it in a safe place so you do not lose it. Once everything is separated, remove the two remaining sheet metal bolts running through the retainer plate and into the firewall. Place the entire assembly in a bag along with the switch if so equipped.

Dimmer Switch

Remove the two small 5/16 headed sheet metal screws from the foot actuated dimmer switch. Then, remove the switch and place in a bag with the screws.

Fresh Air Vents

On non-air-conditioned cars, you will find a round flapper on either end of the firewall with a cable wire attached to it. These are the fresh air

Make note of how the accelerator pedal and cable are attached as well as any switch and wire connectors you may find, depending on the options of the car. The accelerator cable must be removed from the pedal assembly before the unit can be removed from the car. Keep the wiring pigtails, attaching screws, and any other hardware together in a tagged bag.

CHAPTER 8

vents that are actuated by one of the knobs on the kick panel. Follow the cable down from the vent flapper lever and find a small retainer and screw holding the cable to the side panel. Remove these on both sides.

Next, locate the small slide clip retainer that keeps the flapper held into the round duct. Slide this retainer off and gently remove the flapper assembly from the duct. Once removed, twist slightly so that you can remove the cable end. Do this for both sides. Place all the items in bag.

Firewall Pad

The last thing you will need to remove is the insulated firewall pad that is held onto the firewall by a series of plastic pushpins. If you are replacing the pad, it is easiest to cut all the ends flush with the engine compartment side of the firewall and then remove the remaining parts from inside the interior. The pad will simply fall down and you can now remove it. These are seldom in good enough condition to reuse, so a suitable replacement will need to be found.

Carpet Removal

Since virtually everything else in the cab of the car has been previously removed, you can now simply pull the front and rear carpeting from the car that you had been using as a pad. If you didn't before, take note and document how it was cut in and installed. If the carpet is original to the car, photograph and take note how it was cut under the seats and around the shifter hole and console and retain for later use as a template.

Again, be on the lookout for any paperwork, build sheets, or other relics that may have been laid under the carpet when it was installed at the factory or just placed there in the life of the car. If found, be very careful in their removal, as these may be very valuable to you and the car. Many times these may be stuck to the top or bottom of the sound deadener and can be very difficult to remove without damaging them. They may also be very badly stained. Utmost caution must be exercised here.

Sound Deadener and Wiring Harness Removal

In most cases and depending on originality, you will find a sound deadener under your carpeting. If original, it will be a heavy, thick tar paper and is normally stuck to the

The firewall pad will need to be removed from the cab of the car before any bodywork and painting is done. These pads are held on with plastic push plugs. Cutting them flush to the firewall on the engine side will make them easier to remove. Simply push the rest of the plugs into the cab of the car and discard. These will come with the new firewall pad.

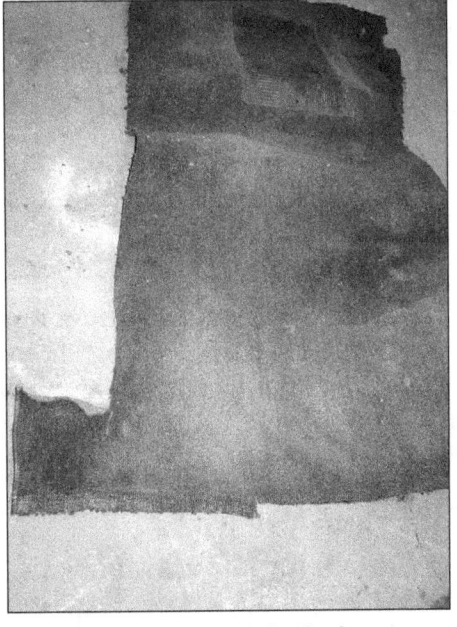

If your carpet was original, always document before and after removal how it was laid in and cut around for such things as seats, dimmer switch, console, shifter, etc., and use the old carpet as a template when replacing with the new one.

If original, you will find a tar paper type of sound deadener under the carpeting. This padding wards off heat as well as deadens highway noise. It should be replaced; a similar product is available through your interior supplier. Use a heat gun to aid in the removal of it but only after documenting how it was originally installed.

190   CHEVELLE RESTORATION AND AUTHENTICITY GUIDE: 1970–1972

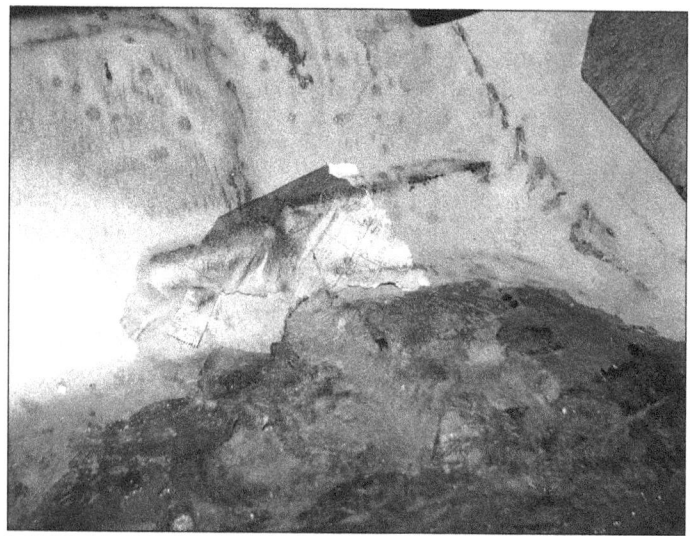
When removing your carpet and sound deadener, take your time! There are many pieces of history to the car that may be found both under the carpet as well as the sound deadener. Some of those items such as a build or broadcast sheet can add thousands of dollars to your car's value, so it is imperative that they be removed very cautiously from the car.

Make note of any wiring you find under the carpeting or sound deadener and how it was installed, clips that were holding it down, routing, etc., as well as where the connections were made on the tail end so you can reinstall them exactly how they were originally found. The wires you may come across could be: intermediate harness, defroster, rear speakers, power convertible top, trunk release, and possibly others.

floor of the car. If it is in good shape and you are only doing a cosmetic restoration, it might be okay to simply leave it there. Removing it will only damage it.

If you are doing a rotisserie restoration or repairing floorpan damage, this will have to be removed and should be replaced. Photo document exactly how the original was installed so that when replacing with the aftermarket pieces you will know how they should lay in.

Using a heat gun and a wide putty knife will help immensely in the removal of the sound deadener, though it is usually best to try and remove as much as you can by hand before going to the heat gun. Heat a small area starting at the edge and slowly work the tar paper loose with the putty knife. Do not get the area too hot; this can also melt the tar paper or catch it on fire. Only a slight amount of heat is required to work it loose. Even a hot air hair dryer will work. Also, take care to not damage any wiring that is under the tar paper, such as the intermediate wiring harness, rear speaker harness, rear defroster harness, or power top harness, and as always, stay very vigil for any paperwork.

Once the pad has been removed, it is time to remove the above-mentioned harnesses. Photograph how the harnesses were run and where the rear plug-ins were found so you can replicate them upon reinstallation.

Removing the Harnesses

Start by unplugging harnesses at their rear most destination, be it speakers, defrosters, rear taillight harness, or power top hydraulic pump. This would also be a good time to separate the dome light harness from the rear intermediate harness. This junction plug can be found just above the driver-side rear wheel tub and will normally be an orange and white wire. For now, you can leave the orange and white harness lay loose.

Once that is completed, unplug the intermediate harness from the rear taillight harness while also sliding the intermediate harness clips from the bottom side of the trunk weatherstrip rail. The rear taillight harness plug is normally found on the driver-side rear just underneath the weatherstrip channel.

Lastly, check for any trunk release or trunk light pigtails and unplug those from the intermediate harness. The intermediate harness and plastic sheathing are held to the floor with a series of metal straps folded over on top of the plastic sheathing. Gently bend these up ever so slightly and just enough to remove the harness from the floor. These can be delicate

CHAPTER 8

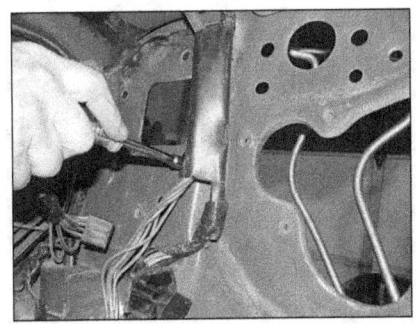

If not already done earlier, remove the two 5/16 headed sheet metal screws holding the intermediate harness to the firewall. These may not be on all years, so do not panic if they are not there. Once removed, remove the entire plastic sheathing and harness as a unit and store away.

and are only held on by one spot weld, so be gentle. Once that and any other harnesses lying on the floor have been unplugged, bag and tag them and put them into safe storage.

Remove the two 5/16 sheet metal screws holding part of the plastic sheath just to the right of where the fuse panel mounts on some Chevelles. Now simply snake the intermediate harness up through the rear seat divider and remove it from the cab of the car.

You have now completed your interior removal. Once your door panels, carpet, and seat covers arrive, you can reinstall them in the reverse order.

Installing the Sound Deadener

You have now reached that point in your restoration where you will want to replace the carpet. This is one job you are more than capable of doing and should not have to sub out to someone else. It is very simple to install when you follow a few simple tasks. For starters, you should only need a tape measure, carpet knife, carpet shears, hole punch, center punch, hammer, chalk, and a razor blade. Most of these tools you should have in your toolbox.

Our particular installation is being done on a bench-seat column-shift Chevelle. The other installations such as manual floor shift nonconsole, manual shift with console, and floor shift automatic will be fairly similar with slight changes in the way the carpet is cut out for the shifter, console, and/or bucket seats. Carpets will come in two sections, front and rear.

Make sure that all of your wiring, including the intermediate harness, speaker harness, defroster, and power convertible top harnesses, is all in place before putting the sound deadener in. If your car has a console, make sure the console pigtail harness is also installed under the carpet. For safety sake and also to protect your carpet, it is highly recommended that you put some small rubber nipples on the seat track studs (three per side) if your car has bucket seats. One of these studs to the kneecap when kneeling in the car will make you appreciate the corners.

Lay your sound deadener onto the floorpan following the directions that come in the kit. There is no need to glue or otherwise adhere the sound deadener to the floor. Once you have it laid in, move on to the carpet. It is

When starting your carpet installation, be sure that your floor is clean and dry. Do a thorough vacuuming and make sure all of your tools are at hand to install the sound deadener and carpet.

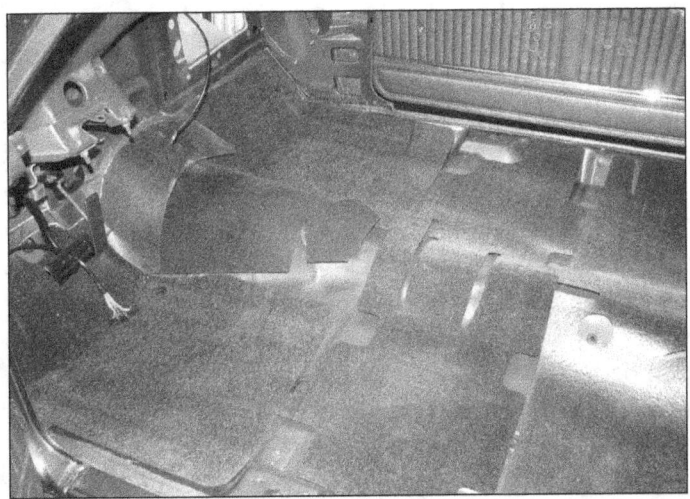

Starting with the sound deadener, make sure your intermediate electrical harness, speaker harness, rear defroster, rear speakers, or power top harnesses are all installed before you lay down your sound deadener.

Also make sure that all your floor drain plugs are in place and caulked. You can install your rear seat belts now, but waiting until the carpet is completely in place would be better.

Start with your rear carpet section. Lay it in place and ensure that it is lying flat in the rear footwell and over the driveshaft hump. Locate your inner front seat belt mounts on the driveshaft tunnel and mark the hole.

best if you leave the sound deadener and carpet installation to the very last (before seat installation) so you do not snag or dirty the carpet while working on the rest of the interior. It can also be installed anytime during the interior restoration.

Admittedly, it is easier to install the carpet before the kick panels, heater box, firewall pad, and e-brake pedal are in, but you run a huge risk damaging the carpet if it is done that early into the interior install. The series of photos in this section were done early on to better show the installation, but you need to decide which best suits your particular situation. Leave your seat belt installation until all of the carpet is in place.

Installing the Rear Carpet Section

Start with the rear carpet section first. It will work much better for you if you first laid your carpet out in the sun to get it nice and warm, as it will form much better to the floor if you do this. It is not mandatory, as most carpets are heat pressed from the factory. These are designed to fit your car, especially in the area near the back footwell as well as from up and over the area just under the rear seat.

You will notice that your carpet came several inches wider than needed. Do not panic when you see it sticking out both sides of the interior. Much of this will be trimmed off during the install. Place your rear section of carpet into the back area and tap into those areas to depress the carpet into the footwells. You will also want to make sure the heat-pressed hump area of the carpet is centered directly over the driveshaft hump. Once you are centered, use white chalk to mark the front and rear edge with a small line. This will help to keep your carpet visually centered over the hump.

While holding the carpet down and centered, move your hands outward while pushing the carpet down and holding it tight to the floor. Locate the hole for the inner side belt

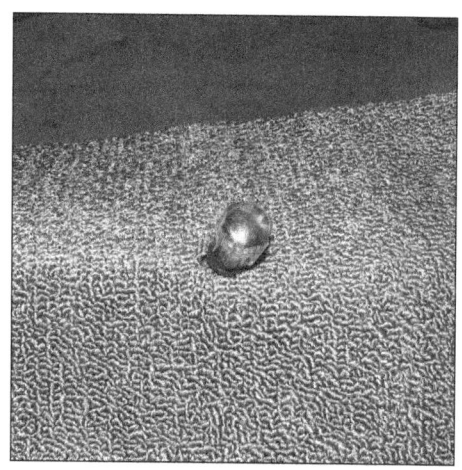

Using a hole cutter or other means, locate the mounting hole. Be sure the carpet is pulled tight and is lying flat before you drill the hole.

attachment points on either side of the driveshaft hump. While holding the carpet tight and making sure it is still centered as well as sitting in the footwell where it should be, use an ice pick or center punch and cut through the carpet and into the seat belt holes. Once you locate the seat belt hole, open it up with a hole punch or cut it just large enough for the bolt to fit

Use a hammer to tap a hole through the carpet, or simply cut it with a scissors or a carpet knife. Only cut the hole large enough to fit the seat belt attaching bolt.

Do the same for the outer retractable seat belt mounts. Locate the hole and cut it in the same manner. Using your seat belt bolts, place a large washer on them and tighten all four of them to the carpet. This will keep the carpet in alignment while you make your other cuts.

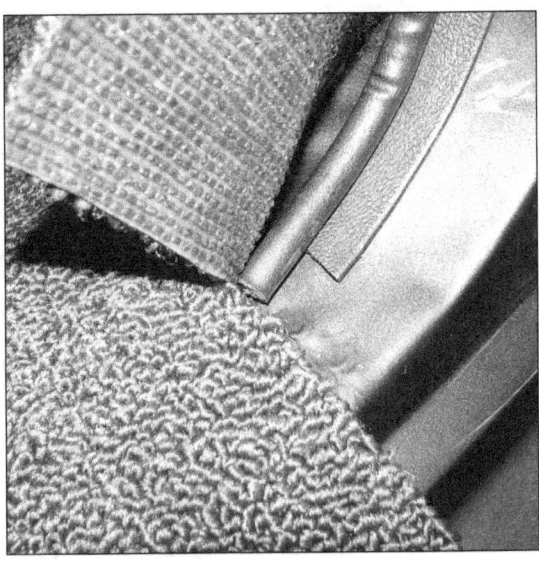

Place your doorjamb windlace on the car and carefully cut the carpet around it. Leave everything a little long until you have completed the installation. You can then go back and do your finish trimming. This will ensure a tight fit.

Do the same on the inside of the windlace. Leave just a little extra material, as you want the carpet to conceal as much of this as possible without overlapping it.

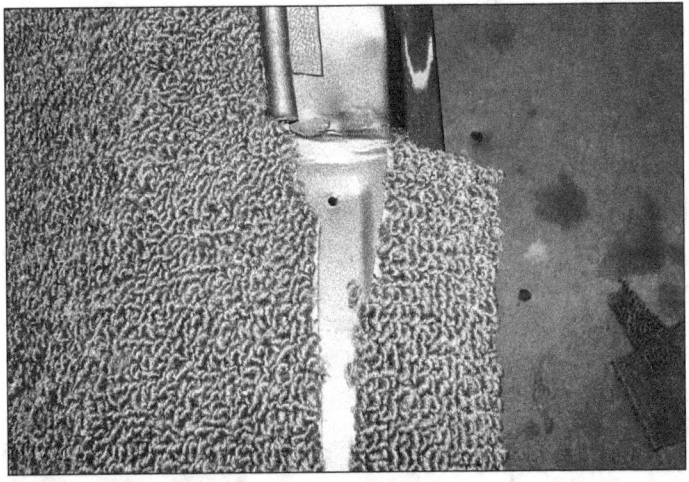

Cut lengthwise along the door-jamb even with the screwholes for the sill plate. Be careful to not cut this too short. The sill plate needs to hold the carpet down in this area.

Cut around the rear seat bottom hold-down bracket, leaving a small gap between the carpet and the bracket. This area can be seen after the seat is installed, so you want to be close and neat with your cuts.

through. Put a large washer on the seat belt bolts and tighten them to the carpet. This will hold the carpet in place on the tunnel while you proceed to attach the rest of the carpet.

Now that the driveshaft hump area is secured, move outward to the door sill area while pushing the carpet down and making sure it stays flat on the floor and in the footwell area. When you get to the outer edge of one side of the carpet, find the mounting hole for the retractable seat belt. Again, use an ice pick or center punch to cut a hole open just large enough for another seat belt bolt to fit through. Attach a washer and secure to the floor. This will keep the entire rear carpet piece from moving around while you trim it and install the front half.

Now that you have the carpet secured, you can start cutting it in around the door sill, jamb area, and rear seat hold-down brackets. As with any part of the carpet install, cut the carpet long and allow for extra material as you can always go back and trim after everything is in place.

Starting with the doorjamb, install the doorjamb windlace on both jambs to use as a guide to determine how much to cut around. Hold the carpet down firmly and cut the carpet just even with the leading edge of the doorjamb. Now cut the carpet parallel and alongside the flap of the windlace at the base of the floor. Do not cut this short; extra material can always be trimmed back later.

Using the sill plate attaching holes as a guide, cut the carpet lengthwise along the door sill so that the screw holes are just barely exposed. Do not cut this area short. You want the sill plate to be able to be laid over the carpet and help hold it at the floor.

Locate the rear seat mount holes on the floor using the ice pick or other tool. Mark it with a circle in chalk. Do not cut the hole this time. These use a flap cut in the carpet to conceal the seat track foot.

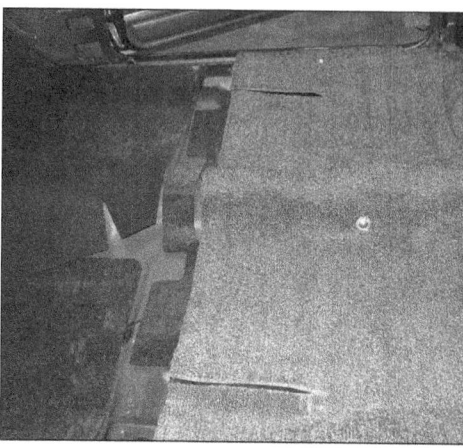

On factory installed carpet, a slit was made from the front attaching point to the rear attaching point on both bench seat tracks as well as all four bucket seat tracks. These cuts were made to try and conceal the unsightly tracks and feet.

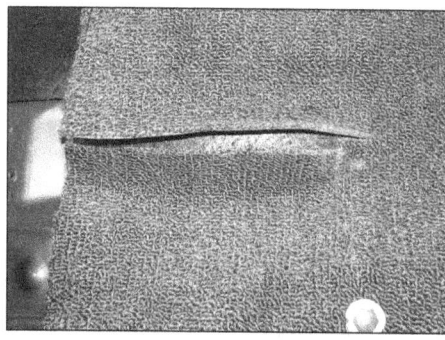

Using a straightedge, draw a chalk line 1 inch inboard of the front and rear attaching points for the seats and to a point just inboard front and rear of the seat mounts. From here, make an L-shaped cut so that the flap will conceal the foot.

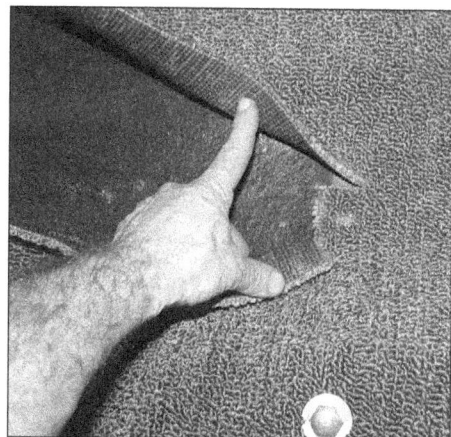

This would be the driver's side rear cut. The passenger's side would be just the opposite so as to conceal the track and foot from that side as well.

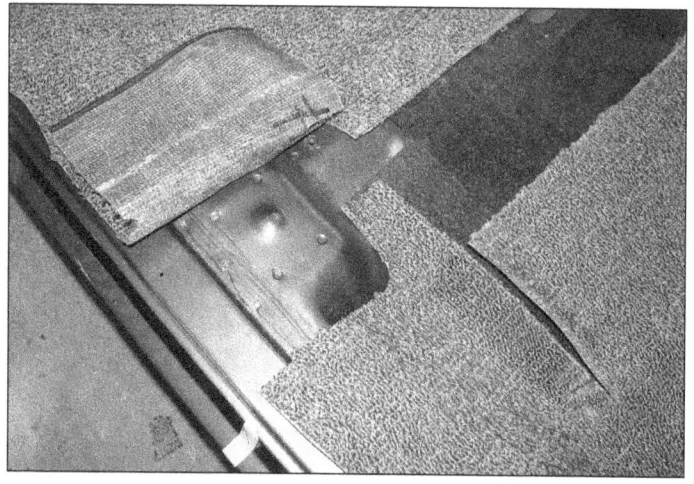

Cut around the floor protrusion on the rear carpet and remove this piece. Doing so will allow the front carpet to lay over the rear but will not be a double thickness, making it hard to get the sill plate to lie flat.

Cut around the rear seat hold-down brackets with enough material removed to allow the wire hold-down on the seat to fit into the bracket. About a 1/2 inch clearance around the bracket is sufficient. Once all is cut in and secured, locate the seat track holes or bucket seat studs.

If you notice any bulges in the carpet, especially over the driveshaft hump, you can try applying some steam to that area to try and help it lay down. If that does not work, use some extra carpet scraps or padding and lay it under the carpet in the area of the bulges. This will help the carpet lay more firmly.

Regardless if your car has a bench seat or bucket seats, use the ice pick and locate the outboard rear seat track attaching bolt hole. This time, instead of cutting a hole for the bolt, simply mark the hole with a circle. If your car has bucket seats, move inboard and locate the rear seat track stud. Mark a chalk circle around the stud as well.

Using a straightedge, find the front outboard seat track stud or hole (depending on which seats you have) and the rear hole. Move the straightedge an inch inboard of those two points and draw a straight chalk line. Then using the same chalk, draw a two-sided flap around each mounting area. When cut correctly, this will not only create a flap to help conceal the length of the track but also the feet of the seat track.

Cut around the protrusion in the floor on either side as well as an approximate 4-inch section across the middle of the bench seat cars and a smaller cut-out section on bucket seat cars. We will save the underseat cutout until you have the front carpet in place to use as a guide as to where to make the cut.

Where the floorpan protrudes up on either side of the floor near the sill plates, cut back the front corners of the rear carpet section to follow the contour. This will allow the front carpet to lay down tighter to the floor instead of trying to install the sill plates over two thicknesses of carpet. This completes the rear carpet installation, and you can now move on to the front section.

Installing the Front Carpet Section

The front carpet section is slightly trickier. Start by laying the front half of the carpet in the cab and press it into place, making sure all of the wrinkles are out and it is form fit to the driveshaft tunnel.

Make sure the carpet is centered on the floor. If your car has a floor-mounted non-console 4-speed and you ordered the correct carpet, make sure you lay the pre-formed carpet shifter area directly over the cutout in your car's floor and use this as a guide to center the carpet.

Lay your sill plate on the door sill and line up the screw holes, making sure it is where it should be mounted. Use a piece of tape laid on the car's floor under the sill plate to mark the center line of the "Body By Fisher" logo. The rear finish seam of the front carpet section should lie directly centered in the "Body By Fisher" nameplate on the sill plate. Do this for both sides. Then just as you did for the rear carpet section, cut the excess material from the door sill area using the door sill screw holes as a guide. Make sure that the carpet has not moved and is lying completely flat on the floor.

Moving to the front of the sill plate mounting area, cut the carpet perpendicular to the sill plate where the side vent bulkhead meets with the door sill. Only cut as far back as the inside edge. In all likelihood, your kick panels are now in place, but for the sake of understanding, the photos will depict them not installed so as to better show how to cut the carpet in. Cut the carpet alongside and parallel to the side vent bulkhead, leaving the carpet about an inch longer than the floor to allow for it to fold up and under the plastic kick panel when installed. If your kick panels were already installed, cut the carpet in the same manner. Using a tool with a 90-degree bent end, pull the carpet up and under the kick panel.

Do the same for the 45-degree angled floor section between the floor and the firewall pad, cutting

You want your front and rear carpet to overlap the Body By Fisher emblem as close to dead center as you can. The rear carpet will actual lay under the front carpet for several inches.

INTERIOR

When laying your front carpet down along the sides of the vent well area, cut it long until you get both sides fitted in. If your kick panels are installed, use the same procedure but wait to tuck them under until all the carpet is completely fitted. In either case, you will also need to make a small slit where the two angles meet to allow them to fold.

Lay your carpet up and over the firewall pad and cut it about 1 inch longer than where the two overlap all along the top. Remove that cut piece of carpet and tuck the balance behind and under the firewall pad, making sure the pad fits tight and does not bulge out.

If your kick panels are not installed and you are sure your carpet is laid where you want it to be, go ahead and cut the carpet back to about an inch long. This will allow the carpet to tuck up and under your kick plates and not reveal the floor coloring. You also want to make sure to leave the area around the vent opening clear enough to allow the caulking that is on the vent to fit against the metal and not on top of the carpet.

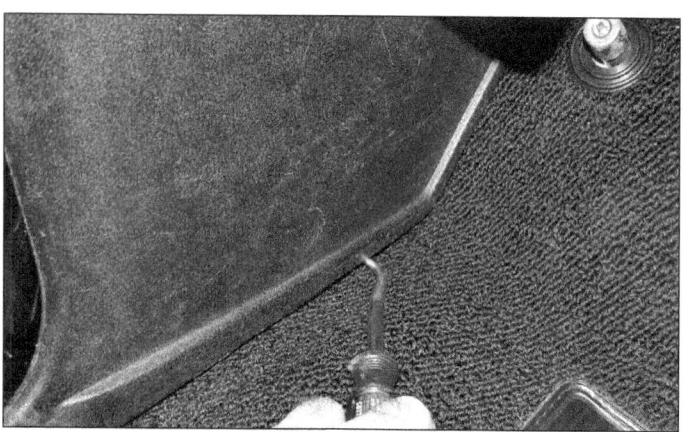

If your kick panels are already installed, use an L-shaped tool to help fold the carpet up and behind the kick panel. This makes it much easier to get the carpet to tuck up and behind the kick panel.

the carpet at least an inch long to allow for the carpet to fit under the kick panel and hide the painted floor and side vent bulkhead area. You will also need to make a slight cut where the carpet that lies flat on the floor meets the angled carpet, making the 45-degree bend to allow it to lie flat next to the kick panel and be tucked underneath it without kinking. Cut back only the piece that fits up under the kick panel and not the piece that lies on the floor. Do the same for the other side.

It is best to have already installed your firewall insulation pad for the next step. Making sure the carpet is lying flat against the floor, the 45-degree firewall bend, and against the firewall pad, measure and mark the carpeting about 1 inch long where it will tuck underneath the firewall pad. Cut the carpet horizontally along this line from one side of the car to the other and then gently tuck it up and under the firewall pad. Again, great caution must

CHAPTER 8

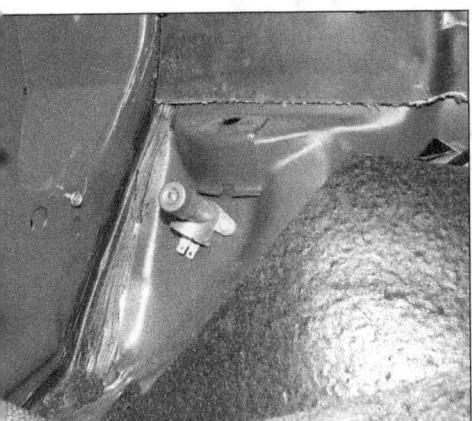

Cutting in the dimmer switch can be tricky, so take your time here. Only make the cuts once you determine that your carpet is exactly where you want it. Make sure everything is lying flat on the floor and not bulged up, as this will throw off your location.

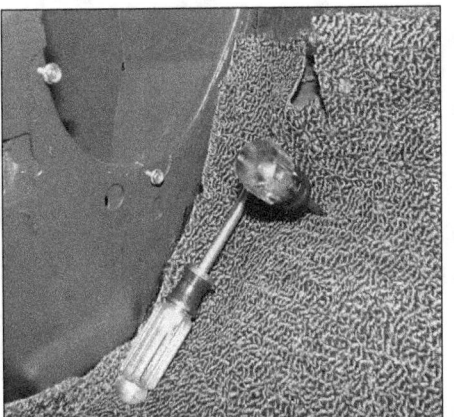

Using your ice picks or other pointed tools, find the two mounting holes through the carpet for the dimmer switch. Once located, mark and remove the tools and place your dimmer switch directly over the holes. Using your chalk, draw a round circle on the carpet where the switch will protrude through.

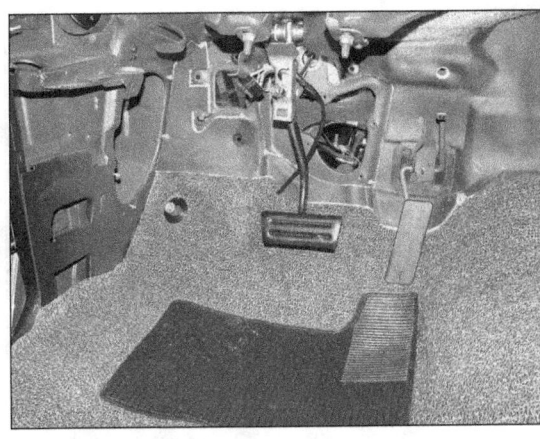

Using the dimmer switch escutcheon, cut the dimmer switch hole just large enough so that the escutcheon can be installed over the hole. You will want to install it from behind and gently push the carpet into the recess of the escutcheon.

be used here to make sure the entire front piece of carpet is lying flat on the floor and contoured to the tunnel before you cut or you will expose portions of the painted floor.

You can now cut the hole for the dimmer switch. You will need to take your time here and pay special attention because if you make a wrong cut here, you will have an unsightly hole. Just like before, make sure the front carpet is lying exactly where it needs to be before you cut any holes. Using two ice picks, find the two mounting holes for the dimmer switch through the carpet. Then, using the dimmer switch as a template, lay it over the top of the carpet and place the two ice picks back into the holes to align it. Draw a chalk line in a circle on the carpet where the switch would protrude through the carpet. Next, and here is where you want to take your time, use your dimmer switch grommet that came with your carpet. Cut a hole in the area that you drew the chalk circle and ONLY large enough to allow the front of the grommet to

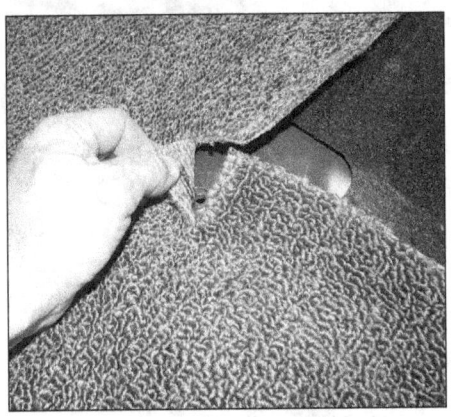

Now you can cut the flaps for the front seat mount and track into the front carpet using the same method you used to cut the rear. Be very careful not to cut the flaps too large or in the wrong area. Fixing these without the proper tools is nearly impossible.

slip up into the carpet cutout. The top half of the grommet will conceal the hole to some degree, so do not make it too large. This will complete the dimmer switch cutout and installation.

Moving on to the front seat track

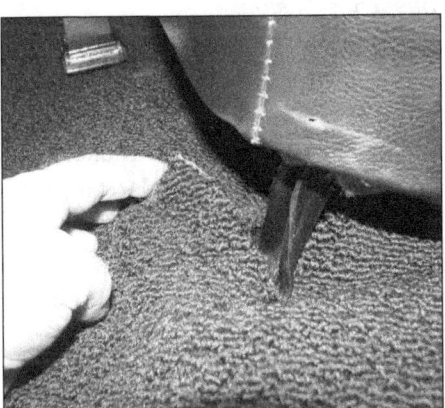

If cut correctly, this is what the driver-side front foot and track area will look like. As you can see, it conceals most of both so they are not readily visible when you open the door and look in.

mounting area, chalk the carpet in a similar fashion to how you did the rear. Use the rear track cutout as a guide to chalk the front. Draw a chalk line lengthways until just behind the front seat track mounting hole, then make your L-shaped chalk line so that the flap will conceal the foot of the front track mount. It will work best if you have a loose track that you

INTERIOR

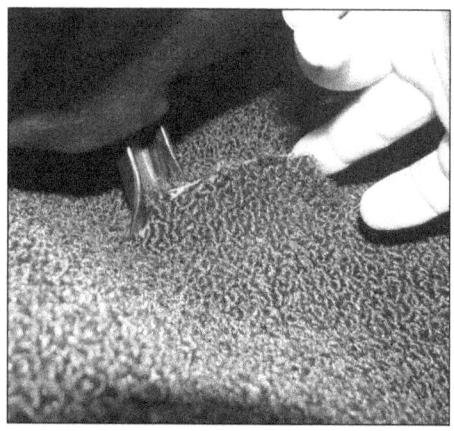

This is how the driver-side rear foot will look when properly cut in. This happens to be a bench seat mount, but bucket seats will be cut very similarly. Repeat these same cuts on the driver's inboard side; make sure the cuts are done the opposite way on the passenger's side.

Use a chalk line to outline the area of the carpet that will be removed under the seat. In this case, a bench seat. You do not have to make these cuts unless you are looking for a concours restoration.

This is what the carpet will look like after you have made the cuts. Notice how the front carpet overlaps the rear carpet and that the sound deadener is now exposed.

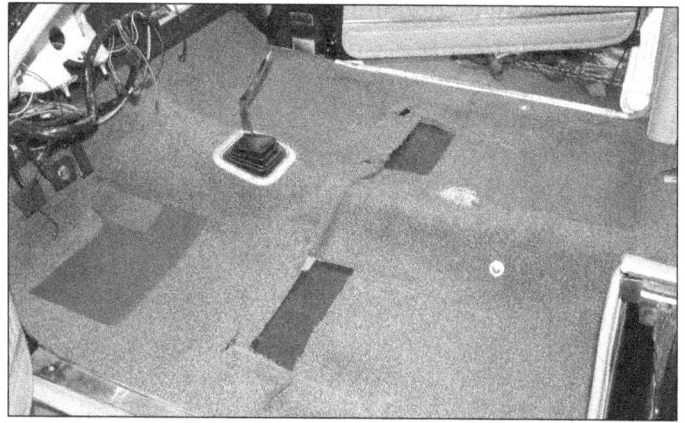

The bucket seat cars are cut with only the carpet cut out under the seat, not across the console. Again, you can elect to skip this step if it is not important to be factory exact.

can use before you make your cuts to ensure the cuts are where they need to be before you actually make them. Once you are happy with your lines, use your carpet knife to cut along the chalk lines. You will have to make four cuts for the bucket seats or just two for the bench seat.

What you want to achieve with these track and foot cutouts are flaps that help conceal both the length of the track and both front and rear seat track feet when looking in from the open door. Care must be taken to make the cuts only long enough to conceal both the track and the mounting feet without interference to the track or the feet and to ensure the flaps will lay as flat as possible when the tracks are installed.

Factory carpet had a cutout under the seat regardless of whether it had a bench seat or bucket seats. You can copy that installation method or simply leave your carpet as is in this area; it depends on the type of restoration you are doing. The difference in the cutout was that for the bench seat the cutout ran from the driver-seat track across the entire floor to the passenger-seat track and about 4 inches wide whereas the bucket seat–equipped cars the cutout was between the left seat track over to the right seat track on each side

CHEVELLE RESTORATION AND AUTHENTICITY GUIDE: 1970–1972   199

CHAPTER 8

Using the manual floor shift cutout in the floor as a template and using your carpet knife, cut the carpet out only as big as the hole. You may have to remove the carpet underlayment around that area as well in order to get it to lie flat. Your cutout will be either square for the non-console or rectangular for the console cars.

After you have cut out the carpet, you can install the rubber shift boot, metal shifter plate retainer, and metal shifter trim plate to the floor. This will also hold the carpet in place.

and was *not* cut out over the driveshaft hump.

To do this, start from the rear edge of the front carpet section, measure 4 inches toward the front of the car. Use your chalk and mark this along several points across the carpet from the driver's side to the passenger's side with the outer seat track cuts being the stopping point for your cutout for bench seat–equipped cars or make the cut out from the left seat track to the right seat track on both sides of the driveshaft hump for bucket seat cars. Refer to the photos for a visual explanation.

When satisfied with your layout, cut along the chalk line and remove this piece. Depending on how your rear carpet section was laid in, you may now also have to remove a small piece of the rear carpet section that is now exposed so that you end up with an approximately 4-inch opening to the floor and sound deadener below.

The final area to address is the cutout for the shifter, be it manual non-console, manual console, or automatic console. Obviously, there will be no cutouts needed for a column shift automatic. Starting with the manual non-console car, cut out the carpet using the square hole in the floor shifter hump as a guide. The same is true for the console-equipped manual transmission, though this time you will use the rectangular cutout in the floor shift hump as a guide. Once completed, you can now install the rubber shift boot, metal shifter plate retainer, and metal shifter trim plate to the floor, which will also hold the carpet in place.

For automatic console–equipped

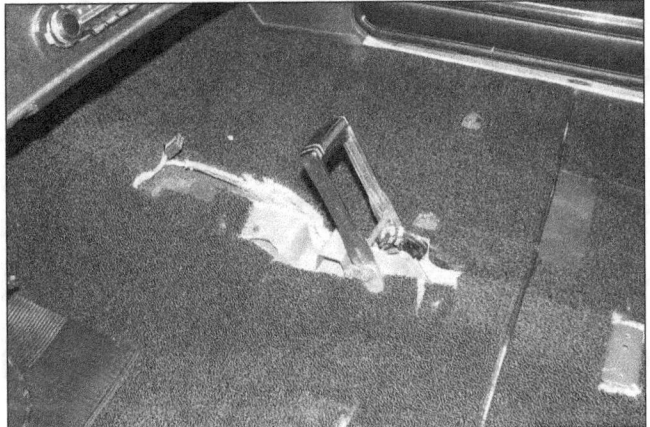

On both manual shift or automatic shift console equipped cars, cut around the area of the shifter just large enough to expose the shifter as well as the front and rear console mounts. Make sure your console wiring is pulled through as well.

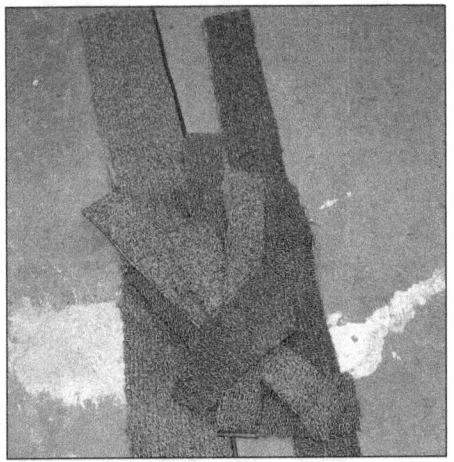

Don't throw away your carpet scraps. They can be used in several areas of the carpet installation as a filler.

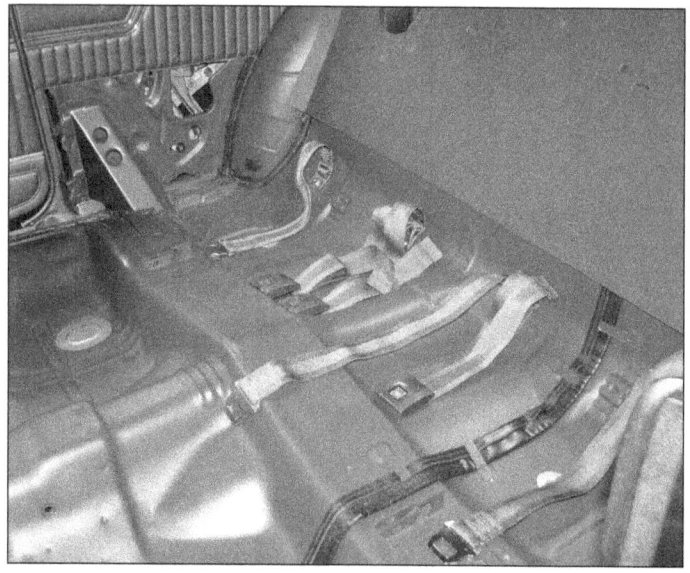

There is a right way and a wrong way to install rear seat belts. This is the correct way. Make sure the belts are installed with the strap facing upward at the bolt mount area, that the tags are on the bottom side of the strap, and that the buckles lie flat when laid on the seal.

Your interior is done. Back away and soak in the beauty of all your hard work. Small details taken care of during the installation will go a long way to the appearance of the total installation.

needs to be. You are now ready to install the console.

You have gathered a nice pile of carpet scraps by this time. Do not throw away them away; you can use these to fill any puffy areas of the carpet, particularly in the driveshaft hump area to take up any dead space the carpet may have left. They can also be used under the carpet where you made the cuts for the console, allowing you to push the carpet out into the sides of the console for a nice clean finish.

A quick trimming of loose fibers and a good cleaning with a vacuum and you are done and ready to install your seats. Install the rear seat belts first, then install the rear seats. Start with the passenger-side rear seat belts and install the male tongue on the first bolt followed by two female buckles on the next bolt, the male tongue and female buckle on the next bolt, and finally the remaining male tongue on the last bolt on the driver's side. Make sure the belts are installed in the bolt so that the belt loops up first. You will also want to make sure that the tags are facing down and that the female buckles will lay correctly without being twisted before you tighten the bolts permanently.

If your car is console equipped, install that first and then the seats, followed by the front seat belts and sill plates. Take care when installing the seats to make sure and get the front and rear track mounting feet under the carpet without tearing or gouging it. This is where a buddy will come in handy, especially with a bench seat. Congratulations, your carpet installation is now finished with minimal hassles or issues, and your interior restoration is looking new again.

cars, make a cutout just slightly larger than the automatic shifter plate where it attaches to the floor. Make a parallel cut up to the front console mount and open it up just large enough for the front console mounting flange to fit through the carpet. Do the same for the rear console mount. If your carpet is humped up in the center over the driveshaft hump, you can make a parallel cut from front to back, allowing the carpet to lay flat. However, be very careful to not cut too much so that it can be seen when the console is installed. You can use your console as a template and test fit it, making small cuts until you are satisfied it is where it

CHAPTER 9

DETAILS, FACTS, AND MYTHS

The devil is in the details. If you are building or having a concours-quality Chevelle built—spending $40,000 to $100,000 to freshen up or completely restore your Chevelle—correct details are a must, and you should expect details to be done properly. If you are just having some bad sheet metal replaced, or new seat covers and door panels installed, or rebuilding the suspension and driveline for your personal pleasure and local shows, maybe some of the finer details are not that important. Even then, you should not accept incorrect details on your Chevelle.

Whether you are doing your own restoration or having a quality restoration facility do a majority of the work that you cannot do or do not feel you have the time to do, it is always advantageous to photograph and document the process. Not only will this be a tremendous help in putting the Chevelle back together, it is something you can record and save for that restoration book of photos you may want to display along with your Chevelle and to document just how your Chevelle was assembled. If you are farming out areas of your project, be sure to convey requests for detailed before, during, and after photos of work being done or make arrangements to visit the facility doing the work and photograph it yourself.

Engine Emission Control Information Labels

Engine emission control information labels are affixed to the radiator-support panel and provide specifics on some tune-up information, such as what ignition timing, dwell, and idle RPM should be for a given engine/transmission combination. Where applicable, multiple engines in a given year may yield the same specifications. Typically, these information labels are affixed to the support panel on the driver's side and are readable when looking at the car from the front.

Like many other assembly stations, the worker simply looked for the label's broadcast code found on the build sheet and did not have to remember or look up which label went with what engine/transmission that was installed in the car.

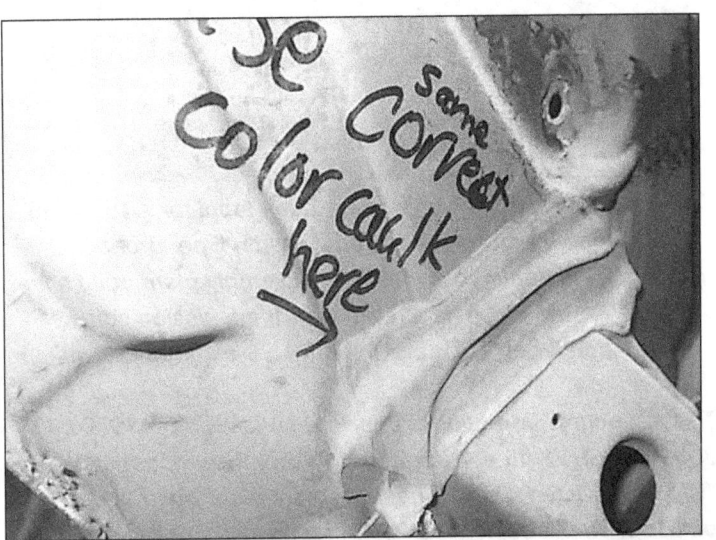

When disassembling your Chevelle in preparation for a concours restoration, always take notes and photographs if possible. Details, such as the caulking material and colors used at various seams both inside and out, are shown here. While some of these areas may never been seen, documenting procedures will score points and may be of interest to others with their restoration.

202   CHEVELLE RESTORATION AND AUTHENTICITY GUIDE: 1970–1972

DETAILS, FACTS, AND MYTHS

1970 Arlington

Label Broadcast Code	Engine – Transmission
AO	307 – After February*
AQ	L65
AR	L34 – Manual/Automatic
AZ	LS6/LS6 – Manual/Automatic (Late)*
DM	307 – Through February*
DP	L34 – Manual (Early)*
DT	LS6 – (Early)*

1970 Atlanta

Label Broadcast Code	Engine – Transmission
AO	307 – After February*
AQ	L65 – Starting 03-26*
AR	L34 – Manual Starting 03-11*
AS	LS5 – Manual Starting 03-23*
AT	L34 – Automatic Starting 03-12
AW	LS5 – Automatic
AZ	LS6 – Starting 03-11*
CR	L48 – Starting 04-30*
DM	307 – Through February*
DN	L65 – Through 03-06*
DP	L34/LS5 – Manual Through 03-06
DO	L48 – Through 12-18*
DQ	L34/LS5 – Automatic Through 03-10*
DT	L78/LS6 – Through 03-10*

1970 Baltimore

Label Broadcast Code	Engine – Transmission
AG	L65 – Manual
AO	307 – After February*
AR	L34 – Manual Starting 03-09*
AS	LS5 – Manual Starting 03-31*
AT	L34 – Automatic Starting 03-10*
AZ	LS6 – Starting 03-03*
CR	L48 – Automatic (Late)*
DD	L48 – Automatic (Early)*
DM	307 – Through February*
DN	L65 – Automatic/Manual 3-Speed
DP	L34/LS5 – Manual Through 02-24*
DQ	L34/LS5 – Automatic Through 03-02*
DO	L48 – Manual
DO	LS3
DT	L78/LS6

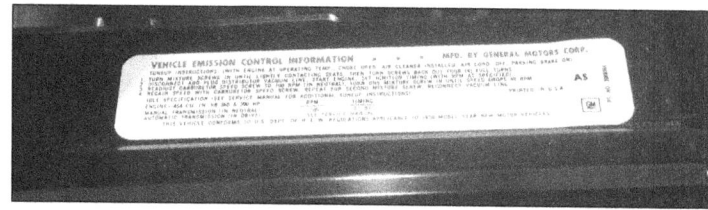

An emission control information label is shown for a 1970 LS5 454-ci engine. Broadcast code "AS" is depicted on the final assembly plant build sheet at Arlington, Atlanta, Baltimore, and Van Nuys in box 104 and was used for the manual transmission only.

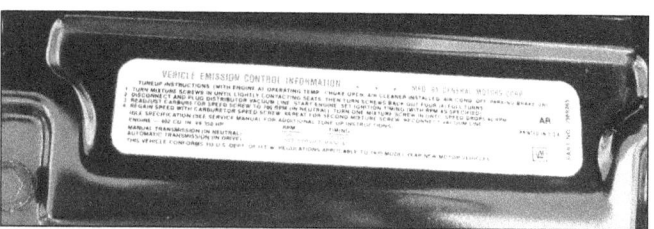

An emission control information label is shown for a 1970 L34 402-ci engine with a manual transmission. Broadcast code "AR" is depicted on the final assembly plant build sheet in box 104. This label is a revision of emission control information label "DP" used in early L34-engined Chevelles with a manual transmission.

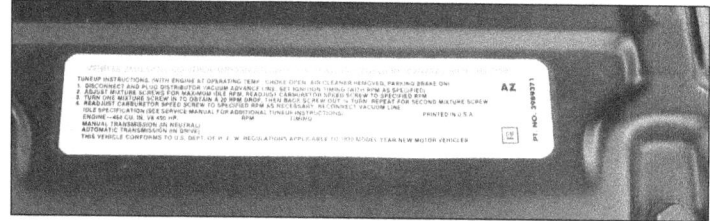

This is an emission control information label for a 1970 LS6 454-ci engine regardless of transmission type. Broadcast code "AZ" is depicted on the final assembly plant build sheet in box 104. This label is a revision of the emission control information label "DT" used in early LS6-engined Chevelles.

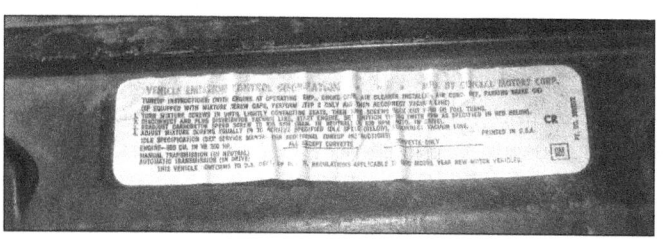

This is an emission control information label for a 1970 L48 350-ci engine with a 4-barrel carburetor. Broadcast code "CR" is depicted on the final assembly plant build sheet in box 104. This label is a revision of emission control information label "DO" used in early L48-engined Chevelles regardless of transmission type.

CHAPTER 9

1970 Kansas City	
Label Broadcast Code	Engine – Transmission
AO	307 – After February*
AQ	L65 (LATE)*
AR	L34 – Manual Starting 03-11*
AT	L34 – Automatic Starting 03-10*
AW	LS5 – Automatic Starting 03-11*
CR	L48 – Automatic Starting 04-08*
CS	LS3
DM	307 – Through February*
DN	L65 (Early)*
DO	L48 – Manual (Automatic Early)*
DP	L34/LS5 – Manual Through 03-04*
DQ	L34/LS5 – Automatic Through 02-25*
DT	L78/LS6

1970 Van Nuys	
Label Broadcast Code	Engine – Transmission
AO	307 – After February*
AQ	L65 (Late)*
AR	L34 – Manual Starting 03-11*
AS	LS5 – Manual (Late)*
AT	L34 – Automatic Starting 03-18*
AW	LS5 – Automatic Starting 03-10*
AZ	LS6 – Starting 04-01*
CR	L48 – Starting 03-23*
DM	307 – Through February*
DN	L65 (Early)*
DO	L48 – Through 03-17*
DP	L34/LS5 – Manual Through 02-21*
DQ	L34/LS5 – Automatic Through 02-21*
DT	L78/LS6 – Through 02-21*

* The following data was taken from what are believed to be legitimate build sheets. Those noted with an asterisk (*) are dates of build sheets, so it is almost impossible to say the exact date when one label code would supersede another. The Arlington, Texas, plant date is even more difficult to ascertain since an actual date is not present on those sheets, but it is assumed they would change around the same time frame as other plants. As expected with any running change, it is possible older labels were used until their supplies were exhausted.

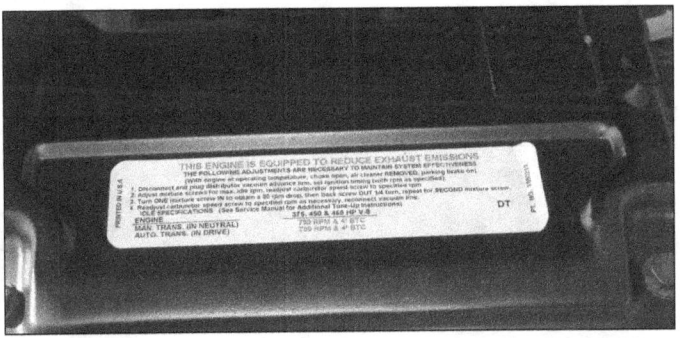

An emission control information label is shown for 1970 L78 402-ci and 1970 LS6 engines used early in the 1970 model-year run. Broadcast code "DT" is depicted on the final assembly plant build sheet in box 104. This label is a revision of emission control information label "AZ" used in early LS6-engined Chevelles.

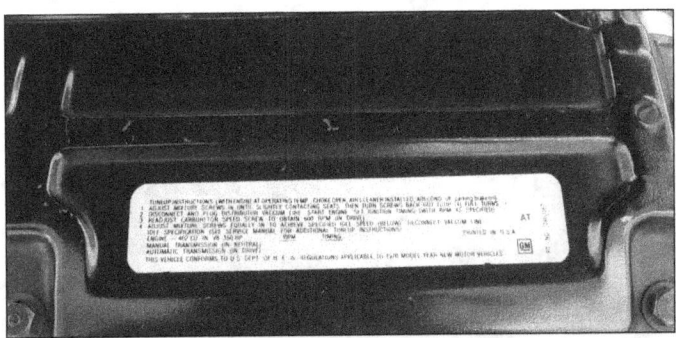

Here is an emission control information label for a 1970 L34 402-ci engine with an automatic transmission. Broadcast code "AT" is depicted on the final assembly plant build sheet in box 104. This label is a revision of emission control information label "DQ" used in early L34-engined Chevelles with an automatic transmission.

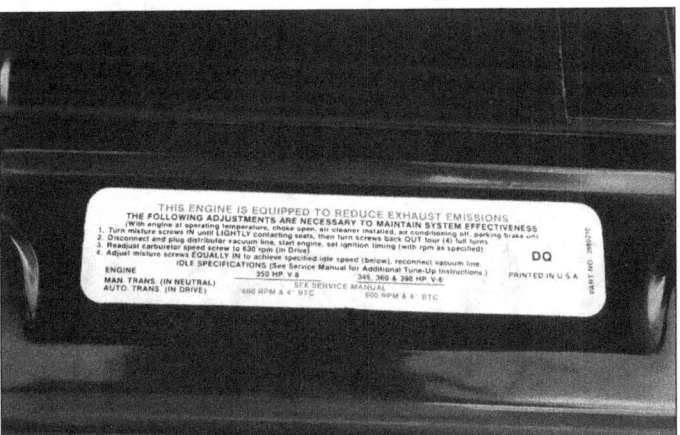

Here is an emission control information label for a 1970 L34 402-ci engine with an automatic transmission and an LS5 454-ci engine at Atlanta, Baltimore, Kansas City, and Van Nuys. Broadcast code "DQ" is depicted on the final assembly plant build sheet in box 104. This label was revised to "AT" used in late L34-engined Chevelles with an automatic transmission, "AS" for the LS5 with a manual transmission, and "AW" for an automatic transmission.

DETAILS, FACTS, AND MYTHS

1971 Arlington

Label Broadcast Code	Engine – Transmission
AO	307
AP	L65
AQ	L48
AT	LS3
AU	LS5

1972 Arlington

Label Broadcast Code	Engine – Transmission
LC	307
LG	L65
LL	L48
LT	LS3
LX	LS5

1971 Baltimore

Label Broadcast Code	Engine – Transmission
AO	307
AP	L65
AQ	L48
AT	LS3
AU	LS5

1972 Baltimore

Label Broadcast Code	Engine – Transmission
LC	307
LG	L65
LL	L48
LT	LS3
LX	LS5

1971 Kansas City

Label Broadcast Code	Engine – Transmission
AO	307
AP	L65
AQ	L48
AT	LS3
AU	LS5

1972 Kansas City

Label Broadcast Code	Engine – Transmission
LC	307
LG	L65
LL	L48
LT	LS3
LX	LS5

1971 Van Nuys

Label Broadcast Code	Engine – Transmission
AO	307
AP	L65
AQ	L48
AT	LS3
AU	LS5

1972 Van Nuys

Label Broadcast Code	Engine – Transmission
LC	307
LG	L65
LL	L48
LT	LS3
LX	LS5

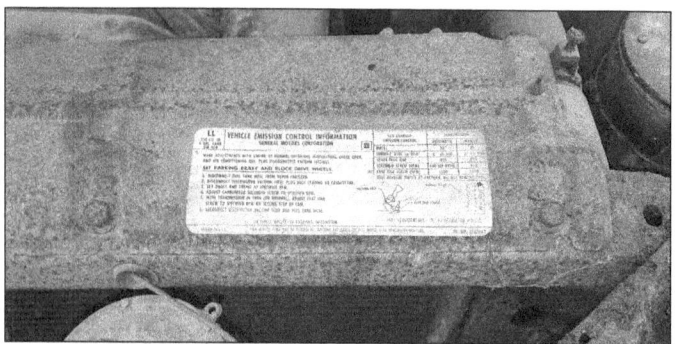

This emission control information label is shown for the 1972 L48 350-ci engine with a 4-barrel carburetor regardless of transmission type. Broadcast code "LL" is depicted on the final assembly plant build sheet in box 91.

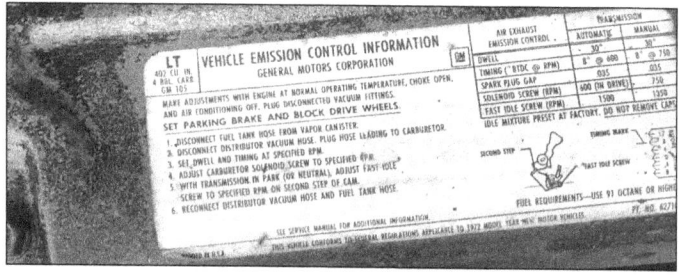

Here is the emission control information label for a 1972 LS3 402-ci engine. Broadcast code "LT" is depicted on the final assembly plant build sheet in box 91 and was used for all transmissions: manual or automatic. Since the LS3 engine was available both with and without the Z15 SS option, the label is specific for the LS3 whether SS optioned or not.

CHAPTER 9

Tire Size/Pressure Labels

Like emission control information labels, tire pressure labels were affixed to the car and located on the driver-side door to specify the tire size and load range along with suggested inflation pressure. These labels also have a part number and broadcast code that appears on the broadcast sheet in box 105 for 1970 Chevelles (box 92 for 1971 and 1972 Chevelles).

The 1970 model year saw a number of different labels, but no discernable pattern has emerged for the

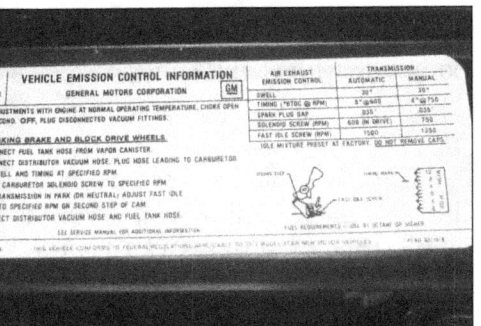

The emission control information label is shown for a 1972 LS5 454-ci engine. Broadcast code "LX" is depicted on the final assembly plant build sheet in box 91 and was used for both the M22 and TH400 transmission. Since the LS5 engine required the Z15 SS option, the label will only be found on Z15 SS-optioned Chevelles.

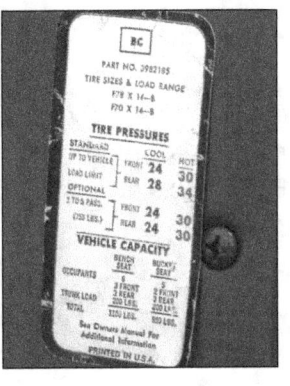

This tire pressure label was found on many Chevelles—both SS-optioned and non-SS-optioned. Assembly plants varied in the possible labels they used, and there does not appear to be any logical reason for using one label over another when the same tire is used, even on the same bodystyle, and "BC" appears to be the most common.

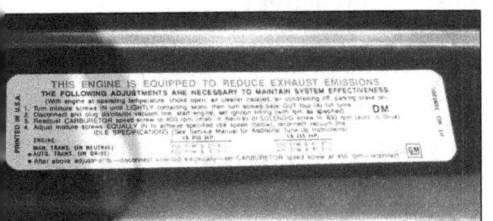

The emission control information label is shown for the base 307-ci engine in 1970. Broadcast code "DM" is depicted on the final assembly plant build sheet in box 104. Note this emission control information label not only depicts the 307-ci engine with a rated 200 hp but also has timing information for a 265-hp V-8, which is the LF6 400-ci small-block engine used in full-size Chevrolets.

Be alert for aftermarket emission control information labels being sold by aftermarket suppliers with incorrect or unverified broadcast codes. Aftermarket emission control information labels may or may not be 100 percent correct with wording or font. Be sure you purchased one with the correct broadcast code for your application if you are replacing yours.

Tire Codes for Atlanta

Atlanta has been found with three different labels: "BC," "BD," and "EZ."

Label	Tire	RPO	Notes
BC	F70x14 white stripe	PY4	
	F70x14 raised white letter	PL4	
	F78x14 black sidewall	PX5	
BD	F70x14 white stripe	PY4	
	F70x14 raised white letter	PL4	
EZ	F70x14 white stripe	PY4	
	F70x14 raised white letter	PL4	
	F78x14 white stripe	PX6	

Tire Codes for Baltimore

Baltimore has been found with eight labels: "BC," "BD," "BI," "BF," "DL," "EZ," "FG," and "FQ."

Label	Tire	RPO	Notes
BC	F70x14 white stripe	PY4	
	F70x14 raised white letter	PL4	
	F78x14 white stripe	PX6	
BF	G78x14 black sidewall	PK1	Concours wagon
	G78x14 white stripe	PK2	Concours Estate wagon
BD	F70x14 raised white letter	PL4	
BI	G70x14 white stripe	PX8	El Camino – early SS
DL	F70x14 raised white letter	PL4	El Camino – late SS
	F78x14 black sidewall	PX5	El Camino
EZ	F70x14 white stripe	PY4	
	F70x14 raised white letter	PL4	
	F78x14 black sidewall	PX5	
	F78x14 white stripe	PX6	
FG	G78x15 white stripe	PU8	Monte Carlo
FQ	G78x15 black stripe	PU7	Monte Carlo
	G70x15 white stripe	P90	Monte Carlo

Tire Codes for Kansas City

Kansas City has been found with seven labels; "AM," "BC," "BD," "BH," "BI," "DL," and "EZ."

Label	Tire	RPO	Notes
AM	E78x14 white stripe	PL3	
BC	F70x14 white stripe	PY4	
	F70x14 raised white letter	PL4	
BD	F70x14 white stripe	PY4	
	F70x14 raised white letter	PL4	
BH	F70x14 white stripe	PL4	El Camino – late SS
BI	G70x14 white stripe	PX8	El Camino – early SS
DL	F70x14 white stripe	PY4	
	F70x14 raised white letter	PL4	
	F78x14 black sidewall	PX5	
	F78x14 white stripe	PX6	
EZ	F70x14 white stripe	PY4	
	F70x14 raised white letter	PL4	

Tire Codes for Van Nuys

Van Nuys with eight labels: "BC," "BD," "BH," "BI," "BL," "DL," "EZ," and "FQ."

Label	Tire	RPO	Notes
BC	F70x14 white stripe	PY4	
	F70x14 raised white letter	PL4	
	F78x14 black sidewall	PX5	
	F78x14 white stripe	PX6	
BD	F70x14 raised white letter	PL4	
	F70x14 red stripe	PY5	
BH	F70x14 white stripe	PY4	
	F70x14 raised white letter	PL4	
BI	G70x14 white stripe	PX8	
BL	F78x14 white stripe	PX6	
DL	F70x14 white stripe	PY4	
	F78x14 black sidewall	PX5	
	F78x14 white stripe	PX6	
EZ	F70x14 white stripe	PY4	
	F78x14 black sidewall	PX5	
	F78x14 white stripe	PX6	
FQ	G70x15 white stripe	P90	Monte Carlo
	G78x15 white stripe	PU8	Monte Carlo

implementation of one label over another.

EZ

The "EZ" labels are found on Atlanta non-SS-optioned Chevelles for the F78x14 tires, while the same "EZ" label, along with "BC" and "BD," are found on F70x14 tires for SS-optioned Chevelles.

FQ

The odd "FQ" labels from Baltimore and Van Nuys can be attributed to its use limited to the Monte Carlo bodystyle with G70x15 tires.

BI

The "BI" label was used by Baltimore for the El Camino with G70x14 white-stripe tires; the "DL" label was used for El Caminos with F70x14 raised white-letter tires regardless of engine size or transmission type. Kansas City used the "BI" label for El Caminos with G70x14 white stripes tires; "DL" and "BH" were used for F70x14 raised white-letter tires regardless of engine size or transmission type. Van Nuys used the "BI" label for the El Camino with G70x14 white-stripe tires; the "BH" label was used for El Caminos with F70x14 raised white-letter tires.

The other labels are not so distinctive in their use. Options—such as engine size, transmission type, air-conditioning, etc. that one might assume would call for different tire pressures, and hence a different label—do not seem to matter, and this applies to both the sport coupe and convertible bodystyles. Several of the broadcast-coded labels are also used on non-SS-optioned Chevelles with F78x14 tire sizes as well.

1971

The 1971 model-year tire pressure labels are just as confusing, considering all SS-optioned Malibus used the same wheel and F60x15 tire combination.

The Arlington plant used "AS," "AT," and "AY." Data is limited, but it appears "AS" was used on M22-transmission Malibus and "AT" and "AY" used on those with an M40 transmission.

The Baltimore plant used "AS," "AT," and "CA." The "CA" tire pressure label was used on El Caminos, but "AS" and "AT" defy any apparent logic. "AS" is found with virtually all available engines with the SS option, while "AT" only appears with the LS5 engine.

The Kansas City plant used "AS," "AT," "BP," and "CA." Like the Baltimore plant, "CA" is used for the El Camino; "BP" is used on the Monte Carlo with G70x15 tires. Both "AS" and "AT" are found with every engine.

The Van Nuys plant used "AA," "AS," "AT," "AY," "BB," and "BP." Unlike the other two plants that assembled El Caminos, "BB" is used for the El Camino; "BP" is used for the Monte Carlo; "AA," "AS," "AT," and "AY" are used for varying engines with no discernable differences in equipment.

Like aftermarket emission control data labels with incorrect or undocumented broadcast codes, be aware of aftermarket incorrect or undocumented label broadcast codes.

Tires

A variety of tire sizes were possible at the assembly plants. Instead of having workers trying to read the tire

Tires were stenciled with their build sheet broadcast code. As one would expect, the four on the ground would not have the stencil last very long and the spare probably would not last much longer. The code "L8DS 5" is found on 1970 build sheets in box 93 and is applicable for the PL4 F70x14WH LTR tire or PS4 F70X14 BS BLTD, depending on how the assembly plant coded the verbiage.

size on the sidewall, tires were stencil painted on the tread with the same broadcast code found on the build sheet.

Several tire manufacturers supplied original-equipment tires to General Motors. Two that are found most often are Firestone and Goodyear with Uniroyal and General being two other tire suppliers.

Part of the 1971 and 1972 Z15 SS Equipment option change was the use of 15-inch wheels and F60x15 tires and the design of the SS wheel. They were first introduced with the 1970 Z28 Camaro. GM documentation for 1971/1972 Chevelles refer to them as "SS (Trans AM)" wheels, shown here on this 1972 SS with Firestone Wide Oval tires. (Photo Courtesy Domenick Scorziello)

SS Door Emblems

This has been a controversial point for owners of 1970 Chevelles for years and causes a very controversial bench racing session every time it is discussed. Researching literally hundreds of 1970 broadcast sheet (aka build sheet) documents from every US assembly plant, with the exception of the Flint assembly plant that did not use the same broadcast sheet format paperwork, all RPO Z25-optioned (SS396) Chevelle sport coupes

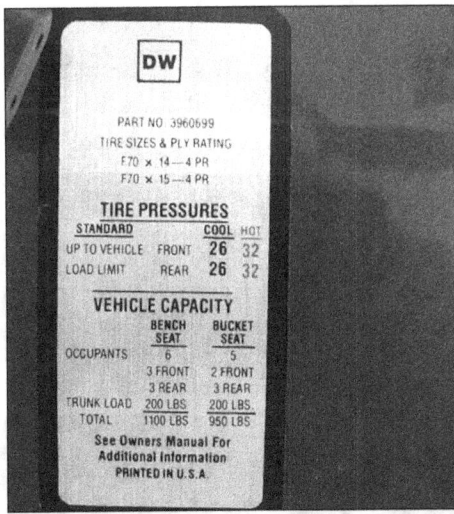

One of many aftermarket tire pressure labels, this one is coded with "DW," which is not a valid broadcast code for a 1970 tire. For 1970 Chevelles, look in box 105 for your correct tire pressure label code. In 1971, only the Baltimore plant has a two-letter code.

This 1972 spare carries the stencil "UDDL 1" for the F60-15-B-B-BB-LTR 15-inch tire used on 1972 SS-optioned Malibu. The code "UDDL 5" is found in box 43 on 1972 build sheets. The same 1971 SS-optioned F60x15 tire is coded "J8DL 5" on the build sheet. The number "5" on tire code of build sheet means the Chevelle was to receive five of the same tire.

and convertibles have the SS door emblems called out on the broadcast sheet in box 107 for the door panels. Not one RPO Z15-optioned (SS454) Chevelle sport coupe or convertible have the SS door emblems listed.

The door panel for either an SS-optioned Chevelle or a non-SS-optioned Chevelle are identical in color and style; the only difference between the two is when the SS396 option is listed on the broadcast sheet, the computer program also prints the B22 DR EMBLEM SS information to inform the trim shop to use the SS emblem instead of the Malibu emblem.

When the SS454 option was released in early November 1969, apparently the computer programmers in the final assembly plants failed to include the B22 option when RPO Z15 was ordered. There are many documented early SS454-optioned Chevelle sport coupes and convertibles with Malibu door emblems. Since the B22 option was not noted on their copy of the broadcast sheet, the workers simply added the Malibu door panel emblem.

Whether this "error" was discovered at the assembly plants and some kind of internal memo was issued to the trim shop to double-check for the Z15 SS454 option and use SS door emblems is not known; no such internal memos have appeared to date. It is also possible that some dealers caught on and possibly due to customer complaints began exchanging the Malibu emblem for an SS emblem to placate their customers. To prevent any future complaints, these dealers may have instructed their prep people to check for this and change the emblems before delivery to a customer, and the customer would never know.

It has also been reported that some very early 1970 SS396 Chevelle sport coupes and possibly convertibles were delivered with 1969 SS396 door emblems. Whether this is true or not, I'll leave it up to you, the reader. Anomalies like this are almost impossible to document as being factual, and if you decide to use a 1969 SS396 emblem, be prepared for a heated discussion.

El Caminos, whether SS optioned or not, did not receive any SS or Malibu emblem on the door panels due to the position of the vent window regulator in any year.

All 1971 and 1972 model-year Chevelle sport coupes and convertibles, regardless of engine size, with the SS option received SS door emblems.

Wheels, Hubcaps, and Wheel Covers

The 1969 through 1972 model year SS Equipment–optioned Chevelles were equipped with special SS wheels, and as such, there were no optional wheels or wheel covers available with any SS option that were ordered. Non-SS-optioned Chevelles came standard with stamped steel wheels and hubcaps with a variety of optional wheel covers and wheels available.

The 1969 and 1970 SS wheels were essentially the same design with the offset being a bit different: 0.40 inches on the 1969 SS wheel and 0.34 inches on the 1970 SS wheel. Both are 14x7 inches. The 1969 SS wheel is stamped with an identification code of YA where the 1970 SS wheel is stamped AO. It should be noted that early model year 1970 SS-optioned Chevelles were equipped with the 1969-version wheel stamped "YA." Atlanta made the change sometime between September 19 and September 24, 1969; Baltimore made the change between November 20 and November 25, 1969; Kansas City made the change between November 5 and November 10, 1969; Van Nuys made the change between September 26 and September 29, 1969. It is not known at this time when or if Arlington and Flint made the change.

The 1971 and 1972 SS wheels were essentially the same design with the offset being a bit different: 0.34 inches on the 1971 SS wheel and 0.30 inches on the 1972 SS wheel.

The 1969 SS396-optioned Chevelle was the first year the SS option included its own special 14x7-inch wheels. The SS wheels were not available as an option on any other Chevelle, and SS-optioned Chevelles were not available with any other wheel. All 1969 and early 1970 SS wheels are coded "YA" and are so stamped.

CHAPTER 9

Both the SS396 and SS454 option in 1970 included its own 14x7-inch SS wheel design. Early 1970 wheels were stamped and coded "YA," but they were soon changed and stamped and coded "AO." Assembly plants varied on their change of codes as supplies of the earlier "YA"-coded wheels were exhausted and their computers programed for the new code.

The optional ZJ7 rally wheel was first offered as an option in 1968 and was optional on all Chevelles except the 1969–1972 SS-optioned Chevelles and the 1971/1972 YF3 Heavy Chevy. Various sizes were available on other Chevrolet models and are one of the most popular wheels for non-SS Chevelles today. Be sure to check wheel dates and codes to see if they are correct for your year if you are doing a concours restoration. These were never standard SS wheels and were only available as an option with the 1968 SS396.

Part of the 1971 and 1972 Z15 SS Equipment–option change was the use of 15-inch wheels and F60x15 tires and the design of the SS wheel. First introduced with the 1970 Z28 Camaro, GM documentation for 1971/1972 Chevelles refer to them as "SS (Trans AM)" wheels. They are shown on this 1971 SS with Goodyear Polyglas GT tires.

Both are 15x7 inch, and Chevrolet refers to them as Trans-Am wheels in their documentation.

Rally Wheels

An optional rally wheel in 14x6-inch size was available under RPO ZJ7 for 1970 through 1972 Chevelles, but the RPO ZJ7 wheels in 1970 were a different design than the RPO ZJ7 wheels in 1971 and 1972. The 1970 rally wheel design was first introduced as part of the 1967 disc brake package (and not available as a separate option in 1967) and featured a slotted design. The same design of rally wheel was also used on Corvettes and Monte Carlos, but those were 15-inch wheels.

The 1971 and 1972 RPO ZJ7 wheel design is 14x6 inch with a 0.88 inch offset.

Heavy Chevy

Around March 1971, Chevrolet introduced a new option package, RPO YF3, and dubbed the car a "Heavy Chevy." Opinions vary on how the car received its name; the most-likely reason is the timing of the option and how heavy was a popular mod term in the early 1970s.

DETAILS, FACTS, AND MYTHS

Optional ZJ7 rally wheels were available on 1972 Chevelles except those that were ordered with the Z15 SS Equipment option or the YF3 Heavy Chevy option.

The wheels are 14x6 inches with special hubcaps and trim rings. They are shown here on this 1972 Malibu with optional PL3 E78x14 white-stripe tires.

When the YF3 Heavy Chevy option was ordered, these 14x7 rally wheels were part of the package. The 14x6 wheels included the bright hub cap and lug nuts but no outer trim ring.

Since the advertised curb weight of the 13437 Chevelle sport coupe is listed in GM documentation as 3,394 pounds and the 13,637 Malibu sport coupe is 46 pounds heavier at 3,440 pounds, the name certainly did not reflect the weight of the car. The RPO YF3 option was only available on the V-8 series 13437 (1971) or 1C37 (1972) base Chevelle. The option consisted of special black or white "HEAVY CHEVY" decals on the hood, fenders, and trunk lid; special side stripes; a black-accented grille; special domed hood with locking pins; 14x6-inch rally wheels with special center caps; and bright lug nuts without the bright outer ring.

Nothing was done to the interior with the RPO YF3 Heavy Chevy option. Seats were limited to the available 13437/1C37 colors (blue, black, or jade for 1971 and black, blue, green, or tan for 1972). Bucket seats were not available as an option. Floors were vinyl-coated rubber material (no carpeting), and door

Both 1971 and 1972 base-Chevelle-series (133/134xx in 1971 and 1C37 in 1972) interiors are fairly sparse. This 1972 Chevelle door panel shows a faux burl wood trim strip. The 1971 door panel was very similar with a white Mylar strip.

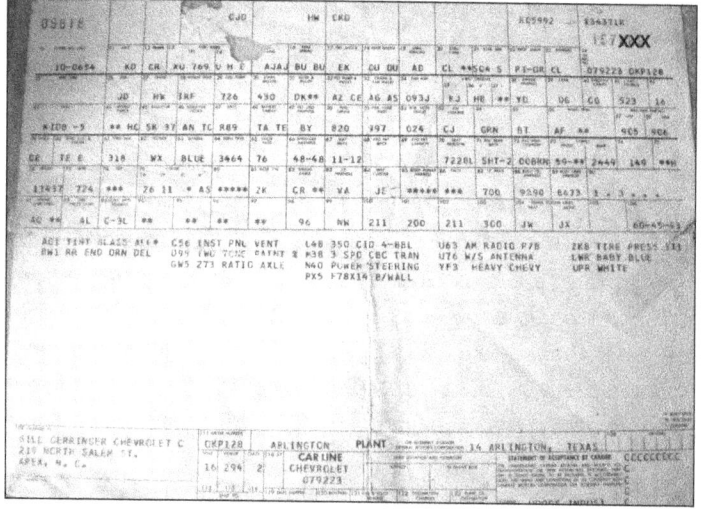

This 1971 Arlington assembly plant build sheet shows the YF3 HEAVY CHEVY option in box 107. Also note in box 107 the item listed as BW1 RR END ORD DEL. This indicates the "Chevelle by Chevrolet" emblem on the trunk is not to be installed due to the HEAVY CHEVY decal location. (Photo Courtesy YF3 Registry)

CHAPTER 9

Another piece of paperwork verifying the YF3 HEAVY CHEVY option is the dealer's invoice from Chevrolet. Shown here as 1AYF3AB HEAVY CHEVY PACKAGE with a suggested retail price of $142.20.

When the option RPO YF3 Heavy Chevy was ordered on a 1971 or 1972 base Chevelle sport coupe, the normal "Chevelle by Chevrolet" script was eliminated from the trunk lid to allow the placement of the "HEAVY CHEVY" decal shown here on this 1972 Flame Orange Chevelle. (Photo Courtesy YF3 Registry)

Any V-8 engine and any transmission could be ordered in the base Chevelle, with or without the RPO YF3 option, except the RPO LS5 454 engine or the M22 Muncie 4-speed transmission. The close-ratio M21 was dropped from the Chevelle options list in 1971.

The RPO YF3 option was basically a dress-up option, and it takes some kind of documentation such as dealer's invoice or build sheet showing the YF3 option to verify a true Heavy Chevy.

Headlamps and Grilles

The 1970 model year would be the last year for Chevelles to come equipped with individual low- and high-beam headlamps. While some will argue the 1970 Monte Carlo isn't a true Chevelle, the Monte Carlo was built at the same assembly plants as other Chevelles, was VIN sequenced with other Chevelles (meaning when a Monte Carlo-series vehicle followed a Malibu-series vehicle, the Monte Carlo's VIN number was one number higher than the Malibu-series vehicle), carried the GM "13" series designation, and was still considered an A-Body car.

Many applicable options (such as radios, air-conditioning, and the like) that would be available on any other Chevelle would be lumped in sales figures with those optioned to Monte Carlos. One feature the 1970 Monte Carlo did not share with other 1970-model-year Chevelles was the headlamp arrangement; 1970 Monte Carlos had a jump on the single-headlamp feature that would grace all other Chevelles in 1971 and 1972. One feature the 1970 Monte Carlo did share with 1970 Malibus was the bright trim below the headlamp that was present on early model-year Chevelles.

panels differed from the Malibu as well. The 1971 base Chevelle has a white, Mylar strip on the door panel where the 1972 base Chevelle has a simulated burl-wood strip. The "Chevelle by Chevrolet" emblem on the trunk was removed because the "HEAVY CHEVY" trunk decal is located in that spot.

A bit of trivia here, in 1970 Chevrolet rebadged the entry-level Chevelle from "300 Deluxe" to "Standard"; in 1971, "Standard" was replaced with "Chevelle." The entry-level Chevelle for 1971 and 1972 is actually a Chevelle "Chevelle," the upscale Malibu was still a Chevelle Malibu–confusing, eh?

Both SS Equipment options in 1970 (RPO Z25 for the SS396 and RPO Z15 for the SS454) were accompanied by several changes in the grille and trim of the standard Malibu. Aside from the blacked-out grille that had been a signature feature since the 1965 Malibu SS, the centered bowtie emblem was swapped for and "SS" emblem, and the Malibu's bright center vertical bar was removed.

The grille emblem "CHEVELLE" was used from 1970 through 1972. Although the part numbers were different for each of the three years, the placement was the same.

The 1970 model year continued the theme from 1969 of the centered bowtie emblem, although for 1970 the bowtie emblem was now silver instead of blue as it had been in 1969. Also, note the park/turn signal lamps for non-SS-optioned Chevelles in 1970 are amber lenses with clear bulbs.

Like the 1970 Malibu series, the early Monte Carlo sport coupes have this bright trim below the headlamp. Just why Chevrolet decided it was no longer to be used is not known; possibly it was just to save a few dollars on each car.

A very common mistake on 1970 SS-optioned Malibus is using the bright center vertical bar that comes with most aftermarket 1970 grille kits. There are no early and late versions that allow for the vertical bar to be correct on a 1970 SS-optioned Malibu.

The small bright trim below the headlamps was standard fare on early 1970 Malibus regardless of having the SS option or not. For some unknown reason, this trim piece began to disappear around February 1970. It is a small detail many restorers overlook and can be a hard piece to find today.

Correct placement of the "CHEVELLE" emblem for 1970 is shown. Note the emblem is located on the driver's side of the grille in the lower section and centered vertically between the blacked-out horizontal bars. In 1970, the hood-locking pins were included with the RPO ZL2 Cowl Induction hood option and were not available separately.

CHAPTER 9

Attention to detail is something often overlooked like the placement of the "CHEVELLE" emblem on this 1970 grille. The emblem should be located one space up from its current location, between the second and third horizontal bars on the lower section of the grille.

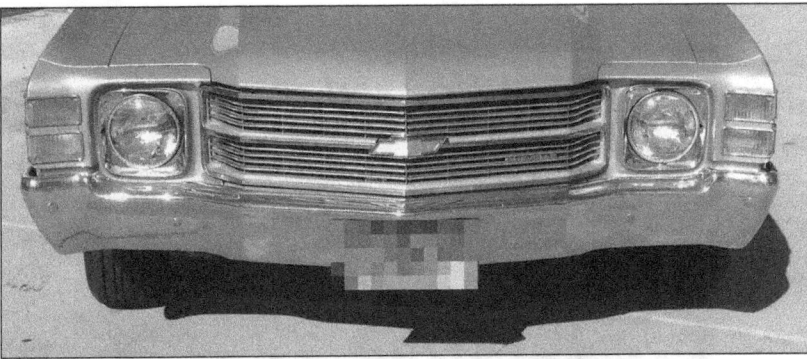

A very common mistake on 1970 SS-optioned Malibus is using the bright center vertical bar that comes with most aftermarket 1970 grille kits. There are no early and late versions that allow for the vertical bar to be correct on a 1970 SS-optioned Malibu.

All SS396- and SS454-optioned Malibu sport coupes built at the Oshawa, Ontario, assembly plant have the entire grille blacked out, not just the small horizontal grille bars. Also note the bright trim below the headlamp indicating a pre-February dated build. (Photo Courtesy Jack Aparicio)

The RPO Z15 SS-optioned Malibu grille for 1971 only differed from the 1971 Malibu grille with all but the center horizontal bar being blacked out and the use of an SS emblem in place of the bowtie emblem. Part of the Z15 option for 1971 was the inclusion of a domed hood (regardless of engine) and hood-locking pins.

The 1971 models saw a typical minor front grille/headlamp and taillamp change from 1970. A single headlamp incorporated both low and high beam for the first time in a Chevelle, if you don't count the 1970 Monte Carlo. The non-SS-optioned Malibu grille is silver with a bowtie centered on the middle horizontal bright bar. Parking and turn signal lamps were moved from the bumper to the leading edge of the front fenders and wrapped around the side of the fenders for better side visibility. The SS option for 1971 again blacked out the grille and traded the bowtie emblem for an SS emblem along with a domed hood and hood-locking pins for the first time on the standard SS domed hood.

Grille Emblems

Part numbers for various grille emblems vary from the original assembly instruction manual to a circa 1972 Chevrolet Parts & Accessories Catalog as was often the case. This occurred because either new part numbers were assigned or parts of similar design were combined into one service part number.

The 1970 base Chevelles did not have a bowtie emblem while the Malibu series did. Both the base Chevelle series and Malibu series, except sedan pickups and station wagons, have a "CHEVELLE" nameplate on the driver-side lower grille;

DETAILS, FACTS, AND MYTHS

The standard 1972 Malibu grille featured four wide bright horizontal bars along with six thinner horizontal bars that were blacked out with a bright leading edge. The bowtie emblem used since 1969 was dropped from the center of the grille for 1972.

The first of four possible parking/turn lamp and headlamp bezel combinations for 1972 is the blacked-out headlamp bezels and clear lens with amber bulb parking/turn lamp lens. Sport coupe, convertible, station wagon, or El Camino makes no difference.

The second of four possible parking/turn lamp and headlamp bezel combinations for 1972 is blacked-out headlamp bezels and an amber lens with a clear bulb parking/turn lamp lens. It makes no difference if it is a sport coupe, convertible, station wagon, or El Camino.

The third of four possible parking/turn lamp and headlamp bezel combinations for 1972 is bright headlamp bezels and a clear lens with an amber bulb parking/turn lamp lens. It makes no difference if it is a sport coupe, convertible, station wagon, or El Camino.

The fourth of four possible parking/turn lamp and headlamp bezel combinations for 1972 is bright headlamp bezels and an amber lens with a clear bulb parking/turn lamp lens. It makes no difference if it is a sport coupe, convertible, station wagon, or El Camino.

sedan pickups and station wagons have a "CHEVROLET" nameplate. Neither SS option had any effect on the nameplates.

The 1971 and 1972 followed suit with 1970 for bowtie, "CHEVELLE," and "CHEVROLET" emblems and nameplates, but only 1971 Malibu have a bowtie emblem, and this was dropped in 1972 due to the revised design of the grille itself.

Very few styling changes were made in 1972. The Malibu-series grille now featured four bright wide horizontal bars with the two thinner bars between each being bright highlighted as well.

The 1972 headlamp bucket and parking/turn signal lamp color often has restorers bewildered. According to the 1972 Chevelle "STANDARD EXTERIOR EQUIPMENT" matrix from Chevrolet (revised December 1971), the base Chevelle series (131/132/133/134xx) was to get bright headlamp bezels with bright rings and an amber parking lamp lens with a clear bulb. The Malibu series (135/136xx) was to get black headlamp bezels with birth rings and a clear parking lamp lens with an amber bulb.

Research has shown the headlamp bezel color along with the parking lamp lens and bulb color varied at each plant throughout the model year with no regard to series, bodystyle, or time of production at an individual assembly plant. Each of the four possible combinations was found throughout the production run at every US assembly plant. Aside from the mostly blacked-out grille on an SS-optioned Malibu, the SS option did not appear to have any influence on the parking lens color or headlamp bezel being blacked out.

Many owners surveyed during research either did not know why their 1972 Chevelle had the parking lens or headlamp bezels they did, indicating the items may have been changed before they acquired the car or were never changed at all, while others confessed to changing one or the other because they like the particular feature better than what their car had when they bought it.

Taillamps

Taillamps in 1970 and 1971 had a running model year change. In 1970, the early taillamp lens has a flat clear lens that was changed to a more domed-shaped area to aid a driver behind you seeing the backup lens area; this change was done sometime in the February 1970 time frame.

The 1971 Malibu series revised both the inner and outer two lenses, while the base Chevelle series remained essentially the same throughout the year with no bright trim.

This is an early (pre-February 1970) taillamp lens. Note the white backup lens is flat. This caused an issue with safety as it was difficult for a driver behind you to see it. Early lenses would be used as assembly-plant supplies were exhausted, so there is no definite date for any plant.

An early model year 1971 taillamp and backup lamp assembly is shown. The clear area of the backup lamp is much smaller than the late version as is the raised portion of the taillamp. The bright outer right was also eliminated in the late revision.

Due to safety issues, the 1971 taillamp and backup lamp on sport coupes, convertibles, and sedans were revised to increase the size of the clear center bump on the backup lens, and the bright ring around the outside of the red section was removed. This same lens carried over to the 1972 model year.

ZL2 Special Ducted Hood Air System and Engine Compartment

This is also known as the cowl-induction or flapper hood system. This hood was an option on all 1970 through 1972 SS-optioned Malibu sport coupes, convertibles, and sedan pickups (El Camino) with any 402- or 454-ci engine and was not an option on 1971 or 1972 SS-optioned Chevelles with either 350-ci engine. The cowl-induction system has been around since the early 1900s. The base of the windshield has a higher static pressure area that what is under the hood. The cowl-induction system (it's more than just the hood) forces air from the base of the windshield into the carburetor.

In actuality, the ZL2 cowl-induction system on a 1970 through 1972 Chevelle is more of a gimmick of the 1970s than a functional system. Buick, Oldsmobile, and Pontiac had Ram Air in one form or another, Chrysler Corporation had its Air Grabber, and Ford had forward-facing hood scoops. Whether any of these systems actually showed any increase in horsepower or not is questionable. The addition of these various systems did not reflect any changes in their respective engine horsepower ratings. Tests have shown very little, if any, horsepower gains. Considering the Chevelle's cowl-induction system is only operating at full

The entry-level Chevelle taillamp and backup lamp assemblies have no bright trim rings in 1971 or 1972. Many 1971 and 1972 Chevelle owners like to use these unadorned lenses for their cleaner look, but be prepared to be docked if you're having your restoration judged on a point system.

DETAILS, FACTS, AND MYTHS

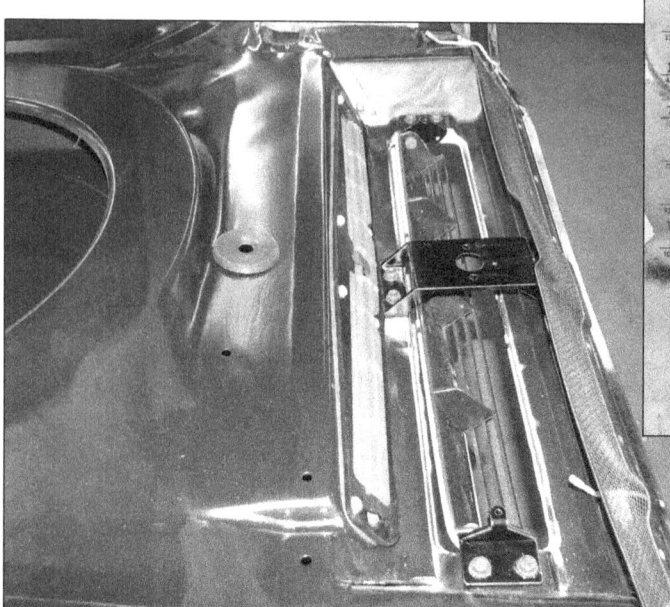

The underside of the ZL2 Special Ducted Air System shows the outer flapper door in the open position. It is shown here during restoration without the actuating hardware attached.

A relatively rare dual-snorkel air cleaner assembly is featured on this restored 1970 LS6 engine. Just why some non-ZL2 Special Ducted Air System hood optioned Chevelles got this air cleaner assembly over the more common open-element type isn't known.

throttle (or very little vacuum such as revving the engine at idle) it's more of a cool look thing than truly functional.

In 1970 the RPO ZL2 had reported sales of 28,888, in 1971 that dropped severely to 4,079 and 1972 was down to 3,659. There is no known accurate breakdown of how many ZL2 hood options were sold with any of the three available bodystyles or with which 402- or 454-ci engine.

The ZL2 hood option relies on two factors to operate: engine vacuum and an electrical system. Both systems use doors—or "flappers," if you will—to monitor and regulate the airflow from outside to the carburetor air cleaner housing assembly. The flapper door is the most notable feature of the system along with the "COWL INDUCTION" script on each side of the hood's dome feature. This flapper is only open under wide open throttle (or fast acceleration) or when the engine is off due to low (or no) engine vacuum. Under normal driving conditions when engine vacuum is present, the flapper door remains closed.

The vacuum actuator has a rubber diaphragm and rod that connects to the hood's flapper door. A vacuum hose is connected to a metered valve that allows full vacuum to slowly close the flapper door without slamming it, while at the same time allows the door to open rapidly with no restrictions during full throttle. Due to its one-way nature, it is color coded to prevent it from being installed backward. The intake manifold has a vacuum fitting to supply the vacuum. The particular vacuum fitting is coded on the build sheet in box 23, depending on the car's other equipment, such as air-conditioning or not, or M40 automatic transmission or not.

Air inducted into the engine compartment is drawn into a special opening on the underside of the ZL2 hood. Air is drawn from the outside when the hood's flapper door is open. When the hood's flapper door is closed, air is supplied by the single-snorkel air cleaner assembly.

The vacuum actuator on the ZL2 Special Ducted Air System hood option is part of the system that controls the opening and closing of the hood flapper assembly.

CHAPTER 9

The electrical switch (transmission throttle control) to activate the ZL2 hood flapper is attached to the gas pedal on a special bracket. The particular type of transmission dictated which electrical connections were used.

The ZL2 hood air cleaner assembly is a cross between the open-element design and a closed design with snorkel(s) for the air intake.

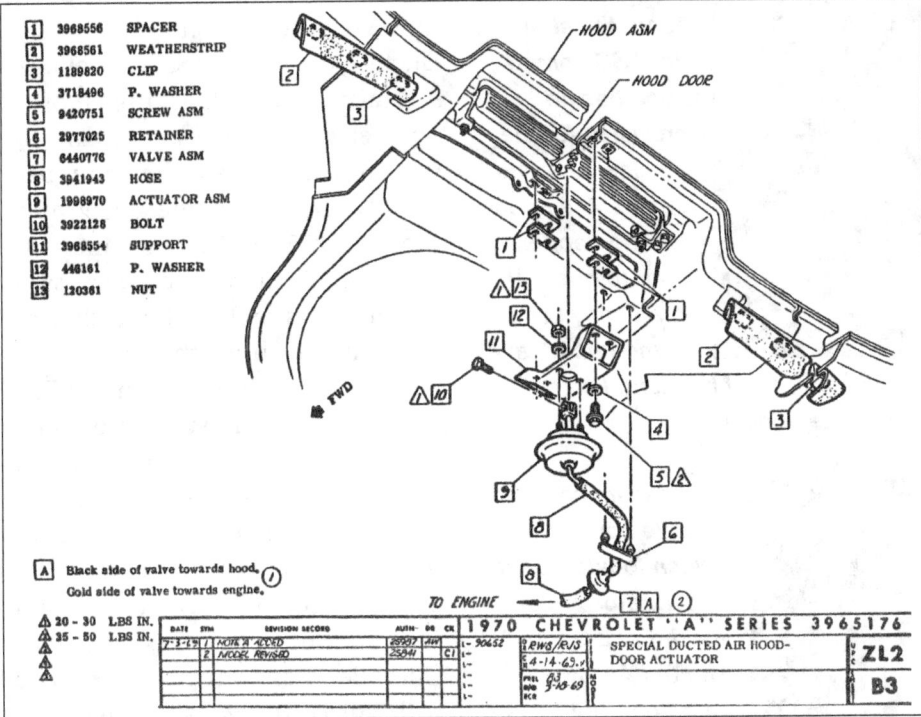

This is an exploded view of the position and mounting of the RPO ZL2 Special Ducted Air System option actuator assembly and the one-way valve from 1970.

The vacuum actuator pod assembly is on the ZL2 Special Ducted Air System hood. This pod would open the flapper door when little to no engine vacuum was available, such as when the engine was off or under heavy throttle.

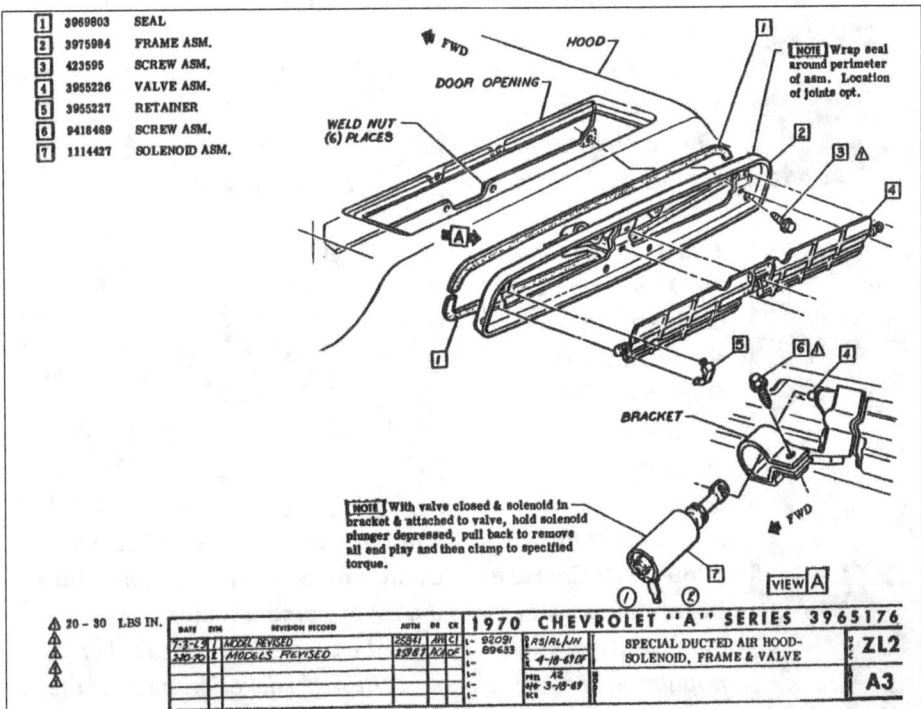

An exploded view depicts the flapper door, the seal, and frame along with the solenoid assembly and how the solenoid is to be installed.

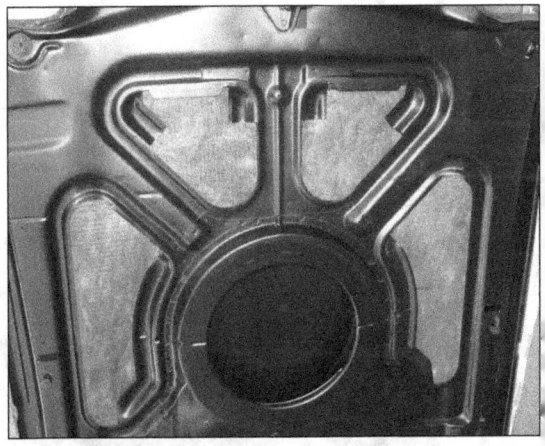

The underside of late ZL2 Special Ducted Air System hood is shown. The late hood differed from the early design with different-size insulation cutout areas and horizontal creases in the sheet metal just in front of the air cleaner housing area that allowed the hood to buckle in the event of a front-end collision.

DETAILS, FACTS, AND MYTHS

Compared to the ZL2 Special Ducted Air System hood, the standard SS domed hood has no provision for the air cleaner to seal against the hood and no flapper door to open. This is an early style domed hood, and when you compare the insulation cutout areas and lack of horizontal crease, you can see the differences between early and late hood styles.

The transmission throttle control switch located on the accelerator pedal for the ZL2 Special Ducted Air System hood option is shown. The two pink wires activate the flapper, while additional wiring (orange wires) is needed for a TH400 transmission to activate the kick-down feature.

This is an unrestored 1970 LS6 engine compartment with the ZL2 Special Ducted Air System hood option. Note the screens in the cowl area. These are not truly correct for any 1969–1972 Chevelle but are aftermarket items that are very popular as they keep leaves and small rodents out of the cowl area.

Air Cleaners

The dual-snorkel air cleaner assembly is a bit of an oddity. This unit was used on non-ZL2 Special Ducted Air System LS6 Chevelles by several assembly plants in lieu of the open-element air cleaner assembly in several instances and has only been found on LS6-engined Chevelles; the L34, L78, and LS5 engines used the open-element air cleaner assembly. From researching build sheets, 5 from Atlanta used the dual-snorkel air cleaner assembly beginning May 20, 16 from Baltimore started on January 23, 2 have been found on Kansas City LS6 Chevelles, 1 to date for Van Nuys, and only 2 for Arlington.

Air cleaner box 55 on your 1970 build sheet will have a two-letter code for the air cleaner assembly your Chevelle was originally equipped with. All 1970 ZL2 Special Ducted Air System hood optioned Chevelles will have the code "DG" in this box regardless of engine size or horsepower rating. All 1971 and 1972 ZL2 Special Ducted Air System hood optioned

The base unit of the ZL2 Special Ducted Air System air cleaner. Note the silver flame arrester on the tube from the passenger-side rocker cover and "REAR" sticker on back of the base. It seems redundant since the air cleaner base will only go on one way but who's to question.

CHAPTER 9

The lid of the open-element air cleaner assembly is actually two pieces. The lower piece has service information rolled into the metal itself, then black paint filled this rolled-out area with service instructions. This lower portion was then combined with the upper portion to form the lid. (Photo Courtesy Les Saville)

Chevelles will have code "DH" in Air Cleaner box 53. The open-element air cleaner assembly will have code "SS" for 1970; the open-element air cleaner assembly was discontinued after the 1970 model year. The dual-snorkel air cleaner assembly is coded "CO" for 1970, which is also the only year for this air cleaner assembly.

Final assembly plants did not always follow hard and fast rules. As noted, the "SS" coded air cleaner assembly was the norm for non-ZL2 Special Ducted Air System hood optioned Chevelles, but research on the Kansas City plant turned up two "CO" coded open-element air cleaner assemblies on LS6 engines with a positraction 4.10:1 rear-end gear ratio and one "CP" coded open-element air cleaner assembly on an LS6 engine with a positraction 3.31:1 rear-end gear ratio. These (at least) three anomalies are found in late April and late June.

PCV Hose Routing

The routing of the positive crankcase ventilation (PCV) hose varied in 1970. All assembly plants except the Arlington assembly plant routed the PCV hose around the front of the carburetor.

The Arlington final assembly plant routed the PCV hose around the rear of the carburetor.

The more common non-ZL2 Special Ducted Air System hood optioned open-element air cleaner assembly shown here is found on L34, L78, LS5, and LS6 engines. This air cleaner assembly is coded as, ironically, "SS" on all plants' build sheets with a notable exception. Atlanta coded this same air cleaner as "CP" on L78 engines.

A relatively rare dual-snorkel air cleaner assembly is featured on this restored 1970 LS6 engine. Just why some non-ZL2 Special Ducted Air System hood optioned Chevelles got this air cleaner assembly over the more common open-element type isn't known.

All plants except Arlington in 1970 routed the PCV hose around the front of the carburetor. Note the engine lift on the driver-side front of the engine. On 1970 LS6 Chevelles, this is left natural like the thermostat housing and not painted orange like it would be on a cast-iron intake manifold.

DETAILS, FACTS, AND MYTHS

The Arlington final assembly plant in 1970 routed the PCV hose around the back of the carburetor instead of around the front. Also shown here is overspray not only on the bellhousing but on the aluminum intake manifold as well.

A driver-side view of an LS6 engine shows the carburetor spacer for ZL2 Special Ducted Air System hood. This example is an Arlington car as noted by the PCV hose being routed to the rear of the carburetor.

In 1970, the Arlington final assembly plant routed the PCV hose behind the ZL2 Special Ducted Air System air cleaner assembly and used this hard-to-find clip to retain the PCV hose.

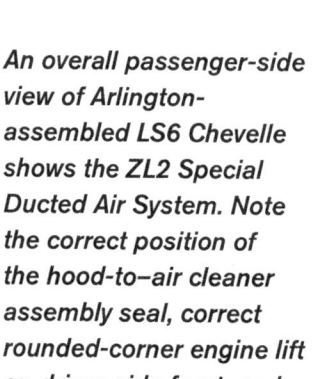

Both the 396- and 454-ci engines in 1970 Chevelles used a low-profile intake manifold that required a carburetor spacer to allow the ZL2 Special Ducted Air System hood to seal against the air cleaner assembly. This was true regardless of engine (396/454) or carburetor (Rochester/Holley). Also visible here is the support bracket for the dual-feed fuel line.

It is often the little details that can make or break a concours restoration. This 1970 LS6 Holley carburetor is one example. Note the white stripe on the hose, markings on the divorced choke cover, and fuel-line support brace also found on the L78 engine.

An overall passenger-side view of Arlington-assembled LS6 Chevelle shows the ZL2 Special Ducted Air System. Note the correct position of the hood-to–air cleaner assembly seal, correct rounded-corner engine lift on driver-side front, and PCV hose routed behind the carburetor.

Corvettes and Chevelles used the same low-profile intake manifolds where applicable. Due to the low-profile intake manifolds that were originally designed to fit under a Corvette hood, the ZL2 option on a 1970 through 1972 Chevelle required a spacer between the carburetor air horn and the air cleaner assembly.

CHAPTER 9

The original Holley carburetor on a 1970 LS6 engine shows the spacer used for RPO ZL2 Special Ducted Air System hood option. Note the throttle-return spring is color coded green and is attached to the throttle bracket.

Cowl-Induction Electrical System

The electrical portion of the cowl-induction system controls the inner-flap door. The inner-flap door directs the air intake from the high-pressure area of the windshield base to the hood. This inner-door valve is mounted on the hood frame just before the flapper door. The electric solenoid is attached to the air valve door with a plunger rod. An electrical relay is mounted on the firewall, typically on the wiring channel along with a switch that mounted on the accelerator pedal. The switch also acts as a passing gear or kick-down switch on TH400 automatic transmission–equipped Chevelles.

Power Steering

Power steering was always an option on 1970 through 1972 Chevelles and was not part of any SS option. It is impossible to say just how many 1970 through 1972 SS-optioned Malibus were ordered with power steering. While it is known that 508,181 Chevelles were ordered with power steering in 1970, 1971 saw sales drop a bit to 477,812, and 1972 sold 418,747 units; just

This restored power steering pump was used on all 1970 Mark IV engines when RPO N40 was ordered with correct "AZ" broadcast code sticker for identification to the assembly-line workers responsible for its installation at final assembly. Both Atlanta and Van Nuys build sheets show an "AZ-AB" broadcast code.

The power steering pulley was not part of the power steering pump. The pulley used was based on the engine; both the L78 and LS6 received a deep-groove pulley, part number 3941105.

how they were distributed throughout the Chevelle lineup for those three years is not known.

Miscellaneous Body and Paint

Painters on both sides of the assembly plant production facilities (Fisher Body and final assembly) did not always use great care when painting their sections of the car. Let's not say their work was haphazard, but given the amount of time they had to do their part, attention to detail was not always their prime concern. If something really bad happened, the car would be pulled from the line (if applicable) or flagged for repair at final assembly.

Bellhousing

The bellhousing is one area where engine assembly would not

An engine with a manual transmission was shipped from the engine plant with the flywheel, clutch/pressure plate assembly, and bellhousing. One of the last steps before shipping was to paint the engine, and not a great deal of care was taken; overspray is common on the bellhousing and other components the engine was shipped with. There is no right or wrong way to determine amount of overspray.

DETAILS, FACTS, AND MYTHS

always take the greatest care when painting the engine, and overspray is quite common. There is no right or wrong way to do this, but bellhousings were not always 100-percent natural, and they were seldom painted completely with the engine.

Trunk

The trunk is another area that did not always get full coverage of either the lower body color or the spatter paint. One can reproduce the paint as found in a concours restoration or one can "over restore" their Chevelle for personal pride.

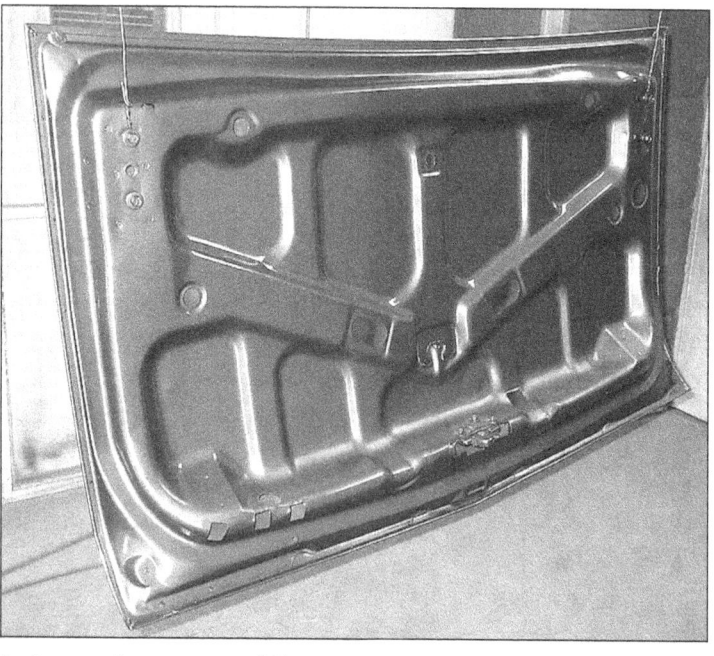

Pictured is the underside of a 1970 Chevelle decklid built at the Arlington final assembly plant. Note the lack of paint coverage in the various support brace holes and the inside edge of the rear support bracing. The red oxide primer is clearly visible in the numerous holes, and coverage of the rear support bracing is spotty. It is another reason to take lots of pictures before you begin disassembly of your Chevelle.

The rear inside trunk area of a 1970 Chevelle built at the Arlington final assembly plant is shown. Note the sparse coverage on the rear lip and zero coverage of the trunk floorpan and inside of rear quarter panels. These areas would be later painted with spatter paint, so there was no need for the body painter to cover these areas.

Inside the trunk area of the same 1970 Arlington Chevelle shows that not much attention to detail was given here. The majority of the trunk and trunk floor was, at this point, left untouched by the color painter as they knew spatter paint was to be applied later in assembly process.

When the spatter paint was applied, coverage was limited to what the painter could (or would) reach and what would typically be visible under normal viewing conditions. Hence, much of the rear bulkhead was not covered, and not much care was given to the leading edge rear of the trunk. If you are lucky enough to find an original-paint Chevelle that you are restoring, areas such as these are great candidates for taking a lot of photos to document why you restored the car the way you did.

The spatter painters only had a few seconds to do their task, and coverage was not as complete as you may wish to do your restoration. Keep this in mind as you decide to do a driver/local show quality restoration or a concours restoration.

The rear area of the trunk shows spatter paint coverage would be on par with the rest of the trunk area. The trunk latch would have already been installed and would get the same spatter paint as the rest of the trunk area.

Miscellaneous Chassis and Driveline

The disc brake system on 1970 Chevelles evolved from an early two-piece rotor to a single-piece design. Just when the change was made varied from plant to plant as inventory was being exhausted. If you are not certain what your 1970 Chevelle should have, and you have a build sheet, check the broadcast code in box 12 "STRG KNUCKLE." The Arlington plant codes changed from the early "DK" to the later "DT" in mid-April; Atlanta plant codes changed from "AS" to "DT" between 04-30 and 05-05; Baltimore plant codes changed from "DK" to "DT" on 03-11; Kansas City codes changed from "DK" to "DT" on 03-18; Van Nuys changed codes from "AS" to "AS-R" between 01-04 and 02-18, then again to "DT-R" between 03-11 and 04-01. Knowing the correct broadcast code will let you select the correct reproduction sticker.

Positraction-equipped Chevelles have a tag of some kind either on the rear-end assembly center section fill plug or on one of the bolts holding the rear cover on. Some early model year 1970 Chevelles may have used the earlier tag as supplies were exhausted.

Chassis were initially assembled upside down; hence the identification sticker appears upside down when the chassis is upright. The sticker shown here with broadcast code "XU" is for a Malibu sport coupe, "XV" for Malibu convertible, "XV" for El Camino, and "XS" for Monte Carlo and is applicable to the 1970 model year.

Frame identification differs for the 1971 and 1972 model years. A Malibu sport coupe is coded "CR," the Malibu convertible is coded "CS," the El Camino is coded "CJ" in 1971 and "CH" in 1972, and the Monte Carlo is coded "CM."

Freshly cleaned and prepared disc-brake dust-shield covers should be natural in color as they are stamped from galvanized steel and should not be zinc plated. The caliper bracket is gold cadmium plated.

An early 1970 two-piece rotor can be easily identified by the lack of the groove in the face of the rotor itself. The early rotors also required a different steering knuckle. Check your build date and final assembly plant if you're not sure which you should have.

This late 1970 single piece rotor can be identified by the single groove in the rotor itself; early two-piece rotors do not have this groove. Check your build date and final assembly plant if you're not sure which you should have.

A tag found on all positraction rear ends is used to remind the owner and technician servicing the rear end that special lubricant is required for the Positraction assembly.

The frame-identification sticker is typically found on the kick up for the rear axle, and the sticker is upside down since the chassis components were assembled with the chassis upside down for ease of installation.

D88 Stripes and Hood Pins

A common misconception is RPO D88 hood and deck stripes were part of the Z25 or Z15 SS Equipment option in 1970, 1971, or 1972. It was not included in the option; D88 hood and deck stripes were part of the RPO ZL2 Special Ducted Hood Air System that was an option on any 1970, 1971, or 1972 SS Equipment–optioned Malibu with a big-block V-8 L34, L78, LS3, LS5, or LS6 engine. The 1971 and 1972 SS Equipment–optioned Malibu ordered with either the L48 350-4 or L65 350-2 small-block V-8 could not order the RPO ZL2 hood system.

The D88 stripes were also optional on any non-SS Equipment–optioned Malibu sport coupe, convertible, or sedan pickup regardless of engine type or size. When the ZL2 option was ordered, the stripes could be deleted from the option via a Fleet & Special Order (F&SO) request, resulting in what is commonly referred to as stripe delete. On a non-ZL2-optioned Malibu by not ordering the D88 option does not constitute "stripe delete" any more than not ordering a radio would be "radio delete" or not ordering bucket seats would be "bucket seat delete."

Hood pins (or locking pins, as Chevrolet often referred to them) are a little different. Hood pins were part of the ZL2 option in 1970, but in 1971 and 1972, hood pins became part of the SS Equipment option Z15—whether the ZL2 hood was ordered or not—and they were part of the YF3 Heavy Chevy option. Hood pins came standard with the SS and YF3 domed hoods in 1971 and 1972.

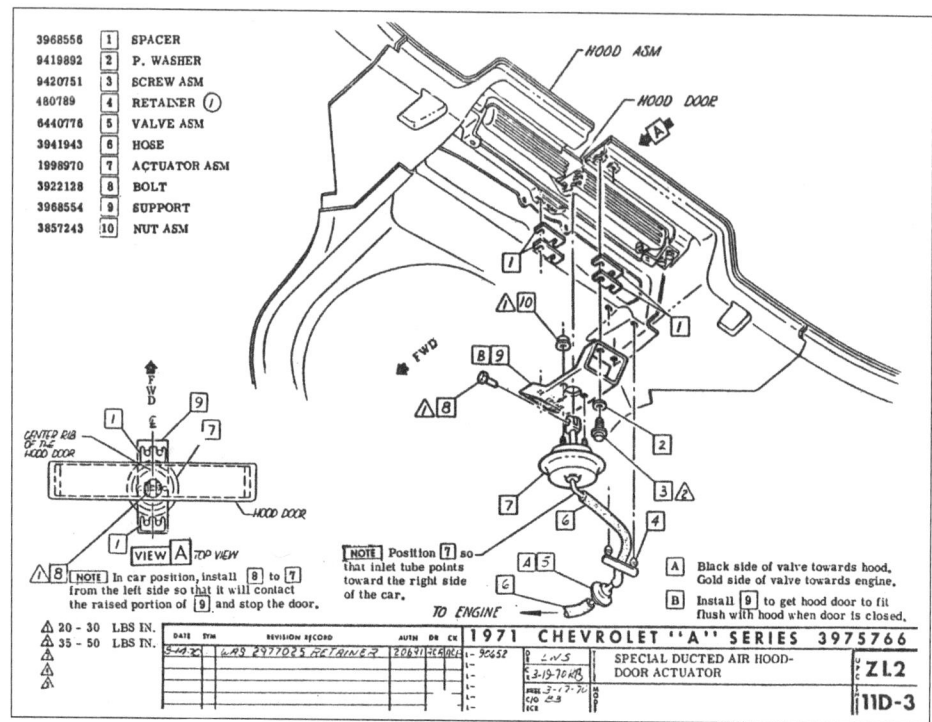

An exploded view shows the position and mounting of the RPO ZL2 Special Ducted Air System option actuator assembly and the one-way valve with added instructions on positioning of the flapper door and actuator assembly support bracket from 1971.

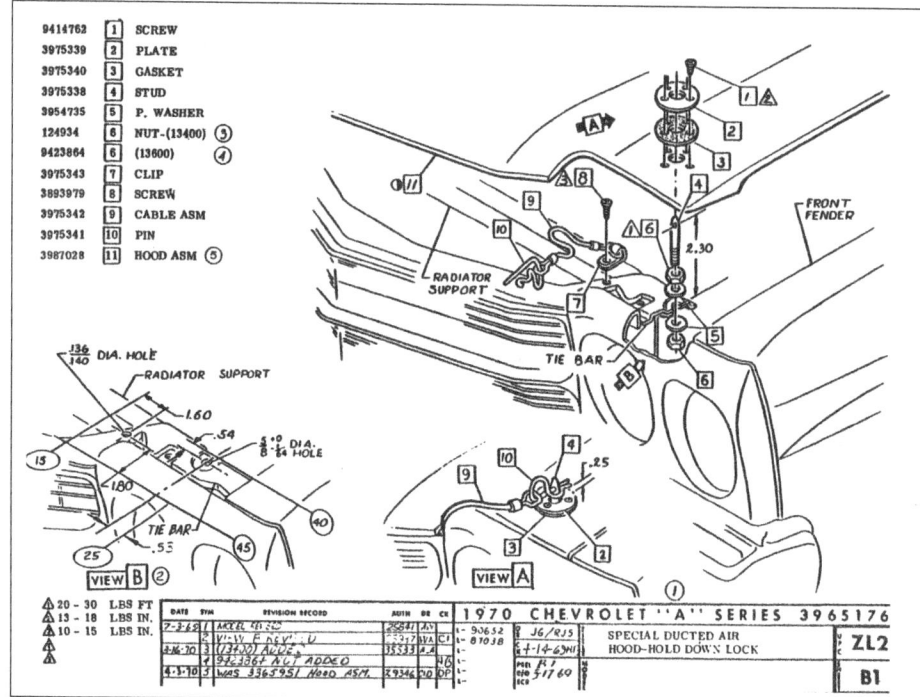

This diagram shows hood pin positioning on 1970 SS Equipment–optioned Malibus when RPO ZL2 Special Ducted Air System hood was ordered. In 1970, the hood pins were one part of the entire RPO ZL2 option and could not be deleted like the D88 stripes could be. Hood pins were not a separate option in 1970 and could not be ordered by themselves.

CHAPTER 9

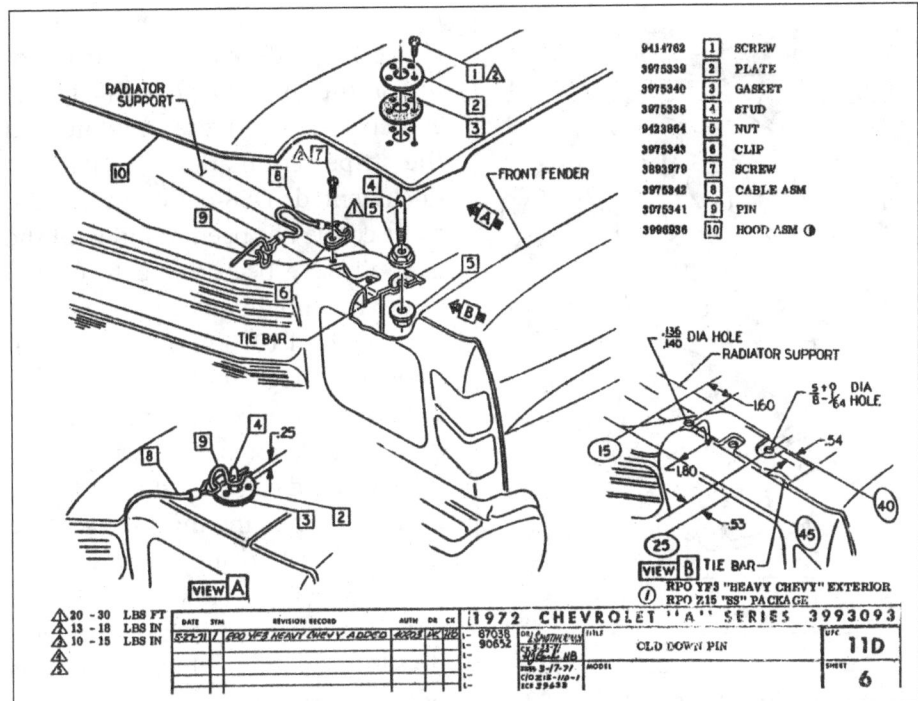

The 1971 and 1972 standard SS Equipment–optioned domed hood is the same as was used on the 1971 and 1972 base Chevelle with the RPO YF3 Heavy Chevy option, and both were equipped with hood pins where the standard SS Equipment–optioned 1970 Malibu domed hood did not have hood pins.

The second 1970 AIM drawing with a redrawn-and-redesigned date of June 4, 1969, shows the stripe's locations and measurements a bit different than the original. Considerations for the vinyl top option are also included, showing the stripes on the rear with the note to "End paint stripe at lid opening. RPO C08 only." To date, most documented vinyl top–optioned Malibu sport coupes with stripes have shown the stripes not stopping at the decklid opening but rather extending to the rear window molding like non-vinyl top–optioned Malibu sport coupes.

An added note on view B shows "paint over edge of decklid opening." The verbiage was also included on the original version but more strongly pointed out with the first revision. Also note the stripes continue to have squared outer corners in the drawing. The drawing also

1970 D88 Stripes

The 1970 factory assembly instruction manual shows three versions of D88 stripes. The first version (dated April 28, 1969) shows the various measurements and stripe locations. Note that although this is a rough drawing and not an engineering drawing, the stripe outer corners appear to be square and not rounded. There are documented original Malibus from both the Arlington assembly plant and the Kansas City assembly plant with square outer-corner stripes. Most that have been found are relatively early model year Malibus, but at least one Arlington Malibu with a build date in June 1970 has been found. Whether these were flukes (as other Malibus from the same time frame have the rounded outer-corner stripes) or it was simply a painter not knowing or adhering to the AIM is not known.

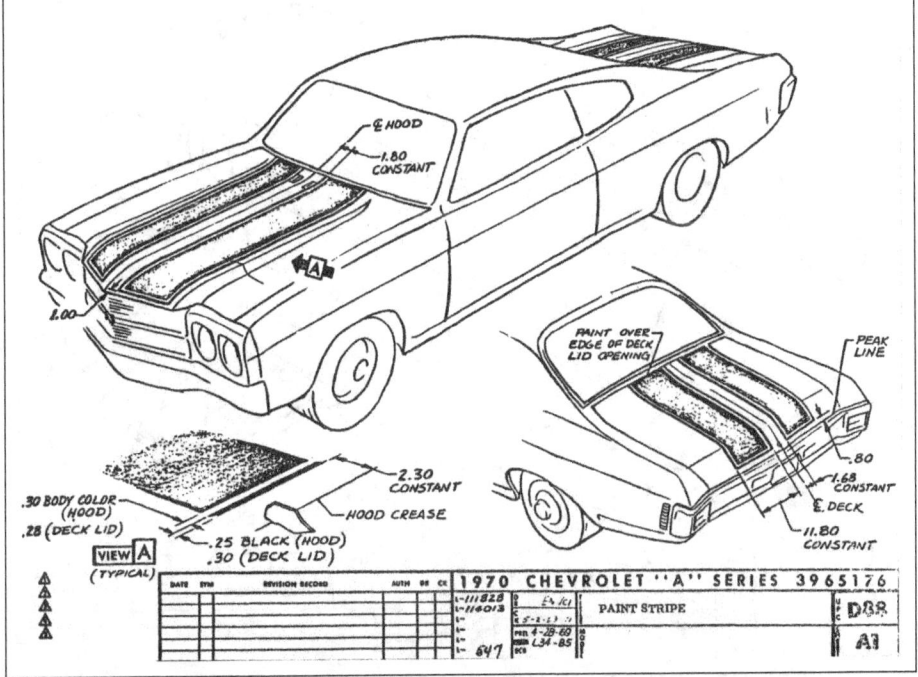

An initial drawing of RPO D88 shows the stripes for 1970. Although this is just a drawing, note the square outer corners of the stripes, which may be the cause of some plants doing square corner stripes in 1970. Several measurements were changed in the first revision of this drawing.

DETAILS, FACTS, AND MYTHS

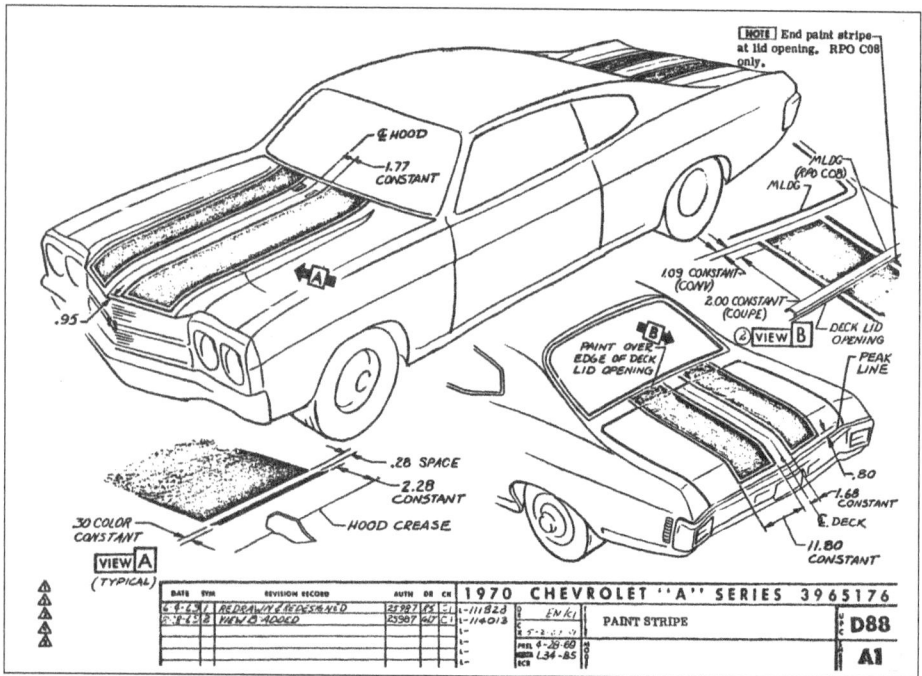

This shows the first revision of RPO D88 stripes for 1970 dated July 4, 1969. Note there are still the square outer corners, but several of the measurements were changed from the initial drawing.

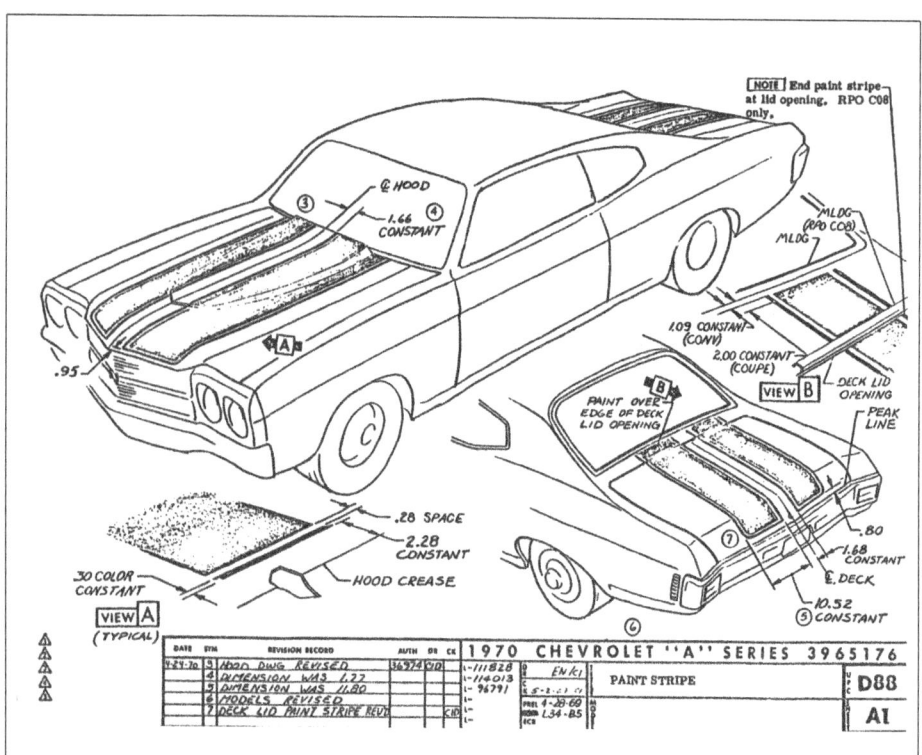

The second revision of RPO D88 stripes for 1970 dated April 24, 1970, now shows the outer corners rounded off. A few minor changes in measurements are also found with this revision, most notably the width of the trunk stripes were narrowed from 11.80 to 10.52 inches.

indicates the stripes on the panel between the decklid and rear molding on the sport coupe with a gap of 2 inches between the molding and the stripe termination. To date, no documented D88-optioned Malibu sport coupe has been found with the gap; all have been found to extend under the molding.

The third 1970 AIM drawing with a revision date of April 24, 1970, shows a change in a few of the measurements, most notably the wider hood stripes as indicated by the centerline distance to the innermost stripe going from 1.77 to 1.66 and a narrower rear stripe going from 11.80 to 10.52. Also note on this second revision the stripe drawing has rounded corners on the outermost stripe.

The dilemma is which group of measurements should you use? The original drawing is probably not a good choice since it was revised before production began, so that leaves a choice between the first and second revisions. For the first revision, it's recommended to use a rounded outer-corner stripe unless you have proof your 1970 Malibu has original square outer-corner stripes now; if it does, be sure to document with quality photos. If your Malibu was built prior to the second revision date of April 24, 1970, it is recommended you use the measurements for the first revision and rounded outer corners; if April 24, 1970, or later, the second revision is recommended. Chances are low that anyone will be able to see a difference between 1.66 and 1.77 for the hood stripes, but he or she could very well know about the 10.52 versus 11.00 width of the deck stripes.

On a daily driver, these measurements may not be critical but on a concours restoration, it's just as easy to do it right as it is to do it wrong.

Note the hood pins on the standard SS domed hood of this SS Equipment–optioned 1971 Malibu sport coupe. A few 1970 and 1971 SS Equipment–optioned Malibus have been found with these square corner stripes. When doing your restoration, be sure to photo document these if your Malibu was so equipped.

The more common round-outside-corner stripes are shown on this 1970 SS Equipment–optioned Malibu sport coupe. Just like 1971 and 1972 when the ZL2 Special Ducted Air System hood was not ordered, RPO D88 stripes were optional.

1971 D88 Stripes

The 1971 AIM drawing for D88 stripes shows no change in the measurements from the final revision of 1970. The 1971 drawing shows the same 2.00 gap on sport coupes as 1970, but as in the case of 1970, no original documented Malibu sport coupe has yet been found with this gap. Another anomaly to be aware of in the drawing is how the thin stripes are all shown with rounded corners, but the inside corners should be square and only the outside corners should be rounded. As in 1970, the D88 stripe option was available on any L6 or V-8 Malibu sport coupe, convertible, or sedan pickup. While still optional with the Z15 SS Equipment option, stripes were standard with the ZL2 hood option.

Several 1971 Malibus have been seen with square-corner stripes; whether these are original (or repaints of originals) cannot be confirmed. As before, unless you have a true, original-paint survivor car with square-cornered stripes, it is probably best to conform to the AIM and use round corners.

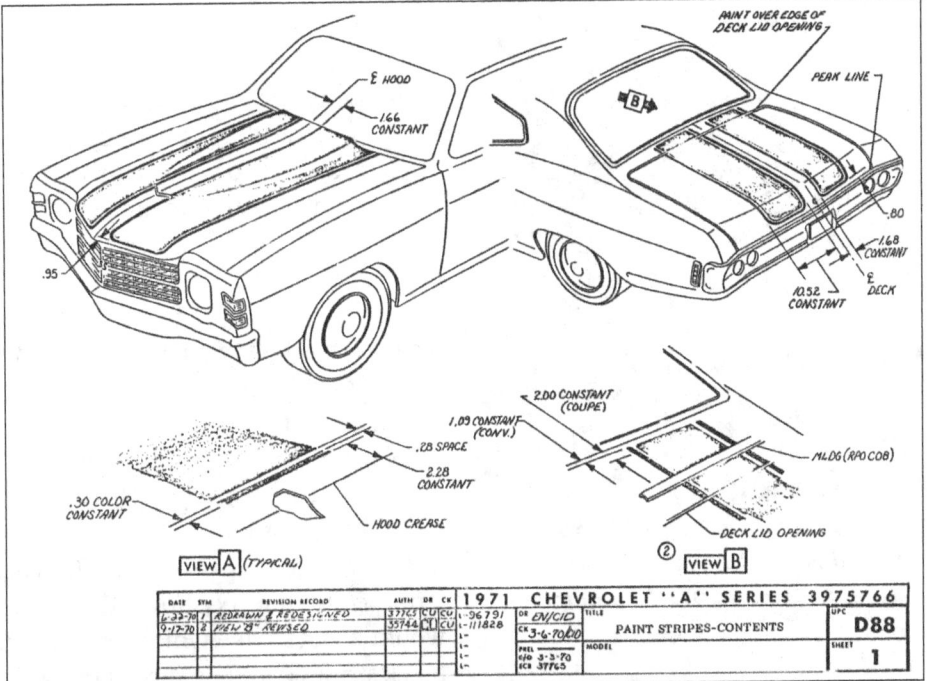

This is the RPO D88 stripe drawing for 1971. Measurements are essentially the same as the 1970 second revision. View B was revised to clarify that the paint stripe should extend from trunk lid opening to and under the molding when a vinyl top was ordered.

1972 D88 Stripes

The 1972 AIM drawing for D88 stripes shows no change in the measurements from the final revision of the 1970 and 1971 drawing. The 1972 drawing shows the same 2.00 gap on sport coupes as 1970 and 1971, but

DETAILS, FACTS, AND MYTHS

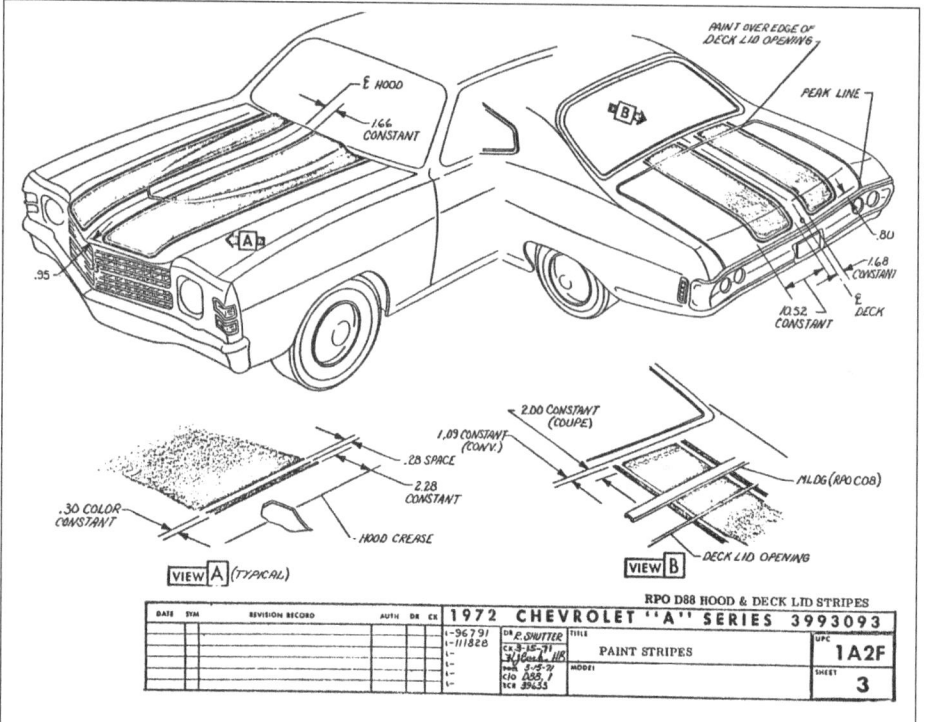

The RPO D88 stripe drawing for 1972 has the same measurements as the second revision of 1970 and the 1971 drawing.

Optional RPO D88 stripes adorn the hood of this Flame Orange 1972 SS Equipment–optioned Malibu sport coupe. Note this is not optioned with the RPO ZL2 Special Ducted Air System hood. Both 1971 and 1972 SS Equipment–optioned Malibus still came with hood pins.

rounded. As in 1970 and 1971, the D88 stripe option was available on any L6 or V-8 Malibu sport coupe, convertible, or sedan pickup. While still optional with the Z15 SS Equipment option, stripes were standard with the ZL2 hood option.

Note in every drawing for each year the stripes were designed to stop just before the rear window molding on sport coupes and convertibles. All original-paint survivors found to date have the stripes extending under this molding.

D88 Stripe Colors

For all three years, stripes were only available in either black or white appropriate to the model year. For 1970, the standard color of the stripe depended on two major factors: the lower-body color of the car and the upper-body color of the car or vinyl top or convertible top if applicable. The interior-color choice had no bearing on the stripe color. Two colors in particular had no stripe color options at all: black Malibus received white stripes, and white Malibus received black stripes regardless of the top color. Several other colors were also limited to either black or white stripes, but the standard color could be overridden by a buyer with a F&SO request, such as Black Cherry, Fathom Blue, or Forest Green in 1970. The stripe color matrix shows this color would always have white stripes, but black stripes could be special ordered. Again, with the exception of a white or black Malibu, the suggested stripe colors in the following tables could be overridden at the buyer's request.

as in the case of 1970 and 1971, no original documented Malibu sport coupe has yet been found with this gap. Another anomaly to be aware of in the drawing is how the thin stripes are all shown with rounded corners, but the inside corners should be square and only the outside corners

CHAPTER 9

1970 Stripe Colors

Exterior Color Code	Sport Coupe without Vinyl Top	Sport Coupe with Vinyl Top					Convertible	
		White	Black	Dark Green	Dark Blue	Dark Gold	White	Black
10	Black	Black	Black	Black	Black	---	Black	Black
14	Black	White	Black	---	Black	---	White	Black
17	Black	---	Black	---	---	---	---	Black
19	White	White	White	---	---	---	White	White
25	Black	White	Black	---	Black	---	White	Black
28	White	White	White	---	White	---	White	White
34	Black	White	Black	---	---	---	White	Black
45	Black	White	Black	Black	---	---	White	Black
48	White	White	White	White	---	---	White	White
50	Black	White	Black	---	---	Black	White	Black
55	Black	White	Black	---	---	Black	White	Black
58	Black	White	Black	---	---	Black	White	Black
63	Black	White	Black	---	---	---	White	Black
75	Black	White	Black	---	---	---	White	Black
78	White	White	White	---	---	---	White	White

All 1970 standard two-tone models have white stripes except the Astro Blue (25) lower and Fathom Blue (28) upper combination that will have black stripes.

1971 Stripe Colors

Exterior Color Code	Sport Coupe without Vinyl Roof Cover		Vinyl Roof Cover or Convertible Top				
	Regular	Optional	Black	White	Blue	Brown	Green
11	Black	---	Black	Black	Black	---	---
13	Black	White	Black	White	---	---	---
19	White	---	White	White	White	---	White
24	Black	White	Black	White	Black	---	---
26	Black	White	Black	White	Black	---	---
42	Black	White	Black	White	---	---	Black
43	Black	White	Black	White	---	---	Black
49	Black	White	Black	White	---	---	Black
52	Black	White	Black	White	Black	Black	Black
53	Black	White	Black	White	---	---	---
61	Black	White	Black	White	---	---	---
62	Black	White	Black	White	---	Black	---
67	Black	White	Black	White	---	Black	---
75	Black	White	Black	White	---	---	---
78	Black	White	Black	White	---	---	---

All 1971 standard two-tone combinations received white stripes only since only white was offered as a top color in the United States. Stripe colors are automatically selected for compatibility to the vinyl roof cover or convertible top color. The same stripe colors and restrictions are applicable to the YF3-optioned Heavy Chevy Chevelle V-8 sport coupe.

1972 Stripes

With two exceptions, Midnight Bronze (68) and Antique White (11), either black or white stripes could be specified by the buyer. Midnight Bronze was limited to white stripes, and Antique White was limited to black stripes. The top color (solid, vinyl, or convertible) had no bearing on the color of stripe that could be selected. The Chevelle V-8 sport coupe optioned with the YF3 Heavy Chevy option could specify black stripes with all exterior colors or white stripes with any exterior color except Antique White.

Appendix A

Pre-Restoration Checklist

It is strongly suggested you make a checklist of things to look for and test when looking for that car of your dreams. Whether you are looking for a daily-driver candidate or a Chevelle you plan to do a full, concours restoration on, you should have an idea of what you are looking for, what works, and what does not work on the car.

Often our heart overrules our brain when buying a car, and looking for a nice Chevelle is no different. Before handing over a lot of cash or writing a check for that shiny Chevelle, step back and take a deep breath. The last thing you want to do is hand over a fistfull of cash only to find basic safety items such as lights, wipers, brakes, etc. are not in good working order. At least you should be aware they need immediate attention.

Even if your plans are to begin a full-blown, body-off-frame restoration, you need to know what you are getting and what needs attention. As a buyer, knowing what that Chevelle is going to need is a very good negotiation tool. For example, is the shiny paint hiding a ton of body filler, meaning you are going to need to replace floorpans, major body panels, etc.? Suspension, brakes, and driveline components may be on the list to refresh or replace anyway, so they may not be as important during inspection. Look for the number of original parts that the Chevelle has. Many components, especially engine items such as the distributor, carburetor, and air cleaner assembly are unique to a specific year and engine and can be difficult, expensive, and time consuming to find in a usable or rebuildable condition.

If your goal is to build a nice daily driver, seemingly little things such as windshield wipers, the wiring, heater, air conditioner, glass, etc. are things you will have to address at some point, and that can affect negotiations on the final price of the Chevelle.

	Good	Bad	Repair	Replace	Notes
Brakes/Chassis/Suspension					
Ball joints					
Brake pads/rotors/drums					
Fuel tank/lines					
Shocks/springs					
Tie-rods/center link					
Tires/wheels					
Electrical					
Brake lamps (L/R)					
Backup lamps					
Clock					
Dash lamps					
Dome lamp (headlamp switch)					
Dome lamp (door switch)					
Emergency flashers					
Gauges (water/oil/amp/tach)					
Headlamps (low/high beam)					
Heat/AC fan switch					
High-beam indicator					
Horn					
Ignition lock					
Radio/stereo					
Taillamps					
Turn signal lamps (L/R)					
Wiper switch/motor					
Engine Compartment					
Air cleaner unit					
A.I.R. system if applicable					
Carb fuel leak/lines					

APPENDIX A

	Good	Bad	Repair	Replace	Notes
Brackets/braces					
Decals/stickers					
Distributor/wires/coil					
Exhaust					
Horn relay					
Power steering/brakes					
Radiator/support					
Wiring harnesses					
Exterior (Body)					
Bumpers/guards					
Chrome/bright trim					
Dents/rust					
Doors open/close					
Emblems					
Fender/hood/trunk fit					
Glass					
Hood open/close, hinge play					
Paint					
Panel fitment (doors/hood/trunk)					
Trunk open/close, fitment					
Interior Items					
Brake/clutch pedals/pads					
Brake switch					
Carpets					
Console					
Convertible top condition					
Convertible top operation					
Dash pad/carrier					
Door handles/locks					
Door/window fuzzies					
Floor mats					
Gas pedal/automatic switch function					
Glass condition					
Headliner					
Heater/A/C operation					
Park brake operation/pad					
Rear view mirror/door mirror(s)					
Seat belts					
Seat condition					
Seat operation front/rear					
Shifter operation					
Speedometer/odometer					
Steering wheel/steering column					
Windows operation					
Other Mechanical					
Rear end noisy?					
Driveshaft thump or seem out of balance?					
Does car drive straight?					
Does car stop straight or pull?					
Are there any vibrations, speed?					
Engine function, miss, surge, etc.					

Appendix B

CHASSIS AND ENGINE COMPARTMENT PAINT COLORS

Every day I receive phone calls, texts, and emails asking me what color and/or gloss level a particular part on a Chevelles should be, and every day I cheerfully answer the question, never thinking that maybe I should just write up some sort of reference guide to help the general Chevelle population. Maybe now was a good time.

I will be fairly general because there are many different colors, shades, and gloss levels found under the hood, not to mention the many types of plating (that could be a book all by itself). Instead, I will be rather generic for home restorers so they can be close enough for the weekend outdoor car show and be proud to show off their engine and chassis.

Many home restorers are happy just to have black parts black and plated parts plated, while others have asked for specific paint codes. I will try and help those who are doing home restorations, since most shops and professional restorers will know the specific codes needed already.

As with any painting steps, make sure you follow all the guidelines detailed in chapter 6. All of your efforts will be for not if they are not followed to the fullest. It is also understood that many of you may be restoring only some of the car and not all of it. In other words, you may be restoring your engine compartment with some of the major components still installed, such as the engine and transmission, and will have to work around those. As with any painting process, cleanliness is critical.

There are many paints that are designed specifically for the area or component that you are painting, such as Chevrolet engine orange, chassis black, stainless steel, radiator black, etc. Two of the best sources I know of for these are Eastwood (eastwood.com) and Details Wholesale (detailswholesale.com/dealers). Detail Wholesale's site provides a list of dealers by state or area where these paints are sold.

Some of you will be using aerosol paints rather than shooting through a gun. If you are restoring your engine compartment with the engine and

---

CHEVELLE RESTORATION AND AUTHENTICITY GUIDE: 1970–1972

transmission in place, you will get far better results by removing all the peripherals on the engine and underhood to allow you more clearance to the compartment without clutter in the way. Items such as carburetor, distributor, alternator, exhaust manifolds, plug wires, pulleys, radiator, wiring harness, and many other items can be removed so that you can better clean the area and spray on the new primer and paint without getting those items covered in overspray. Ultimately, it is best if you are leaving the engine and transmission in the car to leave just the engine long block, brake master cylinder, and booster and wheel tubs. Remove as much of everything else that you can.

It is imperative to clean and spray in a well-ventilated area, wear proper painting clothes and respirators, and take appropriate action to cover the body and any areas you are not painting to protect them from overspray.

Underhood Details

This basic outline provides the colors that you will be working with. It will get you started toward a presentable undercarriage and engine compartment.

- Frame, front control arms, and lower rear trailing arms: semigloss black (if painting black, the upper trailing arms are flat black). Some plants did not paint the rear trailing arms or transmission crossmember, so these could be painted natural steel as well.
- Rear differential: same semigloss black or natural steel, depending on the plant.
- Front and rear coil springs: either natural cast iron or semigloss black.
- Front and rear sway bars: semigloss black or natural cast iron.
- Shocks: shock gray.
- Steering linkage: natural cast iron.
- Brake calipers: natural cast iron or semigloss black.
- Caliper brackets: gold cadmium.
- Disc brake backing plates: originally galvanized steel. Bright zinc is acceptable when restoring.
- Tie-rods: natural cast iron.
- Tie-rod sleeves and clamps: natural steel.
- Steering box (power or manual): natural cast iron with natural aluminum top plate.
- Firewall, wheelhouses, and core support: semigloss black.
- Radiator: gloss black.
- Radiator top plate: semigloss black.
- Cooling fan: gloss black.
- Crank, water pump, and power steering pulleys: gloss black.
- Power steering pump: gloss black.
- Power steering bracket: gloss black.
- Upper/lower alternator brackets: semigloss black.
- Alternator: natural aluminum.
- Alternator fan: originally galvanized, but high-performance is bright zinc, low-performance is semigloss black.
- Fan clutch: natural aluminum with gold cadmium center face and natural steel shaft and mount.
- Heater housing on firewall: gloss black (Kansas City plant sprayed undercoating over the top edge and face of the firewall).
- Heater fan housing: semigloss black.
- Air-conditioner dog house: natural black fiberglass.
- Air-conditioner compressor and brackets: semigloss black.
- Hood hinges and upper/lower hood latch: dark gray phosphate.
- Most small underhood brackets: semigloss black.
- Exhaust manifolds: natural cast iron (special paint for exhaust).
- Brake booster, proportioning valve bracket, and master cylinder cover: gold cadmium.
- Master cylinder: either semigloss black or natural cast iron.
- Proportioning valve: either semigloss black or natural cast iron.
- Metering valve: either natural cast iron or natural brass, depending on plant.
- Windshield washer pump: the base is natural aluminum and canister is bright zinc.
- Horns: gloss black.
- Voltage regulator: gloss black cover with galvanized or zinc base.
- Ignition coil: gloss black.
- Coil bracket: galvanized or zinc.
- Distributor: natural cast aluminum.
- Fuel and brake lines: natural steel.
- Battery tray: semigloss black.
- Intermediate steering column shaft: semigloss black.
- Rag joint: natural cast iron.
- Upper CV joint housing on intermediate shaft: semigloss black or dark gray phosphate.
- Engine, cylinder heads, water pump, oil pan, valve covers (when not chromed), intake (when not aluminum), harmonic balancer: all Chevrolet orange.
- Air cleaner (when painted): semigloss black.
- Bellhousing: natural cast aluminum.
- Transmission (both manual and automatic): natural cast aluminum.
- Driveshaft: natural steel.
- Fuel tank: natural galvanized steel.
- Fuel tank straps: semigloss black
- All parking brake cables: natural steel.
- Bottom side of hood: semigloss black.

Appendix C

ENGINE ASSEMBLY PROCESS

The engine assembly process at both Flint and Tonawanda varied slightly due to their own standard operating procedures. The assembly process here is general in nature and does not go into detail for each step at each plant. One caveat here: today's engines built at various GM engine assembly plants are built very different from how these plants operated 40 and 50 years ago. Modern robotics has taken over much of the process.

In a nutshell, these show the sequence of engine assembly and not the nuts-and-bolts process. It should be noted the cylinder heads were assembled separately from the engine assembly.

Flint Engine Assembly

Raw castings enter plant
Block machining (boring/broaching) in one to two days and block washed
Block begins upside down. Bore sizes on oil pan rail broadcast ahead to piston hook-up area
Galley plugs
Camshaft
Main bearing caps removed, crankshaft installed, caps reinstalled
Flywheel and pressure plate or flex plate depending on transmission type
Cam and crankshaft gears, timing chain
Piston installation
Front engine cover and seal
Harmonic balancer
Oil pump shaft and oil pump
Windage tray bolts if applicable
Oil pan
Clutch housing (manual transmission only)
Engine turned upright
Top Dead Center determined and timing pointer aligned
Camshaft lifters installed
Cylinder heads installed
Rocker arms and balls installed
Intake manifold installed, engine lift brackets if applicable
Oil filler tube if applicable, water outlet and thermostat
Valves adjusted
Valve covers installed
Miscellaneous brackets/braces and switches installed
Build date/suffix code stamped [1]
Water test with vacuum gauge
Oil cavity test
Paint assembly
Distributor installed
Ignition coils and spark-plug wires installed
Spark plugs installed
Temperature and pressure switches installed
Exhaust manifolds installed
Spark-plug wire supports, heat shields, other miscellaneous brackets/braces installed as needed
Component verification
Racked and readied for shipment

Tonawanda Engine Assembly

Raw castings received from other parts of the Tonawanda engine plant
Block machining (boring/broaching) and block washed
Galley plugs
Transmission alignment pins
Camshaft installed
Main bearing caps removed, crankshaft installed, main caps reinstalled
Flywheel and pressure plate or flex plate depending on transmission type
Camshaft and crankshaft gears, timing chain
Pistons installed
Front engine cover and seal
Harmonic balancer
Oil pump shaft and oil pump
Windage tray bolts (if applicable)
Oil pan
Top Dead Center determined and timing pointer aligned
Engine turned upright
Camshaft lifters installed
Build date/suffix code stamped [2]
Cylinder heads installed
Rocker arms and balls installed
Valves adjusted
Intake manifold installed, engine lift brackets if applicable
Water outlet and thermostat installed
Water pump installed
Spark plugs installed
Distributor installed
Miscellaneous brackets/braces installed
Exhaust manifolds installed
Vacuum test
Valve covers
Paint assembly
Hot test
Water and oil drained
Racked and readied for shipment

[1] All small-block (283/307/327/400) V-8 engines have the date and suffix code stamped on the right portion of the engine pad as you face the block. Final assembly plant partial VIN was stamped on the left side of the engine pad when applicable. All L6 engines have the date and suffix code stamped on a machined pad by the distributor.

[2] The engine assembly date and suffix code was stamped on

APPENDIX C

Tonawanda Mark IV engines before the cylinder heads were installed. Now you can see how that information was stamped behind that big plug on the front of the passenger-side cylinder head. All Mark IV engines (396/402/427/454) have the date and suffix code stamped on the left portion of the engine pad as you face the block. Final assembly plant partial VIN was stamped on the right side of the engine pad or another location on the engine block such as the rough cast area by the oil filter or on the bellhousing flange.

1970–1972: 350/396/402/454 Engine ID codes

1970

Code	Size	Carburetor	Horsepower	RPO	Transmission
CNI	350	2	250	L65	Manual-3/4
CNJ	350	4	300	L48	Manual-4
CNK	350	4	300	L48	Powerglide
CNM	350	2	250	L65	Powerglide
CNN	350	2	250	L65	TH350
CRE	350	4	300	L48	TH350
CGR	402	4	330	LS3	Manual-3/4
CKN	402	4	375	L78	Manual-4
CKP	402	4	375	L78/L89	TH400
CKQ	402	4	375	L78	Manual-4 *
CKR	402	4	330	LS3	Manual-4
CKS	402	4	330	LS3	Manual-4 *
CKT	402	4	375	L78/L89	Manual-4
CKU	402	4	375	L78/L89	Manual-4 *
CTW	402	4	350	L34	TH400
CTX	402	4	350	L34	Manual 4
CTY	402	4	350	L78	TH400
CTZ	402	4	350	L34	Manual-4 *
CRQ	454	4	360	LS5	TH400
CRR	454	4	450	LS6	TH400
CRT	454	4	360	LS5	Manual-4
CRU	454	4	360	-LS5	Manual-4 *
CRV	454	4	450	LS6	Manual-4
CRX	454	4	450	LS6	Manual-4 *

Notes:
Neither the 250-ci 6-cylinder nor the 307-ci V-8 are listed here.
The 400-ci 2-barrel Turbo-Fire V-8 small-block is not listed here and was only available in the Chevelle line in the Monte Carlo.
The 350-hp 396-ci engine is actually 402 ci, and the 396 name was only used with the SS Equipment option.
The 350-hp 396-ci engine only uses RPO L34 internally, there was no L34 option as such to order since this was the base engine with RPO Z25.
The 360-hp 454-ci engine only used RPO LS5 internally, there was no LS5 option as such to order since this was the base engine with RPO Z15.
Both the 360- and 450-hp 454-ci engines could only be ordered with either the optional TH400 3-speed automatic transmission or the heavy-duty M22 4-speed manual transmission.
* Heavy-duty clutch
Number found on Vintage Vehicle Services Report

1971

Code	Size	Carburetor	Horsepower	RPO	Transmission
CGA	350	2	245	L65	Manual-4 *
CGB	350	2	245	L65	Powerglide
CGC	350	2	245	L65	TH350 *
CGK	350	4	270	L48	Manual-3/4
CGL	350	4	270	L48	TH350
CJD	350	4	270	L48	TH350
CJG	350	4	270	L48	Manual-3/4 *
CJJ	350	4	270	L48	Manual-3/4
CLA	400	4	300	LS3	Manual *
CLB	402	4	300	LS3	TH400
CLL	402	4	300	LS3	Manual-4
CLP	402	4	300	LS3	TH400 **
CLR	402	4	300	LS3	Manual
CLS	402	4	300	LS3	HD 3-speed MC1
CPA	454	4	365	LS5	Manual 4 #
CPD	454	4	365	LS5	TH400

Notes:
Neither the 250-ci 6-cylinder nor the 307-ci V-8 are listed here.
The 350-ci engines L65 and L48 as well as the 402-ci engine LS3 were the same whether ordered with or without the SS option.
* Includes Monte Carlo
** Monte Carlo only
# The 365-hp 454-ci engine could only be ordered with either the optional TH400 3-speed automatic transmission or the heavy-duty M22 4-speed manual transmission.

APPENDIX C

1972

Code	Size	Carburetor	Horsepower	RPO	Transmission
CAR	350	2	165	L65	TH350 NB2
CDA	350	2	165	-L65	Manual-3/4 NB2 *
CDB	350	2	165	L65	Powerglide NB2 **
CDD	350	4	175	L48	TH350 NB2 *
CDG	350	4	175	L48	Manual-3/4 NB2
CKA	350	2	165	L65	Manual-3/4 *
CKB	350	2	165	L65	TH350 *
CKD	350	4	175	L48	TH350 *
CKK	350	4	175	L48	Manual-3/4
CMD	350	2	165	L65	TH350 NB2
CTL	350	2	165	L65	TH350 *
CLA	402	4	240	LS3	Manual-4 (1)
CLB	402	4	240	LS3	TH400 * (1)
CLS	402	4	240	LS3	Manual-3 (1)
CTA	402	4	240	LS3	Manual-4 A.I.R
CTB	402	4	240	LS3	TH400 A.I.R. *
CTH	402	4	240	LS3	Manual-3 A.I.R.
CTJ	402	4	240	LS3	TH400 A.I.R.
CPA ***	454	4	270	LS5	Manual-M22
CPD ***	454	4	270	LS5	TH400 *
CRW	454	4	270	LS5	TH400 A.I.R. *
CRX	454	4	270	LS5	Manual-M22 A.I.R.

Notes:

Neither the 250-ci 6-cylinder nor the 307-ci V-8 are listed here.

The 350-ci engines L65 and L48 as well as the 402-ci engine LS3 were the same whether ordered with or without the SS option.

* Includes Monte Carlo

** Monte Carlo only

*** To date, no 1972 Chevelle build sheet has been found with either a CPA or CPD engine code.

Tonawanda engine plant production records do not show CRW engine code but rather CRN for "A" and "B" body LS5 with TH400. No 1972 Chevelle has been found with this engine code.

The 270-hp 454-ci engine could only be ordered with either the optional TH400 3-speed automatic transmission or the heavy-duty M22 4-speed manual transmission.

NB2 – California required equipment includes A.I.R. and camshaft with longer valve overlap

A.I.R. stands for Air Injection Reactor

(1) 402-ci engines coded CLA, CLB, and CLS are shown in numerous publications, but there is an ongoing debate if any of these 402-ci engines without A.I.R. were ever installed in a 1972 Chevelle, regardless of final assembly plant. GM's own "Restoration Kit" shows these three codes but does not mention A.I.R. All 1972 builds sheets found to date with the LS3 engine are coded either CTA or CTB; no CLA, CLB, or CLS coded build sheets have been found to date.

Appendix D

Driveshaft Stripe Colors

As noted in chapter 5, driveshafts were often color-coded to assist the assembly-line worker in selecting the correct driveshaft for a particular engine/transmission/bodystyle application.

Color combinations are for the sport coupe/convertible and El Camino/four-door sedan/station wagon where applicable. Note several plants changed their reported color schemes during the production year. These are noted by the last-known build sheets with the first colors listed and the earliest-known build sheets with the second colors listed.

It is assumed the L34 and L78 color schemes changed at the same time. Not all engine/transmission combinations have been found to date.

1970 Arlington

Engine	Transmission						
	Manual 3	M20	M21	M22	M35	M38	M40
350 (L65)	-	-	-	-	-	BR-PK	-
396 (L34)	-	PK-OR	PK-OR	-	-	-	BL-BK
454 (LS5)	-	-	-	PK-BL	-	-	GR-OR
454 (LS6)	-	-	-	PK-BL	-	-	GR-OR

1970 Atlanta

Engine	Transmission						
	Manual 3	M20	M21	M22	M35	M38*	M40
307 (L14)	BR-PK	-	-	-	BR-PK	BR-PK	-
350 (L65)	-	-	-	-	-	BR-PK	BR-PK
350 (L48)	-	-	-	-	-	PK-OR	PK-OR
396 (L34)	-	PK-OR	PK-OR	-	-	-	BL-BK
396 (L78)	-	-	BL-YE	-	-	-	BL-BK
454 (LS5)	-	-	-	PK-BL	-	-	GR-OR
454 (LS6)	-	-	-	PK-BL	-	-	GR-OR

* Atlanta coded the M38 TH350 as M40 CBC TRANS after October

1970 Baltimore

Engine	Transmission						
	Manual 3	M20	M21	M22	M35	M38	M40
307 (L14)	-	DJ	-	-	DJ	DJ	-
350 (L65)	DJ	DJ	-	-	-	TJ	-
350 (L48)	-	OE	-	-	-	OE/DE*	-
396 (L34)	-	TG**	TG**	-	-	-	-
396 (L34)	-	DL**	DL**	-	-	-	-
396 (L78)	-	TG**	TG**	-	-	-	-
396 (L78)	-	DL**	DL**	-	-	-	-
454 (LS5)	-	-	-	-	-	-	PB GO***
454 (LS6)	-	-	-	PB PW****	-	-	GO GD****

* El Camino dated 02-23
** TG used through 11-10 and DL beginning 11-14
*** PB used through at least 04-01 and GO from at least 04-16
**** El Camino

1970 Kansas City

Engine	Transmission						
	Manual 3	M20	M21	M22	M35	M38	M40
307 (L14)	BK-PK	-	-	-	BR-PK	BR-PK	-
350 (L65)	-	-	-	-	BR-PK	BR-PK OR-OR*	-
350 (L48)	-	BR-PK GR-OR*	-	-	-	BR-PK OR-YE*	-
396 (L34)	-	BL-YE PK-OR*	BL-YE PK-OR*	-	-	-	BL-PK BR-OR*
396 (L78)	-	BL-YE PK-OR**	BL-YE PK-OR OR-BL	-	-	-	BL-BK
454 (LS5)	-	-	-	-	PK-BL PK-WH*	-	GR-OR GR-YE*
454 (LS6)	-	-	-	-	PK-BL	-	GR-OR GR-YE*

* El Camino
** PK-OR after at least 10-29

1970 Van Nuys

Engine	Transmission						
	Manual 3	M20	M21	M22	M35	M38	M40
307 (L14)	-	-	-	-	BR-PK	BR-PK OR-OR* WH-PU**	-
350 (L65)	-	-	-	-	-	BR-PK OR-OR**	-
350 (L48)	-	-	-	-	BR-PK	PK-OR OR-YE* WH-PU**	-
396 (L34)	-	BL-YE PK-OR***	BL-YE PK-OR***	-	-	-	BL-BK BR-OR*
396 (L78)	-	BL-YE PK-OR***	BL-YE PK-OR***	-	-	-	-
454 (LS5)	-	-	-	-	PK-BL	-	GR-OR BK---**
454 (LS6)	-	-	-	-	PK-BL	-	GR-OR

* El Camino
** Monte Carlo
*** Change from BL-YE to PK-OR sometime between 10-20 and 11-18

1971 Arlington

Engine	Transmission					
	Manual 3	M20	M21	M22	M35	M38	M40
350 (L65)	–	–	–	–	–	BR-PI	–
350 (L48)	–	–	–	–	–	PI-OR	–
402 (LS3)	–	–	–	–	–	–	BL-BK
454 (LS5)	–	–	–	PI-BL	–	–	GR-OR

1971 Baltimore

Engine	Transmission						
	Manual 3	M20	M21	M22	M35	M38	M40
307 (L14)	–	–	–	–	OR-OR	BR-PK	–
350 (L65)	–	–	–	–	–	BR-PK OR-OR*	–
350 (L48)	–	BR-PK	–	–	–	–	–
402 (LS3)	–	BL-BL	–	–	–	–	BL-BK
454 (LS5)	–	–	–	PK-BL	–	–	GR-OR

* El Camino

1971 Kansas City

Engine	Transmission						
	Manual 3	M20	M21	M22	M35	M38	M40
307 (L14)	OR-OR	–	–	–	–	BR-PK	–
350 (L65)	–	BR-PK	–	–	–	BR-PK OR-OR*	–
350 (L48)	BR-PK	BR-PK	–	–	–	PK-OR OR-YE*	–
402 (LS3)	–	BL-BL	–	–	–	–	BL-BK*
454 (LS5)	–	–	–	PK-BL	–	–	GR-OR

* El Camino

1971 Van Nuys

Engine	Transmission						
	Manual 3	M20	M21	M22	M35	M38	M40
307 (L14)	–	–	–	–	–	BR-PK OR-OR*	–
350 (L65)	–	–	–	–	–	BR-PK OR-OR*	–
350 (L48)	–	–	–	–	–	PK-OR	–
402 (LS3)	–	–	–	–	–	–	BL-BK BR-OR*
454 (LS5)	–	–	–	–	–	–	GR-OR BK---**

* El Camino
** Monte Carlo

1972 Arlington

Engine	Transmission						
	Manual 3	M20	M21	M22	M35	M38	M40
350 (L65)	–	–	–	–	–	BR-PK	–
350 (L48)	BR-PK	–	–	–	–	–	–
402 (LS3)	–	–	–	–	–	–	–
454 (LS5)	–	–	–	–	–	–	–

1972 Baltimore

Engine	Transmission						
	Manual 3	M20	M21	M22	M35	M38	M40
307 (L14)	–	–	–	–	–	BR-PK	–
350 (L65)	–	BR-PK	–	–	–	BR-PK	–
350 (L48)	BR-PK	BR-PK	–	–	–	PK-OR	–
402 (LS3)	PK-OR	BL-BL	–	–	–	–	XX-XX/ BK---*
454 (LS5)	–	–	–	PK-BL	–	–	–

* Monte Carlo

1972 Kansas City

Engine	Transmission						
	Manual 3	M20	M21	M22	M35	M38	M40
307 (L14)	–	–	–	–	–	–	–
350 (L65)	–	–	–	–	–	BR-PK OR-OR*	–
350 (L48)	–	–	–	–	–	PK-OR OR-YE*	–
402 (LS3)	–	–	–	–	–	–	BL-BK BR-BL**
454 (LS5)	–	–	–	–	–	–	–

* El Camino
** Monte Carlo

1972 Van Nuys

Engine	Transmission						
	Manual 3	M20	M21	M22	M35	M38	M40
307 (L14)	–	–	–	–	–	–	–
350 (L65)	–	BR-PK	–	–	–	BR-PK	–
350 (L48)	–	BR-PK	–	–	–	PK-OR OR-YE*	–
402 (LS3)	–	BL-BL	–	–	–	–	BL-BK
454 (LS5)	–	–	–	PK-BL	–	–	GR-OR

* El Camino

Where there are no known combinations as of this printing, it can only be assumed the assembly plants would be consistent. For example, since the Kansas City assembly plant used PK-WH for the LS5 and LS6 engines with manual transmission in the El Camino it would be logical to assume Baltimore and Van Nuys used the same color scheme since all plants used the same PK-BL (or PB) for the LS5 and LS6 with manual transmission in the sport coupe and convertible.

Several of the color combination abbreviations are easy to break down; others, not so much. Those that are known are listed here: B/BL, Blue; BK, Black; BR, Brown; G/GR, Green; P/PI/PK, Pink; O/OR, Orange; YE, Yellow; WH, White.

Source Guide

American Autowire
150 Heller Place
Bellmawr, NJ 08031
800-482-WIRE
americanautowire.com

AMK Products
800 Airport Road, Dept. E
Winchester, VA 22602
540-662-7820
amkproducts.com

Auto City Classics
28433 Hwy. 65 NE
Isanti, MN 55040
800-828-2212
autocityclassic.com

Bill Hodel Smog Parts
330-832-0871

Brake Boosters, Inc.
Steve Gregori
2496 N. Zediker Ave.
Sanger, CA 93657
559-875-0290
brakeboosters.com

Coker Tire
1317 Chestnut St.
Chattanooga, TN 37402
866-516-3215
cokertire.com

Dale McIntosh
info@ls6registry.com
www.ls6registry.com and
www.registries.macswebs.com
www.chevellestuff.com

Dan Duffy Polishing
989-551-1520

Details Wholesale
Jay Nixon
12285 World Trade Dr., Suite D
San Diego, CA 92128
800-760-3382

Eastwood
263 Shoemaker Road
Pottstown, PA 19464
800-343-9353
eastwood.com

Gardner Exhaust
Eric Gardner
15 Glenn Pond Dr.
Red Hook, NY 12571
845-758-8003
gardnerexhaust.com

Gary's Steering Wheel Service
2677 Ritner Hwy.
Carlisle, PA 17015
717-243-5646
garyssteeringwheel.com

Ground Up
91 Great Hill Road
Naugatuck, CT 06770
866-358-2277
ss396.com

The Horn Works
Gary Steinkellner
967 Hackett St.
Beloit, WI 53511
608-361-0095
carhornrestoration.com

Inline Tube
15066 Technology Dr.
Shelby Township, MI 48315
800-385-9452
inlinetube.com

Kelsey Tire
1190 East Hwy. 54
Camdenton, MO 65020
P.O. Box 564
800-325-0091
kelseytire.com

Kolor Korrect
732-846-1044
kolorkorrect.com

Legendary Interiors
121 West Shore Blvd.
Newark, NY 14513
800-363-8804
legendaryautointeriors.com

MacKay Engines
Jeff MacKay
9230 Swigert Road
Rochester, IL 62563
217-498-8250

Muscle Car and Corvette Nationals
Bob Ashton
P.O. Box 182068
Shelby Township, MI 48318-2068
586-549-5291
MCACN.com

MuscleCar Restoration and Design
209 State Rte. 125 West
P.O. Box 24
Pleasant Plains, IL 62677
217-626-2277
musclecarrestorationanddesign.com
www.facebook.com/muscle-car-Restoration-and-Design

Paragon Corvette Reproductions
8040 S Jennings Road
Swartz Creek, MI 48473
800-882-4688
paragoncorvette.com

Quanta Restoration Products
743 Telegraph Road
Rising Sun, MD 21911
410-658-5700
gastanks.com

Redline Gauge and Clock
469 Windy City Road
Humboldt, TN 38343
731-571-0766
redlineg.com

Restoration Service
Steve Hackel
14600 S. Kilpatrick Ave., Unit #34
Midlothian, IL 60445
708-687-4183
restorationservice.net

Super Car Registry
yenko.net

Super Car Restorations
5290 Rte. 553 Hwy.
Clymer, PA 15728
724-254-0553
scr553.com/

Team Chevelle
Chevelles.com

Trim Parts
2175 Deerfield Road
Lebanon, OH 45036
513-934-0815
trimparts.com

Vintage Muscle Car Parts
Eric Jackson
306 Lang Ct.
Union, OH 45322
937-836-5927
vintagemusclecarparts.com

www.ingramcontent.com/pod-product-compliance
Lightning Source LLC
Chambersburg PA
CBHW081442070526
44586CB00019B/2202